An Auto

VOLUME 1
1880–1911

By The Same Author

An Autobiography, Volume 2: 1911–1969 (*forthcoming*)

History and Politics

International Government
Empire and Commerce in Africa
Co-operation and the Future of Industry
Socialism and Co-operation
Fear and Politics
Imperialism and Civilization
After the Deluge (*two volumes*)
Quack, Quack!
Principia Politica
Barbarians at the Gate
The War for Peace

Criticism

Hunting the Highbrow
Essays on Literature, History and Politics

Fiction

The Village in the Jungle
Stories of the East
The Wise Virgins

Drama

The Hotel

A Calendar of Consolation: A Comforting Thought
for Every Day in the Year

AN AUTOBIOGRAPHY

LEONARD WOOLF

With an introduction by Quentin Bell

VOLUME 1

1880–1911

Oxford New York Toronto Melbourne
OXFORD UNIVERSITY PRESS
1980

Oxford University Press, Walton Street, Oxford OX2 6DP

OXFORD LONDON GLASGOW
NEW YORK TORONTO MELBOURNE WELLINGTON
KUALA LUMPUR SINGAPORE JAKARTA HONG KONG TOKYO
DELHI BOMBAY CALCUTTA MADRAS KARACHI
NAIROBI DAR ES SALAAM CAPE TOWN

First published in two volumes as Sowing *and* Growing *by*
The Hogarth Press Limited 1960, 1961
First published as an Oxford University Press paperback 1980
at the suggestion of Kate Bath

British Library Cataloguing in Publication Data

Woolf, Leonard
An autobiography.
Vol. 1: 1880–1911
1. Woolf, Leonard
2. Publishers and publishing—Great Britain—Biography
I. Title
070.5'092'4 Z325.W/ 79-41286
ISBN 0-19-281289-0

Note: References to what was the present at the time of writing have not been updated in the paperback edition

Typeset by Blackmore Press, Shaftesbury, and printed in Great Britain by Cox & Wyman Ltd, Reading

CONTENTS

Illustrations

Maps

Introduction

Leonard Woolf was an intelligent, a sensitive and very truthful man. This is the kind of thing that I need to say in this introduction; this, and my reasons for saying what I do. Others are as able as or more able than I to say that this book is a thoroughly 'good read' (as indeed it is). But I have had to use it as biographical material and to find out whether Leonard is indeed truthful: here then I speak with a certain authority.

But before doing so I want to try to introduce *him*. I knew him for about half a century, but I remember him best in middle and old age when he was a long, thin man, finely, elegantly constructed with a sharp semitic nose, deep grey eyes and a sensitive mouth. The lines of his face, which fell habitually into a mournful or even a grim expression, could be very much transformed when, as often happened, he smiled. His hands, particularly when he was gardening or driving a car, had a look of muscular intelligence like the hands of a craftsman. But the first impression, and it was an enduring impression, was of someone strange from a distant land. When I was a child I was slightly amazed to find that he could speak English so well (I may have been a little confused by having been told that he came from Ceylon). But my father also felt this; Lytton Strachey described him as a camel driver, while his future wife told him that he seemed 'foreign'.

I cannot be sure about that distant land in which my infant understanding and my adult imagination placed him. Certainly it was beyond the Hellespont, somewhere in the East, and it was gorgeous but harsh; one had laboriously to extract a meagre living amidst the bitter herbs and rocky wastes of that country and the best that one could ever hope for was a crumb or two of manna blown from across the mountains by an icy wind. To pursue this fantasy a little further, it was because he or his forebears had, as I imagined, scratched a living from that inhospitable desert, that, when he could cultivate the genial humus of Sussex, he found it child's play to make the land yield milk and honey.

There was no real incongruity in the fact that, despite this exotic appearance, Leonard was at times exceedingly British and almost

John Bullish in his insistence upon the particular virtues of the English. Few people—apart from some eccentric foreigners—have ever been so insistent upon the pre-eminent merits of our cooking. Also there was an intellectual boldness, an uncomfortable intransigence about him which reminded me rather of French than of English friends. There was something unyielding and a little fierce in his way of arguing, which was intimidating, and although he could feel charm in others he did not allow it to affect his judgements, nor did he have any sympathy with weakness or procrastination. I would not like to have been a minor official when Leonard was a colonial administrator, and to have found myself having to confess to some little human weakness or official equivocation.

But 'the grissily Wolf' as Dora Carrington called him 'was charming', and this she said even at a time when she had behaved rather badly, was being examined, and had every expectation of finding Leonard both foreign and ferocious. Indeed I think that one may say that, although he would stand for no nonsense, even the most seductive nonsense, and although there were those, particularly his colleagues in the Hogarth Press, who found him difficult, still, essentially he was a very kind man. There must have been many occasions when he found me almost unbearably exasperating but I do not remember him saying anything that was really malevolent or unkind. Nor, in my experience, did he ever harbour a grudge. Indeed, some of those who knew him only in his later years may think that I have said too much of the forbidding aspect of the man. But it was real enough and so was his kindness; this latter quality earned him a kind of bonus; it is pleasant when pussy purrs upon the hearthrug; but it would be more than pleasant, it would be downright reassuring, to hear a tiger purr (if tigers do purr). Leonard's benevolence was considerable but it was made more considerable still by the intimidating gravity which he sometimes displayed; it had the charm of the unexpected. Women felt this very much, for women are in some respects less immodest than men; men tend to believe, often without the faintest justification, that they are the intellectual equals of all other men; in consequence they take it for granted that they will be taken seriously. Leonard seemed to take everyone very seriously and anyone who might meet him in discussion was treated with intellectual courtesy. Women found this astonishing and flattering and it was perhaps for this reason that, in many ways, Leonard found women better to work with than men. It must also be said that although he tried to be scrupulously fair in argument and was never either evasive or dismissive, he very rarely conceded defeat and was in truth uncommonly stubborn in his opinions. I should like to think that these few sketchy and heavily corrected contours may provide the reader with a faint image of the man, although I have hardly suggested his gift for laughter and for imaginative sympathy. The essential outline which I have attempted to describe is gaunt and severe, but that image has to be qualified by the understanding that his was a very humane and a very kindly personality. He was a person who cared for other people and for animals, even for his tiresome dogs and his perfectly horrible pet monkey. But the aspect of the man which most concerns us here was his honesty, and of his passionate desire to tell the truth on any and every subject there can, to my mind, be no doubt.

These memoirs are essays in veracity; also, and this is something different, he strove to be accurate. In 1968 I gave it as my opinion that he was our most accurate writer on Bloomsbury. This, at the time, was true, and if in the Biography, the Letters and the Diaries of Virginia Woolf we have been able at some points to supplement or even to correct his information, of his desire to write the truth there is still no doubt whatsoever. His two main sources, apart from his memory, were his own diaries and those of Virginia Woolf, and when he has these to help him he practically never goes wrong; it is when there are no diaries on which to rely that he makes mistakes. One of these, oddly enough, is the date of his return from his honeymoon. In the same way, and for the same reason, he is at times misleading when he refers to events which took place in England at a time when he was in Ceylon; but as I said these are minor errors.

Leonard valued intellectual probity and this was one of his grand characteristics. It was a passion which led him to noble and disinterested actions but it could sometimes be a source of weakness in that at times it prevented him from doing things that he wanted to do. Both as a novelist and as a politician he was in a way inhibited by his own honesty.

As a writer of fiction he entered that difficult and perplexing terrain in which, although truth is respected, it is sometimes best conveyed by means of falsehood. Just as the draughtsman must, by a species of falsification and selection, achieve the seemingly impossible task of delineating solid objects upon a flat surface, so the writer of fiction may make his events more real by imposing upon them a form which does not, or need not, exist in nature. In *The Village in the Jungle* Leonard comes so close to direct reporting of that which he has seen that we are continually held, delighted and horrified by what he has to say. It need not, I feel, have been a work of fiction and would have been better if he had not imposed a fictional form upon it. As it is, the book is damaged by the necessities of a story which lacks form. Of *The Wise Virgins* I speak without assurance; to me it seems a failure (some people say that it is a masterpiece). It was written under great stress and with some anger; he describes his family, his wife's family and himself, and everyone or almost everyone is made odious, so odious that it is difficult to feel any sympathy for anyone. Again, for the purposes of his fiction his people act in an uncharacteristic way and in truth he is not at ease with the form that he has chosen. He made some other attempts at fiction but they were few and, so it seems to me, he discovered finally that it was a genre that did not suit him. It would have been difficult, under any circumstances, for Virginia's husband to have written novels.

He is certainly much more at home in the world of politics and his political works are extensive. It is rash to generalise but I fancy that he is at his best in works which are in the main historical, as for instance his admirable *Empire and Commerce in Africa*. Here he tells a plain story with force, lucidity, and some humour.

He had a passionate dislike for the kind of intellectual legerdemain which makes dogma seem respectable. In *Quack, Quack!*, a book too topical to have survived, he made a statement of faith, or rather of doubt, which, for its clarity and honesty, deserves I think to be rescued from oblivion; for here, in the last section of his book, there is an attack upon certain tendencies of thought, or perhaps one should say of rhetoric, which are still with us. We still suffer from fraudulent mystics, transcendental word-mongers, and priest-craft. Indeed if a single superstition has died during the past fifty years then I think it must be that which sees the destinies of mankind prefigured at the bottom of teacups, and this, alas, not because we have become more reasonable but because tea-bags are more convenient. Thus when Leonard denounces the dangerous windbags of his time, Spengler and Count Keyserling, Radhakrishnan and Bergson, he is denouncing the kind of intellectual confusion and chicanery which still flourishes, prospers hugely, disseminates dangerous myths and needs to be attacked.

Spengler he takes as the grand example of the intellectual–political quack, impressive, at times brilliant, he is condemned for his complete lack of intellectual probity or humility—'my work is the result of inspiration such as has not been known in the human race for thousands of years'. Leonard finds Spengler not only pretentious and ridiculous but also dangerous. His manner of arriving at what he calls 'truth' is to search in his blood, his guts, his solar plexus, anywhere so long as it is not his head, and to assert things because in some undefinable way he 'knows' them. The process is terribly like the deep intuitive illuminations of Hitler, the message drawn from the blood and soil of Germany. The transcendent truths of the Nordic myth have exactly the same intellectual character as the splendid certainties of Spengler, and sure enough when it became politically convenient to forget certain passages in *The Decline of the West* this feat was accomplished. Herr Spengler's doctrines became, in 1933, quite indistinguishable from those of the rulers of Germany. On a rational view this adaptation would appear to be unjustifiable, but the beauty of this kind of argument is that it rises above mere reason, and this, for someone who is anxious to placate a tyrant, is certainly a great convenience.

The metaphysical quacks of whom Bergson, Radhakrishnan and Count Keyserling are taken as examples are in their argumentative methods very similar to Spengler.

> By metaphysical quackery I mean the abandonment of and contempt for reason as a means of truth in non-political speculation and the substitution for it of so-called intuition, magic and mysticism. A determined and honest application of reason to the universe as we know it seems inevitably to lead to scepticism and agnosticism, to a disbelief in what appear to be absolute truths, to a conviction that the truth which seems to us most certainly true and most rigorously proved, the belief which we are totally unable not to believe, even reason itself, all these are dubious and precarious and may well be merely delusions and superstitions, the shadow dreams of shadows.

This, as Leonard himself allows, is not a comfortable position for the intellect, and, if one accepts a scepticism which extends even to the operation of reason itself, may one not forgive those who find in the promptings of faith or intuition a way past the insurmountable difficulties which confront the sceptic? In such a tempest of doubt surely the hapless swimmer may grasp at whatever spars or whatever straws seem to give him some buoyancy—always provided that the straws and spars are of a respectable kind—a wave-born cross or a floating mantra and not a Nordic myth?

But this is just what Leonard will not permit. To say that, because we cannot know, we must assert, is in his view wholly dishonest. The fact that we should very much like to be provided with unchallengeable certainties concerning the nature of the universe does not mean that they are obtaïnable, and the only true conclusion that we may draw from the discovery that we do not know what we would so much like to know is quite simply that indeed we do not know.

Moreover, if we do attempt to cut the Gordian knot of doubt, arguing that since reason cannot take us where we want to go there must be a mode of apprehension which transcends reason, our conclusions are invalidated by our own argument, for to argue is to reason, and yet it is the purpose of our argument precisely to dethrone reason.

As may be imagined, Leonard is not in sympathy with religion. He regards it rather as liberal-minded men regard sodomy or drug addiction. It is all right so long as you keep your vices private. Let the solitary anchorite regard his navel or count his beads; undertaken in the privacy of a hermit's cell this is a harmless occupation. But when the religious man begins to preach or to proselytise he becomes a public danger. Scepticism is the mother of toleration; religion, and in particular organised religion, breeds persecution. Nor can it very well be otherwise, for, if we abandon reason, we cannot dispute either with rationalists or with nonconformists. In default of reason we must rely upon arguments that all can understand, those of the *Index Librorum Prohibitorum* or the stake.

I have done my best to summarise Leonard's arguments, although I am well aware that I have not the equipment needed for such a task. The attempt had to be made, partly because the argument which he developed in *Quack, Quack!* was of central importance in his view of the world and partly because the book exhibits both his strength and his limitations.

Moreover I must note in passing that while rereading that book I have been struck by its strange topicality. In the very large volume of literature devoted to the study of Virginia Woolf there is a kind of lunatic fringe, and in this of late it has been possible to find authors who are ready to denounce Leonard, to find in his rationalism an unsympathetic and insensitive quality which, so the story goes, made him incapable of making his wife happy. There is a distinct air of quackery about such writers, a rejection of reason and indeed a sublime disregard of nearly all the available evidence. They too have their place in the records of intellectual dishonesty which Leonard so carefully examined.

From this it may be perceived that, in so far as I understand them, I am in sympathy with Leonard's views. At all events I find it difficult not to admire such a dedicated pursuit of so forbidding a theory and I do think that in demolishing the prophets of the higher or transcendental nonsense he was doing something well worth doing and doing it with great force.

A deep distrust of specious argument and a passionate belief in the value of intellectual integrity seem to me to be very admirable things; but they are not, it must be allowed, a part of the usual equipment of a successful politician, and Leonard was a politician. He went into the world of practical politics, not simply as a thinker but rather to go to the grass roots. And this meant, not merely that on polling day his was one of the tiny band of motor cars which sported the Labour colours in the Lewes Constituency, but also that he was personally involved in the day to day business of the Women's Cooperative Guild or the ward Labour Party. It must be allowed that in practice, as a candidate and as an expert adviser to his party, he did not achieve success as the world usually measures that commodity.

It is easy, nor is it wholly wrong, to explain his relative failure by invoking a familiar idea of the remote intellectual, that is to say the image of one who stands upon some cold eminence from which he can see very well what his fellow men ought to be doing, but where he is so much raised above the common emotions that he cannot descend to those lower altitudes where policies are converted into effective action.

The image is at once true and false. It is true enough that Leonard never thumped a tub and that, precisely because the resonance which results from that exercise is so great and gives to arguments a force which, intellectually, is not properly theirs, he would always have found the effort too distasteful to be accomplished with the enthusiasm which is its necessary ingredient. But, this being conceded, it would be wrong to think of him as one so cerebral in his approach to life as to be quite separated from his fellows by a 'superior' Cambridge arrogance.

If he ever had that quality he lost it in Ceylon. I have only to recall the many times that I myself have heard him, patiently, quietly, without the faintest air of condescension or of 'side', explaining to the Rodmell Labour Party some difficult question concerning the League Covenant or the taxation of land. He had only one aim in view, to make a difficult proposition clear; there was an honesty and a simplicity about him to which those audiences responded. His clarity gave them greater acuteness than they knew themselves to possess; his manifest sincerity was entirely lovable.

Virginia noticed the same thing in him, as also his perfect respect for those who, without being brilliant or in any striking way successful, were in the truest sense respectable.

> Leonard went off at 10 a.m. to give his second lecture at Hampstead. The first was a great success, as I knew it would be. He finds the women much more intelligent than the men; in some ways too intelligent, & apt on that account, not to see the real point. He has another to give this afternoon, so he is staying up at Hampstead, lunching with Lilian, & perhaps seeing Janet. No one except a very modest person would treat these working women, & Lilian & Janet & Margaret as he does. Clive or indeed any other clever young man, would give himself airs; and however much he admired them pretend he didn't.

The truth about Leonard, as I suppose about any human being, is too complex to be expressed in a formula. I cannot even agree with his own estimate. At the end of a lifetime of thankless work on committees he declared that it had all been time wasted.

He was wrong. He achieved more than he would admit. The work of those who, like Leonard, will commit hemselves to the prosaic side of politics, giving their wisdom and experience and asking nothing in return, is of inestimable value, and certainly the country needs such men badly. I believe that Leonard was able to persuade us to do sensible things and to prevent us from committing even greater follies than those of which we have been guilty. As an old man he returned to Ceylon; it cannot often happen that when a period of imperial rule is over and a people has won its liberty a returning civil servant, and a severe one too, is kindly received. Leonard had something like a hero's welcome. The long hours in committee rooms had after all borne some fruit.

'What a life he has led', said E. M. Forster, 'and how well he has led it.'

QUENTIN BELL

Sowing
1880 – 1904

D. D. D.

Amico meo mihi

R. I. P.

1

Childhood

I very rarely think either of my past or my future, but the moment that one contemplates writing an autobiography—and I am sitting down with that intention today—one is forced to regard oneself as an entity carried along for a brief period in the stream of time, emerging suddenly at a particular moment from darkness and nothingness and shortly to disappear at a particular moment into nothingness and darkness. The moment at which officially I emerged from non-existence was the early morning of 25 November 1880, though in fact I did not personally become aware of my existence until some two or three years later. In the interval between 1880 and today I have lived my life on the assumption that sooner or later I shall pass by annihilation into the same state of non-existence from which I suddenly emerged that winter morning in West Cromwell Road, Kensington, so many years ago. This passage from non-existence to non-existence seems to me a strange and, on the whole, an enjoyable experience. Since the age of sixteen, when for a short time, like all intelligent adolescents, I took the universe too seriously, I have rarely worried myself about its meaning or meaninglessness. But I resent the fact that, as seems to be practically certain, I shall be as non-existent after my death as I was before my birth. Nothing can be done about it and I cannot truthfully say that my future extinction causes me much fear or pain, but I should like to record my protest against it and against the universe which enacts it.

The adulation of the deity as creator of the universe in Jewish and Christian psalms and hymns, and indeed by most religions, seems to me ridiculous. No doubt in the course of millions of millions of years, he has contrived to create some good things. I agree that 'my heart leaps up when I behold a rainbow in the sky', or 'the golden daffodils, beside the lake, beneath the trees, fluttering and dancing in the breeze', or 'the stars that shine and twinkle on the Milky Way'. I admit that every now and again I am amazed and profoundly moved by the beauty and affection of my cat and my dog. But at what a cost of senseless pain and misery, of wasteful and prodigal cruelty, does he manage to produce a daffodil, a Siamese cat, a sheepdog, a housefly, or a sardine. I resent the wasteful stupidity of a system which tolerates the spawning herring or the seeding groundsel or the statistics of infantile mortality wherever God has not been civilised by man. And I resent the stupid wastefulness of a system which requires that human beings with great labour and pain should spend years in acquiring knowledge, experience, and skill, and then just when at last they might use all this in the service of mankind and for their own happiness, they lose their teeth and their hair and their wits, and are hurriedly bundled, together with all that they have learnt, into the grave and nothingness.

It is clear that, if there is a purpose in the universe and a creator, both are unintelligible to us. But that does not provide them with an excuse or a defence. However, as I said, nothing can be done about it, and having made my protest, I must now think about my past. When I do think of my past and of the genes and chromosomes of my ancestors, for they after all are a highly important part of my past, I am a little surprised to see where they have landed me. I write this looking out of a window upon a garden in Sussex. I feel that my roots are here and in the Greece of Herodotus, Thucydides, Aristophanes, and Pericles. I have always felt in my bones and brain and heart English, and more narrowly a Londoner, but with a nostalgic love of the city and civilisation of ancient Athens. Yet my genes and chromosomes are neither Anglo-Saxon nor Ionian. When my Rodmell neighbours' forefathers were herding swine on the plains of eastern Europe and the Athenians were building the Acropolis, my Semitic ancestors, with the days of their national greatness, such as it was, already behind them, were in Persia or Palestine. And they were already prisoners of war, displaced persons, refugees, having begun that unending pilgrimage as the world's official fugitives and scapegoats which has brought one of their descendants to live, and probably die, Parish Clerk of Rodmell in the County of Sussex.

For my father's father was a Jew, born in London in the year 1808. His name was Benjamin Woolf and he died in 1870 at the age of sixty-two in Clifton Gardens, Maida Vale. On his death certificate his occupation is given as 'gentleman', but he was in fact by occupation a tailor who had done extremely well in his trade.[1] The first record of him and his business is found in the London directory

[1] I owe nearly all the accurate facts about my grandparents to my nephew, Cecil Woolf, who did a good deal of research into our ancestry.

of 1835, in which he appears as Benjamin Woolf, Tailor, 87 Quadrant, Regent Street. Sixteen years later he opened a second shop in Piccadilly, and four years later a third shop in Old Bond Street. He is described sometimes as 'tailor and outfitter', and sometimes as 'tailor, outfitter, and portable furniture warehouse', and in his shop at 48 Piccadilly as 'waterproofer'. He had seven sons and three daughters, and it is curious that three of the children married into the de Jongh family (my mother's family) and two of them married sisters, Louisa and Sarah Davis of Glasgow. His will is a formidable document covering many pages and he leaves considerable property, but with the proviso that none of it is to pass to any of his children if they marry out of the Jewish faith.

There still exist in London some tailor shops with WOOLF BROTHERS over the window—there used to be one in Holborn until Hitler dropped his bombs on it—and I used to think that perhaps they were the remains of my grandfather's business[1] which might well have made me a very rich man. It didn't, because, although my grandfather lived in a large house in Bloomsbury—I was once told that it was in Tavistock Square, but it may have been in Bedford Square—and had his seven sons, none of his sons went into the business. Like so many Jews of his class, he had an inordinate admiration for education and he educated his sons out of their class. I never knew any of my paternal uncles, but I doubt whether any of them benefited very much from their education, unless one can count one of them a success, for he certainly was, by all accounts, an extremely brilliant and amusing scoundrel.

Two vast oil paintings of my paternal grandparents hung, during my childhood, on the wall of our dining-room, together with what was always referred to as 'the little Morland' and a large pastoral scene, with sheep and goats, ascribed to Teniers. They—my grandparents—died before I was born, but their portraits which loomed so large over so many meals have indelibly impressed upon my mind their features and characters. I remember him as a large, stern, blackhaired, and blackwhiskered, rabbinical Jew in a frock coat, his left hand pompously tucked into his waistcoat, while she, who was born Isabella Phillips in 1808 and died in 1878 at the age of seventy,

[1] This is probably mere fantasy, but it is just possible because 1879 is the last directory to contain an entry for Benjamin Woolf and 1879 the first to contain an entry for Woolf Brothers.

was the exact opposite: pretty, round cheeked, mild, and forgiving. Yes, it was all, no doubt, as it should be—the male forbidding and the female forgiving. She probably had a good deal to forgive, certainly from her children, all of whom, with the exception of my father and one of my aunts, must have been pretty tough people. The look of stern rabbinical orthodoxy in my grandfather's face was, I think, no illusion, for traditionally his family was just like that. His mother, my great-grandmother, we were told, used to walk to synagogue with hard peas in her boots in the evening of every Day of Atonement until she was well over seventy, and she stood upright on the peas in her place in the synagogue for twenty-four hours without sitting down until sunset of the following day, fasting of course the whole time. That in the Woolf family about the year 1820 was considered to be the proper way to atone for your sins. I feel a faint sneaking agreement with my great-grandmother, or rather I would if I had ever had a sense of sin. I presume that my unconscious is the usual cesspool of sadistic and masochistic guilt revealed by psycho-analysis, but I have never been able to detect in myself, even in childhood, a conscious sense of sin. But if there has to be this abominable doctrine of guilt and atonement, then I would approve of my great-grandmother's habit of doing the thing thoroughly.

My mother's family had none of the toughness and sternness of the Woolfs. The de Jonghs—her maiden name was de Jongh—were all of them rather soft. My mother was born in Holland of Jewish parents in Amsterdam. Her father was a diamond merchant, and the whole family migrated to London when she was still a child. I do not know why they migrated,[1] continuing the unending pilgrimage which, as I said, began in Palestine and Persia about 2,500 years ago. They must have been pretty prosperous, for the pilgrimage landed them in Woburn Lodge, that very pleasant kind of country house which, until just before the 1939 war, survived at the top of Tavistock Square beneath the caryatids of St Pancras Church. Thus my maternal and paternal grandparents, my father, my mother, and I myself all lived in or practically in Tavistock Square. When my mother first went, as a child, to live in Woburn Lodge, in the road just outside was a turnpike which was only opened to residents in

[1] My sister thinks that my grandfather often had to visit London and Paris on business, and that he liked London so much better than Amsterdam that he decided to transfer himself, his wife, and his ten children to England.

the Square by a ducal retainer who sat in a kind of summerhouse next to it. That must have been, I suppose, in the 1860s. When I went to live at No. 52 Tavistock Square in 1925, the turnpike and the Duke of Bedford's retainer had gone, but the Square had not changed much otherwise since my mother's childhood. When she was over eighty, I walked with her one day across the Square to Woburn Lodge which was then empty and she stood in the melancholy little garden looking into the deserted rooms, which, she said, were exactly the same as they were when she was a young girl. But we were even then standing at the beginning of the end. For a year or two later they pulled down the north side of the Square and built up a very high and, architecturally, absurd building; and then, later still, in 1940 came the bombs which destroyed nearly all the south side, including No. 52, which, though we had moved to Mecklenburgh Square, we still had on lease from the Bedford Estate.

My mother's parents had ten children, most of them not only soft, but rather feckless, and they drained away most of my grandfather's prosperity by the time that I knew him. I knew both my maternal grandparents, as they lived to be nearly ninety. There was, in fact, something antediluvian about the de Jonghs, or at least they seemed to belong to a different century from ours. It was characteristic of them that my mother's nurse used to describe vividly to her the Napoleonic wars and how the French soldiers marched into the Dutch village where she lived as a young woman and were quartered on her parents. My grandparents, when I knew them, lived in a small house in Addison Gardens, and once a week we as children used to walk with my mother or with nurses or later with a governess from Lexham Gardens to Addison Gardens to have tea with them.

It was the cleanest house and they were the cleanest people I have ever seen anywhere. My grandmother was always sitting by the window of the front ground-floor room in a black ebony chair which had an immensely high straight back rising several feet above her head. She never, so far as I know, stopped knitting, the needles going faster than I have ever seen in the hands of any other knitter. A large black cap was on the whitest hair, and beneath it was the round, pink face of an incredibly old Dutch doll. When she came to see us, the black cap was brought in a special basket made for the purpose. She was the kindest and roundest of women, and, though she had never, I think, read a book or had suffered from an abstract idea or had experienced the grinding of the intellect—which for most people is as unpleasant as the dentist's drill—somehow or other she seemed to have learnt to defeat fate. She was born round about 1800 in Groningen, a provincial town in the north-east of Holland, and in 1890 she sat in the window behind the lace curtains in Addison Gardens, having borne ten children and welcomed thirty grandchildren and having moved, imperturbable, from Groningen to The Hague and Amsterdam and thence to Woburn Lodge and Addison Gardens, passing on her way the whole of the nineteenth century.

Here is a curious example of a family tradition which must have had absolutely no foundation in fact: my grandmother's maiden name was Van Coeverden, and the family tradition was that it was one of her ancestors who in the eighteenth century discovered and gave his name to Vancouver Island. In fact the island was named in 1794 after an Englishman, George Vancouver, a captain in the British navy who first went to sea at the age of thirteen in the *Resolution*, the ship commanded by the great Captain Cook. It is, however, possible that she had a good deal of non-Jewish blood in her ancestry. Some of her children and grandchildren were fair-haired and facially very unlike the 'typical' Jew. She had a very nice, small, eighteenth century, black-and-white portrait of one of her male ancestors and he looked completely non-Jewish; the curious thing is that one of my brothers, who had fair hair, was so exactly like him that at first sight the picture seemed to be a portrait of him in eighteen-century fancy-dress.

I am not one of Rousseau's latter-day disciples who believe in the nobility of the noble savage and in the wisdom of peasants, children, and imbeciles. From the ignorant I expect and I get ignorance and from the stupid, stupidity. But there are people—usually in my experience dogs or old women—extremely simple and unintellectual who instinctively know how to deal with life and with persons, and who display an extraordinary and admirable resistance to the cruelties of man, the malevolence of Providence, and the miseries of existence. My grandmother, sitting so upright in her ebony chair behind the white lace curtains, unconquered by the nineteenth century and her ten children, was one of them; she defied fate even in Addison Gardens. She died at the age of eighty-eight.

My grandfather was a very different type of person. He was a tall, gentle, rather silent man with a long white beard. No one could have mistaken him for anything but a Jew. Although he wore coats and trousers, hats and umbrellas, just like those of all the other gentlemen in Addison Gardens, he looked to me as if he might have stepped straight out of one of those old pictures of caftaned, bearded Jews in a ghetto, straight-backed, dignified, sad, resigned, expecting and getting over two or three millenia nothing but misery from the malignancy of fate and the cruelty of man, and yet retaining somewhere in the small of their backs or the cockles of their hearts a fragment of spiritual steel, a particle of passive and unconquerable resistance. In the house my grandfather always wore a brightly-coloured smoking cap, and I never saw him without a book and a cigar. I daresay that he too cherished in the small of his back and the cockles of his heart that particle of steel which alone enabled him to walk so upright, and alone can account for his survival, but I must admit that I never saw any evidence of it. Life and ten children and the nineteenth century seemed to have been too much for him, and, instead of defying, he had just yielded in silent melancholy to his fate. And at eighty-one, he was knocked down and killed in Walham Green by a horse-drawn omnibus.

The first experience of the misery of disgracing himself, so far as I can remember, came to me in my grandparents' house in Addison Gardens. The chairs and sofa in the sitting-room were covered in shining black horsehair. To sit on them in knickerbockers and stockings was, for a child of four or five years old, torture, for the stiff black hairs pricked you unmercifully on the bottom and behind the knees whenever you moved. I must have been about that age when one warm day the irritation in the lower half of my body, as I wriggled about in agony on the sofa, was too much for me and I had a violent impulse to cry and to make water at the same time. Unfortunately I fought heroically against both impulses until it was too late. The waters burst from me in two places simultaneously, pouring down my cheeks and my legs, and the old servant had to take me into the kitchen where I sat ignominously wrapped in a blanket while my knickers and stockings were washed and dried.

I suppose some people would say that in this story, in this 'misery of disgracing oneself', I have disproved what I said above, namely that I cannot remember ever having had a sense of sin. Isn't that feeling of disgrace the sense of sin? I would myself say no, and the distinction is, I believe, of immense importance in the psychology of the child and of the man or woman who grows out of the child. My father was a believing, but not an orthodox, Jew. He was a liberal

Jew and a member of what was called the Reformed Synagogue. Jews of his generation and outlook were not much concerned with sin. They and their children escaped the psychological impact of crucifixion and redemption, of heaven and hell. It is true that there was the yearly Day of Atonement, but oddly enough my parents, unlike my great-grandmother, never seemed to connect it in any way with their or our sins. At any rate, I don't think I ever heard the word 'sin' mentioned in our house; we were never beaten and hardly ever punished. Some things were, of course, wrong and some so terribly wrong it was inconceivable that any small Woolf would do them. We were, like all children, 'naughty', particularly if we quarrelled or fought or did not eat up what was put on our plates at breakfast or lunch. The standard of behaviour, what was expected of a 'little gentleman' or a 'little lady' by nurses and governesses in the 1880s in Lexham Gardens, was pretty high. But both my parents were cheerful and kindly and good natured and took an extraordinarily optimistic view of God and his ordering of the universe. In consequence we were, as I remember it, extremely good children, yet not subjected to a perpetual stream of 'Don't do this' or 'Don't do that', and so with little, if any, *sense* of sin: indeed, until I went to school about the age of ten I was scarcely aware intellectually of the existence and importance of sin. To retain this innocence at St Paul's Preparatory School or later at the private school in Brighton to which I went for two years was, of course, impossible, and I soon had an encyclopaedic knowledge of wickedness in man, woman, and child, both from the schoolmaster's point of view and that of the dirty and dirty-minded little boy. But by that time, I think, I had become inoculated against any feelings of personal guilt, for, though I often did things which I knew were considered to be wrong, I cannot remember ever to have felt myself to be a sinner.

This looking back at oneself through middle age, youth, childhood, infancy is a curious and puzzling business. Some of the things which one seems to remember from far, far back in infancy are not, I think, really remembered; they are family tales told so often about one that eventually one has the illusion of remembering them. Such I believe to be the story of how as an infant I fell into a stream near Oban which I heard so often that eventually it became part of my memory. What genuine glimpses one does get of oneself in very early childhood seem to show that the main outlines of one's character are moulded in infancy and do not change between the ages of three and eighty-three. I am sure that my attitude to sin was the same when I lay in my pram as it is today when I sit tapping this out on the typewriter and, unless I become senile, will be the same when I lie on my deathbed. And in other ways when I can genuinely remember something of myself far off and long ago, I can recognise that self as essentially myself with the same little core of character exactly the same as exists in me today. I think that the first things which I can genuinely remember are connected with an illness which I had when I was about three. It was a very severe attack of scarlet fever which also affected my kidneys and in those days scarlet fever was a dangerous disease. I can remember incidents connected with the illness and I think they are genuine memories; they are so vivid that I can visualise them and myself in them.

The first is of a man coming into the room and applying leeches to my back. I insisted upon seeing the leeches and was fascinated by them. Twenty-five years later, one day in Ceylon during the rainy season, I was pushing my way through thick, wet grass in the jungle. I was wearing shorts and suddenly looking down I saw that my two bare knees were black with leeches. And suddenly I was back, a small boy of three, lying in bed in the bedroom high up in the Lexham Gardens house with the kindly man rather reluctantly showing me the leeches. I doubt whether in the intervening twenty-five years I had ever recalled the man with the leeches, but there in a flash the scene and the man and the leeches and my feelings were as vivid to me as the leeches on my knees, the gun in my hand, and the enveloping silence of the jungle.

When I look into the depths of my own mind (or should one say soul?) one of the characteristics which seems to me deepest and most persistent is a kind of fatalistic and half-amused resignation. I never worry, because I am saved by the feeling that in the end nothing matters, and I can watch with amusement and detachment the cruel, often undeserved but expected, blows which fate rains upon me. In another incident of my scarlet fever (though it became a family story), I seem to see this streak in my character already formed in the three-year-old child. At one moment my illness took a turn for the worse and I was, so it was said, upon the point of death. They called in Sir William Jenner, the Queen's doctor and a descendant of the Jenner who invented inoculation. He was a kindly man and I was fascinated by the shape of his nose. He prescribed a draught of the most appalling taste. I drank it down, but on his second visit—presumably next day—I sat up in bed with a second dose in the glass in my hand unable to drink it despite all the urging of my mother and Sir William. At last I said to them—according to my mother, with considerable severity—'If you will *all* go out of the room, I will drink it.' I do not really remember that, but I do vividly remember the sequel. I remember sitting up in bed alone and the resignation with which I drank the filthy stuff, and the doctor and my mother coming back into the room and praising me. Sir William sat down on my bed and said that I had been so good that I would be given what I wanted. What did I want? 'A pigeon pie', I said, 'with the legs sticking out.' 'You cannot', he explained and his explanation was not unexpected by me, 'be given a pigeon pie with the legs sticking out just yet, but you will be given one as soon as you are quite well. But isn't there something—not to eat—which you would like now?' I remember looking carefully into his kindly old face and saying: 'I should like to pull your nose.' He said that I might, and gently, not disrespectfully, but as a kind of symbol or token, serious but also, I believe, deep down amused, I pulled Sir William Jenner's nose.

But I must return to my father, Sidney Woolf.[1] He was sent by his father to University College School and afterwards, I think, to Kings College, London, or to University College in Gower Street. He was extremely intelligent and had a quick, powerful mind, so that he did very well at school. One of his elder brothers had become a solicitor and for a time my father joined him, but he had always determined to become a barrister. After some years as a solicitor, he was called to the bar. He was a first-rate lawyer and almost immediately successful; at the age of forty, as a Q.C., he made, I believe, over £5,000 a year. He was born at No. 87 Quadrant, Regent Street in 1844, married my mother in 1875, begat on her ten children, and died in 1892 after a few weeks' illness, at the age of forty-seven. I presume that, like every male, I was in love with my mother and hated my father, but I can find no trace of either the love or the hate in my memories, or indeed in my unconscious when, as occasionally happens, the id intrudes upon my ego. I was eleven when my father died. I admired him greatly and certainly thought that I was fond of

[1] His name on his birth certificate is Solomon Rees Sydney Woolf, but he was always known as Sidney Woolf.

him, and I think that he was both fond and proud of me, because as a small boy I was intelligent, reserved, and had a violent temper, and so in fact resembled him. He was certainly intelligent, reserved, and quick-tempered, but also very nervous and highly strung, and, though normally very kind, more intolerant of fools and their folly than almost any other man whom I have known. Though not an orthodox Jew, his ethical code of conduct was terrific, but he was not, in my recollection of him, either passionately on the side of righteousness or violently against sin. He must have been, I think, one of those rare people whose code of personal conduct is terrific, but whose morality is instinctive, springing from a delicacy or nicety of taste or aesthetic sensibility. This would explain why he was able unexpectedly to do without a sense of sin or the desire to punish sinners. He once said that in his opinion a perfect and complete rule of conduct for a man's life had, once and for all, been laid down by the prophet Micah in the words: 'What doth the Lord require of thee, but to do justly, and to love mercy, and to walk humbly with thy God?' The words were inscribed on his tombstone in the grim and grimy cemetery in the Balls Pond Road.

I can remember the first time that I felt close to my father in a grown up way. I was only six years old, and I know that that was the case because it was the summer of the year of Queen Victoria's Jubilee, and as my father had a very long important case—I think it must have been an arbitration case—during the vacation, we had to take a house near London for our summer holidays so that he could get up and down to town easily. The house was at Kenley. When the rest of the family went off to Kenley, he had to stay on two nights in London, and for some reason I was chosen to stay on with him in Lexham Gardens. I felt terribly proud and important, particularly walking up Lexham Gardens by myself to the mews at the far end near Cornwall Gardens to tell Dennis, the coachman, what time the brougham would be wanted. We drove to the Temple and then walked across Lincoln's Inn Fields to a large room where the case was tried. It too must have been an arbitration case for we all sat round a long table and I sat on a chair next to my father. Mr Bigham, who afterwards became a judge and Lord Mersey, was counsel on the opposite side, and there were heated arguments between him and my father. I thought him to be very rude and a most unpleasant man, and I was amazed when we adjourned for lunch and Mr Bigham patted me on the head and we went off and lunched with him at the Rainbow Tavern, and my father and he were the best of friends. Later on in the afternoon they were at each other again hammer and tongues. Mr Roper, my father's clerk, who seemed to be always arriving with a large red silk bag containing briefs, was very solicitous for my comfort. He must have been almost if not quite an albino, with the palest yellow hair and weak blinking eyes, and when one day, having come down with the red silk bag to a house in the country during one summer holidays, he was given tea, he amazed us by taking jam with his cake. Years afterwards someone might say: 'Do you remember Mr Roper eating strawberry jam with plum cake?', and heads were shaken over the aberration. The case went on for many hours and then in the evening we were driven back to Lexham Gardens and I sat up for dinner with my father. And next day, he drove us down to Kenley with its downs and white dusty road in a phaeton through Croydon and Purley.

My father worked so hard and so continually that we saw less of him than we and, I think, he would have liked. It was always exciting to be with him for he was extremely quick and lively in mind and body—when he was made a Q.C. one of the legal papers described him as having 'an eager and a nipping air'. His energy was once almost the death of me. It was on my seventh or eighth birthday that he gave me a tricycle—it was the days before the 'safety' bicycle was invented, and he and my elder brother, Herbert, already each had their tricycle. On Sunday we all three set off together on our tricycles from Lexham Gardens, along the Hammersmith Road, across the Bridge to Barnes Common, to Sheen and Richmond Park. In those days, after the Castlenau Road you were practically in the country. It seems to me that it was a pretty long ride for a child of seven or eight who had not often been on a tricycle before. But, as it was afterwards discovered, there was something wrong in the bottom bracket of my new tricycle and I had simply to pound along using a good deal of force to make the beastly thing go at all. I can still remember the agony of grinding along the Sheen Road on the way back, the pain of exhaustion made worse by the disappointment in the present which I had so eagerly looked forward to. I managed to conceal my condition from father and Herbert, but when we got back to Lexham Gardens, we were met at the door by my mother, anxious to know how we had enjoyed ourselves. She raised a cry of consternation when she saw me stagger into the hall. It became a tale in the family saga, and she always said that, when she first saw me on the doorstep, my face was absolutely white except for the nose which was a flaming red. In the hall I collapsed and was carried away and put to bed.

My father's intellectual intolerance seemed to be roughly proportionate to his ethical tolerance. If a fool was anywhere in his neighbourhood, he tended to forget any idea of mercy or of walking humbly with or without his God. A stupid or silly remark would drive him frantic, and he showed little mercy to any man, woman, or child who made one. His irascibility when confronted by obstinate stupidity, at one time regularly every Sunday at lunch, produced a remarkable and to some a terrifying scene. Personally I looked forward to these scenes with astonishment, alarm, and at the same time a certain enjoyment. The culprit and victim was a cousin, the orphaned son of one of my father's sisters. In the 1880s a Victorian lunch in a Victorian family like the Woolfs was a formidable, but not altogether unpleasant ritual. It was eminently bourgeois, patriarchal, and a weekly apotheosis of the family. The change from the matriarchy of weekdays to the patriarchy of Sundays was very impressive to a small boy, and to me it was sympathetic. My father practically never stopped working. Every morning immediately after breakfast he was driven in his brougham from Lexham Gardens to Kings Bench Walk, where he had his chambers, and every evening at six the brougham fetched him back just in time for dinner at Lexham Gardens. After dinner and on Saturdays, if he was at home, he worked at his briefs. In the week, therefore, his children saw very little of him. Sometimes I was allowed to go into his dressing-room before breakfast to see him shaved, and sometimes my mother took me in the brougham to fetch him from the Temple—in the summer on such occasions we often stopped at the end of the Mall (or was it Birdcage Walk?) to drink a glass of milk from the Marsham Street cow who grazed of right in the corner of St James's Park. But, as I was saying, this meant that we saw little of my father during the week, and Sunday lunch was a ceremony of some importance, for the whole family, capable of sitting upright and of eating roast beef, sat round the table.

I suppose that in the house in Lexham Gardens towards the end of the 1880s six of the nine children sat round the table at Sunday lunch with my father and mother. There was always an immense sirloin of beef, carved with considerable ceremony by my father.

Bennie—as my cousin was always called—lived alone in London, and he had a standing invitation to our Sunday lunch; he was nearly always there. When I was ten, he must have been about twenty-three or twenty-four. He was almost, to look at, the comic Jew of the caricature, and he was that curious, but not very uncommon, phenomenon, the silly Jew who seems deliberately to exaggerate and exploit his silliness. He was the Jew so accurately described by one of the Marx brothers: 'He looks like a fool and talks like a fool, but don't let him deceive you—he is a fool.' Sooner or later, usually towards the end of lunch, Bennie would contrive to say something of inconceivable imbecility. My father with an effort would restrain himself and ignore Bennie. But Bennie was a masochistic moth who could not keep away from the devastating flame. He would turn with imbecile innocence to my father and ask him whether he did not agree with the imbecility. My father's fingers would begin to beat a nervous tattoo upon the tablecloth and all the little Woolfs fell silent round the table, staring apprehensively at the insensate Bennie. 'But, Uncle Sidney,' he would say, 'Uncle Sidney, it is true, isn't it, that red-haired people in France are not taxed?' 'No, it is not true, Bennie, and no one in the world but you would believe it.' 'But, Uncle Sidney—' and then my father would throw up his hands and let loose upon Bennie's head the torrent of his exasperation.

My mother was a good-looking young woman and we all liked to see her let down her hair, for it reached well below her knees and was extraordinarily thick. She must have been a perfect wife for she adored my father and yet was sufficiently different from him to make life interesting always for both of them. She adored her children and made life very interesting for them when they were small. The best hours of the day were between tea-time and my father's return from the Temple, for we spent them with her in the library playing, when we were quite small, and being read to later on when we were seven or eight or more. She was extremely lively and always ready for a joke both with us and with father. For instance, once when we were all away for the summer holidays in a house in Penmaenmawr, the rain came down in that solid, interminable, relentless way which seems peculiar to the grey mountains of Wales and Scotland. The feeling that there is no reason why it should ever stop, the conviction that it never will stop, induces in the human mind, particularly the child's mind, a feeling of complete despair. My parents and four or five of the elder children sat hour after hour in a largish sitting-room reading and looking out of the window at the grey sky and grey rain streaming down from the grey sky. Late in the afternoon my mother decided that something must be done. She dressed herself up in a black dress, with a black hat and a thick black veil and rang the front door bell. The servant came in and told my father that there was a lady on the door-step who asked to see him on urgent business. With some hesitation he agreed to see her. My mother was shown in and started off brilliantly with a long and somewhat confused story. Father did not recognise her, she played the part so well, and he began cross-examining her in his usual quick, incisive way. Suddenly she got a laughing fit and could not say a word to answer his questions. This was too much for his impatient nature and we rocked with laughter when he burst out: 'My good woman . . .' My mother laughed so much that she had to snatch off the veil and reveal herself.

My mother had for my father and for his memory after his death something of the attitude which Queen Victoria had for Albert, though she was much less exaggerated and completely without the Queen's craziness. I suppose that Victorian matriarchs in widowhood tended to conform to this pattern in which a long life was dominated by the apotheosis of a dead husband. My mother was in many ways an ordinary middle-class woman, but twenty-five per cent of her was a very individual and curious character. She lived to the age of eighty-seven or eighty-eight, and, if she had not insisted upon doing everything for herself—which meant that after the age of eighty she was always falling down and breaking a leg or arm—she might well have lived many more years. Physically, like most of her family, she was tough, though psychologically—again like them—soft. Or rather what made her a curious character was the strange mixture in her psychology of toughness and softness. To hear her talk you would sometimes have concluded that she was living in a world of complete unreality. And so up to a point she did. She lived in a dream world which centred in herself and her nine children. It was the best of all possible worlds, a fairyland of nine perfect children worshipping a mother to whom they owed everything, loving one another, and revering the memory of their deceased father. Nothing that actually happened, no fact, however black, however inconsistent with the dream, made her doubt its reality and its rosiness. That anyone, particularly one of her own children, should doubt or throw doubt on it was the one thing in life which really distressed her. She loved all her nine surviving children, but she loved me less, I think, than any of the eight others, because she felt me to be unsympathetic to her view of the family, of the universe, and of the relation of the one to the other. By nature she was a good-tempered and happy person, and we did not often have family rows or scenes, but every now and then we did have a terrific row, a most distressing scene, and it was nearly always caused by one of her children disturbing my mother's dream.

I remember once at dinner my eldest brother and I, and probably one or two younger brothers, were arguing vehemently about an incident which, according to the papers, had just taken place in one of our wars, probably the Boer war: a gunner of the R.H.A., rushing his gun up to a vital position, looked down and saw his brother lying wounded on the ground. For some reason, to stop his horses or swerve would have been contrary to orders or to the Gunners' tradition and therefore disastrous. Like a good soldier—so the papers said—he shut his eyes and drove over his brother. Was he right? My brother Herbert said he was wrong. I said he was right and gave an interesting account of the thoughts which would pass through my head of the arguments, military and moral, which would determine my action, if, in some future war, I found myself unfortunately driving a gun over the wounded body of Herbert. We had become so interested in the problem that we had completely forgotten the presence of my mother and my sister. Both were in tears and almost in hysterics, and from about 8.30 until near midnight we tried without success to restore the damaged fabric of my mother's dream and calm the fury of feminine distress. My brother did not make the business easy. He was one of those persons who, with the best of intentions, can never leave well alone, and every time that my mother seemed to have got rid of the appalling vision of one of her sons driving a gun over his brother and had begun to recover the rosiness of her fairyland, Herbert, thinking to make everything doubly sure and convince mother that we had all meant the same thing all the time, would begin again with: 'But, mother, you must see that', etc., etc., and we were instantly back where we started at 8.30 with mother and sister in tears.

The curious thing about my mother was that, although she lived in this dream world of rosy sentimentality and unreality, she was at the same time an extremely practical, sensible, hard-headed woman. When my father died, she found herself left with nine children, the eldest of whom was sixteen and the youngest three years old. Though my father had been making a considerable income at the bar, they spent nearly all of it, and suddenly at his death she passed from being very well off into a condition of comparative poverty. She had a little capital, but her income was quite inadequate to educate her nine children in the way that a barrister's children were habitually educated in the 1880s and 1890s. She was also saddled with a long lease of a very large house requiring seven or eight servants and an expenditure which she now could not possibly afford. My father must have been oddly careless about money, for at his own expense he had built a large wing on to the back of the house in Lexham Gardens, though he was the lessee, not the owner, of it. This was a fatal thing to do, for the house thus became much the largest in the street, and so it was now extremely difficult to let, being much larger and more expensive than the kind of house which the kind of people who wanted to live in Lexham Gardens expected to find there. It was indeed a white elephant to us, or an albatross hung round our necks, threatening to ruin my widowed mother and her nine innocent children.

For a year or two it depleted her capital, but just in the nick of time we got rid of it at some cost. She then showed great courage and sound sense. She took a much smaller house in Putney, into which she packed her nine children, a cook, a parlourmaid, and a housemaid, and she determined to spend the whole of her capital on educating her children, in the hope that by the time the money was exhausted they would be in positions in which they could maintain her and themselves. The gamble came off, but it would not have done so unless four of us had got scholarships at St Paul's school and three of us scholarships at Cambridge. From my twelfth to my twenty-fourth year the menace of money hung over us all always and we had to be extremely careful of every penny; but my mother, though she had occasional panics, behaved on the whole with great common-sense, and though we all knew the risks we were running, we did not worry much about it.

The complete break in my life at the age of eleven, caused by my father's death, and the change from considerable affluence to the menace of extreme poverty had a curious effect upon me and in fact all of us. Looking back from 1960 to 1892, when my father died, I think that there was something to be said for the kind of life lived by the Victorian Woolf family in Lexham Gardens and by the many other similar bourgeois families in Bayswater and Kensington. It is, of course, condemned by Karl Marx and his all-red disciples, and it is because I condemn its economic basis and its economic effect upon other classes that I have been a socialist for most of my life. But the social standards of value in Lexham Gardens were very high, much higher than in any proletarian society today or in the proletarian section of a mixed class society. There is much which can be and has been legitimately said against family life on the grand scale, as developed by the middle classes of the nineteenth century: its snugness and smugness, snobbery, its complacent exploitation of economic, sexual, and racial classes. It had an innate tendency to produce the spiritual suburbanism which was the warp upon which so many superior novelists wove their stories between 1890 and 1914, a suburbanism which was in a modern version of that lamentable philistinism which in previous generations had roused the sorrowful protests of Matthew Arnold and the fury and frenzy of Algernon Charles Swinburne. Yet it also had high psychological and aesthetic values, precisely those values which one feels so strongly in the family life as described in Tolstoy's novels. The actual relations between the human beings living in these large households and between the several households related by blood or friendship were, on the whole, in my remembrance extraordinarily human and humane. How much simpler everything would be if everything was either black or white, good or bad.

To return to the economic catastrophe of my father's death, it made us all a little more serious and mature than children between the ages of ten and fourteen are by nature. But it was an economic and materialist seriousness and maturity. I know all that there is to know about security and insecurity, of which much younger generations than mine have sung so many and such pathetic songs. I learned my lesson in 1892 before I was twelve years old. Before my father died, I—and, I think, the whole family—had a profound and, of course, completely unconscious sense of economic security, and, therefore, personally of social security. Money was not talked about or thought about or worried about; it was just there to be spent, not recklessly or extravagantly, but on things which ladies and gentlemen needed or wanted. And the social background, the house and servants and brougham and Sunday sirloin, which were based upon this invisible and unmentioned money, were accepted without question as stable and permanent, like the money. I was aware, at the age of eleven, that all this would send me to a public school, a university, and chambers in the Temple. This sense of economic and social security was, as I have said, innate and unconscious. It was followed suddenly in twenty-four hours by an acute and highly conscious sense of complete economic insecurity. Considering the tremendous reversal of fortune—which has always been assumed in literature to be the essence of tragedy—looking back, I am rather surprised that we did not take the whole thing more tragically. We did not worry much about the thing, but we became almost in a night economically serious and mature. In this we showed a good deal of sense.

We showed good sense because my experience convinces me that money is not nearly as important as we are inclined to believe. Until I reached the age of eleven we were very well off. For the next eleven years of my life we were extremely poor. Then for seven years I was comfortably off. When at the age of thirty-two I resigned from the Ceylon Civil Service, I had no money and no job, and, having married, Virginia and I had to work hard and be monetarily careful. After some ten years I found myself once more, as I had been in childhood, very well off. The point is that in all these economic vicissitudes, though money or its absence made a considerable superficial difference to one's way of life and the volume and quality of one's possessions, I cannot see that it ever had any great or fundamental effect upon my happiness or unhappiness.

In my view happiness and unhappiness are of immense importance, perhaps the most important things in life and, therefore, in an autobiography. It is curious that so little is known about them, particularly the happiness and unhappiness of children. I have pointed out in a serious book on politics, *Principia Politica*, that the apparently innate and profound unhappiness of the human infant, who will go into loud paroxysms of misery without provocation, is unknown in the young of other animals. This primeval pessimism of man must have great psychological and social importance, but autobiographically it is irrelevant, for, as far as I am concerned, I cannot remember anything about my infancy. At the time when my memories begin we were a cheerful and happy family of children, certainly above the average intellectually. But I can vividly recall two occasions when, at a very early age, I was suddenly stricken with an acute pang of cosmic rather than personal unhappiness.

My first experience of Weltschmerz, if that is what it was, must have come to me at the very early age of five or six. Behind the house in Lexham Gardens was a long parallelogram enclosed by the house on the north and on the other three sides by three grimy six-foot walls. It was a typical London garden of that era, consisting of a worn parallelogram of grass surrounded by narrow gravel paths and then narrow beds of sooty, sour London soil against the walls. Each child was given a few feet of bed for his own personal 'garden' and there we sowed seeds or grew pansies bought off barrows in the Earls Court Road. I was very fond of this garden and of my 'garden' and it was here that I first experienced a wave of that profound, cosmic melancholia which is hidden in every human heart and can be heard at its best—or should one say worst?—in the infant crying in the night and with no language but a cry. It happened in this way.

Every year in the last week of July or the first of August, the whole Woolf family went away for a summer holiday to the country. It was a large-scale exodus. First my mother went off and looked at houses. Then we were told that a house had been 'taken'. When the day came, six, seven, eight, and eventually nine children, servants, dogs, cats, canaries, and at one time two white rats in a bird-cage, mountains of luggage were transported in an omnibus to the station and then in a reserved 'saloon' railway carriage to our destination. I can remember country houses in Wimbledon, Kenley, Tenby, Penmaenmawr, Speldhurst, and Whitby which carry me back in memory to my fifth year. And I can remember returning one late, chilly September afternoon to Lexham Gardens from our holiday and rushing out eagerly to see the back garden. There it lay in its grimy solitude. There was not a breath of air. There were no flowers; a few spindly lilac bushes drooped in the beds. The grimy ivy drooped on the grimy walls. And all over the walls from ivy leaf to ivy leaf were large or small spider-webs, dozens and dozens of them, quite motionless, and motionless in the centre of each web sat a large or a small, a fat or a lean spider. I stood by myself in the patch of scurfy grass and contemplated the spiders; I can still smell the smell of sour earth and ivy; and suddenly my whole mind and body seemed to be overwhelmed in melancholy. I did not cry, though there were, I think, tears in my eyes; I had experienced for the first time, without understanding it, that sense of cosmic unhappiness which comes upon us when those that look out of the windows be darkened, when the daughters of music are laid low, the doors are shut in the street, the sound of the grinding is low, the grasshopper is a burden, and desire fails.

There is another curious fact connected with my passion among the spiders in the garden. Forty years later, when I was trying to teach myself Russian, I read Aksakov and the memories of his childhood. His description of the garden and the raspberry canes recalled to me most vividly my spider-haunted London garden and the despair which came upon me that September afternoon. I felt that what I had experienced among the spiders and ivy he must have experienced half a century before among the raspberries in Russia.

The second occasion on which I felt the burden of a hostile universe weigh down my spirit must have been when I was about eight years old. We had arrived in Whitby for our summer holidays and found ourselves in a large, new red-brick house on a cliff overlooking the sea. After tea I wandered out by myself to explore the garden. The house and garden were quite new for the garden was almost bare. Along the side facing the sea ran a long low mound or rampart. I sat there in the sunshine looking down on the sparkling water. It smelt and felt so good after the long hours in the stuffy train. And then suddenly quite near me out of a hole in the bank came two large black and yellow newts. They did not notice me and stretched themselves out to bask in the sun. They entranced me and I forgot everything, including time, as I sat there with those strange, beautiful creatures surrounded by blue sky, sunshine, and sparkling sea. I do not know how long I had sat there when, all at once, I felt afraid. I looked up and saw that an enormous black thunder cloud had crept up and now covered more than half of the sky. It was just blotting out the sun, and, as it did so, the newts scuttled back into their hole. It was terrifying and, no doubt, I was terrified.[1] But I felt something more powerful than fear, once more that sense of profound, passive, cosmic despair, the melancholy of a human being, eager for happiness and beauty, powerless in face of a

[1] It has been pointed out to me that Thomas Traherne seems to have had a similar experience. He writes in *Centuries of Meditation* (Third Century, No. 23): 'Another time in a lowering and sad evening, being alone in the field, when all things were dead and quiet, a certain want and horror fell upon me, beyond imagination. The unprofitableness and silence of the place dissatisfied me; its wideness terrified me; from the utmost ends of the earth fears surrounded me. How did I know but dangers might suddenly arise from the East and invade me from the unknown regions beyond the seas? I was a weak and little child, and had forgotten there was a man alive in the earth.'

hostile universe. As the great raindrops began to fall and the thunder to mutter and growl over the sea, I crept back into the house with a curious muddle of fear, contempt, scepticism, and fatalism in my childish mind.

The child's mind and, since the child is father of the man, the man's mind are supposed to be formed very largely by religion and education. I find it very difficult in retrospect to discover what effect either had upon my mind and character. Both my parents were respectably religious. They believed in God. My mother went to synagogue on Saturday mornings fairly often, my father on the major feasts and festivals. They had us taught Hebrew by a rabbi who looked more like the traditional Jesus Christ than anyone else I have ever seen. He was an incompetent teacher and taught us a smattering of Hebrew, just enough to enable us to repeat a few Hebrew prayers. I cannot remember ever having actively believed in God though I suppose I must at one time have accepted his existence in a passive way. I think myself, though probably very few will agree with me, that my experience with the spiders and the thunder cloud destroyed any belief in God and religion which I may have had before. I know that it was not long after my fourteeth birthday that I announced that I was an unbeliever and would not in future go to synagogue, and I am sure that I had been contemplating this step for some time before I took it. When I solemnly announced to my mother that I no longer believed in Jehovah she wept, but her tears were not very convincing, I think, either to me or to her. She was genuinely distressed, but not very acutely; that I should repudiate the deity and refuse to go to synagogue caused a family sensation, but only a mild one which lasted a very short time.

As regards God himself, it is interesting to observe that by 1894 his position had already become precarious. No one, not even the believers, believed that he would take any steps against me for becoming an atheist. He had become as aloof, intermittent, and tenuous as a comet, and just as ineffective to impinge upon matter or to punish a sinner. Indeed no intelligent person any longer in practical affairs even considered the possibility of God intervening to reward the virtuous or punish the sinner any more than to bring rain to a parched crop or immunity from cholera and smallpox. People did of course still talk as if he could or might do so, but they acted as if he couldn't. In less than a century his position had suffered a change almost exactly like that of the British monarchy. He had become a constitutional instead of an absolute God. He got any amount of reverence and worship from his ministers and people; but all his powers and prerogatives had fallen from his hands into those of priests, the Archbishop of Canterbury or the Pope, of clergymen, churches, and chapels. All that remained to the deity was in fact caput mortuum.

Looking at the event from my point of view, I cannot see that loss of religious faith had any effect at all upon me morally either for good or for bad. I never suffered any of those torments of doubt and pain, remorse and horror, which have been described by their sufferers in many classical nineteenth-century cases of men or women losing their faith. This may perhaps mean that my faith was always rather feeble or that I was never allergic to divinity. When I look into my heart and mind, I find a complete vacuum in certain places which in most other people seem to be full to overflowing. I feel absolutely no desire or necessity to worship. Indeed, I have an instinctive dislike of all gods and Gods, kings, queens, and princes. Unlike many people, I find it impossible to turn an ordinary man or an ordinary young woman into a myth of majesty and beauty, despite (or in part because of) the vast engines of modern propaganda, which in the press, the radio, and television, are employed so successfully to induce the masses to accept the miracle. The cry: 'I must have a God and a faith, or I should have no hope', leaves me cold. I can get no comfort from believing what I want to believe when I know that there is no possible reason for believing it to be true. In fact, however, the universe would for me be a more comfortless place if it owed its origin and laws to one of the Gods whom man has invented than if it was merely the inexplicable phenomenon that on the surface (which is all we see and know) it appears to be. If Jehovah or almost any of the other major deities is our creator and ruler, the lot of man is hopeless, for he is subject to a 'person' who is not only irrational, but cruel, vindictive, and uncivilised. The only tolerable Gods were those of the Greeks because no sensible man had to take them seriously. Of serious, major Gods only two have been civilised: Gautama Buddha and Jesus Christ. Buddha, however, is such an abstraction that he cannot be reckoned as one of the personal deities, and is to be regarded rather as one of the world's great philosophers, inventors of those fairy tales which we call metaphysics or rules of conduct which we call ethics. Christ seems to me to have been a great, but rather unpractical, man, who preached a civilised code of conduct and civilised way of life. If Europe had accepted Christ's Christianity and put it into practice, toning down or even rejecting some few rules of conduct prescribed in the Sermon on the Mount which are too utopian or civilised for human nature as we know it today, our history would have been less horrible and degraded and the world a far happier and far better place. Unfortunately, upon the civilised teaching of Jesus was grafted the dreadful doctrines of sin and punishment and that superstition which for thousands of years has haunted the savage and terrified mind of man—the belief that by killing or crucifying a God, a man, or a goat we can use their blood to wash away our sins. I am glad that I was never taught, as a child, this horrible doctrine of Crucifixion and Redemption.

Another thing which leads people to religion is the practice of praying. Here again I have never felt the slightest desire to pray to a God or to anyone or anything else. The whole business seems to me one of the oddest freaks in human psychology. It is easy enough to understand that if you really believe in a personal deity, and also believe that by the prescribed adulation, adjuration, and supplication you can induce him to do something to your advantage which otherwise he would not do or had forgotten to do—such as to make it rain over your fields, county, or country, or to destroy your enemy, or to forgive your sins—it is eminently sensible of you to pray to him or to hire a shaman, the Rector of the parish, or the Archbishop of Canterbury, as expert intercessor or professional go-between, to do the praying for you. But do nine out of ten of the people who pray or hire the professional prayers—do the professionals themselves, the parish priests and the Bishops and Archbishops, really believe today that they can induce God to make it rain, to destroy Germans or Russians, or to cure a child or a king of cancer or tuberculosis? I doubt whether they believe anything of the kind, and I simply cannot understand how they can go on year after year saying prayers which they know cannot have the slightest efficacy.

But there is an even odder phenomenon than this in the psychology of prayer. Years ago when I was in my early forties, and therefore pretty uncompromising, I was one day eating my bleak plate of roast mutton at the unemotional dinner table in the tenebrous dining-room of 41 Grosvenor Road. In other words I was dining with the Webbs and I was sitting between Beatrice Webb and her sister Mrs Henry Hobhouse. Somehow or other the subject of prayer turned up, and I said with some emphasis that I had never really prayed in my life; I had, of course, said my prayers as a child, the prayers which we were taught, like all well brought up, middle-class children, whatever the religious fold or sty we happened to be born into, to say morning and evening, but I had never prayed with the feeling than I was really addressing or asking someone something. I added that I could not understand how any intelligent person of the twentieth century could get himself into the frame of mind in which praying to God meant something to him. The two sisters fell upon me vigorously, the one from one side and the other from the other. I had met Mrs Hobhouse very rarely, but I knew Mrs Webb quite well and had the greatest respect and liking for her. She was one of the most intelligent persons I have known, but with some large blind spots in her intellectual and aesthetic vision. She told me that she habitually prayed with the utmost intensity and profound spiritual effect.

I tried that day at dinner and later in other conversations with Beatrice Webb to discover exactly what she prayed about and what the profound psychological effect upon her was, but I never got anywhere near an understanding. I do not think that she had any belief in a personal God or that she believed in anything which I should regard as religion, though she may have followed Shaw in the characteristic compromise, in deference to the scientific age, or substituting the Life Force for old bearded Jehovah. But can one pray to a Life Force? At any rate I failed completely to get Beatrice to explain what she prayed about or what the effect was. The nearest that I got to an explanation was that when she prayed she got the same kind of 'release' or relaxation of tension which some people get from confession to a priest or a psycho-analyst.

The explanation of such a psychological idiosyncrasy as this is probably never simple and all sorts of contradictory thoughts and feelings were probably required to combine to make Beatrice Webb pray. At first sight she presented to one a façade of perfect poise and certitude, and with Sidney opposite her to catch and return with such precision the ball of conversation, it seemed fantastic to believe that any doubts or hesitation could ever assail the Webbs in Grosvenor Road. Occasionally one might say something to them which they would not discuss on the ground that it was 'not their subject' and that they knew nothing about it—it is curious to remember that when I first knew them, which was before the 1914 war, foreign affairs was 'not their subject'. But even these flashes of ignorance only added to the impression of their omniscient certitude. For though neither of them was in the least arrogant, one was left with the impression that if the subject had any real importance it would not be 'not their subject'.

Sidney's façade was no façade at all; he was all the way through exactly what he appeared to be on the surface. He had no doubts or hesitations (just as he had never had a headache or constipation); for he knew accurately what could be known about important subjects or, if he did not actually know it, he knew that he could obtain accurate knowledge about it with the aid of a secretary and a card index. When Beatrice talked about religion or prayer, I never remember him to have taken any part in the conversation, though he seemed to follow it with attentive amusement. I am sure that prayer and God meant even less to him than they did to me. But you could not see much of Beatrice without realising that, beneath the metallic façade and the surface of polished certainty, there was a neurotic turmoil of doubt and discontent, suppressed or controlled, an ego tortured in the old-fashioned religious way almost universal among the good and wise in the nineteenth century. I do not think tortured is too strong a word, for, if you watched Beatrice Webb when she was not the hostess, not talking, but attending only to her own thoughts, you would occasionally see a look of intense spiritual worry or acute misery cross her face. This deep-seated maladjustment is confirmed by her autobiography which reveals her as a woman of strong emotions with a profound conflict within herself between what she calls 'the ego which affirmed' and 'the ego which denied'. She had too the temperament, strongly suppressed, the passions and imagination, of an artist, though she would herself have denied this. Her defence against these psychological strains and stresses was a highly personal form of mysticism, and in the consolatory process prayer played an important, if to me incomprehensible, part.

My attitude to prayer and religion appeared to irritate Beatrice, though in general she was, I think, fond of both Virginia and me. (During the war and not long before her death, she told Bobo Mayor that she would like to see us again and would come up to London for the day if Bobo would get us to lunch with her. We went and lunched with her, Mrs Drake, and Bobo. She was more mellow and affectionate than I had known her before; she asked me what I was writing and, when I told her, characteristically said that I must read their *English Local Government*, Vol. IV, *Statutory Authorities for Special Purposes*, and a few days later she sent me a copy of the book. That was the last time I ever saw her.) To return to her attitude towards my attitude to religion, one Sunday when we were staying for a week-end with them at Passfield Corner, the conversation at lunch got on the subject of the teaching of religion in schools. When I said that I did not think it desirable that religion should be taught at all in schools, she was vehemently against me and carried the conversation from the luncheon table to the library. It was the first time that I realised to the full the strength of her passions and mysticism. She seemed to get angry that I mildly maintained my opinion, and marched up and down the room arguing almost violently. Indeed, up and down she marched faster and faster, and as she whisked herself round at each turn faster and faster, talking all the time, suddenly at one of the whisks or turns something in her skirt gave way and it fell on the floor entangling her feet. She stopped, picked it up, and holding it against her waist, continued her march up and down, never for a moment interrupting her passionate argument in favour of the teaching of religion in schools. Sidney and Virginia sat silent all through the discussion.

I do not understand Beatrice Webb's attitude to religion. It was peculiar to herself. As I said, I do not think she was religious or had a belief in God. Mysticism and scepticism were so nicely balanced in her that her mysticism was of the most generalised and intellectualised kind. She was intellectually too honest and austere ever to swallow or accept the religion of a Church, whether Anglican or Catholic. Difficult as I find it to understand her psychology, it is simple compared with that of intelligent intellectuals who, having attained that profound scepticism which is the religion of all sensible men, suddenly contrive to swallow in one gargantuan or synthetic act of faith the innumerable and fantastic doctrines and dogmas of the Church of England or the Church of Rome. I can understand how that Jew of Tarsus, a city in Cilicia, a citizen of no mean city, as he was accustomed proudly to insist, long ago on his way to Damascus with intent to persecute Christians, being a stern orthodox Jew, taught according to the perfect manner of the ancient Jewish law, suddenly in broad daylight seeing a great light from heaven surrounding him and hearing a voice say: 'Saul,

Saul, why persecutest thou me? I am Jesus of Nazareth, whom thou persecutest'—I can understand how Saul of Tarsus suffered instantly on the road to Damascus a complete conversion. But the belief to which he was converted was as simple as the belief from which he was converted. The great light and the voice from heaven convinced him that Jesus of Nazareth had not been a fraud, that he had really come to fulfil what the prophets and Moses had said would come, that he was the first man to rise from the dead—there he was after death appearing on the road to Damascus—and that it was his messianic mission to shew light to Jew and Gentile, teaching them how to repent and turn to God.

The psychology of this kind of conversion, whether through Balaam's ass or the visions of a St Teresa, seems to me completely comprehensible. You believe already in some form of thaumaturgical religion and suddenly a new thaumaturgist or an apparent miracle converts you violently to some other form. But there is no comparison with this in the psychological somersault by which an intelligent sceptic acquires in one mouthful the encyclopaedia of amazing beliefs which successfully turn him into a Roman Catholic or a member of the Church of England. By what process of the mind or the emotions does one acquire sudden belief that the New Testament is a record of fact, that the Athanasian Creed is more certainly true and more significant than the multiplication table, and that those astonishing statements of the citizen of no mean city which the Rector of Rodmell reads to us when we assemble to bury one of our neighbours are not merely matters of fact, but also intelligible? There are one or two quondam sceptics whom I have known well, whom I still regard with admiration and affection, and whose somersault into a Church remains incomprehensible to me. T. S. Eliot is the most remarkable. Tom, when we first knew him, was neither an Englishman nor an Anglican. I helped him to become an Englishman by becoming one of his statutory sponsors, and I am, I think legitimately, proud that I not only printed and published *The Waste Land* but had a hand in converting its author from an American to an English poet. I had no hand in converting him into an Anglican. In later years when he stayed with us at Rodmell, it filled us with silent amazement to see him go to early morning Communion at the village church. I could, if pushed to it, produce an intellectually adequate explanation of the psychological process which brought Tom into the respectable fold of the Church of England, but I have no sympathetic understanding of it as I have of many other mental states in which I do not actually share.

I have wandered forward from my point and my childhood, the point being the effect of religion and education upon me as a child. There is nothing more to be said about the effect of religion. As for education, what a strange, haphazard muddle it all seems to have been when one looks back upon it. The first teaching that I can remember to have received was at a girls' school in Trebovir Road, one of those many Kensington streets which were the waste land of Victorian middle-class dreariness. The school, at which my sister Bella had been for some years a pupil, was kept by a Mrs Cole and it included a kindergarten presided over by a Mrs Mole. Though the rest of the school was for girls only, co-education being in those days unknown, small boys were admitted to the kindergarten and entrusted to the incompetent Mrs Mole. To the incompetent Mrs Mole I was entrusted at the age of five or six. I cannot remember to have learnt anything at all in Trebovir Road except to take an early sexual interest in small girls. For besides the face of Mrs Mole and the face of Mrs Cole and the extremely low table at which we sat in the kindergarten, I can remember only two incidents. One was that I habitually sat illicitly holding under the table the hand of a small yellow-haired girl, and the other was that I somehow or other induced a rather older girl, with black hair, who was not in the kindergarten, to cause an open scandal by kissing me in the hall.

Whether it was considered that my education in other things was too slow or my education in sex too fast at Mrs Cole's school, I do not know, but I was certainly removed from it pretty soon. My memory of what exactly happened to my education after that is hazy, at any rate for a time. We had for many years a governess living in the house, Miss Amy, who came from the Channel Islands and was bilingual in French and English. She taught us French and reading, writing, and arithmetic, all rather incompetently. Fräulein Berger came two or three times a week to teach us German, and I have a dim remembrance of other teachers, male and female, leaving an impression of being despised and dejected, insulted and injured, on my childish mind as they arrived weekly to teach us the piano, dancing, elocution, and other subjects of the same kind which everyone concerned, including the pupils, seemed to assume from the start to be hopeless and useless. It is extraordinary that people like my parents who attached great value to knowledge, books, and things of the mind should have been content, as they appear to have been, in the 1880s to provide such very poor teachers for their small children. Until I came into the hands of Mr Floyd (of whom I will tell more in a moment) at the age of nine, I had never been taught anything to rouse my interest by anyone. Yet I am sure that my parents spent large sums, according to the standards of the time, upon our education. The people who taught us meant well and were all of them kind and decent to us, but they were themselves uneducated and quite uninterested in anything to do with the mind, and they therefore never interested me in anything they were teaching.

My nurse, who was with us for many years and brought us all up, had much less education than our governesses, but she was the first person to interest me in books and in the strange and fascinating workings of the human mind. She was a Somersetshire woman, born and bred on a farm, a rigid and puritanical Baptist. She read a Baptist paper every week from end to end and somehow or other she had got hold of a copy of de Quincey's *Confessions of an English Opium Eater*. This book entranced her; she read it again and again. I find it difficult to believe my memory when it distinctly tells me that Nurse Vicary used to give me a detailed account of what she read in the *Baptist Times* and often read aloud de Quincey to me, and that at the age of four or five I was quite an authority on the politics and polemics of the Baptist sect and often fell asleep rocked, not in a cradle, but on the voluptuous rhythm of de Quincey's interminable sentences whose baroque ornamentations must have been embellished by nurse's mispronunciations and her Somerset accent. But I had the deepest affection for her and for the opium eater, and she was the first person to teach me the pleasure of fear and thrill over public events, the horrors and iniquities of the great world of society and politics as recorded in the *Baptist Times* about the year 1885. I can still feel myself physically enfolded in the warmth and safety of the great nursery on the third floor of the house in Lexham Gardens, the fire blazing behind the tall guard, the kettle singing away, and nurse, with her straight black hair parted in the centre, and her smooth, oval peasant face, reading the *Baptist Times* or the visions of the opium eater. Just as the spider haunted garden remains in my mind as the primary pattern for all the waste lands and desolations into which I have wandered in later life, so the nursery with its great fire, when the curtains were pulled and the gas lit and nurse settled down to her reading, and occasionally far off could be heard the clop-clop of a horse in a hansom cab or four-wheeler, the nursery remains for me the Platonic idea laid up in heaven of security and peace and civilisation. But though in the course of my life I have passed through several desolations of desolation more desolate than the garden with its grimy ivy and its spider webs, I never again found any safety and civilisation to equal that of the gas-lit nursery.[1]

Outside the security of that nursery, terrible and terrifying things happened in the Kensington and London of fifty or sixty years ago. Hushed or whispered stories of Jack the Ripper, I think, penetrated into the nursery, and in my schoolroom days we were all terrified by a little woman, dressed all in black, who on foggy winter nights lurked in the Kensington streets, stabbed unsuspecting gentlemen with a long knife, and then disappeared into the darkness and the fog. There is no doubt that in the eighties and nineties of last century under the prim and pious pattern of bourgeois life, just beneath the surface of society lay a vast reservoir of uncivilised squalor and brutality which no longer exists. It was a class reservoir, and the squalor and brutality welled up, in London at any rate, from those appalling slums inhabited by the 'lower classes'. It was when these dreadful drunken or savage creatures broke out for a moment from their lairs into the life of a small middle-class child that he first knew the paralysing anguish of fear. I can still remember with the most sickening vividness some of the earliest occasions on which I learnt the agony and humiliation of unmitigated fear. The earliest of all is a memory of waking up in the middle of the night and hearing the shrieks of a woman pass along the Cromwell Road at the back of our house, pass along and fade away into the distance, leaving at last complete silence more terrifying even than the solitary shrieking. Next, standing on a chair at the dining-room window, watching the luggage being loaded on to the omnibus to take us all away on our holiday, and suddenly a drunken man in tatters, staggering about, trying to help with the luggage, cursing, swearing, becoming violent, and then finally the horrible sight of his vain struggle with a policeman and his being frog-marched away.

[1] The nurse in the photograph of the Woolf family, plate 2, is not Nurse Vicary. She was a nurse who came and looked after infants in arms; I think her name was Mrs Anselm.

Thirdly, here is another scene. We are returning with nurses or governess down Earls Court Road having just passed the almost rural peace of Holland Walk and the sophisticated civilisation of old Holland House. Suddenly out of a narrow side street, which led to one of the blackest of Kensington slums, two policemen appeared dragging a tall, raging and raving woman. They were followed by a small growling, but cringing crowd. Those who have never seen the inhabitants of a nineteenth-century London slum can have no idea of the state to which dirt, drink, and economics can reduce human beings. The men and women who surged or shuffled into the Earls Court Road behind the two policemen were, like the men and women whom La Bruyère saw in the fields in France, 'animaux farouches'. It is true that they had, like the seventeenth-century agricultural species, 'une voix articulée' and, when they stood on their hind legs, human faces, so that, if nurse had read to me La Bruyère instead of de Quincey, I might have stood in the Earls Court Road of 1885, instead of in the France of 1685, and murmured 'en effet ils sont des hommes'. They were human beings, but they made me sick with terror and disgust in the pit of my small stomach, and the last scene, as the nurses hurried us away, is indelibly imprinted on my memory—the woman flung down in the middle of the road by one policeman, her battered black hat rolling away into the gutter, while the other drove back into their lairs the semi-circle of snarling 'human beings'. Such were the lessons in the sociology of classes which a child might learn in London streets about the time when Queen Victoria was celebrating the fiftieth year of her reign.

Looking back to that scene in a 'respectable' Kensington street, I am struck by the immense change from social barbarism to social civilisation which has taken place in London (indeed in Great Britain) during my lifetime. The woman, the policemen, the nurses, the small boy, the respectable passers-by averting their eyes—all these are inhabitants of a London and a society which has passed away. It can be counted, I suppose, as one of the miracles of economics and education. The slums and their unfortunate and terrifying products no longer exist. No one but an old Londoner who has been born and bred and has lived for fifty or sixty years in London can have any idea of the extent of the change. It is amazing to walk down Drury Lane or the small streets about Seven Dials today and recall their condition only fifty years ago. Even as late as 1900 it would not have been safe to walk in any of those streets after dark. The whole locality was an appalling slum, and its inhabitants, like all those of the innumerable slums scattered over London, were the 'animaux farouches' described in the previous paragraph. They and their lairs, with the poverty, dirt, drunkenness, and brutality, have disappeared; the masses, which had terrified the bourgeoisie ever since they began to march from Paris to Versailles in October 1789, have become the working classes and in England, at any rate, if a socialist dare say so, the working class has become almost indistinguishable, in its way of life, manners, and outlook, from the bourgeoisie. In the last forty years of my life I have got to know the life of the English countryside—in the south of England—as intimately as I know London—indeed, more intimately, for in London one knows intimately only a tiny fragment of its life—and I have seen the same process of profound social change, the emergence of a civilisation out of a barbarism, take place in rural Sussex. In a later chapter I shall have something more to say of this.

I must return once more to my education. In Lexham Gardens the children were divided between the nursery and the schoolroom. I do not remember at what age one was promoted to the schoolroom but I suppose it must have been round about the age of six or seven. Education began in the schoolroom which was presided over by Miss Amy, a tiny little Channel Islander. She looked exactly like a little robin, extraordinarily cheerful and sweet-tempered. I think we were all rather well behaved children, but sometimes I used to try her beyond endurance and she would burst into tears. She had a passion for jam puffs, which were sold at Andersen's bakershop in Earls Court Road, and, when Miss Amy was in tears, I always sneaked out to Andersen's and bought her a jam puff. The jam puff and 'I'm sorry, Miss Amy' always brought immediate forgiveness. At some period of my childhood I was sent to St Paul's Preparatory School. I cannot be quite certain when this took place, but I think it must have been in 1889, when I was nine years old. The only thing which I can remember about it is that I hated the place and was terrified by a boy who occasionally interrupted the relentless slowness of time and the narcotic boredom of the lesson by falling down in an epileptic fit. I cannot remember to have learnt anything at this preparatory school. I am astonished, when I recall the ten years of my education from 1889 to 1899, to find that the human brain could survive the desiccation, erosion, mouldiness, frustration applied to it for seven or eight hours every day and called education. I reckon that, before I went to Cambridge, I must have spent at least 10,000 hours of my short life sitting in some class-room, smelling of ink and boys, being taught by a gowned schoolmaster usually Latin, Greek, or mathematics, and occasionally French or history. An immense number of those 10,000 hours was spent by me and, I think, the master in dense boredom. Of all my masters only two (or possibly four) were interested in what they were teaching and interested in making it interesting. My intelligence must have been considerable to have survived this process of desiccation and attrition.

I was only a term, or possibly two terms, at St Paul's Preparatory School. In 1890, when I was ten years old, I was put under the care of a tutor who came daily to Lexham Gardens to teach me and my elder brother, Herbert. Mr Floyd was a remarkable man, an eccentric who made the task of learning interesting. England, or rather Britain, breeds more eccentrics than most nations, and there is a national flavour to their eccentricity which is difficult to define or describe. In private life they are mostly bores, but they perform a useful purpose in leavening the heavy dough of English society or, to alter the metaphor, they help to keep the pores open to the flow of freedom. It was a good thing for a child of nine or ten to be taught by an eccentric like Mr Floyd who had views of his own, unusual views, about most things and did what he thought right and proper unmoved by the misprision of his superiors or the ridicule of his inferiors.

Mr Floyd was a tall, gaunt, long-legged man, very straight and upright, with thin greying hair and an absurd goatee. He had a large, wide-awake black hat which even in the street was more often in his hand than on his head. He had a curious look in his eyes of abstraction and ferocity. He instituted the following routine for us. After our breakfast Herbert and I walked to High Street Kensington station, where we met him. He then set off down Wright's Lane to Lexham Gardens at a tremendous pace, Herbert on one side and I on the other. We had to run as fast as we could in order to keep up with him, his long legs striding out as in the pictures of the man in the seven-league boots, his head tilted up, the long thin hairs of his head and beard fluttering in the breeze, grasping in one hand an umbrella and in the other a black bag. Nearly everyone turned and looked at us with astonishment as we passed and small streetboys or cads, as we then called them (I don't think they exist in London today), hooted at us. Mr Floyd paid no attention to anything like that.

As soon as we reached Lexham Gardens, we went straight through the hall to the small room overlooking the garden where we had our lessons. Mr Floyd immediately sat down and we sat down one on each side of him. He put his large watch on the table, raised a ruler made of olive wood from Palestine, and said in a solemn voice, 'Tacete', which is the Latin for 'Be silent'. Then for a quarter, a half, or a whole minute, as he chose, we had to sit absolutely motionless and silent. I still possess a little book in which I recorded from 26 March 1890 to 26 May 1891, the length of time each day I succeeded in being silent and motionless or failed. Mr Floyd, in a beautiful hand, has headed the book 'TACE' and has inscribed on the first page:

> Qui non novit tacere, nescit loqui.
> Stultus non novit silentium servare.

He has also written something in Hebrew, which is odd, because I am sure that he was not a Jew.

After 'Tacete' we said the multiplication tables up to twelve as fast as we could. We did this daily until we succeeded in saying them without a mistake for three days running, each time within two minutes. This is not an easy thing to do and it took us quite a long time before we succeeded; it was considered that, having performed the feat, we knew the multiplication tables and need never say them again. There was a good deal to be said for Mr Floyd's system, for, when I went to school, I found I was quicker than most boys in manipulating figures in simple arithmetic. He had also taught me to sit still and be silent on occasions, a rare accomplishment in a boy of ten. He taught me more than this. He had, I think, a genuine, if somewhat eccentric, passion for literature and he made one feel, even at that early age, that the books which we read with him—even Caesar *De Bello Gallico*—had something pleasurable in them, and were not merely instruments of educational torture. I have in my time been subjected, in the name of education, to so much mental torture, particularly the torture of the boredom of being taught by bored teachers, that I am grateful to Mr Floyd for having made me dimly aware at the age of ten that lessons—things of the mind—could be exciting and even amusing. He had for some books the same kind of insatiable love as my nurse had for de Quincey. One of them was *Rasselas*, a copy of which he always carried in his pocket. We read *Rasselas* with him and he pointed out its beauties to us, but, unlike nurse's *Opium Eater*, it is a book which had and has no appeal to me. It seemed to me tedious and tiresome, but there must be something to it, because my mother, who sometimes came and listened to our lessons, became entranced by it. She bought a copy which was usually by her bedside and before she died she must have read the book dozens of times.

One of the pleasant things about Mr Floyd was that he was one of those very rare people who never mind looking ridiculous. He taught us to play fives against a wall on the verandah and he also taught us singlestick, and as he was very tall and we were very small, the spectacle was extraordinarily absurd. But to see Mr Floyd at his best was to see him reading Caesar with my canary sitting on the top of his head. I had a canary, called Chickabiddy, who was so tame that the door of his cage was never shut during the day and he used to fly about the room. I had taught him to come and perch on one's head if one called 'Chickabiddy, Chickabiddy', and it used to be a game we played for two of us to stand at opposite ends of a room and make him fly backwards and forwards very rapidly from head to head. Mr Floyd became very fond of him and he took a liking to Mr Floyd's head. Mr Floyd had a habit of walking up and down the room as he taught us, and Chickabiddy would sit the whole time on his head. The moment would come—eagerly awaited by us—when Chickabiddy would make a mess on the top of Mr Floyd's head. If he was aware of the evacuation, he wiped the mess off with a piece of blotting-paper without interrupting the lesson. Sometimes he did not feel what had happened, and then I, as owner of the bird, said: 'I am afraid, Sir, Chickabiddy has made a mess,' and Mr Floyd would say very politely: 'Thank you, my boy,' and wipe the mess off with the blotting-paper.

When my father died early in 1892, I was eleven years old and Mr Floyd passed out of my life completely: he never came to see us again and I do not know what happened to him. He made a great impression upon me and I have a vivid memory of him, both physically and mentally. I think he must have been a very humane and civilised man, but, young as I was, I felt that he was an unhappy and disappointed man. Well, he passed out of my life and I was sent to a boarding school at Brighton. It was Arlington House in Kemp Town, an expensive preparatory school of which the headmaster was a Mr Burman. My brother Herbert had been sent there in 1891 when my father was still alive and we were well-off. A year later, when my father was dead, we were much too poor to afford the fees of Arlington House. But Mr Burman, who was a stupid, but a very nice and generous man, insisted that Herbert and I should both come to the school at greatly reduced fees, and later on he did the same thing for my four younger brothers. He was one of the most ingrained conservatives I have ever known. Arlington House was a leading preparatory school in Brighton and full of sons of rich people. But Mr Burman was so conservative that he would never change anything; in the first decade of the twentieth century things began to move and change even in middle-class education and Arlington House began to go downhill and eventually Mr Burman had to give it up.

I was at Arlington House for two years from 1892 to 1894. The education which I received was no better and no worse than that usually given at the time to the sons of successful army officers, barristers, clergymen, and stockbrokers. I was taught to play cricket and soccer seriously by masters who thought both games of great importance. One of them, Mr Woolley, was a first-class cricketer and a very good footballer, his attitude to cricket was that of an artist to his art. To be bowled or caught was pardonable; but to play an incorrect stroke or to cut or drive without 'style' was, even though you might hit a four off the stroke, a crime. The whole school was lined up every day in the summer term and did 'bat drill' for a quarter of an hour with Mr Woolley, a handsome, dark, lean, graceful man, facing us with a bat in his hand, like a conductor before his orchestra. 'Forward' or 'off drive', he would say making the stroke perfectly himself, and the whole school would play forward or off drive, and he, like the great conductor, would spot even the smallest boy in the back row if he did not come perfectly straight forward or did not follow through in the drive in perfect style. I was quite good at cricket and in both elevens, and I learned from Mr Woolley the seriousness of games, the importance of style, the duty when you go in to bat of making every stroke with the concentration which an artist puts into every stroke of his brush in painting a masterpiece. Since those days I have played nearly every kind of game from fives and bowls to golf and rugger, and I have played them each and all with the greatest pleasure. But Mr Woolley's teaching had such an effect upon me that I cannot play any game unless I treat it seriously, i.e. each stroke or movement must be correct and above all you must aim at 'style'.

If we were taught to take games seriously by the masters at Arlington House, we were taught to take all other lessons not seriously. We were taught Greek, Latin, arithmetic, algebra, euclid, history, geography, French, and scripture. All the masters were hopelessly bored by all these subjects and so were we. Anyone seen to be good at lessons or rudimentarily intelligent was suspect both to masters and boys; to be a 'swot', i.e. to take lessons at all seriously, was entirely despicable. I was then and have remained all my life a 'swot'; I escaped the unpleasant consequences at Arlington House and later at St Paul's, partly because I had a pretty violent temper and partly because I was sufficiently good at games to make intelligence and hard work pass as an eccentricity instead of being chastised as vice or personal nastiness. I must have been rather intelligent; otherwise I cannot see how I could possibly have learned enough from Mr Burman and his assistants to win, as I did, a scholarship at St Paul's in 1894.

The only thing I learned thoroughly at Arlington House, other than cricket, was the nature and problems of sex. These were explained to me, luridly and in minute detail, almost at once by a small boy who had probably the dirtiest mind in an extraordinarily dirty-minded school. I was at the time completely innocent and I had considerable difficulty in concealing from him the fact that it was only with the most heroic effort that I was preventing myself from being sick. However I soon recovered; one had indeed to develop a strong stomach in things sexual to stand up against the atmosphere of the school when I first went there. The facts are worth recording because they showed me for the first time at a very early age the enormous influence a few boys at the top of a school exercise upon the minds and behaviour of the masses below them. And what is true of a school is true also, I think, of almost every community or society of persons engaged in a common purpose or living in close relationship.

At the age of twelve I was not prudish, for I was much too innocent, and I do not think that I have ever been prudish after the nasty little X removed my innocence. But I have never known anything like the nastiness—corruption is hardly too strong a word—of the minds and even to some extent bodies of the little boys in Arlington House when I first went there. I instinctively disliked it at the time and, when I look back on it, it rather horrifies me even today. It was entirely due to two or three boys at the top of the school. They set the unsavoury tone and dictated the unpleasant manners of all the rest of us. I think they were rather older than boys usually are in a preparatory school, being stranded there as they were too stupid to pass even the entrance examination for a public school. They therefore very soon left in a bunch and my brother Herbert became captain of the school and I succeeded him. Herbert was something of a Puritan and refused to allow what the previous 'monitors' had encouraged. I followed his example, and, as we were both strict disciplinarians, when I left for St Paul's in 1894 the atmosphere had changed from that of a sordid brothel to that more appropriate to fifty fairly happy small boys under the age of fourteen.

No attempt of any kind was made at this school to educate us to become intelligent and responsible members of English society. On the contrary, in so far as anything was done at all, it was calculated to make us unfit to live in any free, civilised society. We were taught nothing of contemporary events, and we were never given the slightest hint that what one learned could have any relation to the life one lived and would have to live. There was not a corner or crevice in Mr Burman's mind which was not obstinately conservative. The only comment that I remember him to have made on public events was continual abuse of Mr Gladstone, whom he regarded as the author of all evil. One day when the school was walking back from Brill's Baths along the front, Mr and Mrs Gladstone drove by in an open victoria. All the way people recognised him and many waved or took their hats off, and he bowed continually and took his hat off to them. He did not look at all the kind of criminal anarchist and traitor whose portrait Mr Burman had drawn for us. My instinct has been, from a very early age, to disbelieve anything which I am told 'on authority' or at the least not to believe it. At the age of thirteen, I think I had already seen far enough through the headmaster to accept everything he said, except on the subject of Latin verbs and the like, with some reserve, and the sight of Mr Gladstone's eagle-like eminence sunning itself in the victoria confirmed my silent determination, since Mr Burman was a conservative, to be myself a liberal.

One of the boys at the school was a grandson of John Bright. Mr Burman never tired of gibing at him for having such an abominable grandfather. This was typical of what the masters at a first-class bourgeois preparatory school thought funny in the eighteen-nineties. But for pedagogic lack of humour the following is hard to beat. The French master at Arlington House was a M. Marot who claimed to be descended from a long line of Counts. He used to ride a horse which was peculiarly angular, and to our eyes he rode very badly. One day when returning from cricket we saw him riding on the front, and, meeting him later in the school, my brother outrageously said to him: 'We saw you riding the old cow, Sir.' M. Marot, who went purple in the face when angry, solemnly punished Herbert by making him write out 500 times: 'I must not call M. Marot's horse a cow.'

I wish I could recall vividly what it felt like to be a boy of twelve or thirteen at a private school in Brighton in 1893. I have a dim remembrance of it and what I do remember is not at all like the usual picture presented to us by adults, whether parents, educationists, or novelists. There were intervals of terrific energy and high spirits, when, for instance, one was playing games or the whole school was romping about the garden or the gym. Otherwise one seemed to live in a condition of almost suspended animation, a kind of underwater existence, for my mental world had to me something of the dim, green twilight which the physical world must have presented, I thought, in Jules Verne's *Twenty Thousand Leagues Under the Sea*. It was a dream world; but it was the actual world of school that one seemed to be dreaming half awake, and always with the feeling that one was just about fully to wake up. I wanted to wake up and, at the same time, was half afraid of doing so. Now at the age of nearly eighty I am doubtful whether I ever have.

One of the reasons for my mental twilight was, I am sure, that I wanted to use my mind, but practically nothing was done to help one to do so—indeed, for the most part one was discouraged from doing so. At home, my mother encouraged us from an early age to read 'good' books, Scott, Dickens, Thackeray, but it is a remarkable fact that until the age of sixteen, when at St Paul's I got into A. M. Cook's form, none of my teachers, except Mr Floyd, ever suggested to me that it was possible to read a work of literature or other serious book for pleasure.

I was not unhappy at my private school; indeed, I was usually quite happy, but it was the happiness of someone only half awake. Looking back, out of the welter of dimly remembered things I can recall a few which I enjoyed immensely. First and most important, food—to be taken out and given a lunch of steak and kidney pudding and ices at Mutton's on the front, after weeks of the rather nasty school food, was marvellous, and I can still recall the deliciousness of a large, hot Cowley bath bun which we were allowed to buy after bathing in Brill's Baths. Then sights—there was a clump of valerian in the garden and on a hot summer day one could watch the humming-bird hawk moths, two or three at a time, come to it. I remember too another entrancing sight connected with butterflies. In the spring we were always taken in coaches for the school treat to Laughton to have a picnic and wander about the woods. And down the glades, which in recollection seem to me to have been carpeted, as they now never are, with spring flowers, gilded in the dappled sunlight, with that extraordinary velvety flight of theirs, dozens of the Pearlbordered Fritillary. I can also recall that it was at Arlington House that I first experienced intense pleasure connected with reading. In very bad weather and in the late afternoon of Sundays, the whole school sat in the big schoolroom in silence and read books which one could take out of a large cupboard, containing the 'school library'. Under the gas jets, on winter evenings, a great fire burning in the huge fireplace, in the silence and comfortable fug, I suddenly found myself transported from the rather boring and always uncertain life to which one had been arbitrarily and inexplicably committed, to the strangest, most beautiful, and entrancing world of *Twenty Thousand Leagues Under the Sea* or *The Log of the Flying Fish*. There is no doubt that I then experienced some of the exquisite pleasure, some purging of the passions, that later came to me, as to Aristotle, from more orthodox literary masterpieces.

In the autumn of 1893 I went to St Paul's School in West Kensington, plunging with a shiver into a much larger and tougher world than I had known hitherto. There I at once began to develop the carapace, the façade, which, if our sanity is to survive, we must learn to present to the outside and usually hostile world as a protection to the naked, tender, shivering soul. At least, I suppose this is true. I have never known anyone who had no carapace or façade at all, but I have known people who had extraordinarily little, who seemed wonderfully direct, simple, spiritually unveiled. They may be highly intelligent and intellectual, but this nakedness of the soul gives them always a streak of the simpleton. They are, indeed, the simpletons—Koteliansky used to translate the Russian word as 'sillies'—the 'sillies' whom Tolstoy thought were the best people in the world. There was something of the 'silly' in Virginia, as I always told her and she agreed, and there was a streak of the 'silly' in Moore. Obviously there is something remarkably good in these streaks, and perhaps if anyone had the courage to be a complete 'silly', to have no façade at all, he would get on just as well as, or better than, the tortoises, the timid souls who live their whole lives behind a shell or mask.

I am afraid that there was never a touch of the 'silly' in me and I soon developed a carapace, which, as the years went past, grew ever thicker and more elaborate. The façade tends with most people, I suppose, as the years go by, to grow inward so that what began as a protection and screen of the naked soul becomes itself the soul. This is part of that gradual loss of individuality which happens to nearly everyone and the hardening of the arteries of the mind which is even more common and more deadly than those of the body. At any rate, I certainly began to grow my shell at St Paul's about the age of fourteen, and, being naturally of an introspective nature, I was always half-conscious of doing so. What the façade hides or is intended to hide in other people can rarely be known with certainty and the psycho-analysts would probably hold that it is even more difficult to know what lies behind one's own. I suspect that the male carapace is usually grown to conceal cowardice. Certainly in my own case, I believe, the character which I invented to face the world with originated, to a very large extent, in fear, in mental, moral, or physical cowardice. It was the fear of ridicule or disapproval if one revealed one's real thoughts or feelings, and sometimes the fear of revealing one's fears, that prompted one to invent that kind of second-hand version of oneself which might provide for one's original self the safety of a permanent alibi. When I said above that I was half-conscious of doing this, I did not mean that I did it deliberately; I did it instinctively, but, being introspective, was half-conscious that a mask was forming over my face, a shell over my soul.

I was five years at St Paul's, from 1894 to 1899, when I went up to Trinity College, Cambridge. My education, in the technical and strict sense of the word, began at the beginning and ended at the end of those five years at school, for though I learned many and very important things in my five years at Cambridge, they were not the educational things which schools and universities are expected to teach one. The education which one received at St Paul's in the last decade of the nineteenth century was Spartan in its intellectual toughness and severity. It was devised and enforced by the high-master, F. W. Walker, a most curious and alarming man. He was a short but solid man, with a red face, rather bloodshot eyes, a straggly beard, a very wide mouth showing black teeth, blackened by the perpetual smoking of strong cigars. He had a deep and raucous voice of immense volume, and he usually roared with it as though in a violent rage, so that one often heard the bellow of the 'old man', as of an enraged bull, echoing down the corridors or through the hall. The 'old man' had developed and encouraged in himself the one-sidedness and eccentricity which are the occupational diseases of schoolmasters; he acted his part with such conscious vigour that he was almost a stage schoolmaster. I do not know anything of his private life, but I should guess that he only cared for two things: first an amalgam of St Paul's School and Greek and Latin, and second an amalgam of good food, good drink, and good cigars.

I was as a boy, and am now, concerned with only the first amalgam, for it determined my education and the equipment of my mind. Despite, or because of, his barbarity and fanaticism the old man became a great headmaster, for, whether the school and the education are judged to be good or bad, they had a character of their own and were created by him. His vision of the school and education was narrow and fanatical. The object of a public school was, in his view, to give the boys the severest and most classical of classical educations. He seemed to be interested only in the clever boys and his object was to turn them into brilliant classical scholars. I think that he and his son, whom he had succeeded in turning into one of the most brilliant of Balliol scholars, the winner of every kind of academic prize and honour, had a genuine love for scholarship and even for classical literature, but their love had become fused and lost in a mixture of classics and St Paul's School, of scholarship and scholarships. For the one test of whether St Paul's School was doing what the 'old man' wanted it to do had become in his view the number and quality of the scholarships which the pupils year by year won at Oxford and Cambridge colleges. It was generally felt that something would be wrong with the universe and with the school if in any year St Paul's did not win more Oxford and Cambridge scholarships than any other public school and, at the least, one Balliol scholarship at Oxford and one Trinity scholarship at Cambridge. And in the eighteen-nineties there was usually nothing wrong with the universe or the school.

In order to turn small boys into scholars the highmaster had devised an extraordinarily intensive system of teaching Latin and Greek. If you came to the school without a scholarship, you were shuffled off at once into an appropriate form, on the classical side if you seemed to be fairly bright, but if not so bright, on the army, science, or history side. If you had won a scholarship, you were not at once drafted into an ordinary form; you were put into what was called 'the Hall'. Physically it was the school hall in which the whole school assembled daily for prayers and occasionally for functions like the annual prize-giving, called the Apposition. I, with all the other scholars of my year, was immediately put into 'the Hall' under Mr Pantin, a kindly but melancholy master. There we sat for a whole term day after day, for the whole school day, doing Greek and Latin composition. We did absolutely nothing else. At the end of it, the foundations of the ancient Greek and Latin languages—their grammar, syntax, vocabulary—had been ground into me as thoroughly as the multiplication tables by Mr Floyd. They had become part of the permanent furniture of my mind. And this process of laying the foundations of scholarship was carried out by Mr Pantin under the personal and terrifying supervision of the highmaster. At least once a day, and sometimes more often, the doors of the hall would be flung open and with an ominous swish of his gown the 'old man' would sail in and flop down, with a growl and a grunt, on the form next to one of us. He then with great care corrected his victim's work in a curiously thin and palsied handwriting, with growls and grumblings and occasionally a roar of rage. As he did this almost daily for a whole term, he got to know personally at once each boy who had won a scholarship and could judge his intellectual capacity, i.e. whether X was a potential Balliol or Trinity scholar and whether Y would never be likely to get anything better than an exhibition at one of the smaller colleges.

The highmaster's character and methods were early revealed to me by the following incident. One afternoon a few weeks after I had been handed over to Mr Pantin and his educational machine for producing classical pâté de foie gras, the highmaster swept into the hall and sat down on the form by my side. He turned and looked at me with a terrifying leer which revealed a satyr's mouth full of black and decaying teeth. He did not say anything until he had finished correcting my work. When he had put the pen down, he turned and gave me another leer. 'Boy', he roared at me, with a roar, not of rage, but of good humour, 'boy, your mother has been to see me. Your mother did not like me.' He then patted me on the head and went off to another apprehensive small boy. When I got home in the evening I heard from my mother, almost in tears, the story of her interview with Mr Walker. She was, not unnaturally, very proud of my having won a scholarship at St Paul's and had asked for an interview with the highmaster in order to discuss with him my brilliant future. She had, I suppose, expected to receive congratulations on being the mother of such a clever small boy. Alas, her lamb was torn to pieces. The boy, said Mr Walker, had been badly taught; his Latin was hopelessly bad and his Greek worse. He knew no grammar and no syntax; he could not do Latin or Greek composition, and his translation was not much better; it was doubtful whether anything could be done with him. After five or ten minutes of this kind of tirade, he paused, and my mother, only just restraining her tears, said: 'But, Mr Walker, what can I do?' '*Do*, Mrs Woolf,' roared the highmaster, '*do*? You've done enough.' And he got up, walked to the door, and opened it for my mother to go out. The interview was over, and the highmaster had attained what was, no doubt, his object: my mother never again asked for an interview to discuss her son's future.

The potential scholar, having spent a term in 'the Hall', was then drafted into the classical form which Mr Pantin and the highmaster considered appropriate. Until you reached the classical VIII form, you also did for a few hours a week French and mathematics; when you got into the VIII, you did nothing but Latin and Greek. But if you were on the classical side, nothing was considered to be of the slightest importance but Latin and Greek. The classical fanaticism of St Paul's in those days may be seen in this. I was, I think, put into the Upper IV for classics, when I escaped from 'the Hall'. Although I had got a classical scholarship, I was, in fact, better at mathematics than classics. I was, therefore, immediately moved up into the VII form for mathematics, i.e. the top mathematical form on the classical side. It was taught by Mr Pendlebury, a first-class mathematician, who had written a first-class school text book. And there I sat under Mr Pendlebury for, I think, three years, never learning anything more than I learnt in the first year, because there was no higher form into which I could be moved and I had to do what each yearly succession of boys did in mathematical Form VII on the classical side.

When I reached the classical VIII form, I did nothing but classics, as I have said. And the intensiveness of the St Paul's system may be seen from this. When I got into the top form of all, the Upper VIII, three or four of the most promising boys (of whom I was one) were withdrawn from the ordinary work of the form for a whole term before they were due to take the Oxford or Cambridge scholarship examinations. Every day we went to the highmaster's house and sat with the highmaster's son, 'Dick' Walker, the great Balliol scholar, who made us all day long translate aloud in turn, without preparation, Homer, Virgil, or some other classical work. In this way we read, so far as I can remember, straight through the whole of the Iliad and the Aeneid, some dialogues of Plato and some Tacitus. We did nothing else at all. It gave one, at any rate for a time, a considerable Latin and Greek vocabulary and some mastery of the art of translating at sight. 'Dick' Walker had such a phenomenal memory that, when we were translating Homer and Virgil, he did not use a book; he knew it all by heart so accurately that he could correct us if we made a mistake without looking at the text.

I said, some pages back, that I wished that I could recall vividly what it felt like to be the small boy who left Arlington House, Brighton, for St Paul's School, West Kensington, about the age of fourteen. I have no doubt that deep down within me, beneath the façade, the carapace secreted by my soul, and beneath the psychological sediment and sludge of sixty years, that little boy still exists intact, so vulnerable, sensitive, eager, nasty, and nice. But I cannot summon him, even like a spirit, from the depths into my consciousness; I can see or feel him merely as a very dim, rather melancholy, emanation of myself. The youth of eighteen who left St Paul's School for Trinity College, Cambridge, in 1899 is the same and yet so different. It would be an exaggeration to say that I can recall vividly what it felt like to be he or that I can remember exactly how he developed out of the small boy in the five years between 1894 and 1899. But there is no need to try to call him up from the depths; he moves recognisably within me, in my heart, my brain, and (if I have a soul) in my soul. For in developing into what he developed into he developed into me.

I had walked into St Paul's School in 1894 a small boy; I walked out of it in 1899 a young man. This passage from boyhood to manhood is in many respects the most difficult and painful period psychologically of one's life. The human caterpillar and chrysalis, infant and boy, emerges as butterfly or moth; in my own case, I may perhaps be said to have emerged as that appropriately named variety of moth, the Setaceous Hebrew Character. The metamorphosis is much more commonly painful—and more painful—than novels and autobiographies admit or depict. I can, of course, speak only for my generation, now old, dead or dying. The modern infant and child, because happier, may perhaps find the passage less difficult, but there are signs that even he does not find it easy. First, one experiences the iron, ruthless impact of society upon the eager, tender, naked ego, upon the 'dear little fleeting soul', the 'animula, vagula, blandula', as Hadrian called it. It would be difficult to exaggerate the instinctive nastiness of human beings which is to be observed in the infant and child no less than in middle or old age. To call it original sin is absurd, for it would mean that we accept as true metaphysical fairy tales or religious nightmares. It is safer to recall and state the bare facts without inventing explanations like the Platonic ideas, Allah, Jehovah, or Jesus Christ. The fact is that at the age of ten, I was a fully developed human being, mean, cowardly, untruthful, nasty, and cruel, just as I was at twenty, fifty, and seventy. And when I observed my companions' actions or caught a glimpse of their thoughts behind the masks of their faces or the curtain of their words, I recognised in them the same intimations of immorality. Yet at the same time there was in all of us—or nearly all of us—I am sure, that animula, vagula, blandula, the gentle, eager, inquisitive, generous, vulnerable guest and companion of our bodies which seemed to have little or no connection with that other tough guest and comrade of the same body. And it was this vulnerable inhabitant of our bodies over which the irresistible steam-roller of society pounded in whatever private or public school to which our parents happened to have sent us, flattening us all out in the image of manliness or gentlemanliness which our parents or lords and masters considered appropriate. Whether the Hyde is more real than the Jekyll, or vice versa, in most human beings, I do not know. I had a feeling, and still have it, that my animula, vagula, blandula, was somehow or other more real, more myself, than the nasty little tough who was, as I thought, deep down and usually out of sight. I daresay that both of these beliefs were illusions. To one of my brothers I was pure Mr Hyde, though he never revealed this to me until he was over sixty and I over seventy in the bitterest letter which I have ever received.

Having read *Genesis* and its story of Cain and Abel, and later Freud and his elaboration of it, the terrible story of the murderous hatred (suppressed of course) of son for father, father for son, and brother for brother, I ought not to have been astonished by this letter. But I was, not so much because my brother so obviously hated me or had seen the so carefully concealed Hyde behind the Jekyll. What shocked me and saddened me was that I should have known someone intimately for over half a century and have liked him, and never in all those years been aware of his hatred and contempt of me. When in Ceylon I for the first time saw in the jungle what nature was really like in the crude relation of beast to beast, I was shocked and at first even disgusted at the cold savagery, the pitiless cruelty. But when I contemplate the jungle of human relations, I feel that here are savageries and hatreds—illuminated by Zeus, Jupiter, Jehovah, Christ, or Dr Freud—which make the tiger and the viper seem gentle, charitable, tender-hearted.

Let me go back to St Paul's School through which I passed on my road to puberty, manliness, and gentlemanliness. My brother's letter shows that my preceptors and guides failed to put my feet on the path which would have landed me in the inner circle of gentlemanliness. But in my journey from form to form and from birthday to birthday I passed inevitably to the other two destinations, puberty and manhood. Sexually the passage to puberty was almost always for my generation a painful and unpleasant business; it certainly was in my case. The first time I ever had violent physical sexual sensations was as a very small boy when, in bed with a cold, I was reading a book called, I think, *The Scottish Chieftains*. The sensations astonished me; they came upon me as I read the description of how one of the chieftains—can it have been Wallace?—dashed down a hill and flung himself—without impropriety, I am sure—upon a lady who was being carried in a litter. I was puzzled by the involuntary physical phenomenon; vaguely I thought it must be somehow or other connected with the cold in my head, but it is perhaps significant that, despite my innocence, I did not report the symptom either to my nurse or to my mother. The facts about copulation and the birth of children were explained to me, as I have said, by a small boy at my private school in the worst possible way and to some extent inaccurately—I was left in some doubt as to the sexual functions of the female navel—when I was twelve years old. I remained a virgin until the age of twenty-five; the manner in which I lost my virginity in Jaffna, the Tamil town in the north of Ceylon, I will relate in a later chapter. In the thirteen years of chastity and youth which intervened my mind and body were continually harried and harassed, persecuted and plagued, sometimes one might even say tormented and tortured, by the nagging of sexual curiosity and desire. How dense the barbaric darkness was in which the Victorian middle-class boy and youth was left to drift sexually is shown by the fact that no relation or teacher, indeed no adult, ever mentioned the subject of sex to me. No information or advice on this devastating fever in one's blood and brain was ever given to me. Love and lust, like the functions of the bowels and bladder, were subjects which could not be discussed or even mentioned. The effect of this was, I believe, wholly bad, leading to an unhealthy obsession and a buttoning up of mind and emotion.

This withdrawal of the self into the inner recesses of one's being behind the façade and the series of psychological curtains which one interposed between oneself and the outside world of 'other people' seems to me, looking back, to have been one of the dominant features in the progress from childhood to manhood. I was not an unhappy youth and we were not an unhappy family. I have already told of the reversal of economic fortune which fell upon us owing to my father's death when I was eleven. When we got rid of the white elephant of a house in Lexham Gardens my mother took her six sons, three daughters, a cook, a parlourmaid, and a housemaid to a house in Colinette Road, Putney. It was an ugly Victorian house, but 'detached', with a small piece of garden in front and a largish square garden with fruit trees behind. To get thirteen human beings into it was a squeeze and it seemed at first very small after the spaciousness of Lexham Gardens. Considering the squeeze and the reversal of fortune, we were an unusually amicable family and quarrels, though sometimes violent, were rare. I was third in the family and I think that the change from wealth to comparative poverty made the eldest three children prematurely serious and grown up. My mother told us exactly where we stood; at the age of thirteen I knew that I must think carefully before I spent a sixpence or even a sixth of sixpence and that my future depended upon my brain and its capacity to win scholarships.

All this gave us—or at least me—as children a kind of grown up seriousness. A sudden reversal of fortune when one is a child impresses upon one, though one is not conscious of it at the time, a sense of the precariousness of life, the instability of one's environment. I know in fact the exact moment when that sense of instability came to me for the first time in my life. To a Londoner the rhythm of London traffic is part of the rhythm of his blood and of his life. I was born to the rhythm of horses' hooves in broughams, hansom cabs, and fourwheelers clattering down London streets, and body and blood have never completely synchronised their beat to the whir and roar and hoot of cars. One of my earliest recollections is of lying in bed high up in a front room of the house in Lexham Gardens, night after night, listening to the clop, clop, clop of a horse in a carriage or hansom cab break the silence of the night as it came down the street past our house. Clop, clop, clop—somehow or other that noise from outside gave one a sense of security, stability as one hugged oneself together under the bedclothes.

Reversal of fortune—to be on top of the world and next moment to be floundering in a bottomless pit, to feel the ground give way under one's feet, the bottom fall out of one's world—the Greek Sophocles recognised as the essence of tragedy. It remains its essence whether in the cosmic tragedy of Oedipus or the parochial tragedy of an eleven-year-old boy in nineteenth century Kensington. The moment came to me in bed listening to the horse's hooves fading away down Lexham Gardens. I remember it as the night before my father died and that somehow or other—perhaps from overhearing the hushed voices of servants—I was aware that he was dying and that his death meant not only the disaster of his death, the loss of him, but also the complete break up and destruction of life as I had known it. And in this curious vision of the future I saw that we were going to be 'poor'. I say that I remember the moment as coming on the night before my father died, but it is possible, indeed probable, that my memory is mistaken, for it is strange that a child of eleven should have been able and allowed to know so much before the catastrophe. But whether it was the night before or the night after death entered, I know the sense of security and stability had suddenly vanished; I could no longer, listening to the horse's hooves, hug myself in the haven of the bedclothes. The bottom had fallen out of the life and the house in Lexham Gardens.

From that moment a kind of unchildlike seriousness came into my life, a sense of responsibility and of the insecurity of material things like houses, food, money. It did not make me unhappy or, after the first shock, worry me. We were, as I have said, a cheerful and united family, lively, energetic, adventurous. I had and still have a passion for any kind of game, from chess to bowls to cricket and fives. I was quite a respectable bat and could play a respectable game at tennis or fives. I therefore enjoyed that important side of private and public school life which was concerned with games. At home we used to play cricket for hours in the back garden with a tennis ball and elaborate rules for scoring runs. My eldest brother, Herbert, and I developed very early a passion for bicycling. He must have been about twelve and I eleven when he acquired on his birthday his first bicycle. It was before the days of pneumatic tyres and we took the incredibly heavy and clumsy machine out into Lexham Gardens in order to acquire the art of riding. After a few minutes' practice he allowed me to try my hand, or rather legs. The seat was too high for me and I could only just reach the pedals, but he gave me a shove and I went off with great speed along the gutter, such speed indeed that I collided violently with a lamp post and the bicycle split in two, the handlebars and front wheel going in one direction, the back wheel, seat, and myself in another. Later we became experts and connoisseurs, saving up our money to buy cycles from a famous cycle shop in Holborn. I got exquisite pleasure from a cycle with handlebars like ram's horns and yellow rims to the wheels. Every day I bicycled to school from Putney to Hammersmith. In the holidays Herbert and I went on bicycle tours. We cycled all over England incredibly cheaply, for we could not afford to spend more than a few shillings a day. Our first expedition was to Oxford, Stratford, Evesham, and the West Country; our longest was to Edinburgh. When I was sixteen, we took our cycles by sea to the north of the Shetlands and cycled down to Lerwick. No one cycled there at that time and we were looked upon as bold adventurers. But one rainy night we were taken in and given beds in a small farmhouse. We were sitting round the fire after supper when there was a knock at the door and there, to everyone's amazement, was another cyclist. He was a young Aberdonian travelling in soap. As we sat talking after he had eaten his eggs and bacon, he saw my father's crest on a bookplate in a book I had been reading. The crest was a wolf's head with the motto THOROUGHLY under it. 'I have a crest too,' he said in his strong accent, 'ay, and a coat of arms. The crest is a cat's head and the motto is SANS PURR; what d'you think of that, lad?'

At the age of fifteen or sixteen, therefore, we did what most boys do and on the surface as boyishly. Yet, beneath the surface, the reversal of fortune had had, I am sure, a darkening and permanent effect. In my own case I can only describe it as this sense of fundamental insecurity, and a fatalistic acceptance of instability and the impermanence of happiness. This fatalism has given me a philosophy of life, a sceptical faith which has stood me in good stead in the worst moments of life's horrors and miseries. For just as, though I believe passionately in the truth of some things, I believe passionately that you cannot be certain of the absolute truth of anything, so too, though I feel passionately that certain things matter profoundly, I feel profoundly in the depths of my being that in the last resort *nothing matters*. The belief in the importance of truth and the impossibility of absolute truth, the conviction that, though things rightly matter profoundly to you and me, nothing matters—this mental and emotional metaphysic or attitude towards the universe produces the sceptical tolerance which is an essential part of civilisation and helps one to bear with some decency or even dignity the worst of Hamlet's slings and arrows of outrageous fortune.

This premature awareness of the seriousness of life accelerated my passage from childhood to manhood and increased the withdrawal of the self into the innermost recesses. Looking back I can see now that there was another thing which strongly encouraged that withdrawal. Though I was not conscious of it for many years, indeed not until I was a young man, from the first moment of my existence, perhaps even before I left my mother's womb, I must have been 'a born intellectual'. The reading of books gave me immense pleasure, but so did 'work' or lessons. Teachers in the days of my childhood and youth practically never explained to their pupils *what* they were teaching. For instance, mathematics, particularly algebra, gave me great satisfaction, though I was never told and never understood until years afterwards at Cambridge when I read Whitehead's little book, *Mathematics*, what on earth it was all about. This satisfaction which I got from mathematics is, I think, closely related to the aesthetic pleasure which came from poetry, pictures, and, most of all, in later years from music. But there were also in it the curious ecstasy which comes from *feeling* the mind work smoothly and imaginatively upon difficult and complicated problems, the excitement of the ruthless pursuit of truth which, perhaps, never entirely leaves one, but which is so intense when one is very young, and finally that astonishing and astonished happiness, described by Keats, which comes to one when some new constellation of thought, some new vision of a profound truth swims into one's ken.

All the characteristics which I have just described are the stigmata of the incorrigible, the born intellectual. England for considerably more than 100 years has been the most philistine of all European countries. This, I suspect, is largely due to the public schools, which during the period gradually established a dominating influence on public life and imposed upon the whole nation their prejudices, habits, morals, and standards of value. The public school was the nursery of British philistinism. To work, to use the mind, to be a 'swot', as it was called in my school days, was to become an untouchable (except for the purposes of bullying) in the hierarchy of the public school caste system. Publicly to have confessed that one enjoyed any of these things would have been as impossible as for a respectable Victorian young lady publicly to confess unchastity and that she had enjoyed it. Overtly the only standard of human value against which the boy was measured was athleticism. Use of the mind, intellectual curiosity, mental originality, interest in 'work', enjoyment of books or anything connected with the arts, all such things, if detected, were violently condemned and persecuted. The intellectual was, as he still is widely today, disliked and despised. This attitude was not confined to the boys; it was shared and encouraged by nearly all the masters.

This contempt of our teachers for what they were teaching and for the boy who wanted to be taught was on the face of it remarkable, but it was really natural and inevitable. In the kind of school to which I went nearly all the masters had been educated themselves in public schools; so too, probably, had their fathers before them. Instinctively and unconsciously and unquestioningly they accepted the standards of value and practised the precepts of public school tradition. They therefore naturally despised the intellect and the arts and anything connected with them, and so any small boy who showed any unusual intellectual ability or interest. To be a swot was just as despicable in the eyes of the masters as in those of the boys. The headmaster of my private school, Mr Burman, as I have said, was the kindest and most generous of men; indeed, I owe a great debt of gratitude to him, for after the reversal of our fortunes he took me and all my brothers one after the other at greatly reduced fees. But he was a Philistine of the Philistines, a dyed in the wool Tory, a pure and perfect product of public school tradition. By the age of fourteen I had learnt from him and the other fifty small boys about me that one of the most despicable of things was to be too intelligent—and that you had to be pretty unintelligent if you wanted to be not too intelligent. Every master who taught me until I reached the age of sixteen or seventeen accepted and inculcated the same doctrine and ethic.

From my very early years I have had in me, I think, a streak of considerable obstinacy. I was lamentably intelligent, and, as I have said, I liked to feel the mind work, I was a born swot for I enjoyed my work. I was, of course, not fully or definitely conscious of this or of the hostility towards it in the world around me, for in childhood and youth, though one feels acutely what goes on in one's own head and in the heads of other people and their often painful interactions, owing to inexperience and diffidence one rarely fully understands or acknowledges what is going on. So I felt, but only dimly understood, the hostility of Mr Burman and of boys and masters at Arlington House and St Paul's to what I now see made me a horrid little intellectual. But, because at the back of my mind and in the pit of my stomach I had this little hard core of obstinacy, I never accepted the standards of value of Mr Burman and of my environment. I did not rebel against them or openly challenge them, but I learned very early, I think, to go my own way behind the shutters of my mind and to be silent about much which went on there.

Being quite good at games and thoroughly enjoying them, I was able to carry this off and escape the penalties which awaited an intellectual in English schools in the last years of the nineteenth century. I was never bullied and, unlike many of my future friends, was never actively miserable at school. But my modus vivendi with masters and boys was attained only by the concealment or repression of a large area of my mental life which had the highest significance for me, and that was how the withdrawal of the ego into inner recesses, of which I wrote above, was encouraged and increased.

I was sixteen before I met anyone among my companions or teachers who showed any sympathy with the side of my life which I had sedulously concealed. When I went up into the VIII form—I think it was the Lower Middle VIII—the master was A. M. Cook, a brother of the editor of *The Daily News*. Cook was an extremely cultivated man; everything about him was quiet but strong including his passion for the arts and his sense of humour. He spotted my inclinations and capacities, I think, owing to my English essays (he made us take the writing of essays very seriously). At any rate, he quite soon asked me to walk round the playground with him during the morning break and for the remainder of the time that I was in his form we always spent this quarter of an hour together. I owe an enormous debt to A. M. Cook. He talked to me not as a master to a pupil or as an adult to a boy, but as an equal to an equal, on the assumption that we both accepted the same standards of intellectual and artistic value and obligations of truth. His taste was both strict and catholic. He encouraged me to read very widely and at the same time always to exercise my own judgment upon what I read. When I went up into a higher form, he gave me a copy of Bacon's *Essays*, beautifully bound in pale blue leather by Zaehnsdorf and inscribed in exquisite handwriting: 'L. S. Woolf first in written work in L.M.8. St Paul's School 1897: from AMC.' The choice of Bacon's curious prose in the pale blue and gold of the Zaehnsdorf binding was characteristic of Cook.

In my last year at school I twice came into contact with people who did not despise the intellect and the arts. G. K. Chesterton had been at St Paul's and was six years my senior. E. C. Bentley, the author of *Trent's Last Case* and the inventor of the clerihew, and R. F. Oldershaw were his contemporaries and they had founded a small debating society which met on Saturday afternoons in rotation in the houses of the members. Bentley and Oldershaw had gone up to Oxford, and, when I knew Bentley first, he was President of the Oxford Union. They continued the debating society after they had left school. It was kept quite small with only eight or nine members and they elected two or three boys still at school. How they came to elect me I cannot remember, but I know that I was both surprised and flattered. G. K.'s brother Cecil was my contemporary and a member; two other boys still at school were, I think, elected at the same time as I was.[1] One was called Myers and the other d'Avigdor,

[1] I rather think that there was a third, namely S. P. Vivian, who eventually became a distinguished civil servant, Registrar-General, with a knighthood.

and it is amusing, in view of the subsequent violent anti-semitism of the Chestertons, to note that three out of the four boys still at school whom they elected to this very exclusive society were Jews.

It was a queer society. The Chestertons were regular attendants and Bentley and Oldershaw came in the vacs. I never liked Cecil Chesterton, partly because his physical appearance was so unprepossessing, and partly because even then he had a streak of that kind of fanatical intolerance which seems to be fertilised, not by profound convictions, but by personal animosities. Gilbert was a very different kind of person. The monstrous obesity from which he suffered in later life had not yet attacked him, but like Cecil, though to a much smaller degree, he was physically unprepossessing. Whereas Cecil seemed to have a grudge against the universe, the world, and you in particular, G. K. gave one the immediate impression of goodwill, particular and general. In those days he had already begun to make his name as a journalist by writing for *The Daily News*. Our debating society was almost entirely political. It sometimes debated a particular political subject and sometimes functioned as a 'mock parliament'. G. K. practically never enlivened us with the paradoxical brilliance for which he was famous as a writer. My memory of him is standing very upright at the table, tearing sheets of paper into tiny pieces and dropping them on the table, while he spoke at immense length on some subject like taxation or bimetallism or the Irish question. His speeches were full of facts and good solid argument.

I do not know what eventually happened to this society the very name of which I cannot remember. (It may have been called The Junior Debater or something like that.) After I left school and went up to Cambridge I dropped out of it, if indeed it continued to exist, and I lost touch with the members, including the Chestertons. Though our little debating society had been so exclusively political and ignored the arts, my enthusiasm for which had been encouraged by Cook, my contact with G. K. and the other members did bring a new breath of intellectual fresh air into my school life. The atmosphere of philistinism at a public school in the last decade of last century was pretty heavy, hostile, menacing to any boy who neither in his beliefs nor in his desires accepted the philistine's standards. It was not just a question of differing in beliefs and tastes. I got on quite well with the boys in my form or with whom I played cricket, football, and fives, but it would have been unsafe, practically impossible, to let them know what I really thought or felt about anything which seemed to me important. It was therefore a surprising relief to find oneself on Saturday afternoons with five or six people to whom one could say what one thought and who accepted the same intellectual standards of value whatever our disagreement might be about other things.

In my last year at school I came across two other people to whom I could talk freely. They were both with me in the top form, and, as they went up to Oxford with scholarships, I never saw them again after I left school. They belonged to the class of persons of whom unfortunately one has come across so many in one's life, the universal rebels who, though they do not know it, rebel against the universe or capitalism or Mr Smith because thay have a personal grudge against something or someone (quite often Mrs Smith). After 1917 very many of these unhappy persons were able to sublimate their private grudges and hatreds, the torture of real or imaginary inferiorities, in the public or oecumenical grudges and hatreds of the Communist Party. But when I was a young man, Karl Marx and the Russian communists had not yet invented the international political lunatic asylum of twentieth century communism in which intelligent people can, in the name of humanity, satisfy animosities and salve their consciences. In those days the inferiority complex had few public outlets and became a kind of spiritual ingrowing toe-nail. My two friends, whom I will call A and Z, had this kind of ingrowing toe-nail. They were virulent intellectuals contra mundum. They despised and, I think, hated practically everything and everyone at St Paul's, but they had a genuine intellectual curiosity and love of literature. When they found that I had the same, though they despised me for playing cricket and fives and for being friendly with all sorts and kinds of boys, they welcomed me as a conversationalist. I used to go into the classroom after cricket and about a quarter of an hour before afternoon school every day and meet them to stand at the window arguing interminably about everything under the sun. Here too I felt that I could say what I thought or felt. As I said, I never saw them again after I had left school. A became, I believe, a clergyman, and Z committed suicide while still at the university. The Church or suicide, it will be observed, were to us in the 1890s what the Communist Party became to a later generation.

2

Cambridge

I went up to Trinity College, Cambridge, in October 1899. As a scientific exhibit, whether for individual or social psychology, my mind was in a curious state. They had turned me at St Paul's into a pretty good classical scholar. In fact, I was good enough to make those in authority think that I might carry off the blue riband of Balliol, Oxford, or Trinity, Cambridge. I was therefore taken out of the Upper VIII for a term or two, and with two or three other boys subjected to the peculiar system of classical cramming or stuffing at the hands of Dick Walker, the highmaster's son, which I have described in the previous chapter. He suddenly advised me to 'sit' for the scholarship examination at Trinity, Cambridge, in March 1899. I had expected to go in for the usual examination later in the year, for the March examination at Trinity was mainly for people already at the college and, though open to outsiders, was very rarely attempted by a boy still at school.

It is almost impossible, I suppose, in old age to remember at all vividly even the miseries—let alone the splendours—of youth. No experience, except the first stages of falling in love, has such a mixture of acutely splendid and miserable torture as that of being 'a new boy'. The first day at school was to me—and I think to the vast majority of the male animals called boys—terrible and terrifying, but also exhilaratingly exciting. You suddenly found yourself in a new, strange jungle, full of unknown enemies, pitfalls, and dangers. It was the feeling of complete loneliness and isolation which made the fear and misery so acute, and the depth of feeling was intensified by the instinctive knowledge of the small boy that he must conceal the fear and misery. And mixed into the misery was the splendour of adventure, the excitement of entering into the new, the unknown jungle.

This terrifying experience of being a new boy is, of course, not confined to one's first days at school. It may happen to one all through life, though naturally it becomes rarer as one grows older, and it is the privilege—or perhaps infirmity—of old age that it is highly improbable that you will experience it after, say, sixty unless you have the misfortune to find yourself in prison or a modern concentration camp. I can remember at least seven such experiences in my own life: three times at the three schools to which I went; the grim days of the examination at Trinity; the first days when I went up to Trinity; the first days in Ceylon in the Civil Service; and the day when I was called up for military service in the 1914 war and entered Kingston Barracks for a medical examination.

The obstinate resistance to misery in the human animal is very remarkable. It may be absurd, but I know that it is true, to say that I was never more miserable than in the few days of March at the Trinity examination. I was the only examinee not in the college; I knew no one; no one spoke to me; I had no idea of where anything was or what I had to do except that I was to go to the Hall for dinner and the examination, and to sleep in a strange and uncomfortable room. Considering the state of nervous tension in which I was, I think it was a miracle that I did well enough to win an exhibition and subsizarship which enabled me to go up to Trinity in the autumn with £75 a year. In the following March at the college exam I converted my exhibition into a foundation scholarship of £100 a year. It is of some social interest to note that in the five years I was at Cambridge I managed to live on £120 a year—the scholarship provided £100 and my family the additional £20. I had to be extremely careful and economical, but never found any serious difficulty in living with friends like Lytton Strachey, Thoby Stephen and Clive Bell, who were well off and spent considerably more.

I entered the new, unknown jungle of Cambridge University and Trinity College as a resident in October 1899. My adolescent mind was, as I say, in a strange condition. I had intense intellectual curiosity; I enjoyed intensely a large number of very different things: the smooth working of my own brain on difficult material; playing cricket or indeed almost any game; omnivorous reading and in particular the excitement of reading what seemed to one the works of great writers; bicycling and walking; work and the first attempts to write—I had won the Eldon Essay Prize at St Paul's, £20 and a gold medal (sold by me many years later to Spink for, I think, £15) for an essay on monarchy, and I know that I got considerable pleasure (and pain) from writing it; people and talk, particularly the kind of people and talk which I wrote about at the end of the last chapter and which I had met so rarely in the jungle of school life that I had little hope of finding them in the new jungle of the university.

When for the first time as an undergraduate I walked through the

Trinity Great Gate into Great Court on my way to the rooms at the top of a staircase in New Court which was to be my lair for two years, I trod cautiously, with circumspection, with no exuberant hopes of what I should find here—for that was what my experience of the human jungle had so far taught me. I had already developed, as I have said, a fairly effective and protective façade or carapace to conceal the uneasiness, lack of confidence, fear, which throughout my life I have been able to repress but never escape.

A symptom and part cause of this psychological flaw is the trembling of my hands which I have had from infancy; excitement or nervousness increase it, but it is never entirely absent. It is hereditary, for my father had it—I remember how, as a small child, I noticed that, when he sat in the library reading *The Times* after breakfast, the paper and his hands perpetually trembled a little. Two of his brothers were afflicted with it and more than one of my brothers. In Ceylon it proved to be a slight nuisance in a curious way. When one sat on the bench as Police Magistrate or District Judge, one had to make notes of the evidence and write down one's verdict and the reasons for it. Normally the tremor does not affect my writing and I would go on quite happily recording the evidence and the pleading of the lawyers if any were engaged in the case. But if I found an accused guilty, almost always a strange, disconcerting thing happened. When all the evidence had been given and the lawyers had had their say a silence fell on the hot court, as I began to write my analysis of the evidence and my reasons for my verdict. I wrote away without difficulty, but again and again when I got to the words: '. . . and for these reasons I find the accused guilty of . . . and sentence him to . . .', my hand began to tremble so violently that it was sometimes impossible for me to write legibly and I adjourned for five minutes in order to retire and calm myself sufficiently to complete the sentence (in two senses of the word).

I used often to wonder what was the explanation of this ironical situation in which the judge, the head of the district, the white 'hamadoru'[1] found his hand refuse to convict and sentence to a week's imprisonment the wretched Sinhalese villager, though he knew that he was legally guilty of the offence and that the sentence was a lenient one. Was it some primeval, subterranean qualm and

[1] This was the title which Sinhalese villagers always gave to the white civil servant; it was said to be something like 'My Lord'.

resistance due to the unconscious consciousness that the judge was no less guilty than the bewildered man in the dock? Or was it a still more subtle subconscious dislike of the majesty of the law as embodied in the judge? My reason has never allowed me to nourish any sentimental illusions or delusions about the law and those who break the laws. I think that I was, by Ceylon standards, a good Police Magistrate and District Judge, always feeling that it was my main duty to temper justice and severity by common-sense, the yardstick of his judicial function for the judge being, not his personal tastes and distastes and ethical beliefs, but the maintenance of law and the laws in the interests of order. In the court at Hambantota they would not, I think, have said that I was a 'lenient' judge. But I have always felt that the occupational disease of judges is cruelty, sadistic self-righteousness, and the higher the judge the more criminal he tends to become. It is one more example of the absolute corruption of absolute power. One rarely sees in the faces of less exalted persons the sullen savagery of so many High Court judges' faces. Their judgments, obiter dicta, and sentences too often show that the cruel arrogance of the face only reflects the pitiless malevolence of the soul.[1]

Such speculation is probably nonsensical and the explanation is probably simple, namely that my hand trembles because in the depths of my being I am physically and mentally afraid. (I used to tell Virginia that the difference between us was that she was mentally, morally, and physically a snob, while I was mentally, morally, and physically a coward—and she was inclined to agree.)

Another curious phenomenon is that the tremor in my hands has always tended to become extreme if I have to sign my name before other people, particularly on cheques or similar documents. This was a nuisance when I was head of a district in Ceylon (I was

[1] The faces of high dignitaries in the Church of Rome and the Church of England often exhibit the same kind of sullen malevolence. Perhaps it is difficult to reach high office in the Law or in the Church without becoming a hypocritical and angry old man. To watch judges at work in the Old Bailey or in the Court of Appeal, when criminal cases come up, will often show that what is said above is not exaggerated. When I used to be summoned to serve on a jury at the Old Bailey, and when I heard Lord Hewart trying criminal cases in the Appeal Court, I was often appalled and disgusted by the arrogant barbarism of the judge. Lord Chief Justices seem peculiarly prone to this kind of infection.

Assistant Government Agent of the Hambantota District in the Southern Province in my last three years in Ceylon), because there was a vast amount of signing of one's name in this kind of way which one had to do. When I came back to England in 1911, I went to a very intelligent and very nice 'suggestion' doctor in Wimpole Street, Maurice Wright, and asked him whether he could cure me. He told me that I had a somewhat rare nervous disorder, called 'familial tremor' because it ran in families; it was very difficult to cure either by suggestion or any other method. Some time ago, he said, a man in a business firm in Bombay had come to him because he had to sign a large number of cheques and as soon as he began to do so, his hand trembled so violently as to make it almost impossible for him to write his name. Suggestion had made him slightly better, but had not cured him. Wright held out little hope of a cure, but thought it just worth while to give it a try. After five or six sessions, he said I was not suggestible and it would be a waste of my time and money to go on with the treatment. He told me that he found a good deal of variation in suggestibility in different professions and occupations; in his experience policemen were the most suggestible of all men. For suggestion to work, he wanted a person to relax but not to become hypnotised; policemen were so suggestible that they almost invariably became completely hypnotised.

Another way in which my trembling hand proved to be a nuisance was when I went out to lunch or dinner; I would clatter my knife and fork on the plate or spill the wine on the tablecloth. Bernard Shaw, who had noticed this, once told me that he had been to F. M. Alexander who had cured him of some nervous affliction and he strongly advised me to let Alexander deal with my tremor. I went to Alexander and he treated me for some time. He was a remarkable man. He was a quack, but an honest, inspired quack. He had himself been suddenly afflected with a nervous disorder and had cured himself by discovering that his loss of muscular control was due to the fact that he had got into the habit of holding his head and neck in the wrong position. From this he went on to maintain that all sorts and kinds of diseases and disorders were due to people getting into the habit of holding their head, neck, shoulders, and spine in this wrong position and his cure consisted in training the patient by exercises to abandon the wrong and acquire automatically the right posture. He said he could certainly cure me and for some time I went to him two or three times a week for treatment at considerable expense. I think that if I had had the patience to go on with the treatment and do the abominable exercises, I might have been cured or at any rate very nearly cured. But I simply cannot bring myself day after day to do physical exercises or remember to hold my head in a particular position, and gradually I gave the whole thing up. But Alexander himself was an extraordinarily interesting psychological exhibit. I feel sure that he had hit upon a very important truth regarding automatic muscular control and loss of control and that his methods could cure or relieve a number of nervous disorders. So far he was completely honest and a genuine 'healer' of the primordial, traditional type. What was fascinating about him was that, though fundamentally honest, he was at the same time fundamentally a quack. The quackery was in his mind and came out in the inevitable patter and his claim to have discovered a panacea. However, as I said, I think his method might have cured me, but I had not the necessary patience to persist with the business and resigned myself to go on trembling slightly all my life. It is one of the consolations of age that it diminishes one's perturbations and fears, and so even one's tremblings.

But I must return to Cambridge in the autumn and winter of 1899. I felt terribly lonely in my first few days at Trinity. I knew practically no one there or indeed at any other college. In my time at St Paul's it was the fashion to enter for Oxford, not Cambridge, scholarships. None of my contemporaries in the Classical VIIIth came up with me and the only Pauline scholar of my year was Maxwell Garnett. As he was a mathematician, I scarcely knew him at school and barely knew him at Trinity. It was only twenty years later, when he was secretary of the League of Nations Union, that I got to know him well.

But suddenly everything changed and almost for the first time one felt that to be young was very heaven. The reason was simple. Suddenly I found to my astonishment that there were a number of people near and about me with whom I could enjoy the exciting and at the same time profound happiness of friendship. It began casually in what was called the screens, the passage through the Hall from Trinity Great Court to Neville's Court. I was looking at the notices on the board after dining in Hall and said something to a man standing next to me. We walked away together and he came back to my rooms. He was a scholar from Westminster, Saxon Sydney-Turner. Saxon was a very strange character with one of the strangest minds I have met with. He was immensely intelligent and subtle, but had little creativeness. In one of the university scholarship examinations they set us for Greek translation a piece from a rather obscure writer which had a riddle in it. Saxon won one of the scholarships and it was said that he was the only person to get the riddle bit right. It was characteristic of him. When, years later, crossword puzzles were invented and became the rage, he was a champion solver. And it was characteristic of him that he was a champion solver, never an inventor, of crossword puzzles and other mental gymnastics, including the art of writing. He had an immense knowledge of literature, but he read books rather in the spirit in which a man collects stamps. He would tell you casually that last night he had read for the second time in three weeks Meister Eckhart's *Buch der gottlicher Tröstung und von den edlen Menschen* much in the tone of voice in which a great stamp collector might casually remark—to *épater* his fellow collectors—that yesterday afternoon he had bought for 2*s*. 6*d*. in a shop in a back street of Soho two perfect specimens of a very rare 1*d*. Cape of Good Hope stamp. Later in life, when he was in the Treasury and lived in Great Ormond Street, he was an inveterate concert and opera goer in London and Bayreuth. He kept a record, both on paper and in his head, of all the operas he had ever been to. Normally with other people he was reserved, spoke little, and fell into long and unobtrusive silences. But sometimes he would begin to talk almost volubly about opera. He would tell you that last night he had been at Covent Garden and heard *Seigfried* for the thirty-fifth time. X had sung Brünnhilde; the great duet in the last act was quite good. X sang well and reminded him of Y whom he had heard sing the same part at Bayreuth, in 1908, Z being Siegfried, when he had been to *Siegfried* for the seventh time. The best performance he had ever heard of the opera was his twelfth, also at Bayreuth; Y was again Brünnhilde and there was the greatest of all Siegfrieds, W. The fourteenth time he saw the opera was . . . and so on.

The rooms which Saxon lived in for many years in Great Ormond Street consisted of one big sitting-room and a small bedroom. On each side of the sitting-room fireplace on the wall was an immense picture of a farmyard scene. It was the same picture on each side and for over thirty years Saxon lived with them ever before his eyes, while in his bedroom there were some very good pictures by Duncan Grant and other artists, but you could not possibly see them because there was no light and no space to hang them on the walls. As time went on, Saxon acquired more and more books and, since he suffered from a variety of ailments, more and more medicine bottles. His bookcases filled up and soon a second and third row, one behind the other, became necessary, and then piles and piles of books covered the floor. There were books upon the tables and chairs, and everywhere there were empty medicine bottles on the books, and the same two pigs, the same two sheep, and the same two dogs looked down upon, one presumes, the unseeing Saxon from the same two pictures on either side of the mantelpiece.

I was up at Trinity for five years. The first two years I had rooms in New Court; in the last three years Saxon and I had a double set of rooms in Great Court. It had one very large room on the first floor and two small bedrooms on the second. Saxon was a short, thin man with a very pale face and straw-coloured hair. He seemed to glide, rather than walk, and noiselessly, so that one moment you were alone in a room and next moment you found him sitting in a chair near you though you had not heard the door open or him come in. We saw very little of each other except in the evenings for he used to get up very late as a rule whereas I was up at eight. We hardly ever had a meal together for he ate very little and at the most erratic hours.

Both physically and mentally Saxon was ghost-like, shadowy. He rarely committed himself to any positive opinion or even statement. His conversation—if it could rightly be called conversation—was extremely spasmodic, elusive, and allusive. You might be sitting reading a book and suddenly find him standing in front of you on one leg in front of the fire knocking out his pipe into the fireplace and he would say without looking up: 'Her name was Emily', or perhaps: 'He was right.' After a considerable amount of cross-examination, you would find that the first remark applied to a conversation weeks ago in which he had tried unsuccessfully to remember the christian name of Miss Girouette in *Nightmare Abbey*, and the second remark applied to a dispute between Thoby Stephen and myself which I had completely forgotten because it had taken place in the previous term.

During the years we were at Trinity, Henry James was at the height of his powers, writing those strange, involved, elusive novels of his last period. We read *The Sacred Fount*, *The Wings of the Dove*, and *The Golden Bowl* as they came out. Lytton Strachey,

Saxon, and I were fascinated by them—entranced and almost hypnotised. I don't know whether we thought that they were really great masterpieces. My enjoyment and admiration of them have always been and still are great, but always with a reservation. There is an element of ridiculousness, even of 'phoneyness' in them which makes it impossible to rank them with the greatest or even the great novels. But the strange, Jamesian, convoluted beauty and subtlety of them act upon those who yield to them like drink or drugs; for a time we became addicts, habitual drunkards—never, perhaps, quite serious, but playing at seeing the world of Trinity and Cambridge as a Jamesian phantasmagoria, writing and talking as if we had just walked out of *The Sacred Fount* into Trinity Great Court. The curious thing was that, whereas Lytton and I were always consciously playing a game in talking or writing like Mrs Brissenden and Mrs Server, Saxon quite naturally talked, looked, acted, *was* a character in an unwritten novel by Henry James.

No human being can be quite as cynical, quite as ironical as facts. While I was in Ceylon—about 1908 or 1909, I suppose—Vanessa, Virginia, and Adrian Stephen went to Rye for the summer and Saxon stayed with them. Henry James was living in Rye then, in Lamb House, and there was also living in the town at the same time, Sydney Waterlow.[1] Sydney, who was a great friend of the novelist, told me that James was shocked by the 'Stephen girls' or rather by their friends. James had known the Stephen children well from their childhood for he was an intimate friend of Sir Leslie Stephen and often came to the house in Hyde Park Gate when their mother was alive. When they came to Rye that summer, he had not seen them for a good many years. He was uneasy at not finding in them the standard of lady-like life and manners which belonged to Hyde Park Gate and the houses and their inhabitants in *The Wings of the Dove* or *The Golden Bowl*. But what upset him most was their friends, poor Saxon and Lytton Strachey, who also came to stay with them. Sydney repeated to me with gusto an interminable sentence in which by parenthesis within parenthesis and infinite reservations, involutions, and convolutions Henry James delicately, regretfully, hesitatingly conveyed his feeling that Saxon was small, insignificant,

[1] The late Sir Sydney Waterlow. Sydney's life was in some ways stranger than fiction. He was an infant prodigy at Eton and a brilliant classical scholar at Trinity College, Cambridge; later in the Diplomatic Service, his last post was Minister in Athens.

silent, and even rather grubby.

Nothing could have been more ironical than the situation there in Rye fifty years ago—the infinitely subtle author of *The Sacred Fount*, with his infinitely sensitive antennae, rendered completely insensitive and obtuse by the mist of social snobbery through which he saw life and people and out of which he often created his shadowy masterpieces. For in 1907 Henry James was in many ways a disappointed man. His reputation was high, but his readers were few. Like so many writers, and with a good deal more reason than most, he felt that the readers, the sales, the success which he knew he deserved evaded him. This saddened him and he was immensely pleased by the appreciation and admiration of younger people like Sydney Waterlow and Hugh Walpole. But Sydney and Hugh were extremely respectable young men, properly dressed, with the right hats on their heads, and carrying an umbrella at the appropriate moment. And now there was the novelist sitting in the same room with two of the most intelligent of the younger generation who understood and admired him far more profoundly, I think, than Hugh or Sydney did, and one of them, Saxon, was almost a creation of the novelist, a character in one of his novels. And all that the sensitive antennae recorded was that the young man was small, silent, and grubby.

All this, it should perhaps be added, did not permanently affect James's respect and affection for Leslie Stephen's family. After Virginia and I married in 1912, I acted for a short time as secretary of Roger Fry's Second Post-Impressionist Exhibition at the Grafton Galleries. One afternoon Henry James came, and after Roger and I had shown him round the pictures—which he did not very much like—we took him down into the basement and gave him tea. When he realised that I had just married Virginia, he got up and shook hands with me a second time and made me a characteristic, ceremonious speech. It went on for quite a time and had many trailing and flowery sentences full of parentheses. But it showed, I thought, genuine kindliness and real feeling for Leslie Stephen and for the great beauty of his wife and daughters. I was amused to see that during tea, as he talked, he gradually tilted back his chair until it was balanced on the two back legs, he maintaining equilibrium by just holding on to the edge of the table. Now the Stephens had told me that when they were children and Henry James came to tea, or some other meal, which he often did, he had a habit of doing this when he talked. As the long sentences untwined themselves, the chair would tilt slowly backwards and all the children's eyes were fixed on it, fearing and hoping that at last it would overbalance backwards and deposit Henry James on the floor. Time after time he would just recover himself, but then indeed at last it one day happened; the chair went over and the novelist was on the floor, undismayed, unhurt, and after a moment completing his sentence.

The tremendous effect of Henry James's later novels upon us at Cambridge between the years 1900 and 1905 may be shown by the following facts. During those years I used sometimes to write down, immediately after they had occurred, conversations or scraps of conversation which had seemed to me significant or amusing. I thought I was recording them verbatim and unembellished, but in fact, as will appear, Henry James—unknown to myself and himself—occasionally took a hand and gave them a perhaps not altogether illegitimate twist. These fragments had, I thought, all disappeared in Ceylon bungalows and in those appalling diaspora of possessions which takes place when one moves from one house to another. But not so very long ago I found in an old notebook two dirty, yellowed, folded sheets of paper—two contemporary records of two such conversations. I propose to give them here.

A word must be said about the dramatis personae in the first conversation. G. was R. K. Gaye, H. was G. H. Hardy, and F. was Walter Morley Fletcher; they were all Fellows of Trinity in 1903 when the conversation took place. Hardy was one of the most strange and charming of men. A 'pure' mathematician of the greatest brilliance, he became an F.R.S. and Savilian Professor of Geometry in Oxford. He had the eyes of a slightly startled fawn below the very beautiful and magnificant forehead of an infant prodigy. He gave one the feeling that he belonged more properly to Prospero's island than the Great Court of Trinity. He lived in a double suite of rooms in Great Court with Gaye, a saturnine classical Fellow who committed suicide some years later. Gaye and Hardy were absolutely inseparable; they were never seen apart and rarely talked to other people. They collected railway tickets (this, I think was really Gaye's mania) and had a passion for every kind of game. They admitted Saxon and me into a restricted acquaintanceship because Saxon had been at Westminster with Gaye, and we played bowls with them in the Fellows' Garden and cricket with a walking stick and tennis ball in their rooms. Fletcher became Secretary of the Medical Research

Council, and F.R.S. and a K.B.E. Here is the record of the conversation to which I had given the title, 'The Cat, the Worms, and the Rats':

When I went into G. and H.'s room, I found them sitting one on each side of the fire in a very dejected condition. On the floor between them sat their cat. They were quite silent and dishevelled and they merely gazed at the cat. The cat's ill, said H. at last in a dull voice. It's got worms, at least that's what the vet said—F. told us to go to him.

Poor thing! I felt I had to say, to break the pause.

It hasn't eaten for two days, he went on. You see, the vet says as soon as it makes the movements preparing to eat, the worms—they're in the stomach, you know—come up into the oesophagus and nearly choke it.

But what are you doing for it? I said.

Well, the vet gave us a powder for it. He said just give it to him and it will kill the worms inside. But that's the worst of these experts, you always think it's quite easy when they are telling you what to do; when you go and try to do it, you find it's impossible. We can't get him to take the powder; we tried to make him take it mixed with milk—the vet told us to—but we could only force a little of it down his throat with a teaspoon and even then he was sick at once. F. says he doesn't believe you can make a cat take anything against its will.

There was a long pause, while we all looked at the cat.

It's in a very emaciated condition, H. was pursuing in a still lower voice, when the door opened and F. came in.

Well, how's the patient? he said with conscientious cheerfulness.

Just the same, said H. You know we can't make it take the powders; it was sick when we forced a little down its throat.

If it was only a dog, I said. You'd simply open its mouth and drop it down. But then of course there are the claws. You can't get hold of a cat.

No, said F., even a dog can't kill a cat easily.

That's because he can't come to close quarters, I said. I suppose if he got it in the back like he does a rabbit, he could quite easily.

I suppose he could, said F. You know a terrier kills a rabbit or rat with a flick just breaking its back. By the bye that reminds me of the most repulsive sight I ever saw—it really was too filthy. It was in France last vac. I was biking in the Rhone valley with J.——

Here H. to whom G. had whispered something broke in: I'm sorry, F., but, before I forget, do you think it's a funny or bad symptom that while the cat is being sick it walks backwards?

Yes, said G., and it also keeps on drawing its head back.

I really don't know, returned F. Well, we were biking through a small village and found there was a fair going on, so we dismounted to have a look. The great attraction was Madame Boug, the champion rat catcher. We found a big crowd awaiting her arrival round a pit. We squeezed in among them and soon she made her appearance. She was a tall, big woman and stark naked except for a tightly fitting red pair of drawers—really quite repulsive, you know. Well, she went into the pit and they loosed about twenty big sewer rats into it too. Then she went down on her hands and knees and chased the rats round. She crawled extraordinarily quickly and every now and then made a dart with her head, caught one by the back in her mouth, gave a little flick, and it was dead. It was quite foul, you know; to see her seize them in her teeth and give that little jerk just like a terrier.

But didn't they bite her? I said.

O yes, he said, in the ears, that was so repulsive. For when there were only three left, she worked them up into a corner and as she was killing one another seized her ear, and I saw another leap up from under her breast right over her neck. I daresay they bit her in the breast too, but it was really so repulsive, you know, that we made off feeling quite sick.

But, said G., as F. got up, I shouldn't have thought her mouth was big enough to seize a rat in.

Ah, said F., she was a big-mouthed woman, quite repulsive, you know.

Then the door closed upon his Goodnight!

May 10th, 1903

The second conversation, which is a good deal more Jamesian, requires a word of explanation. The dramatis personae are St, Lytton Strachey; The G., Thoby Stephen, who was nicknamed The Goth; S-T, Saxon Sydney-Turner; and M., a rather older scholar called Maclaren. 'The method' referred to in the conversation had been invented by Lytton and me; it was a kind of third-degree psychological investigation applied to the souls of one's friends. Though it was a long time before we had any knowledge of Freud, it was a kind of compulsory psychoanalysis. It was intended to reveal to us, and incidentally to the victim, what he was really like; the theory was that by imparting to all concerned the deeper psychological truths, personal relationships would be much improved. Its technique was derived partly from Socrates, partly from Henry James, partly from G. E. Moore, and partly from ourselves. We had already applied the method with disastrous success to Saxon. Here is the conversation:

Sunday night.

I was writing a letter when the St came in. The G. and S-T. were sitting silent round the fire.

Wait a moment! he said.

There was a long pause while he walked up and down. What have you been doing? I said. Two wonderful conversations, was the answer, and then the pacing began again.

It's reached the ultimate, he said at last.

I looked up. O, it's nothing indecent, he said, and—well, it's the penultimate really.

How *did* you do it?

I simply asked him. It's wonderful if it's true. We were hopeless and the method's smashed.

O, I can't believe that.

Yes, but that's the contortion . . . I can't believe it and he can't make me. There are no ups and downs and there are only a few. And he's——

Here the door opened and M. came in. He stood gaping for two minutes and then joined the other two by falling silent into a chair.

He's going—and that of course will be the ultimate—to give me the names.

God!

He began pacing again.

There's no hypnosis even, he went on. The touching and all that—that's not the important part. You see, I *can't* understand it.

But the questions, I said. How could you ask them?

Well, once I *did* think I was lost. But what's so awful for him, poor thing, is that however much he swears it's true, I can't believe him.

Well, you are cruel. I call it sheer brutality.

He stood and drummed on the table with my pen while I lay back in my chair and looked at him. The group round the fire was silent. Suddenly he turned to go and as suddenly came back to the table. There's one thing more, he said. This has certainly been the most wonderful of all.

Then the door slammed.

May 10th, 1903

Let me return for a brief moment to Saxon. I have said that we applied 'the method' to him with disastrous success. Lytton and I were very fond of him—we had become intimate friends long before Saxon and I had the double set of rooms in Great Court. But the more intimately we got to know him, the more concerned we became about his psychological state. He seemed, even at the age of twenty, to have deliberately withdrawn himself from life, to protect himself from its impact and from the impact of persons, emotions, and things by spinning around himself an elaborate and ingenious series of cocoons. He was thus in the process of successfully stifling his creativeness, his sensitive and subtle intelligence, his affections. He was, as I have said, a character in a Henry James novel, but he would also have seemed more alive in *Crotchet Castle* or *Nightmare Abbey* than in the Cambridge of 1900. Beneath the façade and the veils one felt that there might be an atrophied Shelley.

Lytton and I decided that we ought to apply 'the method' to Saxon, to try to make him tear up and break through the veils into life. One evening after dining in Hall we began to apply the third-degree psychological investigation to him about half-past eight and continued it uninterruptedly until five in the morning; when at last he staggered away to bed, we had successfully uncovered the soul of Saxon, but had disastrously confirmed him in the determination to stifle it in an infinite series of veils. Twenty-five years later, I amused myself by writing 'characters' of some of my friends after the manner of La Bruyère. Here is one which was suggested to some extent by recollections of Saxon:

Aristotle sits in a corner of a room spinning, spinning webs around himself. He has been spinning now for thirty years, so that it is rather difficult to see through the web exactly what he really is, sitting there curled up smoking his pipe in the centre of it. Originally before the webs began, if there was such a time—if indeed he did not begin spinning them in his mother's womb—he must have been charming. He might have been Shelley. He might have dreamed dreams of a queer unsubstantial beauty; the fine temper of his mind might have built a philosophy true and beautiful and unintelligible; he might have had bright and delicate affections; he might have been happy, he might have been in love. Years ago, I suppose, all this showed more clearly than it does now. For I think that Heracleitus and Aristophanes must have seen it when they took Aristotle to their bosom. It wanted clear eyes to see through the web even then, it wants still clearer eyes now. You go into a large dirty room full of dead things and abominations and uglinesses. The most abominable thing in it are the books; even the *Phaedrus* becomes a degradation there. All the books are dead, and all the thoughts and words of them have become dust and ashes and desolation. You feel that the Rabelais which you had in your overcoat pocket when you came in has already turned into a skeleton of dry bones. There are books everywhere: on tables and chairs and floor and mantelpiece and bed, and scattered among the books are old bottles of medicine and horrible little boxes of tabloids and capsules and pills. You brighten up when you see a copy of the *Lysistrata* lying upon the table; you open it and find a bottle of laudanum between the leaves, thrust in to mark the place. A thin layer of dust and soot lies upon everything. You sink sadly into a chair and look into the corner and there you see an immense accumulated mass of grey strands, dusty, dirty, tangled. They float about the room brushing softly against your face. You shudder? You try to rouse yourself? You talk loud, brutally, not knowing quite what you are saying? Your noise and excitement, my friend, are quite useless; you had much better sit down again and quitely watch him spinning quietly in the corner. Do you see how the web is growing? There, that long dusty, whitish-grey strand is a list of all the writers on the Higher Mathematics whose names begin with P. A good wrap for the soul? And then there are 124 volumes of Diodorus Siculus and Duns Scotus and Hippocrates and Galen and the Montenegrin poets and the Hottentot philosophers. Fine wraps for the soul? But above all there is the past: to spin the past over the present until what was the present has become the past ready to be spun again over the present that was the future! Quick, let us cover our souls with the litter of memories and old sayings and the dead letters of the dead. And if the dead are ourselves, so much the better; let the rubbish of the past stifle our feelings, let the sap and vigour of our thoughts dry up and ooze away into the dusty accretions which we spin over ourselves. Such is the philosophy of Aristotle. Is he happy? Is the mole or the barnacle or the spider happy? If they are, then Aristotle is too when he has not got the toothache, which is not often. In the very centre of the web, I think, there is still a gentle titillation of unsubstantial happiness whenever he finds another higher mathematician whose name begins with P. or when between 1 and 2 a.m. he explains to Aspasia that the great uncle of his mother's cousin moved in 1882 from Brixton to Balham and that his name was Beeley Tupholme, or even when he sees in his old letters that he was young once with Heracleitus and Aristophanes. It may be that affection still moves him for Aristophanes and Heracleitus and Kyron and Lysistrata and Aspasia, but they move, I think, through the past. The reason of all this? you ask. It may be that God made him—a eunuch; or it may be that the violence and brutality of life were too strong for the delicacy of him; he was terrified by it and by his feelings. He looks sometimes like a little schoolboy whom life has bullied into unconsciousness. Which is really true nobody will ever know, for now he will go on sitting there in his corner spinning his interminable cocoon until he dies. It will be some time before we find out that he really is dead and then we shall go to the large dirty room and push and tear our way through the enormous web which by that time will almost completely fill it, and at last when we stand choking in the centre of it we shall find just nothing at all. Then we shall bury the cocoon.

Lytton Strachey, Thoby Stephen, and Clive Bell all came up to Trinity in the same year as Saxon and I did and we soon got to know them well. We were intimate friends—particularly Lytton, Saxon, and myself—but intimacy in 1900 among middle-class males was different from what it became in generations later than ours. Some of us were called by nicknames; for instance we always called Thoby Stephen The Goth, but we never used christian names. Lytton always called me Woolf and I always called him Strachey until I returned from Ceylon in 1911 and found that the wholesale revolution in society and manners which had taken place in the preceding seven years involved the use of christian names in place of surnames. The difference was—and is—not entirely unimportant. The shade of relationship between Woolf and Strachey is not exactly the same as that between Leonard and Lytton. The surname relationship was determined by and retained that curious formality and reticence which the nineteenth-century public school system insisted upon in certain matters. Now, of course, the use of christian names and their diminutives has become so universal that it may soon perhaps become necessary to indicate intimacy by using surnames.

Lytton was a very strange character already when he came up to Cambridge in 1899. There was a mixture of arrogance and diffidence in him. His mind had already formed in a Voltairean mould, and his inclinations, his passions, the framework of his thought belonged to the eighteenth century, and particularly to eighteenth century France. His body was long, thin, and rather ungainly; all his movements, including his walk, were slow and slightly hesitant—I never remember to have seen him run. When he sat in a chair, he appeared to have tied his body, and particularly his legs, into what I always called a Strachean knot. There was a Strachean voice, common to him and to all his nine brothers and sisters (much less marked in the eldest brother, Dick, who was a major in the army when I knew him, than in the others). It was mainly derived, I think, from the mother and consisted in an unusual stress accent, heavy emphasis on words here and there in a sentence, combined with an unusual tonic accent, so that emphasis and pitch continually changed, often in a kind of syncopated rhythm. It was extremely catching and most people who saw much of Lytton acquired the Strachey voice and never completely lost it. Lytton himself added another peculiarity to the family cadence. Normally his voice was low and fairly deep, but every now and again it went up into a falsetto, almost a squeak.

This squeak added to the effect of his characteristic style of wit. He was one of the most amusing conversationalists I have ever known. He was not a monologuist or a raconteur. Except when he was with one or a few intimate friends, he did not say very much and his silences were often long. They were often broken by a Strachean witticism, probably a devastating reductio ad absurdum—the wit and the devastation owing much to the perfect turn of the sentence and the delicate stiletto stab of the falsetto voice. Many, particularly among the young, as I said, caught his method of talking and ever afterwards spoke in the Strachey voice; so too, many caught his method of thinking and thought ever after with a squeak in their minds. The unwary stranger, seeing Lytton contortedly collapsed in a tangle of his own arms and legs in the depths of an armchair, his eyes gazing in fixed abstraction through his strong glasses at his toes which had corkscrewed themselves up and round to within a foot of his nose, the unwary stranger might and sometimes did dismiss him as a gentle, inarticulate, nervous, awkward intellectual. All these adjectives were correct, but woe betide the man or woman who thought that they were the end of the matter and of Lytton Strachey. I used to tell him that, when he came to see us and we were not alone, I proposed to put a notice on the arm of his chair: BE CAREFUL, THIS ANIMAL BITES.

The animal bit because, behind the gentleness, the nervousness, and the cynicism, there were very considerable passions. They were the passions of the artist and of the man who is passionately attached to standards of intellectual integrity. This may sound priggish to some people, but no man has ever been less of a prig than he was. He suffered the stupid and stupidity, and the philistine and philistinism, with unconcealed irritation which might take the form either of the blackest, profoundest silence or of a mordant witticism. As he could on occasions be ruthless and inconsiderate, I have known his intolerance produce intolerable situations. One summer he came to stay with us at Rodmell for a few days and, when he heard that a well-known literary man, whom I will call X, had taken a cottage in the village, he asked me to have him in to dinner one evening, as he would like to meet him. I deprecated the idea, as X was, like many literary men, rather a bore and not at all 'bright' in the Strachean sense. However Lytton insisted that he had never met X and wanted to meet him, so I foolishly gave way and X appeared the following evening at 7.30. After the first five minutes, Lytton withdrew into himself and a thick cloud of silence, fixing his eyes upon his food or upon the ceiling and tying his legs into even more complicated knots than usual. When X left some three hours later, I do not think that he had heard more than twenty words from the author of *Eminent Victorians*.

This kind of arrogance and rudeness, alternating, as it did, with a curious diffident nervousness, roused a certain amount of hostility to Lytton both among people who knew him a little and often among people who did not know him at all. His physical appearance and voice had that indefinable quality which tends to excite animosity or ridicule at sight in the ordinary man, the Cambridge 'blood' or tough, for instance. To his intimate friends, though he could be momentarily infuriating, he was extraordinarily affectionate and lovable. It should be added that many of his characteristics which superficially irritated or repelled people were due to his health. Though he never during the time that I knew him had a dangerous illness before the final cancer which killed him at the age of fifty-one in 1932, I have the impression, looking back over the thirty-one years of my knowing him, that he was hardly ever completely well, or rather that the standard of his physical strength, health, vitality was, compared with the average human being's, low. One felt that he always had to husband his bodily forces in the service of his mind and that, in view of the precarious balance of physical health, it was surprising how much he accomplished.

The characters in *The Waves* are not drawn from life, but there is something of Lytton in Neville. There is no doubt that Percival in that book contains something of Thoby Stephen, Virginia's brother, who died of typhoid aged twenty-six in 1906. Thoby came up to Trinity from Clifton with an exhibition in the same year as Lytton, Saxon, and I. He gave one an impression of physical magnificence. He was six foot two, broad-shouldered and somewhat heavily made, with a small head set elegantly upon the broad shoulders so that it reminded one of the way in which the small head is set upon the neck of a well-bred Arab horse. His face was extraordinarily beautiful and his character was as beautiful as his face. In his monolithic character, his monolithic common-sense, his monumental judgments he continually reminded one of Dr Johnson, but a Samuel Johnson who had shed his neuroticism, his irritability, his fears. He had a perfect 'natural' style of writing, flexible, lucid, but rather formal, old-fashioned, almost Johnsonian or at any rate eighteenth century. And there was a streak of the same natural style in his talk. Any wild statement, speculative judgment, or Strachean exaggeration would be met with a 'Nonsense, my good fellow', from Thoby, and then a sentence of profound, but humorous, common-sense, and a delighted chuckle. Thoby had a good sense of humour, a fine, sound, but not brilliant mind. He had many of the characteristic qualities of the males of his family, of his father Leslie Stephen, his uncle James Fitzjames Stephen and his cousin J. K. Stephen. But what everyone who knew him remembers most vividly in him was his extraordinary charm. He had greater personal charm than anyone I have ever known, and, unlike all other great 'charmers', he seemed, and I believe was, entirely unconscious of it. It was, no doubt, partly physical, partly due to the unusual combination of sweetness of nature and affection with rugged intelligence and a complete lack of sentimentality, and partly to those personal flavours of the soul which are as unanalysable and indescribable as the scents of flowers or the overtones in a line of great poetry.

Thoby was an intellectual; he liked an argument and had a great, though conservative and classical, appreciation and love of literature. But he also, though rather scornful of games and athletics, loved the open air—watching birds, walking, following the beagles. In these occupations, particularly in walking, I often joined him. Walking with him was by no means a tame business, for it was almost a Stephen principle in walking to avoid all roads and ignore the rights of property owners and the law of trespass. Owing to these principles we did not endear ourselves to the gamekeepers round Cambridge. Though fundamentally respectable, conservative, and a moralist, he was always ready in the country to leave the beaten track in more senses than one. In our walks up the river towards Trumpington, we had several times noticed a clump of magnificent hawthorn trees in which vast numbers of starlings came nightly to roost. I have never seen such enormous numbers of birds in so small a space; there must have been thousands upon thousands and the trees were in the evening literally black with them. We several times tried to put them all up into the air at the same time, for, if we succeeded, it would have been a marvellous sight to see the sky darkened and the setting sun obscured by the immense cloud of birds. But we failed because every time we approached the trees, the birds went up into the air spasmodically in gusts, and not altogether. So we bought a rocket and late one evening fired it from a distance into the trees. The experiment succeeded and we had the pleasure of seeing the sun completely blotted out by starlings. It was several years later that I was to see as large or even larger flights of birds in Ceylon—the great flocks of teal wheeling round the lagoons or the tanks in the Hambantota district.

The following letter which Thoby wrote to me shortly after I went to Ceylon gives, I think, some faint flavour of his character:

46 Gordon Square,
Bloomsbury.
Jan 15, 1905.

Dear Woolf,

I ought to have written to you before this, but the world has been very barren of circumstance, and one feels that a letter ought to contain information in some proportion to the number of miles it has to go. That is probably a fallacy, but anyhow you must have had incidents enough by now among the Obesekeridae to fill an epistle which I hope this will evoke. I have been plodding pretty steadily at the law and becoming crystallised at it—in fact my moustache has disappeared. I was in the New Forest at Christmas, where I got some hunting, one especially rare chivy. From there I walked to Hindhead and stayed some days with Pollock. There were there J. Pollock, his sister and her husband Waterlow (you know the man I suppose), Meredith for a time, and old Bell. I more or less enjoyed it but it was damned funny. Waterlow is a serious cove and devilish Cambridge. "What is poetry? Well, there you ask me a difficult question—I am not sure that it *is* anything—it depends what you mean by being" and so on the old round, till after an hour or two all go to bed leaving Bell and me who shout simultaneously "Now let's talk about hunting." His wife lags behind him but struggles gallantly 'Sidney, Sidney, what do you mean by Mon-og-amy?' However he has a bottom of good sense and is not a bad fellow . . . The good old chapel row[1] is still fermenting. Cornford and Gaye have pamphleteered and Pollock is following with a "legal aspect" one. I have suppressed mine pro tem out of deference to Cornford—who takes I think a rotten line—chapel is either the sublimest function of man or the most pathetic of human fallacies—it's no good being dainty with Christians and chapel's obviously rot and nothing else. I seem to have done nothing and seen nobody and read little of interest for the deuce of a time—I've been reading satires chiefly when I've had time—I think probably all the best things written have been satires except Virgil—and one can worm a quasi-satire out of the bees. I think I am going to make my working men[1] read it. Virgil after all is the top of the tree and Sophocles is thereabouts—next come Catullus and Aristophanes, that is my mature opinion so far as the ancients go. They talk of abolishing Greek at Cambridge and Jackson and Verrall are helping the devils. If they do you'd better become a naturalised Cingalese—and I shall go to the Laccadives. Haynes annoys me rather—I dined with Bell and him the other day—he talks of nothing but suicides, disease and bawdy, and his beastly book—almost he persuades me to be a Christian. Well, my good fellow, I've nothing to say but what's unutterably dull, but I hope I shall hear something enlivening from you some day.

Yrs. ever
J. T. Stephen.

Clive Bell came up to Trinity the same year as we did, 1899, and when we first go to know him he was different in many ways from us and even from the Clive Bell whom I found married to Vanessa Stephen and living in Gordon Square when I returned from Ceylon in 1911. He came into our lives because he got to know Saxon,

[1] Thoby had written and circulated in Cambridge a pamphlet against the practice of compulsory chapel in Trinity College.

[1] Thoby taught at the Working Men's College.

having rooms on the same staircase in New Court. Lytton, Saxon, Thoby, and I belonged, unconcealably and unashamedly, to that class of human beings which is regarded with deep suspicion in Britain, and particularly in public schools and universities, the intellectual. Clive, when he came up to Trinity from Marlborough, was not yet an intellectual. He was superficially a 'blood'. The first time I ever saw him he was walking through Great Court in full hunting rig-out, including—unless this is wishful imagination—a hunting horn and the whip carried by the whipper-in. He was a great horseman and a first-rate shot, very well-off, and to be seen in the company of 'bloods', not the rowing, cricket, and rugger blues, but the rich young men who shot, and hunted, and rode in the point-to-point races. He had a very attractive face, particularly to women, boyish, goodhumoured, hair red and curly, and what in the eighteenth century was called, I think, a sanguine complexion.

Clive became great friends with Thoby, for they both were fond of riding and hunting. In those early days, and indeed for many years afterwards, intellectually Clive sat at the feet of Lytton and Thoby. He was one of those strange Englishmen who break away from their environment and become devoted to art and letters. His family of wealthy philistines, whose money came from coal, lived in a large house in Wiltshire. Somehow or other, Mr and Mrs Bell produced Clive's mind which was a contradiction in terms of theirs.[1] For his mind was eager, lively, intensely curious, and he quickly developed a passion for literature[2] and argument. We had started some reading societies for reading aloud plays, one of which met at midnight, and Clive became a member of them. In this way we came to see a good deal of him and his admiration for Lytton and Thoby began to flourish.

It is necessary here to say something about the Society—The

[1] I do not think that I ever met either of Clive's parents, but I have heard so much about them from him and from others that I have no doubt about the truth of what I say here.

[2] It is worth noting that in those days we set little or no store by pictures and painting. I never heard Clive talk about pictures at Cambridge, and it was only after he came down and lived for a time in Paris and got to know Roger Fry that his interest in art developed. Music already meant a good deal to Lytton, Saxon, and me and we went to chamber music concerts in Cambridge and orchestral concerts in London, but I do not think that it has ever meant much to Clive.

Apostles—because of the immense importance it had for us, its influence upon our minds, our friendships, our lives. The Society was and still is 'secret', but, as it has existed for 130 years or more, in autobiographies and biographies of members its nature, influence, and membership have naturally from time to time been described. There is a good deal about it in the autobiography of Dean Merivale, who was elected in 1830, and in the memoir of Henry Sidgwick, who was elected in 1856, and information about its condition in the early years of the present century can be found in *The Life of John Maynard Keynes* by R. F. Harrod, who was not himself an Apostle. These descriptions show that its nature and atmosphere have remained fundamentally unaltered throughout its existence. The following words from Sidgwick's *A Memoir* are worth quoting:

> I became a member of a discussion society—old and possessing historical traditions—which went by the name of "The Apostles". When I joined it the number of members was not large, and there is an exuberant vitality in Merivale's description to which I recall nothing corresponding. But the spirit, I think, remained the same, and gradually this spirit—at least as I apprehended it—absorbed and dominated me. I can only describe it as the spirit of the pursuit of truth with absolute devotion and unreserve by a group of intimate friends, who were perfectly frank with each other, and indulged in any amount of humorous sarcasm and playful banter, and yet each respects the other, and when he discourses tries to learn from him and see what he sees. Absolute candour was the only duty that the tradition of the society enforced . . . It was rather a point of the apostolic mind to understand how much suggestion and instruction may be derived from what is in form a jest—even in dealing with the gravest matters . . . It came to seem to me that no part of my life at Cambridge was so real to me as the Saturday evenings on which the apostolic debates were held; and the tie of attachment to the society is much the strongest corporate bond which I have known in life.

The Apostles of my generation would all have agreed with every word in this quotation. When Lytton, Saxon, and I were elected, the other active undergraduate members were A. R. Ainsworth, Ralph Hawtrey, and J. T. Sheppard.[1] When Maynard Keynes came up, we elected him in 1903. Sidgwick says that the Society absorbed and dominated him, but that is not quite the end of the story. Throughout its history, every now and again an Apostle has dominated and left his impression, within its spirit and tradition,

[1] Ainsworth became a civil servant in the Education Office; Hawtrey, now Sir Ralph Hawtrey, a civil servant in the Treasury; Sheppard, now Sir J. T. Sheppard, Provost of King's College, Cambridge.

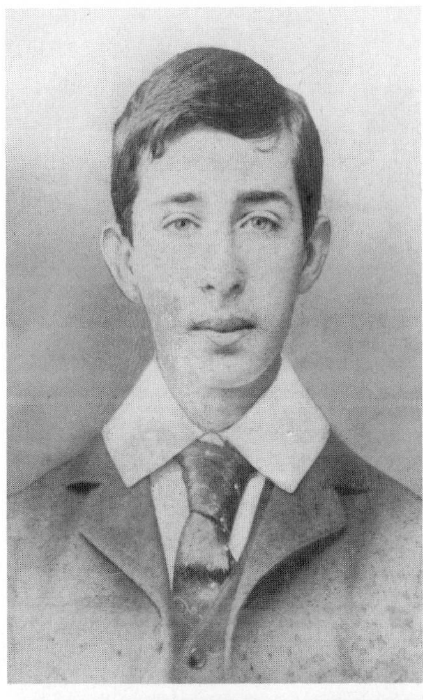

1 The author when a schoolboy

2 The Woolf family in 1886; the author is sitting in the front row on the extreme right

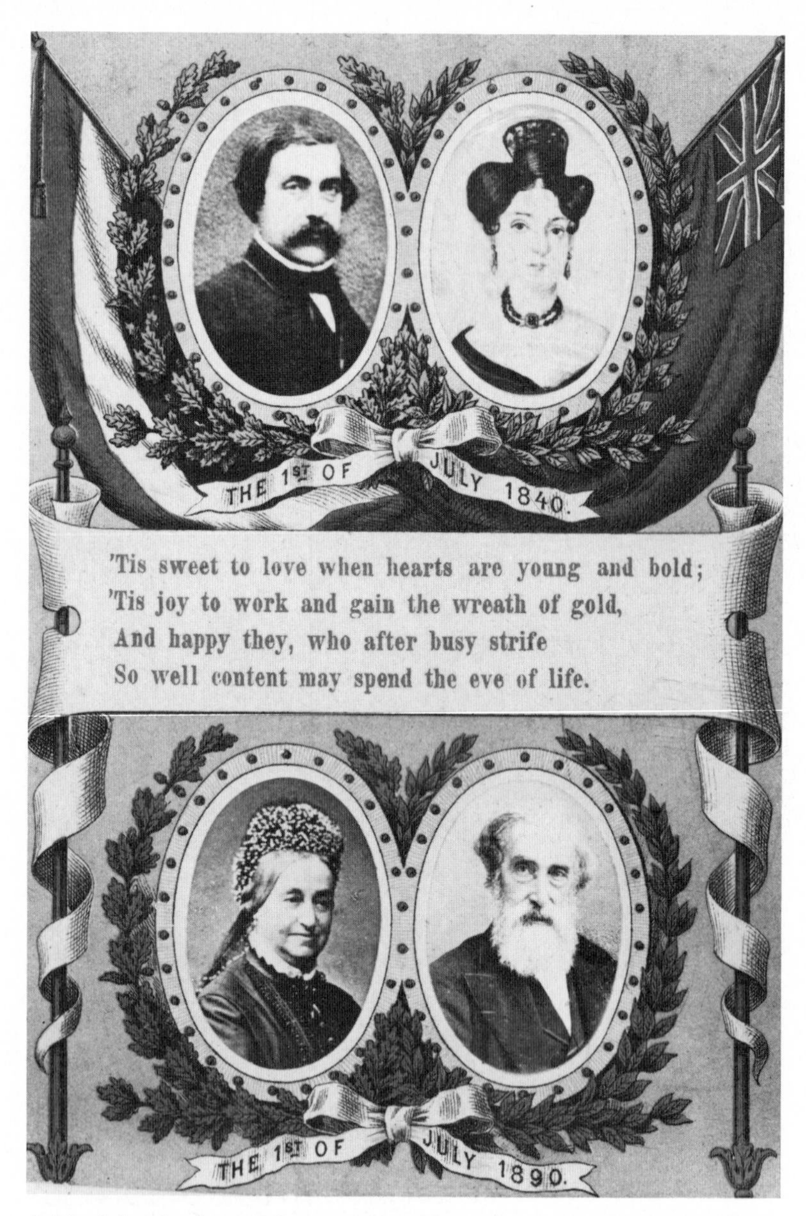

3 The de Jonghs, the author's maternal grandparents, on their wedding day and on their golden wedding day

4 Sidney Woolf, Q.C., the author's father

5 Marie Woolf, the author's mother, in the dress in which she was 'presented'

6 The Shakespeare Society, Trinity College, Cambridge. In the back row Thoby Stephen is second from the left and on the extreme right is Walter Lamb, later Secretary to the Royal Academy. In the front row on the extreme left is Lytton Strachey and on the extreme right the author; second from the right is R. K. Gaye

7 Thoby Stephen, about 1902

8 Vanessa Stephen, about 1902

9 Duncan Grant and Maynard Keynes

10 G. E. Moore

11 Leslie Stephen and his daughter Virginia

12 Virginia Stephen, about 1902

upon the Society. Sidgwick himself was one of these, and a century ago he dominated the Society, refertilising and revivifying its spirit and tradition. And what Sidgwick did in the fifties of last century, G. E. Moore was doing when I was elected.

Mrs Sidney Webb once said to me: 'I have known most of the distinguished men of my time, but I have never yet met a great man.' I had admiration and affection for Beatrice Webb, but when, in her cold and beautiful voice, she pronounced one of these inexorable Sinaic judgments in her tenebrous Grosvenor Road dining-room, gazing through the window across the river at the Doulton China Works, I used to feel that in one moment I should be submerged in despair and desolation, that I was a miserable fly crawling painfully up the Webbs' window to be swotted, long before I reached the top, by their merciless common-sense. But sometimes the fly gave a dying kick, and on this occasion I said: 'I suppose you don't know G. E. Moore.' No, she said, she did not know G. E. Moore, though she knew, of course, whom I meant, and the question of human greatness having been settled, we passed to another question.

The author of Ecclesiasticus probably agreed with Beatrice Webb, for he asked us to praise not great men but famous men—a very different thing. The conversation in Grosvenor Road took place forty years ago, but I still think despite the two impressive authorities that I was right, that George Moore was a great man, the only great man whom I have ever met or known in the world of ordinary, real life. There was in him an element which can, I think, be accurately called greatness, a combination of mind and character and behaviour, of thought and feeling which made him qualitatively different from anyone else I have ever known. I recognise it in only one or two of the many famous dead men whom Ecclesiasticus and others enjoin us to praise for one reason or another.

It was, I suppose, in 1902 that I got to know Moore well. He was seven years my senior and already a Fellow of Trinity. His mind was an extraordinarily powerful instrument; it was Socratic, analytic. But unlike so many analytic philosophers, he never analysed just for the pleasure or sake of analysis. He never indulged in logic-chopping or truth-chopping. He had a passion for truth, but not for all or any truth, only for important truths. He had no use for truths which Browning called 'dead from the waist down'. Towards the end of the nineteenth century there was an extraordinary outburst of philosophical brilliance in Cambridge. In 1902, among the Fellows of Trinity were four philosophers, all of whom were Apostles: J. E. McTaggart, A. N. Whitehead, Bertrand Russell, and G. E. Moore. McTaggart was one of the strangest of men, an eccentric with a powerful mind which, when I knew him, seemed to have entirely left the earth for the inextricably complicated cobwebs and O *altitudos* of Hegelianism. He had the most astonishing capacity for profound silence that I have ever known. He lived out of college, but he had an 'evening' once a week on Thursdays when, if invited or taken by an invitee, you could go and see him in his rooms in Great Court. The chosen were very few, and Lytton, Saxon, and I, who were among them, every now and again nerved ourselves to the ordeal. McTaggart always seemed glad to see us, but, having said good evening, he lay back on a sofa, his eyes fixed on the ceiling, in profound silence. Every five minutes he would roll his head from side to side, stare with his rather protuberant, rolling eyes round the circle of visitors, and then relapse into immobility. One of us would occasionally manage to think of something banal and halting to say, but I doubt whether I ever heard McTaggart initiate a conversation, and when he did say something it was usually calculated to bring to a sudden end any conversation initiated by one of us. Yet he did not seem to wish us not to be there; indeed, he appeared to be quite content that we should come and see him and sit for an hour in silence.

In the early 1890s McTaggart's influence was great. He was six years older than Russell and seven years older than Moore, and these two in their early days at Trinity were first converted to Hegelianism by McTaggart. But Moore, could never tolerate anything but truth, commonsense, and reality, and he very soon revolted against Hegel: Bertrand Russell describes the revolt in the following words:

> Moore, first, and I closely following him, climbed out of this mental prison and found ourselves again at liberty to breathe the free air of a universe restored to reality.

When I came up to Trinity, McTaggart, though regarded with respect and amused affection as an eccentric, had completely lost his intellectual and philosophical influence. The three other philosophers' reputation was great and growing, and they dominated the younger generation. In 1902 Whitehead was forty-one years old, Russell thirty, and Moore twenty-nine. It is a remarkable fact—a fine example of our inflexible irrationality and inveterate inconsistency—that, although no people has ever despised, distrusted and rejected the intellect and intellectuals more than the British, these three philosophers were each awarded the highest and rarest of official honours, the Order of Merit. 1903 was an *annus mirabilis* for Cambridge philosophy, for in that year were published Russell's *Principles of Mathematics* and Moore's *Principia Ethica*. Russell used to come to Moore's rooms sometimes in order to discuss some difficult problem that was holding him up. The contrast between the two men and the two minds was astonishing and fascinating. Russell has the quickest mind of anyone I have ever known; like the greatest of chess players he sees in a flash six moves ahead of the ordinary player and one move ahead of all the other Grand Masters. However serious he may be, his conversation scintillates with wit and a kind of puckish humour flickers through his thought. Like most people who possess this kind of mental brilliance, in an argument a slower and duller opponent may ruefully find that Russell is not always entirely scrupulous in taking advantage of his superior skill in the use of weapons. Moore was the exact opposite, and to listen to an argument between the two was like watching a race between the hare and the tortoise. Quite often the tortoise won—and that, of course, was why Russell's thought had been so deeply influenced by Moore and why he still came to Moore's rooms to discuss difficult problems.

Moore was not witty; I do not think that I ever heard him say a witty thing; there was no scintillation in his conversation or in his thought. But he had an extraordinary profundity and clarity of thought, and he pursued truth with the tenacity of a bulldog and the integrity of a saint. And he had two other very rare characteristics. He had a genius for seeing what was important and what was unimportant and irrelevant, in thought and in life and in persons, and in the most complicated argument or situation he pursued the relevant and ignored the irrelevant with amazing tenacity. He was able to do so because of the second characteristic, the passion for truth (and, as I shall show, for other things) which burned in him. The tortoise so often won the race because of this combination of clarity, integrity, tenacity, and passion.

The intensity of Moore's passion for truth was an integral part of his greatness, and purity of passion was an integral part of his whole character. On the surface and until you got to know him intimately he appeared to be a very shy, reserved man, and on all occasions and in any company he might fall into profound and protracted silence. When I first got to know him, the immensely high standards of thought and conduct which he seemed silently to demand of an intimate, the feeling that one should not say anything unless the thing was both true and worth saying, the silences which would certainly envelope him and you, tinged one's wish to see him with some anxiety, and I know that standing at the door of his room, before knocking and going in, I often took a deep breath just as one does on a cool day before one dives into the cold green sea. For a young man it was a formidable, an alarming experience, but, like the plunge into the cold sea, once one had nerved oneself to take it, extraordinarily exhilarating. This kind of tension relaxed under the influence of time, intimacy, and affection, but I do not think that it ever entirely disappeared—a proof, perhaps, of the quality of greatness which distinguished Moore from other people.

His reserve and silences covered deep feeling. When Moore said: 'I *simply* don't understand *what* he means,' the emphasis on the 'simply' and the 'what' and the shake of his head over each word gave one a glimpse of the passionate distress which muddled thinking aroused in him. We used to watch with amusement and admiration the signs of the same thing when he sat reading a book, pencil in hand, and continually scoring the poor wretch of a writer's muddled sentences with passionate underlinings and exclamation marks. I used to play fives with him at Cambridge, and he played the game with the same passion as that with which he pursued truth; after a few minutes in the court the sweat poured down his face in streams and soaked his clothes—it was excitement as well as exercise. It was the same with music. He played the piano and sang, often to Lytton Strachey and me in his rooms and on reading parties in Cornwall. He was not a highly skilful pianist or singer, but I have never been given greater pleasure from playing or singing. This was due partly to the quality of his voice, but principally to the intelligence of his understanding and to the subtlety and intensity of his feeling. He played the Waldstein sonata or sang 'Ich grolle nicht' with the same passion with which he pursued truth; when the last note died away, he would sit absolutely still, his hands resting on the keys, and the sweat streaming down his face.

Moore's mind was, as I said, Socratic. His character, too, and his influence upon us as young men at Cambridge were Socratic. It is clear from Plato and Xenophon that Socrates's strange simplicity and integrity were enormously attractive to the young Athenians who became his disciples, and he inspired great affection as well as admiration. So did Moore. Plato in the *Symposium* shows us a kind of cosmic absurdity in the monumental simplicity of Socrates; and such different people as Alcibiades, Aristophanes, and Agathon 'rag' him about it and laugh at him gently and affectionately. There was the same kind of divine absurdity in Moore. Socrates had the great advantage of combining a very beautiful soul with a very ugly face, and the Athenians of the fifth century B.C. were just the people to appreciate the joke of that. Moore had not that advantage. When I first knew him, his face was amazingly beautiful, almost ethereal, and, as Bertrand Russell has said, 'he had, what he retained throughout his life, an extraordinarily lovable smile'. But he resembled Socrates in possessing a profound simplicity, a simplicity which Tolstoy and some other Russian writers consider to produce the finest human beings. These human beings are 'simples' or even 'sillies'; they are absurd in ordinary life and by the standards of sensible and practical men. There is a superb description of a 'silly' in Tolstoy's autobiography and, of course, in Dostoevsky's *The Idiot*. In many ways Moore was one of these divine 'sillies'. It showed itself perhaps in such simple, unrestrained, passionate gestures as when, if told something particularly astonishing or confronted by some absurd statement at the crisis of an argument, his eyes would open wide, his eyebrows shoot up, and his tongue shoot out of his mouth. And Bertrand Russell has described the pleasure with which one used to watch Moore trying unsuccessfully to light his pipe when he was arguing an important point. He would light a match, hold it over the bowl of his pipe until it burnt his fingers and he had to throw it away, and go on doing this—talking the whole time or listening intently to the other man's argument—until the whole box of matches was exhausted.

After I went to Ceylon, Moore wrote me some letters which I think, may give to those who never knew him some feeling of his bleak simplicity which was at the same time so endearing, his complete inability to say anything which he did not think or feel, and the psychological atmosphere which surrounded him and which, as I have said, it was both alarming and exhilarating to plunge into. Here are two of his letters:

11 Buccleuch Place
Edinburgh.
March 16, '05

Dear Woolf,

It is very shameful of me not to have answered your letter sooner: it is now nearly three weeks since I got it. I was very, very pleased to get it: I had been wanting to write to you before it came, and was afraid you were not going to write. The reason why I haven't written, in spite of wanting to, is that I don't know what to say. I have begun three letters to you already before this one; but I wouldn't finish them, because they were so bad. I'm afraid I have nothing to say, which is worth saying; or, if I have, I cannot express it.

I do not work any better than I used to, and am just as little interested in anything. As for my work, I have not yet written my review of the "Principles of Mathematics"; and it seems as if I never should. I think I should scarcely get on any faster with my book, even if I had begun that.

Ainsworth and I hardly ever see anyone here. He works very well; and the rest of the time I play the piano to him, or we read together. We have read three of Jane Austen's this term. We have only played golf once a week so far; but we have just been elected members of the club, so that we shall probably play oftener. I think I have improved a little; but I am still very bad indeed.

I went to Cambridge and back a fortnight ago, all within twenty-four hours, to vote in favour of Compulsory Greek. As it turned out, I needn't have gone, for we were 1,500 to 1,000. I found the new brother at Strachey's; but he hardly said anything while I was there, and was not so very attractive at first sight, as I had thought he would be from their description of him.

There is to be a reading-party at Easter; but I almost wish there were not to be: I do feel so incapable of enjoying anything. I wish you could be there. As it is, I don't know who there will be, except Strachey and MacCarthy and ourselves.

My brother has just published a book on Dürer. There is a great deal of philosophy in it, which begins with this sentence: "I conceive the human reason to be the antagonist of all forces other than itself." I do wish people wouldn't write such silly things—things, which, one would have thought, it is so perfectly easy to see to be just false. I suppose my brother's philosophy may have some merits: but it seems to me just like all wretched philosophy—vague, and obviously inconsequent, and full of falsehoods. I think its object is to be like a sermon—to make you appreciate good things; and I sometimes wonder whether it is possible to do this without saying what is false. But it does annoy me terribly that people should admire such things—as they do. I hope you will soon get away from Jaffna. I suppose it is very flat and very hot; and I think there must be more nice Englishmen somewhere in Ceylon.

Ainsworth sends his love.

Yours G. E. Moore.

[1] Thomas Sturge Moore, the poet.

6 Pembroke Villas
The Green,
Richmond, Surrey.
December 1, '08.

Dear Woolf,

I am sending you, enclosed with this, a copy of my last publication. I am sending it, because Strachey said he thought you would like to have it, and at the same time gave me your address. Did I send you the one before, published in 1906? That was a much more interesting and important one. I expect I didn't send it; but I can't feel quite sure that I didn't. If I didn't, and you would like it, I will send you that too. I have always remembered very well that I promised, before you went away, to send you everything I published. But it is so difficult, after such a long time, to feel sure that anyone wants such a promise kept.

I wish I had written to you sometimes: that is to say, if you would have liked to hear from me. The last letter I had from you was in May 1905, nearly four years ago; and I never answered it. I did, in fact, write an answer to it once; but I was ashamed to send it. The truth is I cannot write decently to anyone; I always say such silly things, which don't seem to express what I mean. You said in your last letter to me that you felt something like this too; so perhaps you will understand.

I expect Strachey will have told you about our leaving Edinburgh, and about Ainsworth's marrying my sister.

I have not found that it makes much difference to me, my coming here. I had hoped that I should see a great deal of people that I wanted to see, and that it would be more like Cambridge again. But in fact I hardly ever see anyone except my family.

I was a good deal excited about the marriage, especially when they were first engaged. You known they were only engaged for two months before they married, and of course Ainsworth was constantly coming here. He was very happy; and I wished I could have been engaged too. You know they are coming to live here with me after Christmas. I suppose it is rather an unusual arrangement; but I don't see why it shouldn't succeed.

I don't think you would find me at all altered from what I was. The only difference I notice is that I seem to find it more and more difficult to write anything about philosophy. The only things I have written in all these years, besides a few reviews in the International Journal and some MSS for private persons, are these two papers—the one I'm sending and the one of 1906. I haven't written a line of my book. I have always been engaged either on reviews or on something else, spending no end of time on them with hardly any result. *All* this year I have been trying to write an article on Hume for MacCarthy's New Quarterly, and nothing is done yet, though I've begun it over and over again. I feel very different about it at different times. Sometimes I seem to see how I could do it; very often I feel as if I can't or won't try; and, when I do try, I almost always seem to lose the threat: and there are many other different states of mind too.

Are you coming home this next year? I hope, if you do come, I shall see you a great deal. I have heard very little about you.

Yours very affectionately

G. E. Moore.

This single-minded simplicity permeated his life, and the absurdity which it often produced in everyday life added to one's admiration and affection for him. Like Socrates, he attracted a number of friends and followers as different from one another as Plato and Aristophanes were from Alcibiades and Xenophon. They ranged from Lytton Strachey and Desmond MacCarthy to Sir Ralph Wedgwood,[1] Lord Keynes, and Sir Edward Marsh.[2] Everyone enjoyed Moore's absurdities, laughed at them, and he shared the enjoyment. For although not himself actively witty or humorous, he had a fine, sensitive sense of humour. In conversation Lytton Strachey's snake-like witticisms greatly amused him, but the wit and humour which he liked best, I think, were Desmond MacCarthy's. Desmond was half Irish and his humour had the soft, lovely charm which traditionally is characteristic of Ireland. He was a brilliant talker and raconteur, and he could make Moore laugh as no one else could. And Moore laughed, when he did laugh, with the same passion with which he pursued truth or played a Beethoven sonata. A frequent scene which I like to look back upon is Desmond standing in front of a fire-place telling a long, fantastic story in his gentle voice and Moore lying back on a sofa or deep in an armchair, his pipe as usual out, shaking from head to foot in a long paroxysm of laughter.

During the Easter vac. Moore always arranged a 'reading party'. Only Apostles were asked and only those with whom Moore felt

[1] Ralph Wedgwood was a contemporary of Moore's at Trinity. He was Chief General Manager of London and North-Eastern Railway from 1923 to 1939 and Chairman, Railway Executive Committee from 1939 to 1941. Knighted in 1924, he was created Baronet in 1942.

[2] Eddie Marsh was also a contemporary of Moore's at Trinity. He entered the Civil Service in the Colonial Office in 1896. He was for many years Private Secretary to Winston Churchill, but during his official career he was also Private Secretary to Joseph Chamberlain, Alfred Lyttleton, Asquith, J. H. Thomas, and Malcolm Macdonald. He was a well-known patron of the arts and a man about town with an eye-glass in his eye. But when I was up at Trinity, he still from time to time came up for a weekend and appeared in Moore's rooms.

completely at ease, and that by no means covered everyone even among the elect. Of the undergraduates still up at Cambridge Ainsworth, Lytton Strachey, and I used to go and a certain number of older men who had gone down came, at any rate for the Easter holidays. Desmond MacCarthy, Theodore Llewelyn Davies of the Treasury, Robin Mayor of the Education Office, Charlie Sanger, a barrister, and Bob Trevelyan, the poet, were always asked and always came if they could. We went, twice I think, to the Lizard in Cornwall and once to Hunter's Inn in Devon. I enjoyed these 'reading parties' enormously; I suppose we did sometimes read something, but in memory the days seem to me to have passed in talking and walking—and if they are good, few things can be better than walking and talking. Both were, I think, really very good and it was very exciting for a young undergraduate to be able to form intimate friendships with these older men—friendships which in fact lasted until death ended them.[1] In the evenings Moore sang and played for us, and then we talked and argued again. Moore was at his best on these 'parties'; he liked everyone and was at his ease with them.

I feel that I must now face the difficult task of saying something about Moore's influence upon my generation. There is no doubt that it was immense. Maynard Keynes in his *Two Memoirs* wrote a fascinating, an extremely amusing account or analysis of this influence of Moore upon us as young men. Much of what he says is, of course, true and biographically or autobiographically important. Maynard's mind was incredibly quick and supple, imaginative and restless; he was always thinking new and original thoughts, particularly in the field of events and human behaviour and in the reaction between events and men's actions. He had the very rare gift of being as brilliant and effective in practice as he was in theory, so that he could outwit a banker, business man, or Prime Minister as quickly and gracefully as he could demolish a philosopher or crush an economist. It was these gifts which enabled him to revolutionise economic theory and national economic and financial policy and practice, and to make a considerable fortune by speculation and a considerable figure in the City and in the world which is concerned

[1] Today all are dead. Theodore Davies, a man of extraordinary brilliance and great charm, was killed young in a tragic accident. All the others remained intimate friends for thirty or forty years.

with the patronage or production of the arts, and particularly the theatre and ballet. But most people who knew him intimately and his mind in shirtsleeves rather than public uniform would agree that there were in him some streaks of intellectual wilfulness and arrogance which often led him into surprisingly wrong and perverse judgments. To his friends he was a lovable character and these faults or idiosyncracies were observed and discounted with affectionate amusement.

It is always dangerous to speak the truth about one's most intimate friends, because the truth and motives for telling it are almost invariably misunderstood. In all the years that I knew Maynard and in all the many relations, of intimacy and business which I had with him, I never had even the ghost of a quarrel or the shadow of unpleasantness, though we often disagreed about things, persons, or policies. He was essentially a lovable person. But to people who were not his friends, to subordinates and to fools in their infinite variety whom one has to deal with in business or just daily life, he could be anything but lovable; he might, at any moment and sometimes quite unjustifiably, annihilate some unfortunate with ruthless rudeness. I once heard him snap out to an auditor who was trying to explain to the Board of Directors of a company some item in the audited accounts: 'We all know, Mr X., that auditors consider that the object of accounts is to conceal the truth, but surely not even you can believe that their object is to conceal the truth from the Directors.'

It was this streak of impatience and wilfulness combined with a restless and almost fantastic imagination, which often induced Maynard to make absurdly wrong judgments. But once having committed himself to one of his opinions or judgments, theories or fantasies, he would without compunction use all the powers and brilliance of his mind, his devastating wit and quickness, to defend it, and in the end would often succeed in convincing not only his opponent, but himself. In several points in *Two Memoirs* his recollection and interpretation are quite wrong about Moore's influence, I think. His main point in the memoir is that Moore in *Principia Ethica* propounded both a religion and a system of morals and that we as young men accepted the religion, but discarded the morals. He defines 'religion' to mean one's attitude towards oneself and the ultimate, and 'morals' to mean one's attitude towards the outside world and the intermediate. Moore's religion which we accepted, according to Maynard, maintained that 'nothing mattered except states of mind, our own and other people's of course, but chiefly our own. These states of mind were not associated with action or achievement or with consequences. They consisted in timeless, passionate states of contemplation and communion, largely unattached to "before" and "after" . . . The appropriate objects of passionate contemplation and communion were a beloved person, beauty and truth, and one's prime objects in life were love, the creation and enjoyment of aesthetic experience and the pursuit of knowledge. Of these love came a long way first.'

Although Maynard calls this doctrine which we accepted a 'faith' and a 'religion', he says that Moore's disciples and indeed Moore himself regarded it as entirely rational and scientific, and applied an extravagantly rationalistic, scholastic method for ascertaining what states of affairs were or were not good. The resulting beliefs were fantastically idealistic and remote from reality and 'real' life. The effect of this curious amalgam of extreme rationalism, unworldliness, and dogmatic belief was intensified by our complete neglect of Moore's 'morals'. We paid no attention at all to his doctrine of the importance of rightness and wrongness as an attribute of actions or to the whole question of the justification of general rules of conduct. The result was that we assumed that human beings were all rational, but we were complete 'immoralists', recognising 'no moral obligation on us, no inner sanction, to conform or obey.'

In my recollection this is a distorted picture of Moore's beliefs and doctrine at the time of the publication of his *Principia Ethica* and of the influence of his philosophy and character upon us when we were young men up at Cambridge in the years 1901 to 1904. The tremendous influence of Moore and his book upon us came from the fact that they suddenly removed from our eyes an obscuring accumulation of scales, cobwebs, and curtains, revealing for the first time to us, so it seemed, the nature of truth and reality, of good and evil and character and conduct, substituting for the religious and philosophical nightmares, delusions, hallucinations, in which Jehovah, Christ, and St Paul, Plato, Kant, and Hegel had entangled us, the fresh air and pure light of plain commonsense.

It was this clarity, freshness, and common-sense which primarily appealed to us. Here was a profound philosopher who did not require us to accept any 'religious' faith or intricate, if not unintelligible, intellectual gymnastics of a Platonic, Aristotelian, Kantian, or Hegelian nature; all he asked as to do was to make quite certain that we knew what we meant when we made a statement and to analyse and examine our beliefs in the light of common-sense. Philosophically what, as intelligent young men, we wanted to know was the basis, if any, for our or any scale of values and rules of conduct, what justification there was for our belief that friendship or works of art for instance were good or for the belief that one ought to do some things and not do others. Moore's distinction between things good in themselves or as ends and things good merely as means, his passionate search for truth in his attempt in *Principia Ethica* to determine what things are good in themselves, answered our questions, not with the religious voice of Jehovah from Mount Sinai or Jesus with his sermon from the Mount, but with the more divine voice of plain common-sense.

On one side of us, we were in 1901 very serious young men. We were sceptics in search of truth and ethical truth. Moore, so we thought, gave us a scientific basis for believing that some things were good in themselves. But we were not 'immoralists'; it is not true that we recognised 'no moral obligation on us, no inner sanction, to conform or obey' or that we neglected all that Moore said about 'morals' and rules of conduct. It is true that younger generations, like their elders, were much less politically and socially conscious in the years before the 1914 war than they have been ever since. Bitter experience has taught the world, including the young, the importance of codes of conduct and morals and 'practical politics'. But Moore himself was continually exercised by the problems of goods and bads as means of morality and rules of conduct and therefore of the life of action as opposed to the life of contemplation. He and we were fascinated by questions of what was right and wrong, what one *ought* to do. We followed him closely in this as in other parts of his doctrine and argued interminably about the consequences of one's actions, both in actual and imaginary situations. Indeed one of the problems which worried us was what part Moore (and we, his disciples) *ought* to play in ordinary life, what, for instance, our attitude *ought* to be towards practical politics. I still possess a paper which I wrote for discussion in 1903 and which is explicitly concerned with these problems. It asks the question whether we ought to follow the example of George Trevelyan,[1] and take part in prac-

[1] George Macaulay Trevelyan, O.M., the historian and for many years Master of Trinity College. He was four years my senior at Trinity and, when

tical politics, going down into the gloomy Platonic cave, where 'men sit bound prisoners guessing at the shadows of reality and boasting that they have found truth', or whether we should imitate George Moore, who though 'he has no small knowledge of the cave dwellers, leaves alone their struggles and competitions.' I said that the main question I wanted to ask was: 'Can we and ought we to combine the two Georges in our own lives?' And was it rational that George Moore, the philosopher, should take no part in practical politics, or 'right that we should as we do so absolutely ignore their questions?' My answer in 1903 was perfectly definite that we *ought* to take part in practical politics and the last words of my paper are: 'While philosophers sit outside the cave, their philosophy will never reach politicians or people, so that after all, to put it plainly, I *do* want Moore to draft an Education Bill.'

I have said that we were very serious young men. We were, indeed, but superficially we often appeared to be the exact opposite and so enraged or even horrified a good many people. After all we were young once—we were young in 1903; and we were not nearly as serious and solemn as we appeared to some people. We were serious about what we considered to be serious in the universe or in man and his life, but we had a sense of humour and we felt that it was not necessary to be solemn, because one was serious, and that there are practically no questions or situations in which intelligent laughter may not be healthily catalytic. Henry Sidgwick, in his *Memoir*, looking back in old age to the year 1856 when he was elected an Apostle wrote:

> No consistency was demanded with opinions previously held—truth as we saw it then and there was what we had to embrace and maintain, and there were no propositions so well established that an Apostle had not the right to deny or question, if he did so sincerely and not from mere love of paradox. The gravest subjects were continually debated, but gravity of treatment, as I have said, was not imposed, though sincerity was. In fact it was rather a point of the apostolic mind to understand how much suggestion and instruction may be derived from what is in form a jest—even in dealing with the gravest matters.

I am writing today just over a century after the year in which Sidgwick was elected an Apostle, and looking back to the year 1903 I can say that our beliefs, our discussions, our intellectual behaviour

---

I first knew him, had just become a Fellow of the college. He was a rather fiercely political young man.

in 1903 were in every conceivable way exactly the same as those described by Sidgwick. The beliefs 'fantastically idealistic and remote from reality and real life', the absurd arguments, 'the extravagantly scholastic' method were not as simple or silly as they seemed. Lytton Strachey's mind was fundamentally and habitually ribald and he had developed a protective intellectual façade in which a highly personal and cynical wit and humour played an important part. It was very rarely safe to accept the face value of what he said; within he was intensely serious about what he thought important, but on the surface his method was to rely on 'suggestion and instruction derived from what is in form a jest—even in dealing with the gravest matters.' I think that in my case, too, there was a natural tendency to express myself ironically—and precisely in matters or over questions about which one felt deeply as being of great importance—for irony and the jest are used, particularly when one is young, as antidotes to pomposity. Of course we were young once; we were young in 1903, and we had the arrogance and the extravagance natural to the young.

The intellectual, when young, has always been in all ages enthusiastic and passionate and therefore he has tended to be intellectually arrogant and ruthless. Our youth, the years of my generation at Cambridge, coincided with the end and the beginning of a century which was also the end of one era and the beginning of another. When in the grim, grey, rainy January days of 1901 Queen Victoria lay dying, we already felt that we were living in an era of incipient revolt and that we ourselves were mortally involved in this revolt against a social system and code of conduct and morality which, for convenience sake, may be referred to as bourgeois Victorianism. We did not initiate this revolt. When we went up to Cambridge, its protagonists were Swinburne, Bernard Shaw, Samuel Butler in *The Way of All Flesh*, and to some extent Hardy and Wells. We were passionately on the side of these champions of freedom of speech and freedom of thought, of common-sense and reason. We felt that, with them as our leaders, we were struggling against a religious and moral code of cant and hypocrisy which produced and condoned such social crimes and judicial murders as the condemnation of Dreyfus. People of a younger generation who from birth have enjoyed the results of this struggle for social and intellectual emancipation cannot realise the stuffy intellectual and moral suffocation which a young man felt weighing down upon him in Church and State, in the 'rules and conventions' of the last days of Victorian civilisation. Nor can those who have been born into the world of great wars, of communism and national socialism and fascism, of Hitler and Mussolini and Stalin, of the wholesale judicial murders of their own fellow-countrymen or massacres of peasants by Russian communists, and the slaughter of millions of Jews in gas-chambers by German nazis, these younger generations can have no notion of what the long-drawn out tragedy of the Dreyfus case meant to us. Over the body and fate of one obscure, Jewish captain in the French army a kind of cosmic conflict went on year after year between the establishment of Church, Army, and State on the one side and the small band of intellectuals who fought for truth, reason, and justice, on the other. Eventually the whole of Europe, almost the whole world, seemed to be watching breathlessly, ranged upon one side or other in the conflict. And no one who was not one of the watchers can understand the extraordinary sense of relief and release when at last the innocence of Dreyfus was vindicated and justice was done. I still think that we were right and that the Dreyfus case might, with a slight shift in the current of events, have been a turning point in European history and civilisation. All that can really be said against us was that our hopes were disappointed.

It is true that in a sense 'we had no respect for traditional wisdom' and that, as Ludwig Wittgenstein complained, 'we lacked reverence for everything and everyone.' If 'to revere' means, as the dictionary says, 'to regard as sacred or exalted, to hold in religious respect', then we did not revere, we had no reverence for anything or anyone, and, so far as I am concerned, I think we were completely right; I remain of the same opinion still—I think it to be, not merely my right, but my duty to question the truth of everything and the authority of everyone, to regard nothing as sacred and to hold nothing in religious respect. That attitude was encouraged by the climate of scepticism and revolt into which we were born and by Moore's ingenuous passion for truth. The dictionary, however, gives an alternative meaning for the word 'revere'; it may mean 'to regard with deep respect and warm approbation.' It is not true that we lacked reverence for everything and everyone in that sense of the word. After questioning the truth and utility of everything and after refusing to accept or swallow anything or anyone on the mere 'authority' of anyone, in fact after exercising our own judgment, there were many things and persons regarded by us with 'deep respect and warm approbation': truth, beauty, works of art, some customs, friendship, love, many living men and women and many of the dead.

The young are not only ruthless; they are often perfectionist; if they are intelligent, they are inclined to react against the beliefs, which have hardened into the fossilised dogmas of the previous generation. To the middle-aged, who have forgotten their youth, the young naturally seem to be not only wrong, but wrong-headed (and indeed they naturally often are); to the middle-aged and the old, if they are also respectable, the young seem to be, not only wrong, but intellectually ill-mannered (and indeed they often are). In 1903 we were often absurd, wrong, wrong-headed, ill-mannered; but in 1903 we were right in refusing to regard as sacred and exalted, to hold in religious respect, the extraordinary accomplishment of our predecessors in the ordering of life or the elaborate framework which they had devised to protect this order. We were right to question the truth and authority of all this, of respectability and the establishment, and to give our deep respect and warm approbation only to what in the establishment (and outside it) stood the test and ordeal of such questioning.

It will be remembered that Maynard's *Memoir*, in which he analyses the state of our minds (and Moore's) when we were undergraduates, starts with an account of a breakfast party in Bertrand Russell's rooms in Cambridge, at which only Russell, Maynard, and D. H. Lawrence were present. Lawrence was 'morose from the outset and said very little, apart from indefinite expressions of irritable dissent, all the morning.' And in a letter to David Garnett, Lawrence referred to this visit of his to Cambridge as follows:

My dear David,

Never bring Birrell to see me any more. There is something nasty about him like black beetles. He is horrible and unclean. I feel I should go mad when I think of your set, Duncan Grant and Keynes and Birrell. It makes me dream of beetles. In Cambridge I had a similar dream. I had felt it slightly before in the Stracheys. But it came full upon me in Keynes and Duncan Grant. And yesterday I knew it again in Birrell . . . you must leave these friends, these beetles, Birrell and Duncan Grant are done for ever. Keynes I am not sure . . . when I saw Keynes that morning in Cambridge it was one of the crises of my life. It sent me mad with misery and hostility and rage . . .

Maynard, starting from the breakfast party and this letter, examines the question whether there was in fact something in Lawrence's judgment, some justification for his horror and rage against 'us', whether we were horrible and unclean and black beetles. His account of us, his dissection of our spiritual and intellectual anatomy, leads him to conclude that there was something in what Lawrence said and felt—there was a 'thinness and superficiality, as well as the falsity, of our view of man's heart,' we were 'water-spiders, gracefully skimming, as light and reasonable as air, the surface of the stream without any contact with the eddies and currents underneath.' In this, and indeed in the whole of the *Memoir*, Maynard confuses, I think, two periods of his and of our lives. When our Cambridge days were over, there grew up in London during the years 1907 to 1914 a society or group of people which became publicly known as Bloomsbury. Later in my autobiography I shall have to say a good deal about Bloomsbury, the private nature and the public picture. Here all I need say is that Bloomsbury grew directly out of Cambridge; it consisted of a number of intimate friends who had been at Trinity and King's and were now working in London, most of them living in Bloomsbury.

Lawrence's breakfast party took place in 1914 or 1915. The people to whom he refers are not the undergraduates of 1903, but Bloomsbury, and a great deal of what Maynard wrote in his *Memoir* is true of Bloomsbury in 1914, but not true of the undergraduates of 1903. In 1903 we had all the inexperience, virginity, seriousness, intellectual puritanism of youth. In 1914 we had all, in various ways or places, been knocking about the world for ten or eleven years. A good deal of the bloom of ignorance and other things had been brushed off us. *Principia Ethica* had passed into our unconscious and was now merely a part of our super-ego; we no longer argued about it as a guide to practical life. Some of us were 'men of the world' or even Don Juans, and all round us there was taking place the revolt (which we ourselves in our small way helped to start) against the Victorian morality and code of conduct. In 1914 little or no attention was paid to Moore's fifth chapter on 'Ethics in relation to Conduct', and pleasure, once rejected by us theoretically, had come to be accepted as a very considerable good in itself. But this was not the case in 1903.

Moore and the Society were the focus of my existence during my last years at Cambridge. They dominated me intellectually and also emotionally, and did the same to Lytton Strachey and to Saxon Sydney-Turner. We were already intimate friends, seeing one another every day, before we were elected and got to know Moore well, but Moore's influence and the Society's gave, I think, increased depth and meaning to our relationship. I daresay to a good many people with whom we came into superficial contact we seemed, not without reason, unpleasant. Trinity was such a large college that, when we were up, one soon formed one's own circle of friends and acquaintances and rarely troubled or was troubled by those who belonged to other sets. The hostility of the ordinary man to the scholar and intellectual was therefore a good deal less important and less noticeable in Trinity than in some of the small colleges. It was only on nights of bump-suppers and similar drunks and celebrations that an intellectual or anyone who looked like an intellectual had to be careful to keep out of the way of the 'bloods' and athletes. But I think that we—and Lytton in particular—got a special measure of dislike and misprision from the athletes and their followers—'the little men in waistcoats', as Thoby Stephen called them—on the rare occasions when our paths happened to converge. There was some reason, as I said above, for their finding us unpleasant, for we were not merely obviously much too clever to be healthy 'good fellows', we were arrogant, supercilious, cynical, sarcastic, and Lytton always looked very queer and had a squeaky voice.

It must be admitted that it was not only among the toughs and bloods that we were unpopular. I still possess some letters, written in 1901 and full of the uncompromising ferocity of youth which show this. During my second year at Trinity I had become friendly with a fellow scholar, himself an intellectual of considerable powers. When after a time he seemed to avoid me, I asked him the reason, and he explained his position in letters from which the following are extracts:

"I cannot endure the people I meet in your rooms. Either they or I had to go, and as I was the newest and alone I waived my claim to the older friends and the majority. Strachey . . . &c. are to me in their several ways the most offensive people I have ever met, and if I had continued to meet them daily, I could not be answerable for anything I might do . . . I am not what is known as religious, but I was not going to associate with people who scoffed and jeered at my religion: fair criticism given in a gentlemanly way I do not mind. But the tone of Strachey and even you on matters of religion was not gentlemanly to me . . . I have never been in your rooms without someone coming in whom I do not like, usually Strachey . . . I always spoke to you as a friend to a friend, except when Strachey was with you. Silence is then safer."

As one grows older or even more as one grows old it is easy and pleasant to make either of two mistakes in one's memories of those few years when in one's early twenties one lived in a Cambridge college. One can foolishly idealise and sentimentalise youth and the young, and so oneself as young. Or one can do the opposite and join the many angry old men who are enviously exasperated by the young and therefore remember only the stupidities and humiliations of their own youth. There is a certain amount of truth in each of these views or visions so that either accepted absolutely and unmodified by the other is simply false. My own experience is that I have never again been quite so happy or quite so miserable as I was in the five years at Cambridge from 1899 to 1904. One lived in a state of continual excitement and strong and deep feeling. We were intellectuals, intellectuals with three genuine and, I think, profound passions: a passion for friendship, a passion for literature and music (it is significant that the plastic arts came a good deal later), a passion for what we called the truth.

What made everything so exciting was that everything was new, anything might happen, and all life was before us. We looked before, not after, and our laughter, continual and sincere, was not fraught with pain, just as our pain was as pure as our laughter. We lived in extremes—of happiness and unhappiness, of admiration and contempt, of love and hate. I might any day or hour or minute turn a corner and find myself face to face with someone whom I had never met before but who would instantly become my friend for life. I might casually open a book and find that I was reading for the first time *War and Peace*, *The Brothers Karamazov*, *Madame Bovary*, *Hedda Gabler*, *Urn Burial*, or *The Garden of Proserpine*. I might wake up tomorrow morning and find that I could at last write the great poem that fluttered helplessly at the back of my mind or the great novel rumbling hopelessly in some strange depths inside me. We all wanted to be writers ourselves, and what added to our excitement was that we could share our ambitions, our beliefs, our hopes, and fears. By 'we' I mean pre-eminently Lytton Strachey, Saxon Sydney-Turner, Thoby Stephen, and myself.

The hates, contempts, miseries were as violent—almost as exciting—as the loves, friendships, admirations, ectasies. We were arrogant, wrongheaded, awkward, oscillating between callowness and sophistication. We were convinced that everyone over twenty-five, with perhaps one or two remarkable exceptions, was 'hopeless', having lost the élan of youth, the capacity to feel, and the ability to distinguish truth from falsehood. We were not angry young men in any sense; that psychology of a much later age was alien to ours. Intellectually we were terribly insolent, being contemptuous of, not angry with, authority and stupidity, so that no doubt to those whom we did not like or who did not like us we must have been insufferable.

Here I must again recall the fact, briefly mentioned already, that this period of our early manhood, perhaps the most impressionable years of one's life, was an age of revolution. We found ourselves living in the springtime of a conscious revolt against the social, political, religious, moral, intellectual, and artistic institutions, beliefs, and standards of our fathers and grandfathers. We felt ourselves to be the second generation of this exciting movement of men and ideas. The battle, which was against what for short one may call Victorianism, had not yet been won, and what was so exciting was our feeling that we ourselves were part of the revolution, that victory or defeat depended to some small extent upon what we did, said, or wrote. After the 1914 war, and still more after Hitler's war, the young who are not conservatives, fascists, or communists are almost necessarily defeatist; they have grown up under the shadow of defeat in the past and the menace of defeat in the future. It is natural, inevitable that they should suffer from the sterility of being angry young men. Our state of mind was the exact opposite. There was no shadow of past defeat; the omens were all favourable. We were not, as we are today, fighting with our backs to the wall against a resurgence of barbarism and barbarians. We were not part of a negative movement of destruction against the past. We were out to construct something new; we were in the van of the builders of a new society which should be free, rational, civilised, pursuing truth and beauty. It was all tremendously exhilarating.

And no doubt, looking back after fifty years and two world wars and the atomic age and Mussolini, Hitler, Stalin, and Russian communism, no doubt terribly naïve. Of course, we were naïve. But age and hindsight unfairly exaggerate and distort the naïvety of youth. Living in 1900 and seeing the present with no knowledge of the future, we had some grounds for excitement and exhilaration. The long drawn out, crucial test of society and politics in the Dreyfus case had not yet ended in decisive defeat for the old régime, but the 'pardoning' of Dreyfus foreshadowed their final defeat and the reinstatement of Dreyfus six years later. And what made the Dreyfus case so terribly exciting, so profoundly significant, was that this judicial murder of an obscure Jewish army officer, this trial and conviction of an unimportant captain in the 21st regiment of artillery in France, became, as I said above, a struggle of European and later almost of cosmic importance. One felt that gradually everyone in the world had become involved in it, that everyone was becoming consciously implicated in the struggle between right and wrong, justice and injustice, civilisation and barbarism. The court-martial in the Cherche-Midi prison, the degradation ceremony on the parade-ground with the soldiers drawn up in a great square and Dreyfus raising his arms and crying out to them: 'Soldiers, I am innocent! It is an innocent man who is being dishonoured. Vive la France! Vive l'Armée!', the crowd hissing and shouting: 'A mort! A mort! Kill him! Kill him!', the imprisonment on the Ile du Diable—these events which were contemporary events of our own lifetime assumed symbolic import like the trial and death of Socrates and the scene in the prison at Athens—'Crito, we owe a cock to Asclepius'—or even that other trial before Pontius Pilate in Jerusalem and all the crowd hissing and shouting: 'Let him be crucified! His blood be on us, and on our children.'

I do not think we were wrong in feeling this tremendous significance of the Dreyfus case. It was, what we felt it to be, a struggle between two standards of social and therefore of human value. Two world wars and millions of Dreyfuses murdered by Russian communists and German nazis do not prove us to have been wrong; they merely show that any hope in 1904 that the world might become permanently civilised has not been fulfilled. One should perhaps recall the men and books which in those days of our Cambridge youth filled us with admiration, enthusiasm, hope, for they show the deep currents of revolt operating in the society of our time, and they reveal not only autobiographically our personal psychology, but also—what is more important—the historical psychology of an era.

There was in Trinity an old-established Shakespeare Society which met, I think, weekly to read aloud the plays of Shakespeare. Not content with this, we founded a new society, the X Society, for the purpose of reading plays other than Shakespeare. We read the Elizabethans and the Restoration dramatists with immense pleasure, but we also read two contemporaries, Ibsen and Shaw. The plays of these two writers gave us something over and above the aesthetic pleasure which we got from the poetry of *The Duchess of Malfi*, *Volpone*, or *The Maid's Tragedy*, or the intellectual pleasure which the wit of *The Way of the World* gave us. The poetry, the work of art in *The Wild Duck* or *Hedda Gabler* or *The Master-Builder* gave us and still give me profound pleasure, a pleasure which can rightly be distinguished as purely aesthetic. The dramatic genius, the humour, and the verbal wit in *Arms and the Man* or *You Never Can Tell* gave us and to some extent can still give me great intellectual pleasure. But in all these plays, and pre-eminently in Ibsen's, there was something else, something extraordinarily exciting which belonged to the immediate moment in which we lived and yet went down into the depths of our beliefs and desires and the great currents of history. Not only in such plays as *The Doll's House* or *Ghosts*, but in the strange symbolic words and action of *The Master-Builder* or *The Wild Duck* or *Rosmersholm*, the cobwebs and veils, the pretences and hypocrisies which suppressed the truth, buttressed cruelty, injustice, and stupidity, and suffocated society in the nineteenth century, were broken through, exposed, swept away. When Brack said: 'Good God!—people don't do such things.', when Hilda says: 'But he mounted right to the top. And I heard harps in the air. My—my Master-Builder!', when Relling says: 'Bosh!' to Molvik's: 'The child is not dead but sleepeth', we felt that Ibsen was revealing something new in people's heads and hearts—in our heads and hearts—and that he was giving us hope of something new and true in human relations and that he was saying 'Bosh!' to that vast system of cant and hypocrisy which made lies a vested interest, the vested interest of the 'establishment', of the monarchy, aristocracy, upper classes, suburban bourgeoisie, the Church, the Army, the stock exchange.

We did not think Bernard Shaw to be nearly as great a dramatist as Ibsen. He lacked the poetry, if that is the right word, the creative imagination, which makes *The Wild Duck*, *Hedda Gabler*, *Rosmersholm*, *John Gabriel Bjorkman* so moving, quite apart from any 'message' that they had for our generation. But Shaw did have a message of tremendous importance to us—and to the world—in the years 1899 to 1904. It was the same kind of message which I have tried to describe above as coming to us from Ibsen's Brack, Hilda, and Relling. I still possess a copy of Vol. II of *Plays: Pleasant and Unpleasant* published by Grant Richards in 1901; I have written in it my name and the date, showing that I bought it in November

1902. In the preface Shaw answers his liberal critics who had attacked him for striking 'wanton blows' at idealism, religion, morality, the 'cause of liberty' in *Arms and the Man* and others of his plays. I will quote his own words, because they state contemporaneously, in November 1902, far better than I can today that message which made us recognise him with enthusiasm as one of our leaders in the revolutionary movement of our youth.

. . . idealism, which is only a flattering name for romance in politics and morals, is as obnoxious to me as romance in ethics or religion. In spite of a Liberal Revolution or two, I can no longer be satisfied with fictitious morals and fictitious good conduct, shedding fictitious glory on robbery, starvation, disease, crime, drink, war, cruelty, cupidity, and all the other commonplaces of civilization which drive men to the theatre to make foolish pretences that such things are progress, science, morals, religion, patriotism, imperial supremacy, national greatness and all the other names the newspapers call them. On the other hand, I see plenty of good in the world working itself out as fast as the idealists will allow it; and if they would only let it alone and learn to respect reality, which would include the beneficial exercise of respecting themselves, and incidentally respecting me, we should all get along much better and faster. At all events, I do not see moral chaos and anarchy as the alternative to romantic convention; and I am not going to pretend I do merely to please the people who are convinced that the world is only held together by the force of unanimous, strenuous, eloquent, trumpet-tongued lying.

The novels which a man reads throw light upon his psychology and the psychology of his generation. Very few of the illustrious dead among English novelists meant much to us. In 1903 I read Fielding and Richardson rather because I thought they should have been read, Jane Austen and the Brontës because they gave me pleasure, aesthetic and intellectual. Thackeray and Dickens meant nothing to us or rather they stood for an era, a way of life, a system of morals against which we were in revolt. We were unfair to them and misjudged them aesthetically, as I recognised when much later in life I came to read them again. It was the curious satire of *Crotchet Castle*, so suave and yet so sharp, which struck a note in the past which we could appreciate as in harmony with our mood. Of contemporaries the first to mean something to us was George Meredith. I don't think I ever *liked* him as much as the others of my generation did, for there seemed to be something unreal and phoney in his artificiality. But he appealed to us as breaking away from the cosmic and social assumptions of Thackeray and Dickens, as challenging their standards of morality. I am not sure now that he did and today I feel that we were almost certainly also wrong about Henry James. I have explained already the immense influence which he had upon us. Up to a point we were right and the influence was justified, for the niceties and subtleties of his art and his psychology belonged to the movement of revolt. But he was never really upon our side in that revolt.

There were two novelists, amazingly different from each other, who were very definitely upon our side and whom we recognised with enthusiasm, not merely as writers and artists, but as our leaders. *The Way of All Flesh* by Samuel Butler was published in 1903, a year after his death. We read it when it came out and felt at once its significance for us. The other was Thomas Hardy. *The Return of the Native* and *The Mayor of Casterbridge* seemed to us great novels, and, though we probably overvalued them, we were not far wrong. But those books and still more *Tess of the D'Urbervilles* and *Jude the Obscure* had another importance besides the artistic. The outcry against them came from those who supported what we thought the most degraded and hypocritical elements in Victorianism. *Tess of the D'Urbervilles* was published in 1891 and in the preface to the new edition of 1895 Hardy himself dealt with these critics. He pointed out that 'a novel is an impression, not an argument', and he was not arguing a case in *Tess*. Some of those who objected to his novel were 'genteel persons . . . not able to endure something or other' in the book. Some were 'austere' persons who considered that certain subjects are not fit for art; some objected to a woman who had an illegitimate child being made the heroine of a respectable novel and still more to her being rather provocatively labelled by Hardy in his subtitle a 'pure woman'. Looking back over half a century to this, in these spacious days when solemn judges give solemn judgments that *Ulysses* and *Lady Chatterley's Lover* are not indecent and can be read innocuously by babes and sucklings as well as by pornographic elderly gentlemen, it is almost impossible to believe that in 1900 *Tess* was widely condemned as an immoral book. *Tess* and Hardy were themselves a cause of the change, just as were Ibsen and Shaw, and that was why we, who felt ourselves to be so much involved in this struggle of ideas and ideals, regarded all three of them as in a sense our leaders.

There is another name which I must add to these three, and I am afraid that I will appear ridiculous to practically everyone of later generations by admitting it. For it is Algernon Charles Swinburne.

Late at night in the May term, I like to remember, Lytton, Saxon, Thoby Stephen, Clive Bell, and I would sometimes walk through the Cloisters of Nevilles Court in Trinity and looking out through the bars at the end on to the willows and water of the Backs, ghostly in the moonlight, listen to the soaring song of innumerable nightingales. And sometimes as we walked back through the majestic Cloisters we chanted poetry. More often than not it would be Swinburne:

> From too much love of living,
> From hope and fear set free,
> We thank with brief thanksgiving
> Whatever gods may be
> That no life lives for ever;
> That dead men rise up never;
> That even the weariest river
> Winds somewhere safe to sea.

> We shift and bedeck and bedrape us,
> Thou art noble and nude and antique.

> Thou hast conquered, O pale Galilean; the world has grown grey from thy breath;
> We have drunk of things Lethean, and fed on the fulness of death.

It all sounds, no doubt, silly and sentimental and, what so many people think even more deplorable, so terribly out of date. Of course we were silly and sentimental at the age of twenty, and I do not think there is anything admirable in this kind of crudity and naïvety of the young. Yet the unfledged foolishness is partly due—and was in our case due—to the enthusiasm, the passion with which one sees and hears and thinks and feels when everything in the world and in other people and in oneself is fresh and new to one. This passion is, I think, admirable and desirable, and that is one reason why it irritates us when age and experience, bringing disappointment and boredom, have blurred our sensations, dimmed our beliefs, and castrated our desires.

As to the out-of-dateness of Swinburne and *Dolores* and *The Garden of Proserpine*, and so of the young men and the nightingales, I am not much concerned or troubled by it. I have always thought that to make a fuss or a song about being up-to-date is the sign of a weak mind or of intellectual cold feet or cold heart. Every out-of-date writer of any importance was once modern, and the most modern of writers will some day, and pretty rapidly, become out-of-date. For us in 1902 Tennyson was out-of-date and we therefore underestimated his poetry; today another fifty years has evaporated much of his datedness, and his stature as a poet becomes more visible. I daresay that we overestimated Swinburne's poetry,[1] but I have no doubt that it is generally underestimated today. If I wanted to chant a poem to nightingales singing at midnight and in moonlight, I might still choose the *Garden of Proserpine* or some other poem of Swinburne's and I am sure that it would stand up to the ordeal as well as any song the Sirens have sung. That is no mean or common achievement and would show that there is some poetry in the poem.

Swinburne was something of a legend and symbol to us in the early nineteen hundreds. Immured for the last thirty years of his life by Theodore Watts-Dunton in the grim bourgeois 'residence', The Pines, at the bottom of Putney Hill, 'his life was "sheltered" like that of a child,' as his biographer, Sir Edmund Gosse, wrote 'and he was able to concentrate his faculties upon literature and his dreams without a shadow of disturbance.' His poetry is a kind of distilled lyricism and in this bears some resemblance to Greek lyric poetry, to Pindar and the choruses in Sophocles and Aristophanes, in which sense and sound become one and well up in song. And physically his tiny body, 'light with the lightness of thistledown', seemed to be the perfect ethereal envelope for the lyricist. Living in Putney from 1894 and during my Cambridge years, I had a gleam of reflected glory from the poet. Nearly every morning he walked up Putney Hill and over Wimbledon Common and occasionally I saw him doing this. And once when I was having my hair cut in a shop near Putney station, the door opened and everyone, including the man cutting my hair, turned and looked at the tiny, fragile-looking figure in a cloak and large hat standing in the doorway. I remember very vividly the fluttering of the hands and fear and misery in the eyes.

[1] But not very much, for we retained a certain sense of criticism. We used, as a kind of parlour game, to draw up a Tripos List of all the world's writers of all ages. I still possess one of these Lists compiled by us in 1902. Swinburne is placed in Class I, Division 3, below Browning who is placed in Class 1, Division 2. But we never chanted Browning at midnight to the nightingales.

No one said anything, and after a moment the little figure went out and shut the door. 'That', said the barber, 'is Mr Swinburne.' I have one other memory. Our doctor at Putney was a Dr White, who had played rugger at half-back for England. He was also Watts-Dunton's, and therefore Swinburne's, doctor. He told me that he was sometimes summoned by Watts-Dunton to see the poet. The interview took place in the dining-room in Watts-Dunton's presence. Swinburne sat at a long table and could rarely be induced to say anything, but all the time his little hands played an inaudible tune on the dining-table as though upon a piano. Watts-Dunton, a rather sinister figure, one often saw in Putney. When I took my dog for a walk, I would sometimes meet him in Putney Park Lane, then a very rural lane, arm-in-arm with a beautiful young lady, with whom we had a distant acquaintance, the enormous-eyed, almost Pre-Raphaelite looking, Clare Reich.

To return to Trinity, I have never been what is called 'a good mixer', but I have always felt great interest in and often liking for all kinds of different persons. At Trinity, I had two quite distinct circles of intimate friends. One, which I have so far been dealing with and describing, consisted of intellectuals and scholars with Lytton Strachey, Saxon Sydney-Turner, Thoby Stephen, Maynard Keynes, and G. E. Moore at the centre and at varying distances from the centre Clive Bell, J. T. Sheppard, R. G. Hawtrey and A. R. Ainsworth. Two other persons moved erratically in and out of this solar system of intellectual friendship, like comets, Morgan Forster (E. M. Forster) and Desmond MacCarthy. They were both older than I, Morgan by two years and Desmond by three. Later in life when I returned from Ceylon in 1911 and lived in London, I became much more intimate with them, and I shall have more to say about them when I get to that period of my life. Morgan, I suppose, was still up at King's when I first knew him, though not in my last two years. We did not see very much of him, but he was a fascinating character and what I knew of him I liked immensely. He was strange, elusive, evasive. You could be talking to him easily and intimately one moment, and suddenly he would seem to withdraw into himself; though he still was physically there, you had faded out of his mental vision, and so with a pang you found that he had faded out of yours. He was already beginning to write his early Pan-ridden short stories and *A Room with a View*. You always felt in him and his conversation the subtlety and sensibility together with the streak of queer humour which you always also feel in his books. Lytton nicknamed him the Taupe, partly because of his faint physical resemblance to a mole, but principally because he seemed intellectually and emotionally to travel unseen underground and every now and again pop up unexpectedly with some subtle observation or delicate quip which somehow or other he had found in the depths of the earth or of his own soul. His strange character and our early relationship are shown, I think, in the following letter which he wrote to me just before I left England for Ceylon in 1904:

Harnham, Monument Green,
Weybridge.
14/11/04

Dear Woolf

I nearly was at Cambridge yesterday, but it didn't come off. I don't think, though, that I really wanted to see you again.

This letter is only to wish you godspeed in our language, and to say that if you ever want anything or anything done in England will you let me know. It's worth making this vague offer, because I'm likely always to have more time on my hands than anybody else.

I shall write at the end of the year. I know you much less than I like you, which makes your going the worse for me.

Yours ever
E. M. Forster.

In 1905 Morgan sent me an inscribed copy of *Where Angels Fear to Tread*; he has crossed out the title and written above it 'Monterians'.

Desmond MacCarthy had already gone down when I came up to Trinity in 1899, but in my last years I got to know him quite well as he was a great friend of Moore's and used fairly often to come up and stay with him. Desmond in youth was, I think, perhaps the most charming man that I have ever known. His charm was so much a part of his living person, the tone of his voice, the turn of his sentence, the tolerant or affectionate smile, the wrinkled forehead, the sagacious eye with the humorous gleam in it which reminded me, even when he was young, of the eye of a knowing old dog who understands and appreciates all his master's jokes and can make just as good jokes himself, that sixty years later it is, alas, hopeless to try to convey even a shadow of it to anyone who did not know him. The first time I met him was one weekend when he came up to stay with Moore. He had just returned from a kind of old-fashioned Grand Tour of Europe and he gave us immensely long descriptions of his journeys, particularly in Greece and Turkey. Such pyrotechnic displays or set pieces are usually the most boring type of conversation, but one could listen enchanted by Desmond as a raconteur until one was tired out, not by him, but by pleasure and laughter. He was one of those rare intellectuals who can talk to anyone in any place or 'walk of life' and to whom everyone can talk easily and affectionately. If you went into a tobacconist's to buy a packet of cigarettes with him, it would almost certainly be ten minutes before you came out accompanied to the door by everyone in the shop laughing and talking with him up to the last possible minute. He seemed to me, and to many others of his friends, in those days to have the world at his feet. He had wit, humour, intelligence, imagination, a remarkable gift of words, an extraordinary power of describing a character, an incident, or a scene. Surely, one thought, here is in the making a writer, a novelist of the highest quality. As a human being he remained the same to the end, but as a writer he never achieved anything at all of what he promised. This is not the place to explore the reasons for his failure, interesting though they are, for they belong to a later period of his life and mine, and will therefore be discussed more appropriately when I come to the account of my and of his middle age. In my Cambridge days I remember him only as someone upon whom the good fairies appeared to have lavished every possible gift both of body and of mind. For he was very strong and athletic. He used to play fives with Moore and me and, though I was not a bad player, he was very much better, playing a tremendously fast game and hitting with great power.

So much for the circle of my friends who were scholars, dons, 'intellectuals'. But I moved in a second circle which was almost the exact opposite of this. It was essentially heterogeneous. The kernel of it, so far as I was concerned, consisted of three men, each almost completely different from the other: Harry Gray, who had been at St Paul's, Alan Rokeby Law, who had been at Wellington, and Leopold Colin Henry Douglas Campbell, who had been at Eton. My friendship with them, which outlasted Cambridge, began through Gray. At St Paul's I knew him only by sight for he was on the science side. Somehow or other our paths crossed at Trinity and I went to see him, and it was in his rooms that I met Law and Campbell with whom he had become intimate. Gray was tall, very thin, and graceful, with extraordinarily neat, long hands; his head was very small and all his features small; his face was absolutely without any colour in it except a faint tinge of yellow. Though he was intelligent and very likable, his character in most ways was as colourless as his face. What attracted me in him was that, although lively and affectionate and interested, he seemed devoid of anything approaching passion. He was absorbed in two things, but with an almost impersonal absorption, medicine and music. He was taking the Science Tripos and in later life became a first-class surgeon. He was already, as an executant, a first-class pianist. His playing was brilliant, but singularly impersonal and emotionless, and, when he was not working, he would usually be found playing the piano. It was characteristic of him that he was usually playing Chopin and I used to listen with considerable pleasure and even excitement to the cold and limpid fountains of rhythm and melody which he made Chopin and the piano produce. I liked Gray and he liked me, but in a curiously impersonal way. Years afterwards, when I came back from Ceylon and he had become a distinguished surgeon, he asked me whether I would like to come and see him perform an operation. I have always thought that one should never refuse an experience, so I went to see him take a large growth out of an elderly man's inside. The operation astonished me: it lasted for a very long time and for much of it Gray used only his hands in the man's inside, exerting considerable force. Watching his hands, I was continually reminded by their movements of the way in which he used to play Chopin.

Law was a tiny little man with the palest of straw-coloured hair. At the age of twenty he had the face of a rather puzzled old man and I think that he must have looked much the same at the age of two or even at birth. He and his clothes were wonderfully dapper and he was so tidy that nothing in his rooms might be moved an eighth of an inch from the place appointed for it by him within the room and the universe. He was very affectionate and loyal, so that among his friends all his geese were swans. As he was both conventional and respectable, he would naturally have thought me a blasphemous and predatory goose; he turned me into a swan by seeing that, though brainy and queer, I was a good fellow. I went and stayed with him in his home in Ripley and was fascinated by a glimpse into a stratum of society into which I had never penetrated. He lived an only child with his parents in a small country house and garden typical of the Surrey of those days. His parents were typical too; conservative, conventional, commonplace, they belonged to a not unimportant part of the middle middle-class backbone of nineteenth-century

England. Their intense respectability was strongly tinged with snobbery towards both those above and those below them in the social scale. They had not too much and not too little of everything, including wealth and brains. I cannot remember what Mr Law was or had been, but the family climate was that of the Church and Army, not usually soaring above the rank of an Archdeacon or Colonel, though Mrs Law had a cousin who was a General and had survived the Boer War without the discredit earned by most of the British commanders in South Africa. They must have produced Rokeby rather late in their life; he was not merely the centre of their universe, he was their universe. Their universe was in no sense mine; our standards of value were in most things antagonistic; I had no sympathy for the stuffiness of their postulates, beliefs, ideals. Yet beneath the carapace which class, religion, and public school had formed over their brains and souls, there was something in them and in Rokeby that I liked and found interesting, perhaps because it was so different from anything under my carapace. I made them rather uneasy, but they accepted me as a friend of Rokeby. He died quite young, a few years after he went down from Trinity, and with his death their universe collapsed. They sent me a copy of a biographical memoir of him which they had privately printed.

Leopold Colin Henry Douglas Campbell, who later in life became Leopold Colin Henry Douglas Campbell-Douglas and still later Lord Blythswood, belonged again to a class completely different from that of Law. He was a Scottish aristocrat, tracing his descent from Sir Colin Campbell of Lochow in the fourteenth century, Colin Campbell of Blythswood in the seventeenth century, and the Douglases of Douglas-Support in the eighteenth century. His ancestors were a long line of soldiers; his uncle, the first Lord Blythswood, his father, and one of his brothers were all colonels of the Scots Guards. The aristocratic class and way of life to which Leopold Campbell belonged could scarcely have been more different from or more antagonistic to mine, but I have always enjoyed plunging, with a shudder and shiver, into a strange and alien society of people, as into an icy sea. To aristocratic societies I know that I am ambivalent, disliking and despising them and at the same time envying them their insolent urbanity which has never been more perfectly described than in *Madame Bovary*. Here is Flaubert's description of the old and young men whom Emma met when she was invited to stay with the Marquis d'Andervilliers—so like the old and young men whom I met at lunch in the Campbells' house in Manchester Square in 1903:

Leurs habits, mieux faits, semblaient d'un drap plus souple, et leurs cheveux, ramenés en boucles vers les tempes, lustrés par des pommades plus fines. Ils avaient le teint de la richesse, ce teint blanc que rehaussent la pâleur des porcelaines, les moires de satin, le vernis des beaux meubles, et qu'entretient dans sa santé un régime discret de nourritures exquises . . . Ceux qui commençaient à vieillir avaient l'air jeune, tandis que quelque chose de mûr s'étendait sur le visage des jeunes. Dans leurs regards indifférents flottait la quiétude de passions journellement assouvies; et, à travers leurs manières douces, perçait cette brutalité particulière que communique la domination de choses à demi faciles, dans lesquelles la force s'exerce et oû la vanité s'amuse, le maniement des chevaux de race et la société des femmes perdues.

Leopold's father was a General who had just got through the Boer war without either credit or discredit; he looked like and was essentially a General who had been Colonel of the Scots Guards. Leopold was in many ways true to type, but in some ways a mutation or sport. He talked of huntin', shootin', and ridin', and even in later life frequented 'la société des femmes perdues', but at Eton he suddenly became virulently infected with religion and determined to become a High Church parson. There must have been a gene in the family producing embryos with a tendency to become clergymen rather than colonels, because Leopold's uncle, the second Lord Blythswood, went up to Trinity College, Cambridge, and took orders. My experience is that almost everyone, if you really get to know them, is a 'curious character', and Leopold was no exception. I liked him and he liked me, although—or perhaps to some extent because—we had so very little in common. He had many of the infuriating prejudices and affectations of his class and caste, but he was affectionate and, what is rare, a man of real good-will. He had a singularly open mind in some directions and an appreciation of people; though my mother was in almost every way different from the ladies whom he knew, when he got to know my family, he became very fond of her and she of him. What attracted me in him was the spontaneous gaiety and benevolence in his nature and an unusual mental curiosity. At Cambridge he was preparing to take Holy Orders and in due course he became a High Church parson. Why exactly he went through this exacting process and lived the whole of his life as curate, vicar, or rector of parishes in towns or villages, I never really understood. His religion puzzled me though he never hesitated to talk quite freely to me about it. At a certain psychological level it was perfectly genuine, but the level was only just below the surface of his mind or soul. He took a kind of aesthetic pleasure in the paraphernalia of High Church services, the incense and genuflexions and all the rest of it, or perhaps it is truer to say that the Church was to him exactly what the Scots Guards were to his father, his uncle, and his brother. At any deeper level, religion and Christianity seemed to mean nothing, to have no relevance for him. I feel sure that, if he and I had been walking down Piccadilly and had suddenly come face to face with Jesus Christ, I should have recognised him instantly, but Leopold, if he noticed him at all, would have dismissed him as merely another queer-looking person.

My friendship with Leopold Campbell caused one curious incident. There was an undergraduate at Trinity of our year, whom I will call X and whom we both knew and rather liked. He was a slightly dim person and I was astonished and outraged to hear from more than one acquaintance that he was going about saying that I 'sponged on Campbell'. I was not yet, at the age of twenty, steeled to expect and ignore the malignancy of men or the spurns that patient merit from the unworthy takes, and I went round to the rooms of X on the first floor of a house on King's Parade terribly hurt and terribly angry. There followed a scene of violent emotion in which I exacted a grudging apology and left the room in such a rage that I fell down the stairs from the first to the ground floor.

I had to keep the Gray-Law-Campbell circle as far apart as possible from the circle of my intellectual friends as they were mutually suspicious and antagonistic. By the time I left Cambridge I had become very intimate with Thoby Stephen and Lytton Strachey and knew their families, and so the foundations of what became known as Bloomsbury were laid. Thoby's family seemed to a young man like me formidable and even alarming. When his father, Sir Leslie Stephen, came up to stay a weekend with him, Lytton and I were had in to meet him. He was one of those bearded and beautiful Victorian old gentlemen of exquisite gentility and physical and mental distinction on whose face the sorrows of all the world had traced the indelible lines of suffering nobility. He was immensely distinguished as a historian of ideas, literary critic, biographer, and the first editor of the *Dictionary of National Biography*. In each of these departments the distinction was not undeserved; his *History of*

English Thought in the Eighteenth Century seventy-six years after it was published, according to Mr Noel Annan, Provost of King's College, Cambridge, and a very professional, a very modern, and a very exacting critic, in his book *Leslie Stephen, His Thought and Character in Relation to his Time*, 'still stands as a major contribution to scholarship and in a sense will never be superseded in its scope'. Maynard Keynes, another expert and severe critic, also thought highly of this book. Stephen's literary criticism in *Hours in a Library* and his biographies, deeply etched by his personal prejudices and the conventional ethics of respectable Victorians, are of remarkable quality and are still readable and read. When I found myself, a nervous undergraduate, sitting opposite to this very tall and distinguished old gentleman in Thoby's rooms in Trinity Great Court and expected to make conversation with him—not helped in any way by Thoby—it seemed to me, as I said, formidable and alarming. What added enormously to the alarm was that he was stone deaf and that one had to sit quite near to him and shout everything one said to him down an ear-trumpet. It is remarkable and humiliating to discover how imbecile a not very imaginative, or even an imaginative, remark can sound when one shouts it down an ear-trumpet into the ear of a bearded old gentleman, six foot three inches tall, sitting very upright in a chair and looking as if every word you said only added to his already unendurable sorrows. However it must be said that this awkwardness and terror were gradually dissipated by him. He had immense charm and he obviously liked to meet the young and Thoby's friends. Unlike Henry James, he could see through our awkwardness and even grubbiness to our intelligence, and was pleased by our respect and appreciation. In the end we were all talking and laughing naturally (so far as this is possible down an ear-trumpet) and enjoying one another's company. This must have been about three years before Leslie Stephen died.

The basis of Mr Ramsey's character in *To the Lighthouse*, was, no doubt, taken by Virginia from her father's character; it is, I think, successfully sublimated by the novelist and is not the photograph of a real person stuck into a work of fiction; it is integrated into a work of art. But there are points about it which are both artistically and psychologically of some interest. Having known Leslie Stephen in the flesh and having heard an enormous deal about him from his children, I feel pretty sure that, subject to what I have said above about the artistic sublimation, Mr Ramsey is a pretty good fictional portrait of Leslie Stephen—and yet there are traces of unfairness to Stephen in Ramsey. Leslie Stephen must have been in many ways an exasperating man within the family and he exasperated his daughters, particularly Vanessa. But I think that they exaggerated his exactingness and sentimentality and, in memory, were habitually rather unfair to him owing to a complicated variety of the Oedipus complex. It is interesting to observe a faint streak of this in the drawing and handling of Mr Ramsey.

I also met Thoby's two sisters, Vanessa and Virginia Stephen, when they came up to see him. The young ladies—Vanessa was twenty-one or twenty-two, Virginia eighteen or nineteen—were just as formidable and alarming as their father, perhaps even more so. I first saw them one summer afternoon in Thoby's rooms; in white dresses and large hats, with parasols in their hands, their beauty literally took one's breath away, for suddenly seeing them one stopped astonished and everything including one's breathing for one second also stopped as it does when in a picture gallery you suddenly come face to face with a great Rembrandt or Velasquez or in Sicily rounding a bend in the road you see across the fields the lovely temple of Segesta. They were at that time, at least upon the surface, the most Victorian of Victorian young ladies, and today what that meant it is almost impossible to believe or even remember. Sitting with them in their brother's room was their cousin, Miss Katherine Stephen, Principal of Newnham, with whom they were staying. But Miss Stephen was in her cousin's room for a tea-party, not in her capacity of cousin, but in her capacity of chaperone, for in 1901 a respectable female sister was not allowed to see her male brother in his rooms in a male college except in the presence of a chaperone. I liked Miss Stephen very much, but it could not be denied that she was a distinguished, formidable, and rather alarming chaperone. All male Stephens—and many of the females—whom I have known have had one marked characteristic which I always think of as Stephenesque, and one can trace it in stories about or the writings of Stephens of a past generation whom one never knew, like the judge, Sir James Fitzjames Stephen, and the two James Stephens of still earlier generations. It consisted in a way of thinking and even more in a way of expressing their thoughts which one associates preeminently with Dr Johnson. There was something monolithic about them and their opinions, and something marmoreal or lapidary about their way of expressing those opinions, reminding one of the Ten Commandments engraved upon the tables of stone, even when they were only telling you that in their opinion it would rain tomorrow. And what was even more characteristic and Stephenesque was that usually over this monolithic thought and these monolithic pronouncements there played—if one dare use the word of these rather elephantine activities—a peculiar monolithic humour.

The Principal of Newnham had a liberal measure of this Stephen method of thinking and talking and it was not calculated to put at his ease a nervous young man who met her for the first time. Thoby, a most monolithic Stephen—his affectionate nickname, The Goth, fitted his great stature and monumental mind—was himself a little shy and quite incompetent to deal with a slightly sticky social situation. In such a situation he was inclined to sit silent, smiling tolerantly and deprecatingly. Vanessa and Virginia were also very silent and to any superficial observer they might have seemed demure. Anyone who has ridden many different kinds of horses knows the horse who, when you go up to him for the first time, has superficially the most quiet and demure appearance, but, if after bitter experience you are accustomed to take something more than a superficial glance at a strange mount, you observe at the back of the eye of this quiet beast a look which warns you to be very, very careful. So too the observant observer would have noticed at the back of the two Miss Stephens' eyes a look which would have warned him to be cautious, a look which belied the demureness, a look of great intelligence, hypercritical, sarcastic, satirical.

In the Stephen family there was a vein of good looks, particularly noticeable in the males. There was something very fine in Leslie Stephen's face and his nephew Jim (the famous 'J.K.'), the son of James Fitzjames, must have been a handsome man. The mother of Vanessa and Virginia was born Julia Jackson; when Leslie Stephen married her, she was the widow of Herbert Duckworth. Julia Jackson's mother was one of the six Pattle sisters whose great beauty was legendary. The Pattle genes which caused this beauty must have been extremely potent, for there is no doubt that it was handed on to a considerable number of descendants. It had some very marked individual characteristics—for instance, the shape and modelling of the neck, face, and forehead, and the mouth and eyes—which were and are traceable in the third and fourth generation. It was essentially female for, though it has certainly produced many lovely women, I cannot see any trace of it in the male descendants of the Pattles whom I have known. Julia Jackson inherited a full measure of the Pattle beauty, as one can see in the famous photographs by her famous aunt, Mrs Cameron, herself one of the six Pattle sisters. All this is not irrelevant to my story. No one could deny that the Pattle sisters and their female descendants in the next generation were extraordinarily beautiful, but it was a beauty which was or tended to become rather insipid. It was, I think, too feminine, and not sufficiently female, and there was about it something which was even slightly irritating. Vanessa and Virginia had inherited this beauty, but it had been modified, strengthened, and, I think, greatly improved by the more masculine Stephen good looks. When I first met them, they were young women of astonishing beauty, but there was in them nothing of the saintly dying duck loveliness which was characteristic of some of their feminine ancestors. They were eminently Stephen as well as Pattle. It was almost impossible for a man not to fall in love with them, and I think that I did at once. It must, however, be admitted that at that time they seemed to be so formidably aloof and reserved that it was rather like falling in love with Rembrandt's picture of his wife, Velasquez's picture of an Infanta, or the lovely temple of Segesta.

While I was at Cambridge, I got to know Lytton Strachey's family a good deal better than I did Thoby Stephen's. The Strachey and Stephen families both belonged to a social class or caste of a remarkable and peculiar kind which established itself as a powerful section of the ruling class in Britain in the nineteenth century. It was an intellectual aristocracy of the middle class, the nearest equivalent in other countries being the French eighteenth century noblesse de robe. The male members of the British aristocracy of intellect went automatically to the best public schools, to Oxford and Cambridge, and then into all the most powerful and respectable professions. They intermarried to a considerable extent, and family influence and the high level of their individual intelligence carried a surprising number of them to the top of their professions. You found them as civil servants sitting in the seat of permanent under-secretaries of government departments; they became generals, admirals, editors, judges, or they retired with a K.C.S.I. or K.C.M.G. after distinguished careers in the Indian or Colonial Civil Services. Others again got fellowships at Oxford or Cambridge and ended as head of an Oxford or Cambridge college or headmaster of one of the great public schools.

Stephens and Stracheys were eminent examples of this social development, and, when I got to know them well, I was both interested and amused by the great difference in outlook and postulates of their circle from many of those in the circle from which I came. The Strachey family, as I said, belonged to exactly the same class as the Stephens, but, owing I suppose to its individual genes, it was in many ways extraordinarily different. When I first knew Lytton, they lived in a very large house in Lancaster Gate. I used sometimes to call formally on his mother, Lady Strachey, on Sunday afternoons, according to the strange custom of those prehistoric times, and sometimes I was asked to remain to Sunday supper. Lytton's sister Pippa, who was the most energetic and charming of women and remains so today, ageless in the eighties, decided that we must all be taught by her to dance Highland dances and I went to one or two evening parties at which about twenty young people, including the Miss Stephens, practised this difficult art under the lively and exacting tuition of Pippa.

I stayed with Lytton three years running in the summer in large country houses which his parents rented, once in Surrey, once in Essex, and once near Bedford. In this way I got to know his father and mother and all his brothers and sisters. They stand out in my memory as much the most remarkable family I have ever known, an extinct social phenomenon which has passed away and will never be known again. Lytton's father was Lieutenant-General Sir Richard Strachey, who, like his two brothers, had had an extraordinarily brilliant career in India. He was a remarkable product of his caste in nineteenth-century Britain, a man of immense ability whether in action or intellectually, for he attained eminence as an army officer, an administrator, an engineer, and a scientist. When I knew him he must have been eighty-five years old, a little man with a very beautiful head, sitting all day long, summer and winter, in a great armchair in front of a blazing fire, reading a novel. He was always surrounded by a terrific din which, as I shall explain, was created by his sons and daughters, but he sat through it completely unmoved, occasionally smiling affectionately at it and them, when it obtruded itself unavoidably upon his notice, for instance, if in some deafening argument one side or the other appealed to him for a decision. He was usually a silent man, who listened with interest and amusement to the verbal hurricane around him; he was extraordinarily friendly and charming to an awkward youth such as I was, and he was fascinating when now and again he was induced to enter the discussion or recall something from his past.

Lytton's mother, like his father, came from a distinguished Anglo-Indian family, being the daughter of Sir John Grant. She was a large, tall, rather ungainly woman who often appeared to be completely detached from the world around her. She would walk into a room in a kind of dream-like way, gaze uncertainly about her and then walk out again. I used to think that she had come in to try to find something which she had forgotten and then, when she was in the room, forgot what it was she had forgotten. She would often sit at the head of the Strachey table apparently unconscious of her children's babel of argument, indignation, excitement, laughter. This absentmindedness or distraction was, however, rather deceptive. She was, in fact, tremendously on the spot whenever she gave her attention to anything. She was passionately intellectual, with that curiosity of mind which the Greeks rightly thought so important. She had a passion for literature, argument, and billiards. I was very fond of her and got on well with her, and she liked me, I think. The houses which they took for the summer in the country were necessarily large and always had a billiard-table, and I played many games of billiards with her. She was a magnificent reader of poetry and in the evenings she would read aloud to Lytton and me for hours. The last time that Virginia and I saw her was when she was old and blind, sitting one summer evening under a tree in Gordon Square. We went and sat down by her, and somehow or other we got on the subject of Milton's *Lycidas*, which at St Paul's we had to learn by heart. She recited the whole of it to us superbly without hesitating over a word. The beauty of the London evening in the London square, the beauty of the poem of that old blind Londoner who sat on summer evenings 300 years before in Lincoln's Inn Fields composing *Paradise Lost*, the beauty of Lady Strachey's voice remain one of the last gentle memories of a London and an era which vanished in the second great war.

In 1902 the Strachey family consisted of five sons and five daughters, female and male alternating down the family thus: Elinor (Mrs Rendel); Dick, in the Indian Army; Dorothy (later Madame Simon Bussy); Ralph, married, in the East Indian Railway; Pippa, later secretary of the Fawcett Society; Oliver, married, in the East

Indian Railway; Pernel, later Principal of Newnham; Lytton; Marjorie; James. Their ages ranged from Elinor's forty-two years to James's fifteen; their father, Sir Richard, had been born in the reign of George III two years after Waterloo, and their grandfather, Edward Strachey, far, far back in 1774. These years and dates are not irrelevant to a description and understanding of Lytton and his family. I felt that whereas I was living in 1902, they were living in 1774-1902. At dinner someone might casually say something which implied that he remembered George IV (which he might) or even Voltaire or Warren Hastings, and certainly to Lytton the eighteenth century was more congenial and, in a sense, more real than the nineteenth or the twentieth. The atmosphere of the dining-room at Lancaster Gate was that of British history and of that comparatively small ruling middle class which for the last 100 years had been the principal makers of British history.

At supper on Sunday evenings in Lancaster Gate or still more in the country houses in the summer the number of Stracheys present was to a visitor at first bewildering. In London the family consisted of Sir Richard, Lady Strachey, Dorothy, Pippa, Lytton, Marjorie, James, and Duncan Grant, Lady Strachey's nephew. In the country there was always a large influx of the married sons and daughters, with wives, husbands, and children. The level of intelligence in each son and daughter and in the father and mother was incredibly, fantastically high. They were all, like their mother, passionately intellectual, most of them with very quick minds and lively imaginations. All of them, I suspect, except the two eldest, must have been born with pens in their hands and perhaps spectacles on their noses. Their chief recreation was conversation and they adored conversational speculation which usually led to argument. They were all argumentatively very excitable and they all had in varying degrees what came to be known as the Strachey voice. I have said something about it in describing Lytton. It had a tremendous range from deep tones to high pitched falsetto. When six or seven Stracheys became involved in an argument over the dinner table, as almost always happened, the roar and rumble, the shrill shrieks, the bursts of laughter, the sound and fury of excitement were deafening and to an unprepared stranger paralysing. And these verbal typhoons were not confined to literary discussions and the dinner table. I was once playing croquet with Lytton, Marjorie, and James when I stayed with them in a house near Bedford and a dispute broke out between the three Stracheys over some point in the game. I stood aside waiting until the storm should subside. The noise was terrific. The back of the house, which was, I think, early Georgian, looked down with its, say, eighteen windows upon the lawn where we were playing. By chance I looked up at the house and was delighted to see a Strachey face at each of the eighteen windows watching the three furious gesticulating figures and listening, I think appreciatively, to the noise and excitement.

In my family we were very energetic and, in a mild way, adventurous. I have always liked to do something new or experimental, and my brother Herbert and I thought nothing of setting off on our bicycles at short notice to ride from Putney to Edinburgh or of deciding on a bicycle tour in the Shetlands. Lytton was by our standards very unadventurous, but when I stayed with him in the house near Bedford it struck me that it would be amusing to hire a canoe at Bedford and canoe down the Ouse to Ely where the Cam flows into it and then canoe up the Cam to Cambridge. I induced Lytton, with some difficulty, to agree to do this with me. I reckoned to take about four or five days for the whole expedition. We set off in brilliant, hot, sunny August weather. The Ouse was amazingly beautiful. There was some legal dispute over navigation which had gone on for years, and for years all the locks on the river were closed to boats or barges. The river was entirely deserted except for our canoe and innumerable birds. It seemed to be very high, the water almost topping the banks. One paddled or floated down an immense, lovely, interminable tunnel of blue water, feathery reeds and meadowsweet, bright green fields and bright blue sky, accompanied by an unending escort of flashing kingfishers. In one respect it was a pretty strenuous expedition, since, the locks being closed, every now and again, when one came to a lock, one had to lift the canoe out of the water and carry it round to float it again below the lock. In the evening we tied up and found an inn to stay the night in and it was all extremely pleasant. But the second day it started to rain, heavily and pitilessly, and at Huntingdon, I think, we abandoned the canoe and took a car to Peterborough, where we stayed the night. Next morning it was still raining and dejectedly we returned to Bedford by train.

I stayed up for five years at Trinity. I had come up with a vague intention of eventually becoming a barrister, having as a small child announced that I would be what Papa was and drive every morning in a brougham to King's Bench Walk. But it was not long before I changed my mind and decided to go into the Civil Service, expecting as a scholar of Trinity to be high enough up in the examination to get a place in the Home Civil Service. Meanwhile as a classical scholar I had to take the Classical Tripos. In my day you got your B.A. degree on the Classical Tripos, Part I, and to take Part II was a luxury usually indulged in only by those who thought they might subsequently get a Fellowship. In my third year I got a First Class in the Tripos, but in the third division, which disappointed the authorities, so the Master, the great Dr Montagu Butler, wrote to me, since they thought I should have been placed in the first division. I decided that I would spend my fourth year reading for Part II of the Classical Tripos, Greek philosophy. I did even worse in that than in Part I, for I only got a Second Class. I spent my fifth year reading for the Civil Service examination. This was a great mistake. For the Civil Service you needed to be crammed in as many subjects as possible besides your main subject (in my case classics). In twelve months you crammed into your head as much as possible of subjects called, for instance, political economy, political science, logic. The university was ill-equipped for cramming and one really ought to have gone down and delivered oneself into the hands of a London crammer who knew how to treat the human brain like the goose who is to become pâté de foie gras.

Compared with most scholars I did little work at Cambridge, if work means going to lectures, reading, and stuffing your head with what will give you a high place in an examination. I hate lectures, and, as at Trinity the authorities did not insist upon scholars attending them punctiliously, I went to few. I read voraciously both in Greek and Latin and in English and French, but it was not the kind of diet which wins you very high marks in an examination. I am quite good at exams, but the truth is that I was a really first-class classical scholar when I came up from St Paul's to Trinity, but nothing like as good when I took Part I of the Classical Tripos. When I took the Civil Service examination, I could read Greek and Latin fluently, as I still can, but I had forgotten all the paraphernalia of syntax and writing Greek and Latin compositions. The result was that I got poor marks in the classical papers in which I should have amassed most of my marks and so did extremely badly. The best that I could hope for was a place in the Post Office or Inland Revenue. I was over age for India. I felt that I could not face a lifetime to be spent in Somerset House or in the Post Office, so I decided to take an appointment in the Colonial Service, then called Eastern Cadetships. I applied for Ceylon which was the senior Crown Colony, and I was high enough up on the list to get what I asked for. I found myself to my astonishment and, it must be admitted, dismay in the Ceylon Civil Service.

Looking back I can see that the dismay was natural, but unnecessary. I am glad that I did not go into the Home Civil and did go into the Ceylon Civil Service. My seven years in Ceylon were good for me, and, though they gave me a good deal of pain, they gave me also a good deal of pleasure—and a great deal of pleasure as a memory of things past. But I am glad too that I lived the kind of life at Trinity which was mainly the reason why I did not do well in the examinations. It was, I think, a civilised life both intellectually and emotionally. My intellect was kept at full stretch, which is very good for the young, by books and the way I read them and by friends and their incessant and uncompromising conversation. The emotion came from friendship and friends, but also from the place, the material and spiritual place, Trinity and Cambridge. I must try, before I end this chapter and this period of my life, to say something of the effect of the institution, the college and the university with the surrounding aura of the town and the country, an effect partly of place and partly of history and spirit.

The attitude of a person to the institutions, collectivities, groups, herds, or packs with which he is or has been associated throws considerable light upon his character and upon the hidden parts of it. Biographers and autobiographers, as a rule, say little about it and many people are reticent about their 'loyalties' other than that which Johnson significantly described as the last refuge of a scoundrel.(I propose to use the word loyalty to cover a person's emotions or reactions of a positive and appreciative nature to any group or institution.) When I try to look objectively into my own mind, I detect feelings of loyalty to: my family; 'race' (Jews); my country, England in particular, and the British Empire generally; places with which I have been connected, such as Kensington and London (born and bred), counties, Middlesex and Sussex, where I have lived, Ceylon, Greece; school; Trinity and Cambridge. Some of the evidence for the existence of these loyalties is curious, but unmistakable. For instance, in the case of St Paul's, Cambridge University, England, and the British Empire, if they win in any game or sport, I get distinct pleasure, and pain if they lose. I also want Sussex and Middlesex to win in county cricket, but here for some more complicated reasons I also want Yorkshire and Gloucestershire to win, and there is a conflict of loyalties.

The quality of these loyalties differs profoundly in the different cases. In the case of places like London, England, Sussex, Ceylon I love them for their material beauties or excellences, but also for spiritual qualities, memories, traditions, history. Still more significant is the fact that in some cases, particularly family, race, and school, my feelings are ambivalent. The first wounds to one's heart, soul, and mind are caused in and by the family, and deep down unconsciously one never forgets or forgives them. One loves and hates one's family just as—one knows and they know—one is loved and hated by them. Most people are both proud and ashamed of their families, and nearly all Jews are both proud and ashamed of being Jews. There is therefore always a bitterness and ambivalence in these loyalties. My feelings towards St Paul's school are ambivalent, but in a different way. I hated its physical ugliness, its philistinism, the slow, low torture of boredom that crept over one as one sat hour after hour in the stuffy class-room listening to the bored voice of the bored master. I still hate it, and yet I have at the same time affection for and pride in it. I get irrational pleasure from the knowledge that I was taught in a school which has now existed for 450 years and that it was connected with Erasmus. I like to think that I went to the same school as Milton, Marlborough, and Pepys. I do not feel the same towards another Old Pauline, Field-Marshal Lord Montgomery, as I would if I had been to Eton or Croydon Secondary Modern School; I wish I thought him as great a general as he thinks himself and, quite irrationally, I feel personal regret that he says such silly things.

My loyalty to Trinity and Cambridge is different from all my other loyalties. It is more intimate, profound, unalloyed. It is compounded of the spiritual, intellectual and physical inextricably mixed—the beauty of the colleges and Backs; the atmosphere of long years of history and great traditions and famous names; a profoundly civilised life; friendship and the Society. Soon after I went to Ceylon, Desmond MacCarthy wrote me a long letter in which among other things he described how he had been up to Trinity to the great annual feast, Commem. I will quote what he says, because I think it gives an extraordinarily keen taste of Trinity College and why, even in its most absurd moments, it meant something to Desmond and to all of us. The letter is dated 23 March 1905:

I have only been up to Cambridge twice since I saw you. Once for Commen: I was McTaggart's guest, and I stayed with him. I didn't enjoy the dinner very much—I overate and overdrank to meet his sense of the occasion. We didn't have very good talk. I relish his wit; but he doesn't enjoy my jokes, at least I feel he doesn't, so I cant make them. The scene was just what you remember, neither very easy nor dignified—and yet it made a claim on one's feelings, as standing for something. "The college" "Trinity"—do these words mean much to you? They do mean something to me. Yet there are several things which mean so much more that I find it hard sometimes to believe that I have *any* esprit de corps—(corps d'esprit an old horse dealer, with an excellent French accent, called it as I travelled up in the train). Then the Master got up, holding his glass of wine in both hands and swaying solemnly from side to side in a way that in itself was a benediction, proposed the guests in a speech of admirable blandness and effortlessness and nothingness and as I listened I felt the glamour of success. How fine it is that the college should send out men who become ministers and judges and bishops and how very gratifying it would be to come down as the bigwig of the evening and make a most splendid speech in reply—all this sublimated by the rosy mist of port. And I looked down the table and caught sight of the Davieses[1] their faces set in deep disgust.

"Then McT and Theodore and I went to the reception at the Lodge. The Master stood at the top of the stairs and welcomed us—received us, wrapped us round with romantic ceremonial hospitality. He was the Master of Trinity—the leaders of their generations were there—I was a brilliant young man—it was an Occasion.

"Then we went to Jackson's[2] at home. You know the scene—clouds of tobacco smoke, a roar of conversation—dozens of whist tables with lighted candles on each—clay pipes—boxes of cigars, a piano and someone singing God knows what—the tune coming in gusts as through an opening and shutting door above the babel of voices. Then songs with choruses—school songs, the various representatives of different schools gathering round the piano in turn and shouting with defiant patriotism—then music hall songs—imagine Parry on a sofa in the window, singing and enjoying the fun of the thing—"Oh my darling, oh my darling, oh my darling Clementine"—Then came the event of the evening for me. I got on the sofa with Strachey and had a good talk. First about the people in the room—beginning

[1] Theodore Llewelyn Davies in the Treasury, and his brother Crompton, a solicitor. They were both very good-looking and charming, brilliant intellectually, high-principled, austere.

[2] Henry Jackson, O.M., Regius Professor of Greek and one of the senior Fellows of Trinity, a great scholar and a great character.

with the sour-faced Montague,[1] standing a little way off, whom I wish always to take gently above the elbow and inform that he is not another Dizzy. We talked for a long time about the Society, angels, brothers, and embryos—and felt as tho' we were getting things clear—at least I did—and we agreed.

To stay up at Cambridge for a fifth year, as Saxon and I did, is a curious experience, a little melancholy, though the gentle melancholy was not unpleasant. It was a kind of twilight existence, a respite, a waiting for the business of life to begin. Practically everyone of one's own year had gone down, and though I saw more and more of Moore and Maynard Keynes, it was often a solitary life. I came up for six weeks in the 'long vacation' and that was still more solitary, for only a very few people did that. In some ways, one felt Cambridge, the essence of Cambridge, more intimately in the deserted courts than in term time. I came up ostensibly to read for my exam and I suppose that I did do a certain amount of work. It was a hot summer and the long summer days passed slowly away. There was a strange man called Barwell whom I knew and who also was up 'for the long'. He was said to be a descendant of that Richard Barwell, Member of Council in India, who supported Warren Hastings against Philip Francis. Philip Francis said of Richard Barwell that 'he is rapacious without industry, and ambitious without an exertion of his faculties or steady application to affairs. He will do whatever can be done by bribery and intrigue; he has no other resource.' But Warren Hastings said of him that 'his manners are easy and pleasant.' His descendant, the Barwell whom I knew, seemed to have inherited the qualities which Hastings saw in his ancestor, and I never detected any sign of the sinister characteristics which Francis describes. He was a good deal older than I and had gone down from Trinity before I came up. But he was quite often about the place, and his manners were indeed easy and pleasant. He was what is called a man of the world, almost the first of that curious human species whom I got to know fairly well. I could never be and never shall be, I know well, a man of the world, and I rather despise them with at the same time a sneaking envy of them—but I often get on quite well with them. I got on quite well with Barwell. He liked good food, good wine, and good conversation. He used to take me, an Irish baronet whose name I no longer remember, and a

[1] Edwin Montagu, later Secretary of State for India in Lloyd George's 1916 Coalition Government.

B.A. called Maclaren, in a punt up the river and there we tied up under the willows and ate chicken, drank Burgundy, and talked through the long summer evenings like scholars and men of the world. And as darkness fell we punted slowly and silently back to Trinity.

Slowly the days and weeks passed away, and the Civil Service examination was on us in one of the hottest of London summers. The torture was prolonged for the exam went on for about three weeks. I remember coming out into the blazing sunshine in Burlington Street with Saxon quite often to find Thoby Stephen waiting for us so that we could lunch together, and then back again into the examination room in Burlington House to answer or not answer absurd questions about Logic, or Political Science, or Political Economy.

But even a Civil Service exam ends at last, and on 29 August 1904, I set out with Maynard Keynes on a walking tour from Denbigh. We walked with knapsacks on our backs from Denbigh through Bettws-y-Coed, Beddgelert, and Pwllheli to Aberdaron. There we stayed for a few days with Charlie[1] and Dora Sanger. Then we walked to and climbed Snowdon, ending our tour finally at Carnarvon. Maynard was an extraordinarily good companion and even in those days had a passion for gambling, which I shared. We talked all day and in the evening did what we could to satisfy our gambling passion by playing bezique. Maynard kept the score and I remember him working out the result in the train on our way back to London, the result being that I won a few shillings off him.

The result of the exam was a considerable shock, but somehow or other I had learnt very early in life not to worry about things, to make up my mind quickly, and not to waste one's energies and emotions in regrets. I saw at once that I was not going to sit in Somerset House for the rest of my life and that therefore I must go to

[1] Charles Percy Sanger was a remarkable man. He was an Apostle, but a good deal older than I. He did brilliantly at Trinity and then became a barrister and was at the top of his profession as a conveyancer. He was a gnomelike man with the brightest eyes I have ever seen and the character of a saint, but he was a very amusing, ribald, completely sceptical saint with a first-class mind and an extremely witty tongue, a mixture which I never came across in any other human being. He wrote a very interesting pamphlet about Emily Brontë, which I published in the Hogarth Press, *The Structure of Wuthering Heights*.

Ceylon. The next few weeks, until I finally walked up the gangway of the P. and O. *Syria* at Tilbury, passed away quickly in the atmosphere of a kaleidoscopic dream. I bought tropical suits and a topi at the Army and Navy Stores; I took riding lessons in the Knightsbridge Barracks, a terrifying procedure, and in Richmond Park, which was a pleasant antidote. I passed my medical examination at any rate triumphantly for the doctor complimented me on having the cleanest feet of anyone he had examined that morning —'though,' he added, 'I am bound to say that that is not saying very much.' I travelled up to Stonehaven near Aberdeen and spent a night with my brother Harold on a farm where he was learning agriculture. I spent a night with Moore in Edinburgh. I went through ceremonies of farewell with Desmond, who gave me the Oxford Press miniature edition of Shakespeare and Milton in four volumes which have accompanied me everywhere ever since, with Morgan Forster, Lytton, and Saxon. I had a farewell dinner with Thoby Stephen and his sisters Vanessa and Virginia in Gordon Square. I felt just as I did when as a small boy at school in Brighton I stood in Brill's Baths and looked down at the water so far below and nerved myself for the high dive. I got ready everything which I was to take with me to Ceylon, which included ninety large volumes of the beautiful eighteenth century edition of Voltaire printed in the Baskerville type and a wire-haired fox-terrier. At last I dived; the waters closed over me; I took the train to Tilbury Docks.

GROWING
1904 – 1911

Si le roi m'avoit donné
Paris sa grand' ville
Et qu'il me fallût quitter
L'amour de ma vie!

Je dirois au roi Henri
Reprenez votre Paris;
J'aime mieux ma mie, o gué,
J'aime mieux ma mie.

Foreword

I have tried in the following pages to tell the truth, the whole truth, and nothing but the truth, but of course I have not succeeded. I do not think that I have anywhere deliberately manipulated or distorted the truth into untruth, but I am sure that one sometimes does this unconsciously. In autobiography—or at any rate in my autobiography—distortion of truth comes frequently from the difficulty of remembering accurately the sequence of events, the temporal perspective. I have several times been surprised and dismayed to find that a letter or diary proves that what I remember as happening in, say, 1908 really happened in 1910; and the significance of the event may be quite different if it happened in the one year and not in the other. I have occasionally invented fictitious names for the real people about whom I write; I have only done so where they are alive or may be alive or where I think that their exact identification might cause pain or annoyance to their friends or relations. I could not have remembered accurately in detail fifty per cent of the events recorded in the following pages if I had not been able to read the letters which I wrote to Lytton Strachey and the official diaries which I had to write daily from 1908 to 1911 when I was Assistant Government Agent in the Hambantota District. I have to thank James Strachey for allowing me to read the original letters. As regards the diaries, I am greatly indebted to the Ceylon Government, particularly to the Governor, Sir Oliver Goonetilleke, and to Mr Shelton C. Fernando of the Ceylon Civil Service, Secretary to the Ministry of Home Affairs. When I visited Ceylon in 1960, Mr Fernando, on behalf of the Ceylon Government, presented me with a copy of these diaries and the Governor subsequently gave orders that they should be printed and published.

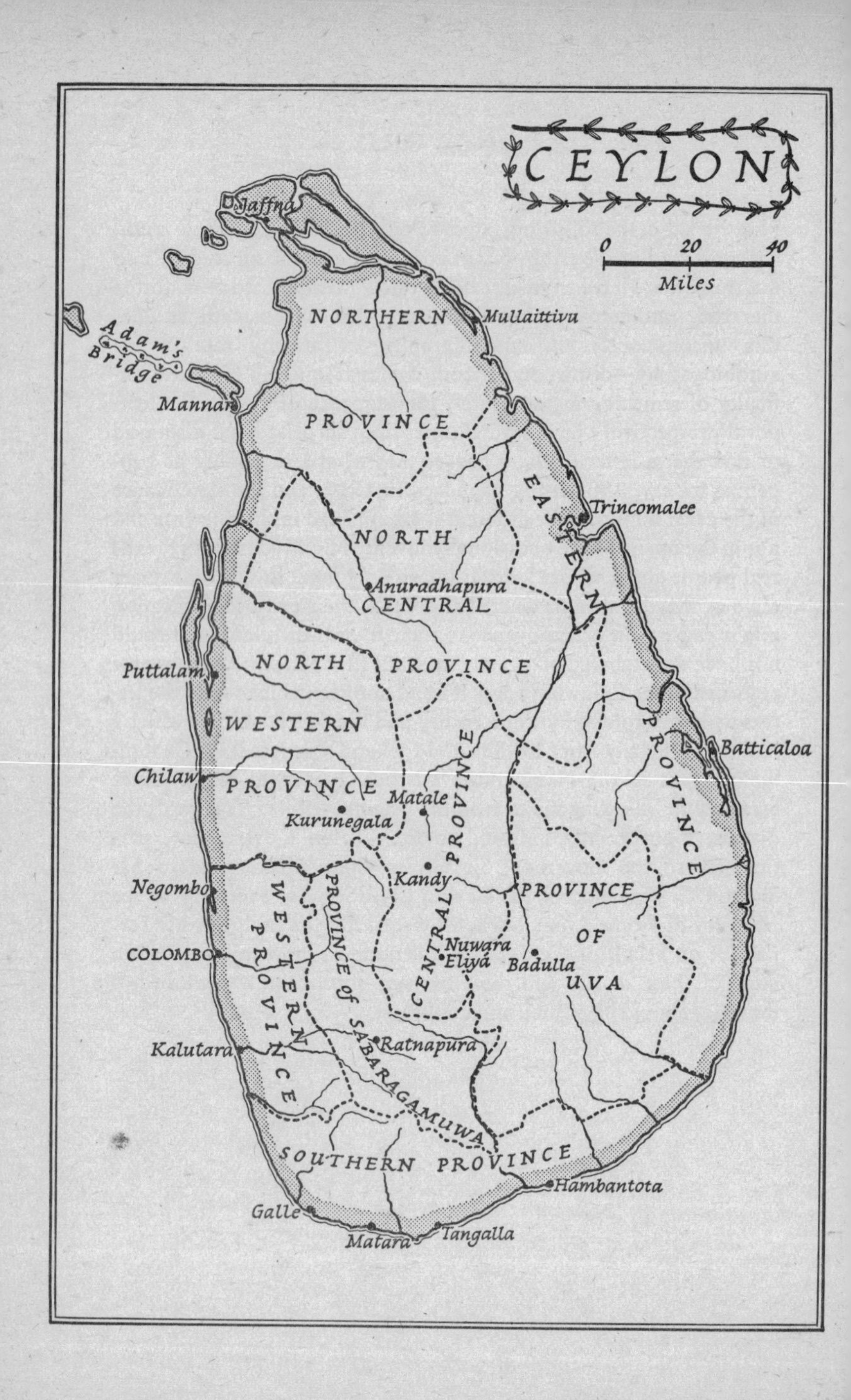
CEYLON
0
20
40
Miles
Jaffna
Adam's Bridge
Mannar
NORTHERN
PROVINCE
Mullaittivu
Trincomalee
EASTERN
PROVINCE
NORTH
CENTRAL
PROVINCE
Anuradhapura
Puttalam
NORTH
WESTERN
PROVINCE
Chilaw
Kurunegala
Matale
CENTRAL PROVINCE
Batticaloa
Negombo
Kandy
WESTERN
PROVINCE
PROVINCE of SABARAGAMUWA
COLOMBO
Nuwara
Eliya
Badulla
PROVINCE
OF
UVA
Ratnapura
Kalutara
SOUTHERN PROVINCE
Hambantota
Galle
Matara
Tangalla

1

The Voyage Out

In October 1904, I sailed from Tilbury Docks in the P. & O. *Syria* for Ceylon. I was a Cadet in the Ceylon Civil Service. To make a complete break with one's former life is a strange, frightening, and exhilarating experience. It has upon one, I think, the effect of a second birth. When one emerges from one's mother's womb one leaves a life of dim security for a world of violent difficulties and dangers. Few, if any, people ever entirely recover from the trauma of being born, and we spend a lifetime unsuccessfully trying to heal the wound, to protect ourselves against the hostility of things and men. But because at birth consciousness is dim and it takes a long time for us to become aware of our environment, we do not feel a sudden break, and adjustment is slow, lasting indeed a lifetime. I can remember the precise moment of my second birth. The umbilical cord by which I had been attached to my family, to St Paul's, to Cambridge and Trinity was cut when, leaning over the ship's taffrail, I watched through the dirty, dripping murk and fog of the river my mother and sister waving good-bye and felt the ship begin slowly to move down the Thames to the sea.

To be born again in this way at the age of twenty-four is a strange experience which imprints a permanent mark upon one's character and one's attitude to life. I was leaving in England everyone and everything I knew; I was going to a place and life in which I really had not the faintest idea of how I should live and what I should be doing. All that I was taking with me from the old life as a contribution to the new and to prepare me for my task of helping to rule the British Empire was 90 large, beautifully printed volumes of Voltaire[1] and a wire-haired fox-terrier. The first impact of the new life was menacing and depressing. The ship slid down the oily dark waters of the river through cold clammy mist and rain; next day in the Channel it was barely possible to distinguish the cold and gloomy sky from the cold and gloomy sea. Within the boat there was the uncomfortable atmosphere of suspicion and reserve which is at first invariably the result when a number of English men and

[1] The 1784 edition printed in Baskerville type.

women, strangers to one another, find that they have to live together for a time in a train, a ship, a hotel.

In those days it took, if I remember rightly, three weeks to sail from London to Colombo. By the time we reached Ceylon, we had developed from a fortuitous concourse of isolated human atoms into a complex community with an elaborate system of castes and classes. The initial suspicion and reserve had soon given place to intimate friendships, intrigues, affairs, passionate loves and hates. I learned a great deal from my three weeks on board the P. & O. *Syria*. Nearly all my fellow-passengers were quite unlike the people whom I had known at home or at Cambridge. On the face of it and of them they were very ordinary persons with whom in my previous life I would have felt that I had little in common except perhaps mutual contempt. I learned two valuable lessons: first how to get on with ordinary persons, and secondly that there are practically no ordinary persons, that beneath the façade of John Smith and Jane Brown there is a strange character and often a passionate individual.

One of the most interesting and unexpected exhibits was Captain L. of the Manchester Regiment, who, with a wife and small daughter, was going out to India. When I first saw and spoke to him, in the arrogant ignorance of youth and Cambridge, I thought he was inevitably the dumb and dummy figure which I imagined to be characteristic of any captain in the Regular Army. Nothing could have been more mistaken. He and his wife and child were in the cabin next to mine, and I became painfully aware that the small girl wetted her bed and that Captain L. and his wife thought that the right way to cure her was to beat her. I had not at that time read *A Child is being Beaten* or any other of the works of Sigmund Freud, but the hysterical shrieks and sobs which came from the next cabin convinced me that beating was not the right way to cure bed-wetting, and my experience with dogs and other animals had taught me that corporal punishment is never a good instrument of education.

Late one night I was sitting in the smoking-room talking to Captain L. and we seemed suddenly to cross the barrier between formality and intimacy. I took my life in my hands and boldly told him that he was wrong to beat his daughter. We sat arguing about this until the lights went out, and next morning to my astonishment he came up to me and told me that I had convinced him and that he would never beat his daughter again. One curious result was that

Mrs L. was enraged with me for interfering and pursued me with bitter hostility until we finally parted for ever at Colombo.

After this episode I saw a great deal of the captain. I found him to be a man of some intelligence and of intense intellectual curiosity, but in his family, his school, and his regiment the speculative mind or conversation was unknown, unthinkable. He was surprised and delighted to find someone who would talk about anything and everything, including God, sceptically. We found a third companion with similar tastes in the Chief Engineer, a dour Scot, who used to join us late at night in the smoking-room with two candles so that we could go on talking and drinking whisky and soda after the lights went out. The captain had another characteristic, shared by me: he had a passion for every kind of game. During the day we played the usual deck games, chess, draughts, and even noughts and crosses, and very late at night when the two candles in the smoking-room began to gutter, he would say to me sometimes: 'And now, Woolf, before the candles go out, we'll play the oldest game in the world', the oldest game in the world, according to him, being a primitive form of draughts which certain arrangements of stones, in Greenland and African deserts, show was played all over the world by prehistoric man.

The three weeks which I spent on the P. & O. *Syria* had a considerable and salutary effect upon me. I found myself able to get along quite well in this new, entirely strange, and rather formidable world into which I had projected myself. I enjoyed adjusting myself to it and to thirty or forty complete strangers. It was fascinating to explore the minds of some and watch the psychological or social antics of others. I became great friends with some and even managed to have a fairly lively flirtation with a young woman which, to my amusement, earned me a long, but very kindly, warning and good advice from one of the middle-aged ladies. The importance of that kind of voyage for a young man with the age and experience or inexperience which were then mine is that the world and society of the boat are a microcosm of the macrocosm in which he will be condemned to spend the remainder of his life, and it is probable that his temporary method of adjusting himself to the one will become the permanent method of adjustment to the other. I am sure that it was so to a great extent in my case.

One bitter lesson, comparatively new to me, and an incident which graved it deeply into my mind, are still vivid to me after more than fifty years. I am still, after those fifty years, naïvely surprised and shocked by the gratuitous inhumanity of so many human beings, their spontaneous malevolence towards one another. There were on the boat three young civil servants, Millington and I going out to Ceylon, and a young man called Scafe who had just passed into the Indian Civil Service. There were also two or three Colombo business men, in particular a large flamboyant Mr X who was employed in a big Colombo shop. It gradually became clear to us that Mr X and his friends regarded us with *a priori* malignity because we were civil servants. It was my first experience of the class war and hatred between Europeans which in 1904 were a curious feature of British imperialism in the East.

The British were divided into four well-defined classes: civil servants, army officers, planters, and business men. There was in the last three classes an embryonic feeling against the first. The civil servant was socially in many ways top dog; he was highly paid, exercised considerable and widely distributed power, and with the Sinhalese and Tamils enjoyed much greater prestige than the other classes. The army officers had, of course, high social claims, as they have always and everywhere, but in Ceylon there were too few of them to be of social importance. In Kandy and the mountains, hundreds of British planters lived on their dreary tea estates and they enjoyed superficially complete social equality with the civil servants. They belonged to the same clubs, played tennis together, and occasionally intermarried. But there is no doubt that generally the social position and prospects of a civil servant were counted to be a good deal higher than those of a planter. The attitude of planters' wives with nubile daughters to potential sons-in-law left one in no doubt of this, for the marriage market is an infallible test of social values. The business men were on an altogether lower level. I suppose the higher executives, as they would now be called, the tycoons, if there were any in those days, in Colombo were members of the Colombo Club and moved in the 'highest' society. But all in subordinate posts in banks and commercial firms were socially inferior. In the whole of my seven years in Ceylon I never had a meal with a business man, and when I was stationed in Kandy, every member of the Kandy Club, except one young man, a solicitor, was a civil servant, an army officer, or a planter—they were of course all white men.

White society in India and Ceylon, as you can see in Kipling's stories, was always suburban. In Calcutta and Simla, in Colombo and Nuwara Eliya, the social structure and relations between Europeans rested on the same kind of snobbery, pretentiousness, and false pretensions as they did in Putney or Peckham. No one can understand the aura of life for a young civil servant in Ceylon during the first decade of the twentieth century—or indeed the history of the British Empire—unless he realises and allows for these facts. It is true that for only one year out of my seven in Ceylon was I personally subjected to the full impact of this social system, because except for my year in Kandy I was in outstations where there were few or no other white people, and there was therefore little or no society. Nevertheless the flavour or climate of one's life was enormously affected, even though one might not always be aware of it, both by this circumambient air of a tropical suburbia and by the complete social exclusion from our social suburbia of all Sinhalese and Tamils.

These facts are relevant to Mr X's malevolence to me and my two fellow civil servants. None of us, I am sure, gave him the slightest excuse for hating us by putting on airs or side. We were new boys, much too insecure and callow to imagine that we were, as civil servants, superior to business men. Mr X hated us simply because we were civil servants, and he suffered too, I think, from that inborn lamentable malignity which causes some people to find their pleasure in hurting and humiliating others. Mr X was always unpleasant to us and one day succeeded during a kind of gymkhana by a piece of violent horseplay in putting Scafe and me in an ignominious position.

It is curious—and then again, if one remembers Freud, it is of course not so curious—that I should remember so vividly, after fifty years, the incident and the hurt and humiliation, the incident being so trivial and so too, on the face of it, the hurt and humiliation. One of the 'turns' in the gymkhana was a pillow-fight between two men sitting on a parallel bar, the one who unseated the other being the winner. Mr X was organiser and referee. Scafe and I were drawn against each other in the first round, and when we had got on to the bar and were just preparing for the fray, Mr X walked up to us and with considerable roughness—we were completely at his mercy—whirled Scafe off the bar in one direction and me in the other. It was, no doubt, a joke, and the spectators, or some of them, laughed.

It was a joke, but then, of course, it was, deep down, particularly for the victims, 'no joke'. Freud with his usual lucidity unravels the nature of this kind of joke in Chapter III, 'The Purposes of Jokes', of his remarkable book *Jokes and their Relation to the Unconscious*. 'Since our individual childhood, and, similarly, since the childhood of human civilisation, hostile impulses against our fellow men have been subject to the same restrictions, the same progressive repression, as our sexual urges.' But the civilised joke *against* a person allows us to satisfy our hatred of and hostility against him just as the civilised dirty joke allows us to satisfy our repressed sexual urges. Freud continues:

> Since we have been obliged to renounce the expression of hostility by deeds—held back by the passionless third person, in whose interest it is that personal security shall be preserved—we have, just as in the case of sexual aggressiveness, developed a new technique of invective, which aims at enlisting this third person against our enemy. By making our enemy small, inferior, despicable or comic, we achieve in a roundabout way the enjoyment of overcoming him—to which the third person, who has made no efforts, bears witness by his laughter.

Civilisation ensured that Mr X renounced any expression of his innate, malevolent hostility to Scafe and me by undraped physical violence on a respectable P. & O. liner, but under the drapery of a joke he was able to make us 'small, inferior, despicable, and comic' and so satisfy his malevolence and enjoy our humiliation to which the laughter of the audience bore witness. Even when I am not the object of it, I have always felt this kind of spontaneous malignity, this pleasure in the gratuitous causing of pain, to be profoundly depressing. I still remember Mr X, though we never spoke to each other on board ship and I never saw him again after we disembarked at Colombo.

2

Jaffna

When we disembarked, Millington and I went to the G.O.H., the Grand Oriental Hotel, which in those days was indeed both grand and oriental, its verandahs and great dining-room full of the hum and bustle of 'passengers' perpetually arriving and departing in the ships which you could see in the magnificent harbour only a stonethrow from the hotel. In those days too, which were before the days of the motor-car, Colombo was a real Eastern city, swarming with human beings and flies, the streets full of flitting rickshas and creaking bullock carts, hot and heavy with the complicated smells of men and beasts and dung and oil and food and fruit and spice.

There was something extraordinarily real and at the same time unreal in the sights and sounds and smells—the whole impact of Colombo, the G.O.H., and Ceylon in those first hours and days, and this curious mixture of intense reality and unreality applied to all my seven years in Ceylon. If one lives where one was born and bred, the continuity of one's existence gives it and oneself and one's environment, which of course includes human beings, a subdued, flat, accepted reality. But if, as I did, one suddenly uproots oneself into a strange land and a strange life, one feels as if one were acting in a play or living in a dream. And plays and dreams have that curious mixture of admitted unreality and the most intense and vivid reality which, I now see in retrospect, formed the psychological background or climate of my whole life in Ceylon. For seven years, excited and yet slightly and cynically amused, I watched myself playing a part in an exciting play on a brightly coloured stage or dreaming a wonderfully vivid and exciting dream.

The crude exoticism of what was to be my life or my dream for the next few years was brought home to me by two trivial and absurd incidents in the next few hours after my arrival. It was a rule of the P. & O. not to take dogs on their boats and I therefore had to send out my dog, Charles, on a Bibby Line vessel. The day after my arrival I went down to the harbour to meet the Bibby boat. Charles, who had been overfed by the fond ship's butcher and was now inordinately fat, greeted me with wild delight. He tore about ecstatically as we walked along the great breakwater back to the G.O.H. and, when we got into the street opposite the hotel, he dashed up to a Sinhalese man standing on the pavement, turned round, and committed a nuisance against his clean white cloth as though it were a London lamp-post. No one, the man included, seemed to be much concerned by this, so Charles and I went on into the hotel and into the palm-court which was in the middle of the building, unroofed and open to the sky so that the ubiquitous scavengers of all Ceylon towns, the crows, flew about and perched overhead watching for any scrap of food which they might flop down upon. Charles lay down at my feet, but the heat and excitement of our reunion were too much for him, and he suddenly rose up and began to be violently sick. Three or four crows immediately flew down and surrounded him, eating the vomit as it came out of his mouth. Again no one seemed to be concerned and a waiter looked on impassively.

Millington and I went round to the Secretariat to report our arrival and we were received, first by the Principal Assistant, A. S. Pagden, and then by the Colonial Secretary, Ashmore. Ashmore had the reputation of being an unusually brilliant colonial civil servant and he gave us a short and cynical lecture upon the life and duties which lay before us. Then we were told what our first appointments were to be. I was to go as Cadet to Jaffna in the Northern Province. As I walked out of the Secretariat into the Colombo sun, which in the late morning hits one as if a burning hand were smacking one's face, the whole of my past life in London and Cambridge seemed suddenly to have vanished, to have faded away into unreality.

I spent a fortnight, which included Christmas, in Colombo and on 1 or 2 January 1905, now a Cadet in the Ceylon Civil Service on a salary of £300 a year, I set out for Jaffna with a Sinhalese servant, my dog, a wooden crate containing Voltaire, and an enormous tin-lined trunk containing clothes. In those days the journey, even without this impedimenta, was not an easy one. Jaffna, on the northern tip of Ceylon, is 149 miles from Colombo. To Anuradhapura, the most famous of the island's ruined cities, which was just about half-way to Jaffna, one went by train. From there northwards the line was under construction, the only section so far opened being the few miles from Jaffna to Elephant Pass through the peninsula. The only way to travel the hundred odd miles from Anuradhapura to Elephant Pass was to use what was called the mail coach. The mail coach was the pseudonym of an ordinary large bullock cart in which the mail bags lay on the floor and the passengers lay on the mail bags.

I had to spend the night at Anuradhapura, and I was asked to dinner by the Government Agent, C. T. D. Vigors, at the Residency. Here I had my first plunge into the social life of a Ceylon civil servant, a life in which I was to be immersed for over six years, but which always retained for me a tinge of theatrical unreality. There was Vigors, the Government Agent of the Province, an athletic, good-looking English gentleman and sportsman, a very genteel maternal Mrs Vigors, and the tennis-playing, thoroughly good sort, belle of the civil service, Miss Vigors. Then there was the Office Assistant to the Government Agent and the Archaeological Commissioner, and there may have been also, but of this I am uncertain, the District Judge and the Police Magistrate. We were all civil servants. They were all very friendly and wanting to put the new boy at ease. The conversation never flagged, but its loadstone was shop, sport, or gossip, and, if anyone or anything turned it for a moment in some other direction, it soon veered back to its permanent centre of attraction. But we were all rather grand, a good deal grander than we could have been at home in London or Edinburgh, Brighton or Oban. We were grand because we were a ruling caste in a strange Asiatic country; I did not realise this at the time, though I felt something in the atmosphere which to me was slightly strange and disconcerting.

It was this element in the social atmosphere or climate which gave the touch of unreality and theatricality to our lives. In Cambridge or London we were undergraduates or dons or barristers or bankers; and we *were* what we were, we were not acting, not playing the part of a don or a barrister. But in Ceylon we were all always, subconsciously or consciously, playing a part, acting upon a stage. The stage, the scenery, the backcloth before which I began to gesticulate at the Vigors's dinner-table was imperialism. In so far as anything is important in the story of my years in Ceylon, imperialism and the imperialist aspect of my life have importance and will claim attention. In 1905 when I was eating the Vigors's dinner, under the guidance or goad of statesmen like Lord Palmerston, the Earl of Beaconsfield, Lord Salisbury, Mr Chamberlain, and Mr Cecil Rhodes, the British Empire was at its zenith of both glory and girth. I had entered Ceylon as an imperialist, one of the white rulers of our Asiatic Empire. The curious thing is that I was not really aware of this. The horrible urgency of politics after the 1914 war, which forced every intelligent person to be passionately interested in them, was unknown to my generation at Cambridge. Except for the Dreyfus case and one or two other questions, we were not deeply concerned with politics. That was why I could take a post in the Ceylon Civil Service without any thought about its political aspect. Travelling to Jaffna in January 1905, I was a very innocent, unconscious imperialist. What is perhaps interesting in my experience during the next six years is that I saw from the inside British imperialism at its apogee, and that I gradually became fully aware of its nature and problems.

After the Vigors's dinner, still an innocent imperialist, I returned to the Anuradhapura Rest House where I was to sleep the night and where I had left my dog, Charles, tied up and with instructions to my boy on no account to let him loose. He of course had untied him and Charles had immediately disappeared into the night in search of me. He was a most determined and intelligent creature, and not finding me in Anuradhapura, he decided, I suppose, that I had returned to Colombo en route back to London and his home. So he set off back again by the way we had come, down the railway line to Colombo. At any rate, two Church Missionary Society lady missionaries, Miss Beeching and Miss Case, who lived in Jaffna, returning by train from Colombo, in the early morning looking out of their carriage window at the last station before Anuradhapura and ten or fifteen miles from Anuradhapura, to their astonishment saw what was obviously a pukka English dog, trotting along wearily, but resolutely, down the line to Colombo. They got a porter to run after him, catch him, and bring him to their carriage. The result was that, as I sat dejectedly drinking my early tea on the Resthouse verandah, suddenly there appeared two English ladies leading Charles on a string.

The missionary ladies were aged about twenty-six or twenty-seven and I was to see them again in Jaffna. Miss Beeching had a curious face rather like that of a good-looking male Red Indian; Miss Case was of the broad-beamed, good-humoured, freckled type. In their stiff white dresses and solar topis, leading my beloved Charles frantic with excitement at seeing me again, on a string, they appeared to me to be two angels performing a miracle. I thanked them as warmly and devoutly as you would naturally thank two female angels who had just performed a private miracle for your benefit, and in the evening I went off with Charles and my boy to the 'coach'. It was only about two months since I had left London, grey, grim, grimy, dripping with rain and fog, with its hordes of hurrying blackcoated men and women, its stream of four-wheelers and omnibuses. I still vividly recall feeling again, what I had felt in Colombo, the strange sense of complete break with the past, the physical sense or awareness of the final forgetting of the Thames, Tilbury, London, Cambridge, St Paul's, and Brighton, which came upon me as I walked along the bund of the great tank at Anuradhapura with Charles to the place where the coach started for Jaffna.

Over and over again in Ceylon my surroundings would suddenly remind me of that verse in Elton's poem:

> I wonder if it seems to you,
> Luriana, Lurilee,
> That all the lives we ever lived and all the lives to be
> Are full of trees and changing leaves,
> Luriana, Lurilee.

One of the charms of the island is its infinite variety. In the north, east, and south-east you get the flat, dry, hot low country with a very small rainfall which comes mainly in a month or so of the north-east monsoon. It is a land of silent, sinister scrub jungle, or of great stretches of sand broken occasionally by clumps of low blackish shrubs, the vast dry lagoons in which as you cross them under the blazing sun you continually see in the flickering distance the mirage of water, a great non-existent lake sometimes surrounded by non-existent coconut trees or palmyra palms. That is a country of sand and sun, an enormous blue sky stretching away unbroken to an immensely distant horizon. Many people dislike the arid sterility of this kind of Asiatic low country. But I lived in it for many years, indeed for most of my time in Ceylon, and it got into my heart and my bones, its austere beauty, its immobility and unchangeableness except for minute modulations of light and colour beneath the uncompromising sun, the silence, the emptiness, the melancholia, and so the purging of the passions by complete solitude. In this kind of country there are no trees and changing leaves, and, as far as my experience goes, there are no Luriana Lurilees.

But over a very large part of Ceylon the country is the exact opposite of the sandy austerity of Jaffna and Hambantota in which I spent nearly six years of my Ceylon life. It is, as in so many other places, mainly a question of rain. In the hills and mountains which form the centre of Ceylon and in the low country of the west and south-west the rainfall is large or very large and the climate tropical. In this zone lies Anuradhapura and nothing in the universe could be more unlike a London street than the bund of the tank in Anuradhapura. Everything shines and glitters in the fierce sunshine, the great sheet of water, the butterflies, the birds, the bodies of the people bathing in the water or beating their washing upon the stones, their brightly coloured cloths. Along the bund grow immense trees through which you can see from time to time the flitting of a brightly coloured bird, and everywhere all round the tank wherever you look are shrubs, flowers, bushes, and trees, tree after tree after tree. And for the next thirty-six hours in the bullock cart all the way up from Anuradhapura to Elephant Pass it was tree after tree after tree on both sides of the straight road. It was a world of trees and changing leaves, and all the lives of all the people who lived in that world were, above all, lives full of trees and changing leaves.

The only other passenger by the coach was a Sinhalese, the Jaffna District Engineer. It was a trying journey. The road from Anuradhapura to Elephant Pass had been cut absolutely straight through the kind of solid jungle which covered and still covers a large portion of Ceylon. If the bullock cart stopped at any time and you looked back along the road as far as you could see and then forward along the road as far as you could see, the road behind and the road in front of you were absolutely identical, a straight ribbon of white or grey between two walls of green. In my last three years in Ceylon, I lived a great deal in this kind of solid jungle country, for it covered half of the Hambantota District where I was Assistant Government Agent. It is oppressive and menacing, but I got to like it very much. It is full of trees and changing leaves, and therefore completely unlike the open scrub jungle of the great treeless stretches of sand which in the south you often find alternating with thick jungle. But it is also quite different from the brilliant luxuriant fountains of tree and shrub in which the villages lie in the Kandyan hills and from the parklike luxuriance of places like Anuradhapura.

Travelling through it by road, all you see is the two unending solid walls of trees and undergrowth on either side of you. The green walls are high enough to prevent the slightest eddy of wind stirring the hot air. The jungle is almost always completely silent. All the way up to Elephant Pass I saw hardly any birds and no animals except once or twice the large grey wanderu monkey loping across the road or sitting in attitudes of profoundest despair upon the treetops. Except in the few villages through which we passed we met scarcely any human beings. In the day the heat and dust were terrific; the bullock cart creaked and groaned and rolled one about from side to side until one's bones and muscles and limbs creaked and groaned and ached. All you heard was the constant thwack of the driver's stick on the bulls' flanks and the maddening monotony of his shrill exhortations, the unchanging and unending ejaculations without which apparently it is impossible in the East to get a bull to draw a cart. So slow was the progress and so uncomfortable the inside of the cart, that the District Engineer and my dog Charles and I walked a good deal, for we had little difficulty in keeping up with the bulls. But at night we lay on the postbags, the District Engineer on one side and I on the other with the dog between us. Each time that the rolling of the cart flung the D.E. towards my side and therefore on to Charles, there was a menacing growl and once or twice, I think, a not too gentle nip.

I left Anuradhapura at 9 o'clock in the evening of Tuesday, 3 January, and the bullock cart with its broken and battered passengers arrived at Elephant Pass at 9 o'clock in the morning of Thursday, 5 January. The town of Jaffna, for which I was bound, was the capital and administrative centre of the Northern Province. It stood upon a peninsula—the Jaffna peninsula—which is connected with the mainland of Ceylon by a narrow causeway, Elephant Pass. As we approached Elephant Pass in the early morning, the country gradually changed. The thick jungle thinned out into scrub jungle and then into stretches of sand broken by patches of scrub. Then suddenly we came out upon the causeway. On each side of us was the sea and in front of us the peninsula, flat and sandy, with the gaunt dishevelled palmyra palms, which eternally dominate the Jaffna landscape, sticking up like immense crows in the distance. Everywhere was the calling and crying and screaming of the birds of the sea and the lagoons. It is an extraordinary change which never lost its surprise, the jet of exhilaration in one's body and mind when after hours in the close overhanging jungle one bursts out into a great open space, a great stretch of sky and a distant horizon, a dazzling world of sun and sea.

From Elephant Pass I took the train to Jaffna. The journey from Anuradhapura, one hundred and twenty-one and a half miles, had taken me forty hours, as I find from a letter which I wrote to Lytton Strachey on the day of my arrival. Today one does the journey easily in four hours. The difference is not unimportant. Up in one's brain and deep down in one's heart and one's belly, the quality of one's life is very much affected by its tempo; the tempo of living is itself enormously affected by the tempo of ordinary transport, the pace at which one normally travels from place to place. In describing my childhood I said that in those days of the eighties and nineties of the nineteenth century the rhythm of London traffic which one listened to as one fell asleep in one's nursery was the rhythm of horses' hooves clopclopping down London streets in broughams, hansom cabs, and four-wheelers, and the rhythm, the tempo got into one's blood and one's brain, so that in a sense I have never become entirely reconciled in London to the rhythm and tempo of the whizzing and rushing cars. And the tempo of living in 1886 was the tempo of the horses' hooves, much more leisurely than it is today when it has become the tempo of the whirring and whizzing wheels. But in Ceylon, in the jungle road between Anuradhapura and Elephant Pass, and again in my last three years in the south of the island, I had gone straight back to the life and transport of the most ancient pastoral civilisations, in which the rhythm of life hardly altered or quickened between the moment when some restless man made one of the first revolutions by inventing the wheel and yoking a bull to a cart and the moment when the restless European and his brand new industrial civilisation began in the eighteenth century seriously to infiltrate into Asia.

I am glad that I had for some years, in what is called the prime of life, experience of the slow-pulsing life of this most ancient type of civilisation. I lived inside it to some extent, at any rate in Hambantota, and felt a curious sympathy with the people, born and bred to its slowness, austerity, harshness, so that something of its rhythm and tempo, like that of the lagoons and the jungle, crept permanently into my heart and my bones. It was almost the last chance for anyone to see it or live in it. The railway was already undermining it in many places and, six years later when I left Ceylon, the motor-car had only just begun to appear, the instrument or engine which finally destroys the ancient rhythm and ways of primitive life. When, less than a year after I had jolted up the road from Anuradhapura to Jaffna in the bullock-coach, I went down to Colombo to take my exam in Tamil, Law, and Accounts, the railway had been completed and I travelled by train all the way to Colombo. As far as the great north road and its villages were concerned the tempo of transport and life had already changed from that of the bullock to that of the locomotive.

The train from Elephant Pass to Jaffna was slow, grunting, grinding. Though I was dazed by the bucketing of the interminable bullock cart and in a state of nervous trepidation and anticipation with regard to what awaited me in my first 'station' at the end of the journey, I was fascinated by what I saw out of the railway carriage window. The Jaffna peninsula is unlike any other part of the island which I have seen (though it may be like parts of the Eastern Province which I never went to). It is inhabited by Tamils, who are Hindus and generally darker and dourer than the Sinhalese. The Tamil crowd swarming on the station platforms or in the villages or in the Jaffna streets has a look and air of its own, much less animated (unless it is angry) and less gay than the Sinhalese in Colombo or Kandy or the Southern Province. I lived for nearly three years in this purely Tamil district; Tamil was the first eastern language which I had to learn and I got to know the people fairly well. They have to work hard and they do work extraordinarily hard to make a living out of a stony, unsmiling, and not, I think, a very fertile soil. I came to like them and their country, though never as much as I like the lazy, smiling, well-mannered, lovely Kandyans in their lovely mountain villages or the infinite variety of types among the Low Country Sinhalese in their large, flourishing villages or the poverty and starvation stricken villages in the jungle.

The Jaffna country is remarkable. It is covered with a chequerboard of innumerable roads and I must have bicycled over practically every one of them by the end of my time there. But it is so dead flat that I never remember having to ride up or down even a modest slope, let alone a hill. It is thickly populated, and, as the Hindu likes to live by himself to himself, every family lives in a house in a compound which is surrounded by a tall cadjan fence. In Jaffna itself and in the villages, the compounds are close packed one against the other often for mile upon mile, so that the road runs on and on between two long lines of cadjan fences. Behind and often overhanging the fences are tall trees so that you feel rather confined and constricted in the hot, windless tunnel. The contrast is all the more striking when every now and again you suddenly come out of the airless heat of the villages into a stretch of open country. Here again is one of those featureless plains the beauty of which is only revealed fully to you after you have lived with it long enough to become absorbed into its melancholy solitude and immensity. Everywhere the lone and level sands stretch far away, interrupted only occasionally by a few black palmyra palms. Out of the enormous sky all day long the white incandescence of the sun beats down upon the earth; towards evening it changes slowly to a flaming red or a strange delicate mixture of pink and blue.

When I arrived in Jaffna, I was met by the Office Assistant, Wilfrid Thomas Southorn, who eventually became Sir W. T. Southorn, Governor of Gambia, and who married my sister Bella. In order that the reader may understand the autobiographical story of the following six years, I must say a few words about the organisation of the Ceylon Civil Service in the year 1905. The island was divided administratively into nine Provinces and some of the Provinces were subdivided into Districts. In charge of the Province was a Government Agent (always referred to as the G.A.), a senior civil servant of twenty years' service or more. The Provincial government office or offices, the kachcheri, was always in the chief town of the Province, and there the Government Agent had his Residence. Districts were in the charge of an Assistant Government Agent (the A.G.A.), a civil servant of anything from six to twenty years' service. The A.G.A. had his Residence and District kachcheri in the 'out-station', the chief town of his District; he was under the orders of and directly responsible to the G.A., but, owing to the long distances and difficulties of transport, he usually had a good deal of independence and scope for initiative. In 1905 the Northern Province was divided into the Jaffna peninsula with the provincial kachcheri in Jaffna town, and on the mainland two Districts, Mannar and Mullaitivu. The G.A. was John Penry Lewis, fifty years old; the A.G.A. Mannar was John Scott, aged twenty-eight, and the A.G.A. Mullaitivu R. A. G. Festing, aged thirty.

In provincial kachcheris the G.A. always had two young civil servants immediately under him who did the office work, checking the accounts, issuing licences, going through all the letters, preparing the files and submitting all important questions for decision by the G.A. with perhaps a précis and, if they had any, their own suggestions or proposals. Of these two the senior was the O.A. (Office Assistant to the Government Agent) who might have anything from one to six years' service; the junior was called a Cadet, and every civil servant when he first arrived was attached to some provincial kachcheri as Cadet. It was in the post of O.A. and Cadet that the young civil servant learnt his job of imperialist administrator and to a great extent determined his future career. For your performance in the role of Office Assistant and your G.A.'s opinion of you had a considerable effect upon your career, for it influenced the minds of the great men far off in the Secretariat in Colombo, the Second Assistant Colonial Secretary, the Principal Assistant Colonial Secretary, and the Colonial Secretary himself, in whose hands rested your fate as regards promotion and appointments. Posts were either administrative, i.e. you were an Office Assistant, an Assistant Government Agent, or a Government Agent, or purely judicial, i.e. you were a Police Magistrate or a District Judge. Generally the administrative posts were considered to be a good deal more desirable than the judicial, and it was the young man who made his mark as O.A. who got rapid promotion to A.G.A. whereas the not so successful would probably find that he got a succession of judicial appointments. It must be admitted that success, in this sense, did not depend entirely upon your competence as a civil servant. A social analysis of the service in my time would, I think, have revealed the curious fact that, if you were thought to be not much of a 'good fellow' or not much of a 'gentleman', this was considered by the Colonial Secretary and his Assistants to qualify you for being a Magistrate or Judge rather than an A.G.A. (though this, of course, did not mean that no Police Magistrates or District Judges were good fellows or gentlemen).

Well, it was as Cadet attached to the Jaffna kachcheri that I arrived in Jaffna on 5 January 1905. The station had a white population of ten or twelve government officers, perhaps ten missionaries, a retired civil servant with a daughter and two granddaughters, and an appalling ex-army officer with an appalling wife and an appalling son. For the purpose of accommodating myself to this society, of avoiding being condemned as not a good fellow or not a gentleman, I had some liabilities and three assets. One liability is the social defect which I have suffered from ever since I was a child, as I showed in the first volume of my autobiography, intelligence. Intelligence and the intellectual produced the same feeling of uneasiness, suspicion, and dislike among the white population of Jaffna and Ceylon as they had on the P. & O. *Syria*, in St Paul's School, and in nearly all strata or pockets of English society. I explained in *Sowing* how in my childhood and youth I had developed, in part instinctively and in part consciously, a façade or carapace behind which I could conceal my most unpopular characteristics. The rather abortive wave of hostility on board the *Syria* against me and my fellow civil servants taught me the necessity of improving the façade and made me more fit to deal with Ceylon civil servants and planters. The process, I suppose, is what is popularly known as 'making a man of him'. It made, let us say, finally a man of me, though the man was and has remained three-quarters sham. What in fact happened was that I had put the finishing touches to a façade behind which I could conceal or camouflage my intellect and also hide from most people, both in Ceylon and for the remainder of my life, the fact that I am mentally, morally, and physically a coward. A particular liability was my ninety large volumes of Voltaire. Socially and psychologically they did me no good, and materially throughout my years in Ceylon caused considerable difficulty when I was moved from one station to another and they suddenly had to be transported over hundreds of miles in country which sometimes was without a railway. I am a little proud of the fact that socially I lived down the ninety volumes and physically brought them back to England in fair condition, neither repudiating Voltaire spiritually and socially nor abandoning him materially.

Of my assets the first, and perhaps least important, was three bright green flannel collars. I do not suppose that anyone now remembers that in 1904 a new kind of collar was suddenly put upon the market for men's clothes. They were of very bright colours, made of flannel, and you attached them by studs to whatever kind of shirt you chose to wear. They were, no doubt, a symptom of the moral breakdown of the Edwardian era, the revolt against Victorianism, particularly in so far as it affected the formal male respectability in dress with its boiled shirt and starched white collar. It is true that they went out as soon as they came in, and it may be that I was almost the only person who had the courage and bad taste to buy them. I know that Thoby Stephen, when he saw me wearing one, said: 'My good fellow, you can't wear that sort of thing', and they were commented upon—as were my brown boots—most unfavourably by Lytton Strachey. In Ceylon for a short time they did me a great service. No one had ever seen anything like them before—or would again—and people were deceived into thinking that I must be a very up-to-date and dashing young fellow.

My second asset was my good dog Charles. I had bought him four or five years before from an advertisement in the *Exchange and Mart*, a paper which was of absorbing interest to us in my boyhood. In term time I used to take him with me to Cambridge, where he was more of a liability than an asset, for I was not allowed to have him with me in my rooms in college. For some strange reason a wizened little Lord X—I have completely forgotten his name and hardly knew him at the time—kept him for me in his rooms in Jesus Lane. Charles was an extremely intelligent and affectionate dog, his one fault being that he was an inveterate fighter and hunter. It was, however, his faults which brought me fame and respect in Jaffna. On the very day of my arrival there he helped me to create a good impression, to develop my façade, and to do something to counteract Voltaire. The mere fact that I had brought a dog with me—which had hardly if ever been done by a civil servant before—was well thought of and began to counteract Voltaire, and the two things, the one so obviously right and the other so obviously wrong, helped to establish for me the privilege, which the most conventional Englishman is surprisingly ready to allow, of being slightly eccentric.

Charles immediately staged a spectacular act or rather acts which won us both approval. On my arrival in Jaffna I was taken in hand by Southorn, who introduced me to Dowbiggin, the Superintendent of Police, and Jimmy Bowes, the Assistant Superintendent of Police. The four of us, accompanied by Charles, walked into the vast ancient Portuguese Fort, where I was to live with Southorn in a bungalow upon one of the bastions. As we approached the steps leading to the great outer walls, a cat suddenly crossed our path and scrambled up and over a wall into a kind of dishevelled garden. In England Charles was well aware that he was not allowed to chase cats, but, I suppose, the imperialist Anglo-Indian spirit had already got hold of him and he thought that in any case a native cat was different. Ignoring my shout to him to come back, he was up and over the wall in a second, and from the tangle of shrubs rose a terrific din of snarls, growls, hisses, shrieks, and groans. Before I could get over the wall there was a sudden silence, and back over the wall came Charles, bloody and very much scratched about the face, but triumphantly carrying in his mouth a large, dead tabby cat. I saw that the dead cat and the rapidity of its murder had immediately given me, as well as Charles, considerable prestige in the eyes of Dowbiggin and

Bowes, and even of Southorn.

But my triumphs and those of the blood-stained Charles were not yet finished. We went up on to the ramparts of the Fort and there Charles at once found among the weeds and bushes a very large snake. He seized it, luckily behind the head, and began to shake it violently as if it were a rat. It was a strange sight. With every shake he gave it, its body gave him a violent blow on the ribs and the tail curled round like the thong of a whip and hit him in the face on the opposite side of his body. The thuds on his ribs, the smacks of the tail on his face, and Charles's grumbling growls resounded regularly for some minutes and then the snake was as dead as the cat. My reputation as a good fellow, a Sahib, a man not to be trifled with, was therefore established within three hours of my arrival, for a civil servant, wearing bright green flannel collars and accompanied by a dog who within the space of ten minutes had killed a cat and a large snake, commanded immediate respect.

By a lucky chance I clinched the matter that same evening and again proved myself to be a man whom one cannot trifle with. My third asset was that I could play a competent game of tennis and a good game of bridge. Dowbiggin, now Sir Herbert Dowbiggin, was not at all meek and mild either in word or deed. He was a bad bridge player, but had bullied the other bad bridge players into accepting him as a kind of dictator of the Jaffna bridge table. Of all this I, of course, knew nothing that evening, when I was taken by Southorn to call on Mrs Lewis, the Government Agent's wife, and found myself with her as my partner playing bridge against Dowbiggin and Southorn. In the third or fourth hand Dowbiggin revoked and, when the last card had been played, I claimed the revoke. He turned upon me, red in the face, and violently told me that I was talking nonsense. Emboldened by Charles, the dead cat, and the dead snake, I told him what cards had been played by whom and turned up the trick which proved that he had revoked. Silence fell upon the bridge table and I felt that something had happened. In fact what had happened, thanks to the green collar, the dead cat, and my ability to play bridge better than Sir Herbert Dowbiggin (whom I got to like very much), was that another dictator had fallen and I, rather like the hero in a boys' school story, had 'made good' my very first day as a new boy. I was accepted as one of them by the Sahibs of the Northern Province and therefore of Ceylon.

The company of white Sahibs of Jaffna and of Ceylon, into which

I now had to fit myself, formed a strange society such as I had never known before and would never know again. It was the product of British imperialism in Asia, and this kind of society, as imperialism is dying out of the world, is itself vanishing, if indeed it has not already vanished. A rather detailed picture of it as it appeared to my bewildered and astonished eyes and mind when I plunged into it in 1905 has a faint historical as well as personal interest. At the top of it were the five civil servants, the G.A., with his O.A. and Cadet, the District Judge, and the Police Magistrate. The G.A. was John Penry Lewis who had been in the service twenty-seven years and was now aged fifty. He was a large, slow, fat, shy man with one of those leathery or rubbery faces which even in middle age, and still more in old age, remains the face of a bewildered and slightly grumpy child, or even infant. He was an intelligent man, but extremely lazy and not fond of responsibility. This kind of inertia and habit of evading definite decisions (particularly when it was really necessary to decide) was, I think, common among civil servants in the higher administrative posts. It was partly due, I suppose, to climate which tended to dry up and sap the vigour of the older administrative civil servants who had inevitably spent a good deal of their lives travelling about in very hot and unhealthy districts. Lewis really took little interest in administration; he had the mind of an antiquarian, a historian, or archaeologist. He was fond of reading and of ferreting out curious facts about his Province. After I became his Office Assistant and he found that I liked responsibility and did not make mistakes, he left more and more work to me, and when he was promoted to Kandy and the Central Province, got me transferred there to be again his O.A. I was a year with him in Kandy where, I think, I did nine-tenths of his work; I know that usually I worked hard for ten or eleven hours a day. We never had much to say to each other, but I liked him very much and I think he liked me.

His wife, Mrs Lewis, was the exact opposite of him. She was the kind of wife which so many slow, silent, shy men marry. Large, plump, floridly good-looking, she never stopped talking at the top of her voice. She exploited what, I think, must have been a thick streak of congenital vulgarity and went out of her way to say the most outrageous things at the most awkward moments. Lewis would say: 'Really, my dear,' deprecatingly, but with a chuckle, when she had reduced some unfortunate young man or woman to blushing misery, for her vulgarity amused him. She did not mean to make people miserable, but she had the mind of a mischievous, not a malicious, gamin. After a time I got on quite well with her and in some ways really liked her, tiresome though she was. She treated me with some caution, which, being so rare with her, I felt to be slightly complimentary (or perhaps uncomplimentary) to me. Listening to Mrs Lewis—and I must have listened to her, silent myself, for an extraordinary number of hours in the years of our acquaintance in Jaffna and Kandy—I was again and again amused and indeed entranced to realise that she was a Jane Austen character complete in face, form, speech, mind—a Mrs Jennings who had stepped straight out of *Sense and Sensibility*, out of the Portman Square of 1813, into the Ceylon of 1905. I, like Elinor, desire to do 'justice to Mrs Lewis's kindness, though its effusions were often distressing, and sometimes almost ridiculous.'

Mrs Lewis, true to the type of all the Mrs Jennings's who have lived since, and indeed before, 1813, was an inveterate matchmaker. In this character she once unsuccessfully tried her hand upon me, the other victim of her artless and embarrassing manoeuvres being a young woman friend of hers who came on a visit of several months to her. On the evening when Miss M's visit came to an end and she had left Jaffna (she lived in another British colony east of Ceylon), sitting on the tennis court after the game was over, I felt the strangeness of a few minutes' complete silence from Mrs Lewis and found that she was observing me with a contemplative eye. She broke her silence by saying to me in a voice which echoed through the courts: 'I hope you kissed Mary good-bye?' The question was meant to be, and was, awkward, for in 1905 kissing was much rarer, less public, and more significant than it is in 1960. This trivial episode gives, I think, a fair picture of how we lived and talked in the Jaffna of those days. Mrs Lewis never again referred to Mary, and even later in Kandy, where the field for the matchmaker was far wider and more favourable, she never again tried to practise her art upon me. In all other ways she remained true to type as long as I knew her. A fragment of her conversation, which I find recorded by me in a letter to Lytton, shows her style: 'Since writing the above I have called on the G.A. They are back from the Pearl Fishery now and I have had the inevitable dinner. Mrs G.A. is the same as ever: her greeting to her husband when he comes into a roomful of people is: "O Pen dear, you really are *too* fat, with your great ugly paunch sticking out before you."'

The two other civil servants were the District Judge and the Police Magistrate. Sanders, the D.J., was a small, fat whisky drinking man of forty-nine whom I never got to know well, because he was soon transferred to another station. Dutton, the P.M., was a strange character; a strange fate, partly due to me, befell him, but I will deal with him and his fate in greater detail later. This, as I have said, was the top stratum of Jaffna society whose social routine was incredibly regular. We all worked pretty hard during the day. When the office and the Courts closed and the Sahibs and their womenfolk feared no more the heat o' the sun, from our various bungalows we converged upon the node of the day and of society, the tennis court in the Fort. In the Ceylon of those days among the white people the evening tennis was a serious business, a ritual, almost a sacrament. Every evening regularly there assembled Mrs Lewis, Sanders, Southorn, I, Dowbiggin, Bowes, and the two lady missionaries, Miss Case and Miss Beeching. Occasionally the Provincial Engineer, Waddell, would come, but it was significant that Dutton was never there. We played hard and seriously for an hour or more, though only Southorn was a really good and I a fairly good player.

When the light began to fade, we put on our sweaters, and, sitting in a circle, drank whisky and soda and talked. This was socially the peak of the Jaffna day, the ritual of British conversation which inevitably followed British exercise. It fascinated me and, in a curious way, I never got tired of its humdrum melancholy and monotony, for it revealed not only the characters of my companions, but the strange quality of our imperialist isolation. Besides the eight people mentioned above, who were players, there were non-players who came apparently for the conversation, sometimes the G.A. and nearly always a Captain X (I have forgotten his name), his wife and his son. Captain X belonged to a past age which seemed remote even fifty years ago. He had been an officer in the army, in a curious regiment of Malays, the Ceylon Rifles, which had been disbanded many years before. (Years later I got to know their descendants very well in the Malay village of Kirinda in the Hambantota District, for, when the regiment was disbanded, the Malay soldiers who did not want to be repatriated to Malaya—and there were quite a considerable number of them—were settled with their families in Kirinda, and had remained there intermarrying ever since.) Captain X was a short, choleric, dictatorial, foul-mouthed old gentleman, almost a caricature of the stage caricature of the curry-eating Anglo-Indian colonel; regularly every evening he laid down the law for all of us, his loud strident voice monotonously revealing his contempt for 'natives' and his irritation with young men like me. His mountainous wife sat nodding her silent and sinister approval. Of the son I can remember practically nothing.

In those days, of course, no 'natives' were members of the Jaffna tennis club. Our society was exclusively white. The only Tamils admitted were the podyans, the small boys who picked up the tennis balls and handed them to us when we were serving, and the great Sinnatamby. I used to watch Sinnatamby with some interest, a big stoutish Tamil in a voluminous white cloth and towering maroon turban. He was the keeper of the courts and served us the drinks. He was extremely respectful, but I sometimes thought that I caught in his eye a gleam which belied the impassive face when some more than usually outrageous remark of the Captain or of Jimmy Bowes echoed up into the heavy scented immense emptiness of the tropical evening sky. He might have been a character in a Kipling story, and I could imagine generations of Sinnatambys standing respectfully behind their white masters in India right back to before the Mutiny—and some of them with that gleam in the eye getting their own back during the Mutiny.

The white people were also in many ways astonishingly like characters in a Kipling story. I could never make up my mind whether Kipling had moulded his characters accurately in the image of Anglo-Indian society or whether we were moulding our characters accurately in the image of a Kipling story. In the stories and in the conversations on the Jaffna tennis court (and off it) there was the same incongruous mixture of public school toughness, sentimentality, and melancholy. When in the tropics the glaring, flaring day ends with the suddenness to which the northerner never becomes insensitive and darkness creeps rapidly up the sky and over the earth, it is impossible not to feel the beauty, the emptiness, the profundity, the sadness in the warm, gently stirring insect humming air. Our talk after the game, as we sipped our whisky and sodas, consisted almost entirely of platitudes, chaff, or gossip, and yet it was permeated by an incongruous melancholy, which, if we had known the word, we might even have called Weltschmerz.

Like all Anglo-Indians and imperialists who were colonial government servants, we were, of course, 'displaced persons'. After two world wars and Hitler we all understand today the phenomenon and psychology of the displaced person. But that was not the case in 1905. Yet we ourselves on the Jaffna tennis court, though we did not know the name, were in fact the phenomenon and had the psychology of people whose lives had suddenly been torn up by the roots, and, in a foreign country, had therefore become unreal, artificial, temporary, and alien. We all pretended to be tougher, more British, more homesick than we really were, yet there was a pinch of truth and reality in all our posturings.

James Stewart Bowes, Assistant Superintendent of Police in Jaffna, was an interesting example of all this. His brother Freddy was in the civil service, highly intelligent, high up, and successful. Jimmy was the failure of the family and had been found a job in the police. He was thirty-three, drank too much and whored too much, and was already becoming fat and flabby. His only accomplishment was that, like his brother, he spoke French like a Frenchman—they had, I think, been brought up in France. His language was of the foulest and his conversation generally lurid smut, but every now and again he would break out into melancholy self-pity and sentimentality. In a letter to Lytton on 27 February 1905, I gave a description of him which is perhaps worth quoting:

> I believe I have made the remark before but I can't help repeating it, that the people in rotten novels are astonishingly like life. All the English out here are continually saying things of which, if you saw them in a novel, you would say 'people don't say those sort of things'. They are always sentimentally soliloquising with an astounding pomposity. There is a horsey superintendent of police here, very loud and vulgar and goodnatured. He took me for a drive the other day in what he calls his 'English gig', and as we bowled along under the palm trees he gave me the following address interspersed with curses at the drivers of bullock carts who got in his way. 'Ah, my dear Woolf, how I hate this bloody island. I shall have something to say to the Almighty when I meet him. I didn't ask for much, a little house in an English shire, with plenty of hunting and six or seven horses and enough money to run up to London for a week when the frost comes—Get out, you ugly stinking fucking son of a black buggered bitch; you black bugger you—I don't ask for much, I'd be as happy as a king—you greasy fat Jaffna harlot, get out of the light, you black swine—and I don't get it.' It went on like this for a full half hour, and if you left out the curses and the language, you would find the same sort of stilted stuff in any of the swarms of 1st class books in the Union library.

I began my life as a civil servant in Jaffna by living with the O.A., Wilfred Thomas Southorn, known to his friends as Tom Southorn.

He was a year my senior. Jaffna was and is a biggish town. Europe has made a deep and wide impression upon the face of all the big towns of Ceylon which I know except upon Jaffna; in Colombo, Kandy, or Galle, the buildings, the private houses, the roads and gardens are Europeanised over quite a considerable area. But Jaffna, except in one or two conspicuous and dramatic places, is pure Tamil. It is what I think all large towns in Europe, and indeed the world, must have been before the nineteenth century, a swollen village or a congeries of villages which have coalesced into what we now call, because of its size, a town. After the nineteenth century in Europe and usually in Asia towns consist of a centre and a suburban area, and beyond the suburban area is 'the country' and villages. The suburb is urban, as a rule horribly and hideously urban, and markedly different from the countryside and the rural village. When you pass from the town and its suburbs into the country you pass from one life or age into another. It is quite different in Jaffna; there as soon as you leave the main street, the esplanade, or the seashore, you are in a typical Tamil village of narrow roads between cadjan fences which hide whitewashed low huts or bungalows, bowered in trees. And the feeling that you are in an enormous village rather than in a town is the stronger because the population of Tamils is so thick on the ground in the Jaffna peninsula that in many places one village has joined up to another and to what is now the municipal area of Jaffna town. The consequence was that if I bicycled out of Jaffna to the opposite coast or to some far off village, as I so often did, even after a year or two when I knew the whole country well, it was extremely difficult to know when and where one had left the town and was in the country and a village.

These topographical details are not unimportant psychologically. They made the feeling of life in Jaffna quite different from anything that I have known elsewhere. And they increased, in a curious way, one's sense of imperialist isolation from the life of the surrounding country, even though at the time one was not really aware of this. For in the few places in the town upon which Europe had left its mark, the impression was dramatic and intense, and it was within these places for the most part that we Europeans worked and lived our lives. There were three such places and if you observed them with an historical and philosophic eye, you might see behind them the course of Ceylon history and the impact of Europeans upon it over three or four centuries. On the main street the Dutch have left their mark; it is half eastern and half Holland, many substantial houses, such as the Dutch built for themselves in Ceylon towns, with the characteristic stoeps. Down on the seashore it is a mixture of Holland and England in a number of houses solidly built, with porticoes and verandahs, in which lived white government servants, some wealthy Tamils, and an old retired Government Agent, Sir William Twynam.

But the third European enclave is the most impressive. It is a relic of the Portuguese occupation. The northern end of the main street opened into an immense esplanade or maidan, green with grass when the monsoons bring rain, but bare brown earth between the monsoons. There the Portuguese had built out of blocks of grey stone an enormous Fort commanding the sea. I suppose the area which it covers must be nearly equal to that of Trafalgar Square; it has a rather beautiful solidity and austerity; it is perfectly intact, the ramparts, walls, and bastions being exactly what they must have been when the Portuguese built them. It was characteristic of our rule in Ceylon that there was practically nowhere any sign of a military occupation. There was not a single soldier in Jaffna or in the Northern Province. The Fort had therefore been given over by us entirely to civilian use. The process must have begun with the Dutch for they built a church in it in the eighteenth century, and a Government House which in my time was only occupied when the Governor visited Jaffna. One side of the Fort had been converted into a prison and along another side a row of bungalows had been built in which lived the Superintendent of Police, the Assistant Superintendent of Police, and the District Judge. And perched up on one of the bastions was a bungalow for the Office Assistant.

It was in this bungalow on the bastion that I lived with Southorn. It was a rather gloomy house, overshadowed by an immense banyan tree which had covered the whole area between the verandah and the edge of the bastion with the tangle of roots and branches which is the sinister method of the banyan's growth. The tree was inhabited by a notorious and dangerous devil, so that the servants disliked the bungalow and would never go near the tree after dark. If you walked to the edge of the bastion and looked down upon the esplanade you saw below you a small erection which looked like a hen coop; in this there lived another devil or God whose power or reputation was considerable, for many people came to worship him. They sacrificed to him dozens of chickens by slicing their heads off with a sharp knife and you saw the headless bodies fluttering about on the ground. On grand occasions goats were sacrificed. At night great flocks of crows came and roosted in the banyan tree and all night through you could hear their melancholy rustling, cawing, and croaking.

The kachcheri was about a mile from our bungalow and every morning we used to bicycle to it down the long main street, Charles running by my side. The town was full of pariah dogs, usually lying about in the middle of the road. The first morning half-way down the main street three large yellow pariahs, each of them twice the size of Charles, flew at him. There was a terrific whirl of growls and snarls, of dogs and dust, and then after a minute or two three yellow dogs ran off into the adjoining compounds whimpering with their long tails between their legs. Charles had only a few superficial wounds. It is a curious fact that he was never again attacked in Jaffna; it was as if the news had been passed round canine society that it was safer to leave him alone, and as he was one of those fighters who never fight unless they are attacked or provoked, he lived the remainder of his short life in honourable peace.

The kachcheri is separated from the road by a small courtyard, and adjoining it at the back is the G.A.'s Residency. Both are solid grey buildings with broad verandahs and date, I think, from Dutch times. Attached to the Residency is what in England we would call a garden, but in Ceylon is called a compound. It was in fact almost a park,[1] with great trees planted so that they gave the whole place an air of beautiful stillness and, what was so rare in the blistering dry heat of Jaffna, of coolness even in the middle of the day. We sat all day in the office working, except for the hour we took off when we bicycled back to the bungalow for lunch or tiffin. I rather doubt whether any European ever really understands an important side of the East and of Asia, ever gets the feel of its castes and classes and individuals into his brain and his bones, unless he has sat hour after hour in a kachcheri, watching from his room the perpetual coming and going along the verandah of every kind and condition of human being, transacting with them the most trivial or the most important business, listening to their requests, their lies, their fears, their sorrows, their difficulties and disasters. There are many things in

[1] I had forgotten when I wrote, that the Jaffna G.A.'s bungalow was actually called 'The Park' not 'The Residency'.

the manners and methods of a Sinhalese or Tamil who comes to a kachcheri to get a cart licence or to buy a piece of Crown land or to protect himself against a dishonest and malignant village headman or to ruin a hated neighbour which are exasperating and distasteful to a European, and many civil servants never really got over this initial annoyance and distrust. However much they liked their work and, up to a point, the people of Ceylon, as they walked into their office in the morning there was below the surface of their minds, when they passed through the crowd on the verandah, a feeling of irritation and contempt.

I too, like everyone else, was at first irritated and contemptuous. But gradually these feelings, when I was left by myself in the kachcheri to deal with the people and their business, began to evaporate and in the end, I think, they died out of me altogether. I liked unobserved to observe the perpetual procession of men coming and going on the verandah, to listen to their requests and enquire into their problems and complaints. We who live in the towns and urbanised villages of northern Europe have a social psychology radically different from that of the Tamils and the Sinhalese. Our ideas and feelings are limited, hard, distinct, brittle, a muted version of the ideas and feelings of the people whom we read about every morning in the *Daily Mail* or the *Daily Express*. Our instinct is normally to tell the truth, even if we don't know—as is normally the case— what the truth is. Our life is dominated by machinery, material as in the railways and social as in the intricate tangle of law and government. We live in a little walled box with a row of walled boxes on each side of us and another facing us. Our life runs between metal lines like the trains and the old-fashioned trams. It has normally nothing to do with the jungle where wild beasts like the leopard and the elephant roam or even the human jungle where the human beast roams. If we have a tree in our back garden, there is no devil, no Yakko in it. Of course, very deep down under the surface of the northern European the beliefs and desires and passions of primitive man still exist, ready to burst out with catastrophic violence if, under prolonged pressure, social controls and inhibitions give way. That is why, as I said before, if you get even a little way below the surface, you find that no one is an ordinary person. But normally the schoolmaster, the Sanitary Inspector, the clergyman, the daily paper, the pavements and lace curtains and police magistrates and High Court judges, the ego and the superego are far too strong for the id, and we may live our whole lives behind our lace curtains in the image, not of God or man, but of the rubber stamp and the machine.

The people on the verandah of the Jaffna and Hambantota kachcheris are, at any rate, not like that. I do not think that I sentimentalise or romanticise them. They are—or at least were in 1905—nearer than we are to primitive man and there are many nasty things about primitive man. It is not their primitiveness that really appeals to me. It is partly their earthiness, their strange mixture of tortuousness and directness, of cunning and stupidity, of cruelty and kindness. They live so close to the jungle (except in the Europeanised towns) that they retain something of the litheness and beauty of jungle animals. The Sinhalese especially tend to have subtle and supple minds. They do not conceal their individuality any more than their beggars conceal their appalling sores and ulcers and monstrous malformations. Lastly, when you get to know them, you find beneath the surface in almost everyone a profound melancholy and fatalism which I find beautiful and sympathetic—just as something like it permeates the scenery and characters of a Hardy novel. The result of these inconsistent and contradictory characteristics was to me extraordinarily fascinating, so that few things have ever given me greater pleasure than, when I had learned to speak Sinhalese, sitting under a tree in a village or on the bund of a village tank and discussing with the villagers their interminable problems, disputes, grievances. And when I revisited Ceylon for the first time, after fifty years, the moment when I felt fully and keenly again the life of the Sinhalese and the Tamils was when I found myself on the verandah of the kachcheris at Hambantota, Kandy, Vavuniya, and Jaffna.

During my first weeks in the Jaffna kachcheri I found the work intolerably dull and boring. The O.A. was responsible to the G.A. for all the work of the office, indeed administratively of the whole Province. All the correspondence passed through his hands and, if he was a first-rate civil servant, whatever was submitted for decision by him to the G.A. would be properly and clearly set out by him with a minute and probably a suggestion or recommendation. If the G.A. was travelling on circuit so that it might well be impossible to get in touch with him, as was often the case, the O.A. might himself have to make a highly important and difficult decision. One of the extraordinary things about the life of an administrative civil servant in those days was the variety of his work. The G.A. was responsible for everything connected with revenue and expenditure in his Province (other than expenditure on main roads, public works, and major irrigation works). He was at the head of the Customs, the prisons, the police. He was responsible for all municipal and local government, for all minor roads and minor irrigation works, for sale or development of Crown Lands, for welfare work, for law and order, and for a great deal of paternal government unknown in European countries for several hundred years. The machinery of his government was a large number of headmen, a village headman in each village and superior or chief headmen in charge of larger areas. Half his time was—or should have been—spent on circuit, in travelling round his Province acquainting himself with the characters and work of his headmen and the conditions of the people, considering possibilities of improvement and development, enquiring into requests and complaints, and settling the interminable disputes and feuds of village life. In these circumstances a vast amount of interesting and important work was open to the O.A., particularly if he was energetic and the G.A. a little lazy. The Cadet was in a very different position. Fresh out from England, completely ignorant, he was the maid of all work, the kitchen maid, the fag who had to learn his job by doing all the dull, mechanical, dirty work of the O.A. At the age of twenty-four I was an arrogant, conceited, and quick-tempered young man. My work in the office consisted of signing my name on licences and routine documents and letters, and of checking the accounts. After some weeks of this, my temper gave way and I told Southorn that I would not go on doing this, that I was just as good as he was, and that I must be given some of the interesting work. Southorn was an unusually good-tempered person; any other O.A. would have told me to go to hell, but he very weakly did what I demanded.

My letters to Lytton show that after that I got a great deal more than my due share of the extraordinary variety of work which a junior civil servant had to do in those days. Indeed within four months of my arrival in Ceylon and three months of my arrival in Jaffna, I was, to all intents and purposes, left for two weeks entirely and solely in charge of the Northern Province, because the G.A. was miles away and out of touch with Jaffna conducting the Pearl Fishery, and Southorn was trying to pass his examination in Colombo. For instance here is the description of an 'enquiry' of a kind which G.A.'s and A.G.A.'s were continually holding, but which seemed very strange to someone who had only two or three months' experience as a civil servant:

April 9, 1905   10.30 P.M.

I am dead tired having bicycled about 35 miles. I had to inspect the stumps of some trees which had been cut down near a big temple. A violent dispute had arisen between two priests and one accused the other of cutting down trees on crown land. I had to decide whether it was crown land or not in the midst of a yelling mob of some hundreds of people. I must now go to bed, although I probably shall not sleep being perpetually kept awake by a big owl I possess. He is a wonderful bird: he looks hundreds of years old with the wisdom and malignancy of a fiend; the beauty and texture of his feathers is indescribable, the most astonishing mixture of greys and browns. All night long he chases a rat round the dog kennel in which I keep him, but as he never catches him and I never feed the rat, they are both slowly dying of starvation. It is questionable whether in the end either will have the strength to eat the other.

Almost the first thing I read in Tamil was this: 'I saw a teacher and his disciple sitting under a tree; the age of the disciple was eighty, and the age of the teacher was eighteen.'

In the end there was no tragedy to the owl. I took him one evening and let him loose and he flew away over the Fort and esplanade. He had been given to me by a police constable. I do not remember how I dealt with the rat.

Here is another letter to Lytton which recalls to me very vividly the atmosphere and savour of those early days in Jaffna:

May 21, 1905

A cataclysm is hourly expected here. Yesterday a headman came to the Kachcheri and reported that a hole had suddenly appeared in a field about 5 miles from Jaffna, that it was still increasing. I bicycled out to the place in the afternoon. It is in the middle of a perfectly flat plain and was the most astonishing sight I have ever seen. It is like a big pond with the water about a foot from the top, there is a curious heaving in the water, every five or ten minutes a crack appears in the earth round the edge, the crack widens and the earth topples over into the water which heaves and swirls and eddies. Hundreds of natives stand round, looking on with the usual appearance of complete indifference, and every time another foot of ground disappears, a long 'aiyo, aiyo' goes up. The water is obviously from the sea which is about a mile and a half from the place and I expect it means that Jaffna Peninsula is going to return to the seabed from which it came. If the sea once begins coming in, there is absolutely nothing to stop it simply pouring over this huge flat plain which is never above and sometimes below sea level. If so, this is my last letter to you—and for dullness is probably only equalled by the first, which, I remember, went to France. But there is nothing to say to you, nothing to tell you of except 'events'. I neither read nor think nor—in the old way—feel. I can tell you that I rode 12 miles, after the usual work, to the northern coast to inspect a leaky ship, in which the Government is sending salt to Colombo: how I was rowed out in the moonlight side by side with the vast fat Chetty contractor who was responsible for the leaky ship: how I climbed about in the hot hold with the water pouring in, and examined the master and crew sitting on a campstool in a little reeking cabin: how I was rowed back through a little fleet of catamarans, fifty or sixty logs of wood bobbing on the sea each with a kneeling figure on it which outlined against the white sea looked like a ghost praying. I can't write about anything else; here are the only realities, and the curious feelings they excite, the only pleasant feelings. Perhaps they are not the only ones; when I read your letters first, you are for the moment real again. I can laugh too over Bob Trey—whose letter God damn it, I shall never answer—and every now and then you raise things even to the pitch of excitement. But for the rest it's either the curious feelings and excitement from these curious rare incidents and sights or else the boredom of work and the nausea of conversation.

The following is perhaps worth quoting as giving a picture of a Ceylon hospital in 1905:

Last week I had another study in sordidity which may amuse you—the Jaffna hospital. I happened to be with Dutton (who is really doing the magistrate's work) when he was summoned to the hospital to take the dying deposition of a man who had had his head cracked in a brawl. I walked over with him. The hospital consists of two long rooms bare and whitewashed, with rows of plank beds down each wall. Horrible looking dishes lay scattered about and on the planks lay three or four natives without any covering but the clothes in which they had arrived, their heads and bodies bandaged, groaning, grunting and spitting on the floor. Outside, and on the verandah and therefore to all intents and purposes in the room, squatted a crowd of patients and their friends talking, quarrelling, chewing betel and spitting it out upon the floor. Among these sat the dying man eating curry and rice out of a big dish, and quarrelling with the man who is accused of having broken his head. We could discover no attendant and so went off to ask the doctor what it all meant. All he could tell us was that he had given strict orders that the man should lie quite still doing nothing as he might fall down dead at any moment. The whole thing was exactly what I imagine the 18th century hospitals were like....

By the by, have you read one of the supremest books, *Pilgrimage to Al-Madinah and Meccah* by Burton? There is no doubt we must go to Egypt and Arabia, and after all 'Voyaging is Victory'. Even here in this squalid little place, you have the curious absorbing people, and now and then there is a strangeness and beauty about a place that you never could have dreamt of in England.

Finally here is an extract from a letter of 4 June 1905, which gives a glimpse of the work of a callow civil servant and of the mood of the moment.

I did not write to you last week, simply because I couldn't; and it was made worse by no letter from you. After a year or two I don't think I shall write letters at all. In a dim way, of course, I can realize what you are doing, and how the hours go, but I don't see how it is possible for you to imagine what actually I am doing all day here. The worst of it is its futile fullness: one is simply overwhelmed in the swamps of petty little things. Pundits and work and tennis and law, it is almost impossible to escape for a moment. They have made me Additional Police Magistrate now: I spend the evenings in trying to learn something about the law; in the day the work is something of a horror and a relief. At first it is a mere whirl: sitting in sheer ignorance up there in the hum of the Court, writing down the evidence, listening to the proctors and witnesses, thinking of questions to ask, trying to make up your mind—all at the same time. I felt that at any moment I might raise your old cry: 'I resign'. But it is a relief after the dreary drudgery of the kachcheri. Its sordidity is almost superb: you see all the curious people and listen to their intimate lying tales. It is impossible to feel that it is real, when I sit up there in the stifling heat and look out over the glaring waste to the Fort and the sea, and listen to an interminable story of how one man smashed in the skull of another with a stone because the latter asked him to repay a debt of 25 cents. It is absolutely incredible how futile life can be: and if one doesn't become engrossed in its futility, I don't see that there is anything to stop one going mad.

My letters to Lytton of this period are extremely gloomy. Diaries and letters almost always give an exaggerated, one-sided picture of the writer's state of mind. He is concerned to reproduce as vividly as possible—to make the reader feel as deeply as possible—a mood, only one of the many moods which chase one another all day and all night long through our minds and bodies. Even to ourselves we habitually exaggerate the splendours and miseries of our life and forget in the boredom of Wednesday the ecstasy of Tuesday—and vice versa. And when it is a letter that one is writing to an intimate friend of one's youth, the passions and prejudices of youth which were so important a part of that friendship exaggerate and distort the picture of our reactions to entirely new circumstances. This is certainly true of the letters which I wrote to Lytton in the early years of my time in Ceylon. I felt keenly the complete loss of the life which I had lived at Cambridge, its friends and friendship. In every conceivable way my life in Jaffna was the exact opposite. Intellectually I was back in school with the old sense of frustration. Much of the work was terribly boring. When I sat down to write to Lytton, all these feelings were so strong that they overwhelmed or eliminated all others. But even in these letters one sees between the lines interest, fascination, even cheerfulness breaking through.

In May 1905, Southorn was moved from Jaffna and this had a considerable effect upon my life there for quite a long time. The Government sent to take his place as O.A. and man called Leak. Normally he would never have been appointed an O.A. for he was a senior civil servant. But he was extremely ill with T.B. and the Government sent him to the dry climate of Jaffna as the best place in the island for him. He was married and had a child so I had to move out of the O.A.'s bungalow and find a home elsewhere. This was by no means easy, as it was impossible to get an empty bungalow in a place like Jaffna and the only solution was to discover a government servant who had the room and was willing to take one in. Eventually I landed myself in the bungalow of the Police Magistrate, Dutton.

Dutton's character and career were odd and I propose to interrupt the narrative of my own life in order to pursue that of Dutton's in so far as I was able to observe it. Dutton was not a pukka Sahib and was not accepted as such by the pukka Sahibs of Jaffna. To begin with he was not a Public School boy and had not been to a university. We were, of course, not all in so high a social category as that, but most of us could pass as 'gentlemen'. Dutton, in the opinion of Jaffna society, couldn't—his origins and his ways came too obviously from that depressing, dun-coloured, lace curtain region where the lower middle-class merges into working class or vice versa. 'A bloody unwashed Board School bugger, who doesn't know one end of a woman from the other', was the description of him given to me when I first came to Jaffna by Bowes or Dowbiggin, and it must be admitted that there was some truth in the portrait. He was a small, insignificant looking man, with hollow cheeks, a rather grubby yellow face, an apologetic moustache, and frightened or worried eyes behind strong spectacles. He always reminded me of Leonard Bast in *Howard's End*. He did not play tennis and he did not play bridge and did not mix at all in the white society of 'the station', living alone in a largish bungalow with a piano, so it was said, and a vast number of books. The policemen, Dowbiggin and Bowes, hated him for being a lenient magistrate, and sitting on the tennis court after the evening's play I suffered hours of boredom listening to their abuse of him and of his decisions.

For these reasons I hardly ever saw him during my first months in Jaffna. Now finding myself without a bungalow, I decided to ask Dutton to take me in. It was a bold step. I knew that the rest of Jaffna's white population would strongly disapprove, but I had built up a reputation of being an extremely competent civil servant and a somewhat formidable 'good fellow' whose lapses from convention or good taste were condoned because, as they said, 'of course, he's slightly mad'—how wrong they were!—so that I felt fairly secure that my career in the 'Service' or in Jaffna society would not be jeopardised, as otherwise it well might have been, by my sharing a bungalow with 'dirty Dutton'. I therefore with some trepidation called upon him to ask him to take me in.

His bungalow appalled me. It was in a side street, smothered in trees, hot, stuffy, full of mosquitoes and geckos—not a breath of air ever found its way in. I found him sitting at a small table typing out incompetently on a decrepit typewriter the poetry which he had written the previous evening. Every evening Dutton wrote poetry, poetry incredibly feeble and of a sickly, sticky simplicity which, had I not read it—hundreds of lines of it—I should not have believed attainable by an adult in the twentieth century. The vagaries of the human mind, the human heart, the human character in real life, so much more unbelievable than the most absurd creations of bad novelists, fill me with amazement. Who could possibly imagine that in 1905 an English civil servant, a Police Magistrate—what we now know to have been an imperialist—would sit hour after hour, day after day, writing poetry about fairies or, as he called them, fays? When not writing poetry, Dutton either read or played, with distressing incompetence, on a wheezy, out of tune piano. Some of the notes of this piano had fallen in pieces and were now tied up with string, and he played on it for hours Gilbert and Sullivan, Mozart, the Gaiety and every other Girl, and impossibly sentimental German abominations.

The books which Dutton read surrounded him. There were hundreds of them, nearly all of them pocket editions and cheap series, like the Home University Library. They were ranged in bookcases which stood at right angles to the walls with narrow passages between them, and they and the piano filled the whole room except for a small space which housed a table, a typewriter, a chair, and Dutton. He was extremely nervous and suspicious and for some time the interview and the conversation were awkward, but eventually, when he found that I had read as many books as he had—or even more—and that I did not think poetry funny, he agreed to take me in, and I and my Voltaire joined Dutton and his Home University Library.

I have hardly ever known anyone so hopelessly incompetent as Dutton was to deal with life, and *a fortiori* with just that particular kind of life into which the cynical malevolence of fate had pitchforked him in Ceylon. The only possible way in which I can imagine he might have cheated fate or God or the Devil would have been for him to have obtained a safe, quiet post in the Inland Revenue or the Post Office and to have lived a life bounded on the one side by Somerset House or St Martin's-le-Grand, and on the other by a devoted mother and a devoted old servant in Clapham or Kew. In Ceylon he lived the life of a minnow in a shoal of pike. The basis of his character was timidity which, as so often, was compensated underneath by boundless self-conceit. His lower class origin superimposed upon his timidity a deep inferiority complex which burst out in the most grotesque intellectual arrogance. He did not mix with his fellow civil servants and the other white inhabitants of Jaffna because he was afraid of them but also because, at the same time, he despised them. He must, I suppose, when a boy, have had a brain a good deal better than the average, and so he won scholarships which lifted him out of the welter of the elementary school into the Ceylon Civil Service. Unfortunately this meant that he was given the kind of education which completely addled his fairly good brain and destroyed every chance of his becoming a rational person. Literature, art, poetry, music, history, mathematics, science were pitchforked into his mind in chaotic incomprehensibility. When later on in Ceylon I became an extremely incompetent shooter of big game and, in cutting up the animals killed by me, saw the disgusting, semi-digested contents of their upper intestines, I was always reminded of the contents of Dutton's mind. As he not unnaturally disliked and temperamentally was frightened of the people and life which surrounded him, he very early escaped from them and it into books and the undigested, sticky mess of 'culture' which they provided for him. His roots began and remained in Peckham, while his mind was full of Keats, the Gaiety Girl, Shakespeare, and fays—the result was lamentable.

In the months during which I lived with Dutton in his bungalow I got to know him extremely well, I came to pity him and with reservations to like him. Deep down under his muddled mind, his flinching and cringing soul, his crazy culture, he was a simple, nice person. My knowledge of books won his respect, and he very soon talked to me quite freely and relied upon my judgment in many things. For instance, he asked me to read the hundreds of thousands of lines of his poetry and tell him what I thought of them. This was a very ticklish business. His poetry was, as I said, incredibly bad, and, when not about fairies and similar poetical paraphernalia, was infected with a curious kind of castrated eroticism. I suspect that Dutton was physically impotent—and this accounts for something in the events which followed; mentally he was certainly a eunuch. He liked to talk about love and women in a way which made me feel slightly sick. His attitude towards them was a cross between that of a sentimental and innocent schoolgirl and that of Don Quixote. He once told me that sexual intercourse seemed to him repulsive, and impossible with anyone with whom one was in love. His naïvety in such matters was extraordinary and led him into doing the oddest things, sometimes as Police Magistrate in his Court. Here is an example.

Some time before I went to live with him, I was riding home gently down the main street of Jaffna. I was returning, I think, from tennis in the Fort. It was evening, soft and sad with the long shadows falling across the street after the fierce heat of the day. The houses had built-out verandahs, screened from the road by great rattan blinds. I was thinking of nothing in particular, riding slowly, relaxed, a little melancholy. Being on a horse I could see over the blinds on to the verandahs. As I passed one of the houses, I happened to look into the verandah and a Burgher girl sitting there smiled at me and I smiled at her. A little further on I was crossing an open space which led down to the seashore and my bungalow. Suddenly I heard a thin voice saying: 'Sah! Sah!' I looked down and there was a minute boy, about seven years old, trotting along by the side of my horse. I asked him what he wanted, and he said: 'Sah! Sah! That young girl ask whether she come to your bungalow tonight.' I very foolishly said yes, and she came and spent the night with me. The 'young girl', I discovered, though the niece of one of my own very respectable clerks, was a notorious Jaffna character—a 'loose liver', as they said; at the moment she was being kept by a Tamil lawyer.

About three months after I went to live in Dutton's bungalow, he told me one evening that he had had a most unpleasant case to try that morning. The Tamil advocate in question had brought a case against a young Burgher girl for abuse and indecent language, alleging that she had come to his house, where he lived respectably with his wife and family, and in the middle of the day, standing in the street, shouted in a loud voice: 'Come out, you son of a whore! Come out, you son of a bitch!' and had added details about the gentleman's life and practices which Dutton could not repeat. After hearing the complainant, the accused, and their witnesses, Dutton came to the conclusion that the woman was technically guilty of abuse, but that morally she was a pure young girl whose chastity had been unsuccessfully attacked by the licentious advocate. This he said in Court, and, after giving the advocate a moral lecture, he said that he regretted having to convict a pure young girl of a technical offence and to fine her ten rupees, and in order to show his own view of the matter he would pay her fine himself. So saying he took ten rupees out of his pocket and handed them to the Clerk of the Court. As the pure young girl was my clerk's niece and had, as I said, a notorious reputation in Jaffna, the whole incident and Dutton's little speech gave the Jaffnese immense pleasure and amusement.

After I had lived some months with Dutton, I began to urge him to mix with other people and suggested that he should come with me one evening to the tennis courts. At first he refused, but I saw that he was rather anxious to do so, and that fear alone prevented him. Eventually he decided to come with me and play tennis, and so one evening, fitted out with tennis shoes and a racket, Dutton appeared, to the astonishment of the habitués, on the courts. Among the habitués or habituées were the two missionaries, Miss Case and Miss Beeching, who came to the courts solely, I think, because they wanted exercise. They obviously and with justification disapproved of the other habitués, including myself, and they very rarely stayed on the courts after play was over. They were bad players and usually played singles together, and I handed Dutton over to them; for the next few months Dutton used to come and play nearly every evening a hopelessly incompetent game of tennis with Miss Case and Miss Beeching. And I think I noticed, without really paying any attention to it, that sometimes the two missionaries would sit on after their game was over, talking in low voices to Dutton.

Then one Sunday I had to bicycle out to a place some ten miles from Jaffna to inspect a piece of land over which there was some dangerous village dispute. On the way back in the evening, to my astonishment I suddenly came upon Miss Beeching and Dutton, standing close together in a dry paddy field, each holding a bicycle and apparently engaged in earnest conversation. I can still see their minute figures, standing there in the gigantic, flat, dusty plain of the Jaffna peninsula, looking helpless, ridiculous, pathetic against the flaming sunset. And I realised that largely owing to me Dutton would marry Miss Beeching—or perhaps it would be more accurate to say that Miss Beeching would marry Dutton. I like, as I have said before, the beauty, solitude, melancholy of great empty sandy plains, but just as when you see two human beings outlined against their flaming sunset, they contrive to make you see the human beings as two manikins, so too they tend to induce in me a feeling of impotence, the dwarfing and dooming of everything human in the enormous unpitying universe. I was depressed that Sunday bicycling back to Jaffna.

Some months later Miss Beeching did marry Dutton. Oddly enough, I cannot remember whether I was or was not at the wedding—I rather think I was not. At any rate, just about that time I was moved to another post, to Kandy hundreds of miles from Jaffna and for a long time I lost all sight of and touch with the Duttons. I saw them only twice again.

The first time must have been some four years later. I was now an extremely competent civil servant; my façade was in full working order. As a result I was Assistant Government Agent, Hambantota, having been given the post over the heads of many of my seniors, including Dutton. I worked sixteen hours a day, had chronic malaria and bad temper, and rarely saw a white man or woman. My fellow whites, when I did meet them, treated me as one of themselves, violent tempered and slightly mad, but on the whole what they called a good fellow. Dutton, despite Mrs Dutton, had remained a failure in every direction; nothing could make him a good fellow, and so he was still a Police Magistrate, and in my last year in Hambantota I heard that he had been made P.M. of Matara, the district which adjoined mine on the way to Galle. As however I practically never left my District, there was no reason why I should ever meet the Duttons. But I did—twice.

The largest town in my District was not Hambantota, the headquarters where I lived, but Tangalla, thirty miles or so away. There was no railway and about once a month I drove or rode to

Tangalla and stayed a night or two there in the Government Rest House. One evening on my arrival I found the Duttons in the Rest House; he had been ordered to come and try a case which, for some reason, the Tangalla Police Magistrate and District Judge—who was Southorn—could not take. The Duttons and I dined together, and after dinner we sat on the verandah with the Indian Ocean a few yards from our toes and talked. The conversation was curious, uneasy, and I felt—I could not say why—that every now and then it became tense and sinister. It was partly that the cosmic surroundings of the Tangalla Rest House once more, as upon the Jaffna plain, made the Duttons—and of course myself—appear to me minute, helpless, infinitely insignificant, almost tragically ridiculous. If I had to show anyone what God can do in the way of tropical nights, I think I should take him to the Rest House verandah at Tangalla. The small, insignificant building lies by itself in a small bay fringed with rocks and coconut palms. The ocean laps against the verandah. The evening air is warm and still and gentle. An enormous sky meets an enormous sea. The stars blaze in the sky and blaze in the sea. Every now and then—it seems almost at one's feet—a long, snake-like, black head rises out of the stars in the sea, remains for a moment motionless above the water looking at the stars in the sky, and then silently slides back into the sea. It seems incredibly mysterious, this black head emerging from the water to gaze at the stars in the sky, even though you know it to be only a turtle coming up to the surface to breathe. There is no sound in this melodrama of a tropical night except a faint lapping of the sea, and now and again a shivery stir of palm leaves. The sky, the sea, the stars, the turtles, the bay, the palms were so lusciously magnificent at Tangalla Rest House that Nature seemed to tremble on the verge—I don't think she ever actually fell over the verge—of vulgarity.

As the Duttons and I talked, we were embedded in, overwhelmed by this starry magnificence. Dutton and Miss Beeching had, I think, both changed. He seemed to have shrunk and she to have swollen. They reminded me of those pairs of insects—some are spiders or worms—in which a very small male is attached to a very large female—fitting ignominiously and neatly into her gigantic body—I sometimes think that this must be the ideal life for a male—and, after performing his male functions, is killed and eaten by her or just dies. Not that I thought that Mrs Dutton would kill and eat Dutton; but she seemed somehow or other to have absorbed what little life and virility he had ever possessed. He spoke very little and sat silent with a vague, apologetic half smile on his face. She on the other hand talked incessantly. She had never liked me, had always disapproved of me, and I felt that her hostility remained. She did not, for instance, make any attempt to conceal her irritation at the fact that I had been given the Hambantota District while Dutton, who was five years my senior, was still only a Police Magistrate. Yet, as the evening wore on, the immense canopy of stars and sky seemed to overwhelm her and break down her reserve, even her hostility. I cannot now remember exactly what we talked about or what she said—it was principally, I think, reminiscences of the days in Jaffna. But I was left with a feeling of tenseness, failure, and unhappiness. And in the feeble light of the oil lamp on the verandah I saw that the Red Indian face was puckered with worry and she looked as if she might at any moment burst into tears. I felt terribly sorry for them, but far more for her than for him. It became indeed so painful, this patter of expressed and unexpressed misery, that I made some excuse and went off to bed, promising to come and see them if I was ever in Matara. I never saw Dutton again.

But I did see Mrs Dutton. Some months later I had to spend a few hours in Matara, and before paying my respects to the A.G.A. of the district I called upon the Duttons. He was away, but I found her at home in a two-storied house. She seemed to have grown even larger than before and was dressed completely in white in a voluminous, bride-like dress of some cambric kind of material. So voluminous was her dress that there emanated from her when she moved about the room the astringent smell of clean, new linen that one notices in large drapers' shops. The house was incredibly clean and shiny and smelt of soap and polish. I felt as if I had entered the hygienic aseptic ward of a hospital—so different from my bungalow with its immense shadowy grey rooms always smelling of books and dogs.

Mrs Dutton had glossy black hair parted in the middle, worried brown eyes, and a complexion the colour of very pale copper. In her white dress she looked tragic and ominous. I felt extremely uncomfortable and wished I had not come. The conversation began calmly with the usual platitudinous gambits, but, as it went on, the feeling of agitation and tenseness which I had felt on the verandah of the Tangalla Rest House returned—also the continued sense of her hostility towards me. She was obviously in a state of almost neurotic misery. And she began to express it, not openly, but obliquely, by continually returning to Dutton, his retiring nature, his failure in the civil service, the prejudice of everyone, including the authorities, against him. The more she said, the more nervous I became, and I began to get what was, I think, probably a delusion that she was accusing me of having been the cause of her marrying Dutton. As always happens when one is nervous, I became more than usually emphatic and sympathetic, and this made her still more agitated and unreserved. Suddenly overcome by panic, I said that I must go. She insisted that I must first see the house, and in terror I followed her upstairs and into their bedroom. Whether my nerves had given way and I was no longer seeing things as they really were, I do not know, but it seemed to me that I had never seen a bedroom like it. It was, like Mrs Dutton herself, a mass of white cambric, the two beds being covered with the most voluminous white mosquito curtains I had ever seen. It looked as if the whole room was filled with bridal veils, and yet, perhaps owing to the overpowering smell of clean linen, it gave me the feeling of unmitigated chastity. It was the linen of nuns and convents rather than of brides and marriage beds. We stood one on each side of the beds and Mrs Dutton broke down. I was so embarrassed and terrified that I cannot really remember exactly what she said, but she told me that her marriage was a complete failure, that Dutton was so queer that he ought not to have married, and that she was completely miserable, and, as she spoke, the tears ran down her cheeks. Keeping the beds between us and looking at her over the top of the immense mosquito curtains, I tried to calm her and eventually got her to stop her tears and come downstairs. In fact, I persuaded her to walk with me to the Assistant Government Agent's bungalow. She would not come in with me, and as we said goodbye in the dusk outside the house, I ventured nervously to pat her on the shoulder. I never saw Mrs Dutton again, and a year or two later, when I had left Ceylon for good, I heard in England that Dutton had died of tuberculosis.

To return to my own life in Jaffna, it was varied and pretty strenuous. Leak was too ill to do any work and so I had to do the work of both the O.A. and the Cadet. I also sometimes had to act as Superindendent of Police. In a letter to Lytton I tell him of an incident which shows the kind of thing one had to do as a Superintendent of Police. A Police Constable came to my bungalow early in the morning and told me that a small boy had disappeared and that it was thought that he had been taken away by a young man in a bullock cart to the coast at Kangesanturai, fifteen to twenty miles away. The parents were in a desperate state, thinking that he might have been murdered, and they had set off for Kangesanturai. I too set off for the same place immediately on my bicycle, accompanied by a Police Sergeant. Some distance from Kangesanturai a policeman was waiting on the road to stop us and take us to the Chief Headman's, the Maniagar's house. There we found a young man and a crowd of relations of the small boy, together with headmen and the policeman.

The story was this: the child had been last seen with a young man in a bullock cart driving towards the coast. The young man was known to keep a dancing girl and therefore to be habitually in debt. The child's relations, when they heard this, set off in a body on the main road to the sea, stopping every bullock cart they met and searching it. At two in the morning they met a cart with the young man in it; they dragged him out, searched him, and found the boy's jewellery on him. Then they took him to the Maniagar's house, beat him with sticks and whips, pushed pins down his nails, and tortured him generally until he confessed. He said that he had taken the boy to Kangesanturai, carried him out into the sea, knelt on him in the water until he was drowned, took his gold ornaments, and then threw the body out into the sea. I set off at once to the sea, accompanied by police, headmen, the accused, and the child's relations. The young man took us to the place where he had thrown the body into the sea. The headmen collected twenty or thirty villagers and all day long we toiled over the burning blinding white sand watching the men wading along the shore searching for the body. We did not find the body. I knew there was a ship lying off Jaffna, the *Serendib*—it was the Government's Pearl Fishery boat—and I sent a note to the captain, telling him what had happened and asking him whether he could help us in the search for the body. Some days later I received the following characteristic letter from him—I found it among my papers, I don't know why I should have kept it for fifty-five years. It is perhaps not surprising that the Master of the *Serendib*, who spent his time coasting round the north of Ceylon, is a year out in the date of his letter:

S.S. *Serendib*
Kangesanturai
June 18th, 1904

Asst. Supt. Police

Sir,

I received your note this morning and came on here immediately to see you but you had gone to Jaffna.

I found it was not possible for me to get under weigh again today as it is blowing very hard to the westward with a rough sea and I think it be a fruitless search besides my coals are running short and have just enough to carry me to Pamban and should I have gone out today I should have had to come back from Delft to Kayts to get some more.

I leave here for Delft at six tomorrow morning and shall keep a good look out on the way.

I don't think the body will have gone seaward yet as it has not had time to float and the way the tides set it will be found on the beach if found at all.

Yours most
respectfully
J. H. Rhodes
Master

P.S. We give a drowned man from 7 to 9 days to float but he must have weighed the child down.

Send the prisoner on board here and I will take him out tomorrow morning with a firebar round his neck and I'll drop him in 9 fathoms.

This letter is written in very fine copperplate handwriting. I do not remember whether the boy's body was ever found or whether the accused was hanged. The headmen's and police methods of dealing with accused people horrified me. In those days, as I soon learned, it was a perpetual—and usually losing—struggle to prevent every kind of pressure, including physical violence and torture, being applied to the accused in order to extract a confession. But if the treatment of the criminal was savage, the treatment of his victim was not much better. In another letter about the same time I described how I had taken the deposition of a dying man:

I rode to a place called Pt. Pedro on Sat. afternoon, partly on business, partly in order to escape Jaffna. It is about 21 miles away. I thought I should come back by a mad way and started out down the coast where there were no roads only sand and palmyra trees. No one ever goes there and the sand has heaped itself up into great curves and ridges. It seemed to be absolutely uninhabited except for one enormous temple standing quite solitary in this wilderness of sand. At last the track I had been following disappeared altogether and I had to haul my bicycle across a dried up lagoon in the direction I imagined my road to lie. Eventually I found myself at a Rest House 12 miles from Jaffna: there I inspected the tracing of a new road and pushed my bicycle through two miles of paddy fields. I got back at 7, scorched, aching, and sore, only to be met by a constable with a letter asking me to take a dying deposition of a man who had been stabbed in a fight. Only a Magistrate can do this so off I dragged myself to the hospital. It is fairly grim; the man was a mass of wounds, he lay on a bare wooden bed in the long gloomy room surrounded by all the other loathsome patients. It took an hour and a half to get his story out of him and it had to be interrupted by the man having to have his urine drawn, a filthy operation. In the end he became unconscious or pretended to be. It must be pleasant to be in a dying condition and be shouted at until you are forced to tell who stabbed you. I shall write an article (strictly anonymous) on Modern Humanitarianism in the East for the *Independent*. I wonder if things are really managed in England as they are here.

At the time I wrote this, I was too inexperienced to be able to take a line of my own. Later when I had found my feet and knew all the snags as well as the ropes, I did what I could. But I was never a full-time Police Magistrate and only acted occasionally as Superintendent of Police, and one soon found, as I said above, that it was extremely difficult to prevent effectively the primitive and illegal methods of the police and headmen in dealing with crime. I am all and always upon the side of law and order, and my time in Ceylon, where I was on the Government side of the fence, strengthened me in this attitude, simply because without law and order, strictly enforced, life for everyone must become poor, nasty, brutish, and short. And the nearer one gets to the criminal, the more closely one has to deal with him, as one does when one is on the Government side of the fence in the administration or on the Bench or in the police, the less sentimental sympathy one gets for him, for he is usually a very nasty and brutish man. But in my case, actual experience from the inside of the administration of law and of what is called justice produced in me an ineradicable and melancholy disillusionment with those whose duty it is to do justice and protect law and order. Too often one watches the line between the criminal and the policeman or the judge growing thinner and thinner. As I pointed out in *Sowing*, the faces of eminent judges of the High Court of Justice suggest that nastiness and brutishness are found upon the Bench as well as in the Dock.

Towards the end of my first year in Jaffna, in 1905, I was again in difficulties over a house to live in. I had to move out of Dutton's bungalow, I suppose because he was to get married, and I could find nowhere to go. At last a Government Surveyor called Shipton offered to take me in for a week or so, but the first day I moved in a catastrophe befell me which for the time solved my housing problem. I got typhoid. I know exactly how I got it. In the north-west shoulder of the mainland across the sea from Jaffna there had been a complete failure of rain and a minor famine had fallen upon the unfortunate inhabitants. We started a relief work in Punakari, the building of a road. The people worked on the road and were paid in rice and every fortnight I sailed across to superintend the work and see that the people received their rice. It was a pretty strenuous operation. I sailed in an open Tamil boat with no protection from the sun and, as the bottom of the boat was usually full of the most ancient and fish-like smelling bilge water, the sun and stench combined were formidable. Punakari was one of the most desolate and out of the way places in Ceylon. There was no road to it from anywhere and that was why I had to get to it by boat. It was an extraordinary desert of sand; thick jungle began four miles from the sea, and between the sand and the jungle stretched a large area of dry, parched paddy fields. In the middle was a small ancient Dutch fort, converted into a Rest House in which I stayed. For several hours I trudged about in the blazing sun inspecting what was being done and the number of workers, and calculating how much rice would be needed for next week. Then I sailed back to Jaffna.

I had to do this every two weeks, and on my return from the third or fourth visit the wind suddenly dropped completely and we lay becalmed.

> All in a hot and copper sky
> The bloody Sun, at noon,
> Right up above the mast did stand,
> No bigger than the Moon.
>
> Hour after hour, hour after hour,
> We stuck, nor breath nor motion,
> As idle as a painted ship
> Upon a painted ocean.

'A weary time! a weary time!' just as the ancient mariner found it. The sun and the glare of the sun upon the sea were intolerable. The bilge was fouler even than usual, the stench more nauseating; flies swarmed over the boat, the bilge, one's hands and face. I had brought some food with me and managed with difficulty to eat a little of it. It would have been much better if I had not, for there is no doubt that the bilge, the food, and the flies combined to give me typhoid.

The afternoon I moved into Shipton's bungalow I had a bad headache and next morning I woke up feeling wretched. I hardly knew Shipton and I did not like to tell him that I felt ill, so I crawled out of bed and joined him at breakfast on the verandah. There is an eastern dish called hoppers, which is I believe a corruption of the Tamil 'appam'; it is a kind of thick rice pancake which many Europeans in my time liked very much. Even at the best of times, when I was not suffering from typhoid fever, I was not very fond of them. That morning when the good Shipton put before me a plate on which sat two hoppers and on each rather greasy hopper sat a rather greasy fried egg, I felt as if my last moment had come. Shipton saw my difficulty and I had to confess that I felt extremely ill. He took my temperature which was very high. He must have been an unusually sensible man, for he did not assume, as nearly everyone else in Jaffna would have assumed, that I had malaria. He decided that I must see a doctor, but the difficulty was that there was no good doctor and no hospital in Jaffna which could take a European. He then took a step which almost certainly saved my life. About six or eight miles from Jaffna there was a village called Manippay in which was an American mission with a small hospital and an American doctor in charge. Shipton went off to Manippay and brought the American doctor to see me. He immediately diagnosed typhoid and agreed to take me into his hospital. I was put on to a mattress, carried out and put into a bullock cart, and driven away to Manippay. There we were confronted with difficulties, though I was in no state to realise them. There was nowhere in the hospital itself any place suitable for a sick European. I had therefore to be placed in a small, completely bare outhouse which had only one small window about ten foot from the floor.

The doctor, who was an extraordinarily nice man, told me that I had typhoid, and that if I laid absolutely as still as possible and ate practically nothing, my temperature, which was over 103, would gradually go down and precisely on the twenty-first day would be normal, 98·4, and I should have recovered. The hospital was terribly under-staffed; he had only one trained nurse, a Tamil girl, who had never touched a white patient and would probably be too shy to do so. This proved to be the case; she came occasionally into the room, but always stood a long way from the bed so that she could not even put the thermometer into my mouth. In the end I always took and recorded my temperature on the chart and it was my Tamil servant Appukutty who nursed me patiently and efficiently for the three weeks. It was a strange three weeks. I lived in a kind of twilight world, physically and mentally. They gave me nothing to eat except from time to time a cup of Benger's food, I think it was called. I have always had an infinite capacity of sleeping when I want to sleep and I slept almost the whole three weeks away. Somewhere, too, deep down in me I had an iron determination not to die. One day after I had been there a week or ten days, I woke to find three white-robed, turbaned headmen standing by my bed. They salaamed and one of them stepped forward and said: 'Sir, we heard that you are ill and dying, so we have come to pay our respects to you.' For a moment I thought it was a dream, but when I realised its reality, I was so much amused by the words and the solemn spectacle that I felt that the crisis was past and that I should certainly recover. And so it was, for punctually on the twenty-first day, when I took my temperature, it was for the first time normal.

I suppose it must have been another ten days or a fortnight before I was allowed to leave the hospital. Since childhood I have rarely had an illness severe enough to be followed by what one can accurately call convalescence. But when I have, the misery and horrors of convalescence have always seemed to me infinitely worse than those of the illness. Typhoid seemed to have drained all strength out of both body and brain. Someone—I forget who—took me for a few days into his bungalow down on the shore of the Jaffna lagoon and one evening I foolishly crawled along the road to the Fort and sat watching the tennis. On my way back suddenly I felt as if my last hour had come; my heart began to beat as if I had an electric drill inside me and the sky turned black while the earth began revolving round me. I sat down by the side of the road and eventually crawled home to bed. Then I got three weeks' leave and went off first to Kandy and then to Bandarawela. Here I stayed in a hotel up in the mountains. It has a most delicious and exhilarating climate. When I first got there, I could miserably totter along for a quarter of a mile; a week later I had completely recovered and could walk five or ten miles and enjoy it. The following extracts from letters which I wrote to Lytton from Bandarawela in January 1906, recall the place and my mood in it:

I was four days in Kandy and three in Hatton, an immense empty hotel surrounded by an interminable series of tea-covered hills, and now I have practically settled down for two weeks here. You can't understand my mood—and I don't think I can give its tone to you at all—without an idea of this country. It has enmeshed me together with my appalling isolation. It is superb; don't you think it always is when you can see vast distances? Well, here wherever you walk you can see over enormous tracts, but instead of, as usually happens in these cases, seeing plains, it is one immense sea of hills. You stand upon one and they rise and fall all round you in great waves, not rugged but desolate, covered with coarse grass, almost bare of trees. It is only to the east that there is anything dark and rugged where they rise up 2,500 feet above this place in a long dark chain covered with jungle. The air is wonderfully soft and clear and the sky a curiously pale blue. I walk out on to these and wander about from 7–9 every morning and 4–6 every evening, the rest of the day I read Voltaire's letters, Huysmans, and Henry James. The only people I talk to are a man who drives a traction engine and an interminable procession of tea-planters. The latter are typically 'good fellows': they ask me to come and stay with them and I accept and then put it off in terror. Somehow or other though I can talk to them there is a horrible feeling of boredom and awkwardness. One must always say the same things in the same cheery way, and, as I do of course, the awkwardness is only felt by myself. I have definitely promised to stay next week with two of them on their estates about 10 miles away: I shall have to but I dread it. . . . An American whom I met at Hatton gave me the following recipe for happily spending one's days: 'Take a quiet walk, have your meals, clean your boots, take out your clothes and see that they are all right, read and answer your letters, talk to anyone you come across, go to bed', and 'fuck your wife' I added and enraged him.

. . . I stayed with the planters some days and, of course, it was much better than I expected. One was a wild maniac of the kind I am always surprised at being able to get on with, typically, this is a repetition, an ordinary very good fellow. The other was curious: he had been at Selwyn destined for the church. He had never thought until he began to read theology and that reduced him immediately to agnosticism. Then he became a private tutor, and tried to reform the method of teaching, his object being to teach people to think. He is rather charming and strenuous and deals largely in philosophy. We had, before an admiring audience on whom he has completely impressed himself, a violent argument about the existence of time and he is now about to begin a study of *Principia Ethica*. One would hardly expect an evening like I had in an isolated hill bungalow on a Ceylon tea estate.

These extracts are from letters written on 13 and 28 January 1906. On 28 January I received a telegram from the G.A. Jaffna asking me whether I was well enough to take up in the middle of February a special appointment as Koddu Superintendent at the Pearl Fishery. It was obviously an extremely interesting job, so I wired back 'Yes', and next day set out to Jaffna.

The Ceylon Pearl Fishery is said to go back to very ancient times. The pearl oyster (Pinctada), which is more nearly related to the mussel than to the edible oyster, breeds on the pearl banks in the Gulf of Mannar some miles off the barren uninhabited coast of the Mannar District in the Northern Province. The oysters breed and produce pearls very erratically. In my day there was a Superintendent of Pearl Fisheries, Hornell, who had a steamer at his disposal and, I think, a dredger. He inspected the oyster banks in the autumn and if he found that there were sufficient mature oysters and the average number of pearls in the samples dredged up was satisfactory, the Government proclaimed a Pearl Fishery for the following February. As the Fishery was in the Northern Province waters, the G.A. Jaffna was in complete charge of it and had to make all the arrangements for it. He took with him four or five white officers. In 1906 he had three civil servants, John Scott, the A.G.A. Mannar, and two specially seconded, i.e. Malcolm Stevenson (three years my senior) and myself, and an Assistant Superintendent of Police.

The Pearl Fishery camp was always at Marichchukaddi, which as the crow flies is about eighty miles from Jaffna. When there is no Fishery, Marichchukaddi is merely a name on a map, a stretch of sandy scrub jungle with the thick jungle beginning half a mile or so inland. There was no road to it, only a rough sandy track along the coast to Mannar, so that the only way to reach it was by sea. There was no harbour and all the bigger boats and steamers from India and Colombo had to lie anchored offshore. About twenty to thirty thousand people came from all over Asia to the Fishery, divers, jewellers, dealers, merchants, traders, financiers, shopkeepers, dacoits, criminals. To house these people the Government, i.e. the G.A., built a large town on the desert of sand, containing bungalows for himself and the other Government officers, huts for the divers, traders, and boutique keepers, a court, police station, prison, and hospital. All these buildings were of timber with cadjan roofs. This temporary town was laid out in regular streets: Main Street, Tank Street, New Street, New Moor Street.

It was, I think, on 15 February that I sailed from Jaffna to Marichchukaddi in an open native boat. It took me a day and a half to reach Marichchukaddi. I lay on a mattress with the sun beating down upon me during the day and the immense canopy of stars seemingly just above my head at night. We had to sail first south-west round Mannar and through the little islands of Adam's Bridge and then south to the Fishery. There is—or was—to me always something extraordinarily romantic in this kind of setting off entirely alone in a small boat into the unknown. The wind would fall and we lay becalmed in an immense silence and then the breeze would again steal up across the water and we would begin once more to go gently through the sea. It really was as though time stood still. One's life, one's universe had been reduced to the bare sea and the bare sky, day and night, sun and stars. Whether or when one was to arrive lost all importance; the complete solitude away from any trace of civilisation or taint of civilised people, with its gentle, soothing melancholy, seemed, as it always does, to purge the passions. When they ran my boat up on to the sandy beach at Marichchukaddi and I jumped down into the sand, I felt that, though my body was unwashed and unshaved, my mind had been curiously cleaned and purified. Naturally I was instantly and appropriately recalled to reality. The G.A.'s bungalow had been built on a small hillock of sand overlooking the beach and I walked up the slope to report my arrival and find out where my bungalow would be. When I reached the top, there was Mrs Lewis sitting outside the bungalow with a table by her side and a gramophone on the table blaring into the evening sky above and the sand and sea below 'Funiculi, funicula'. 'Hallo! Hallo! Mr Woolf. I'm glad to see you', the jolly female voice was louder even than the Neapolitan singers. 'How are you? Come on, come on and have a drink and listen to my new record.' I was back once more in civilisation.

It was certainly a very primitive form of civilisation, apart from Mrs Lewis and her gramophone. The methods on which we ran the Fishery seemed to me antediluvian, primordial. The fishing was actually done by Arab or Tamil divers. There were 4,090 Arabs who came down from the Persian Gulf in dhows. The dhows were commanded by chiefs or sheiks, some of whom, I think, commanded several dhows. There were 4,577 Tamil and Moor divers, most of whom came from India; they fished from open native boats. The Fishery lasted from 20 February to 3 April. Every morning about 2 or 3 a.m., if the wind and sea were favourable, the Superintendent fired a gun which was the signal that the dhows and boats might be launched and sail off to the Pearl Banks. The method of fishing was this: each diver (if he was an Arab, using a bone nose-clip) stood on a large flat stone through which ran a rope held by a man in the boat, called a manduck. At a signal from the diver the man paid out the rope as fast as he could and the diver on the stone was carried to the floor of the sea. There he shovelled oysters into a large basket which was attached to another rope. When he shook the rope, he was hauled up by his manduck into the boat. This went on all day. There were 473 boats divided into two fleets which fished on alternate days; the largest number of boats to go out on any one day was 286. In the afternoon the Superintendent fired a gun out on the Banks and all the dhows and boats raced for the shore.[1]

The Arabs ran their boats up on to the sand and with a tremendous shouting rushed into the koddu carrying their oysters in great baskets. The koddu was an enormous fenced square enclosure with nine open huts running down it from end to end. Each hut was divided into compartments, and each boat as soon as it arrived had to bring in its load of oysters and deposit it in a compartment dividing it up into three equal heaps. The Koddu Superintendent, of whom I was one, then went round and chose two out of the three heaps as the Government's share, leaving the other heap to be gathered up by the divers and to be taken with a roar of shouting out of the koddu.

Later in the evening the Government's oysters were auctioned by the G.A. When the first divers rushed their shares out of the koddu, they were surrounded by a crowd of pearl dealers and merchants who bid against one another for the oysters. Those who succeeded in getting some, hurried away and opened the oysters to see whether the number and quality of the pearls which they contained were above or below average. What they found in these samples determined the bidding at the Government auction in the evening. The method of extracting the pearls from the oysters was primitive and insanitary. The oysters were put into a canoe or dug-out and allowed to rot for several days; when the oysters had decayed, seawater was put into the canoe which was gently rocked and the seawater gradually poured off; there upon the bottom of the canoe was a sediment of sand, putrid oyster, and pearls. As the Fishery went on and the whole camp became full of thousands of putrid and putrescent oysters, a horrible smell hung over it and us night and day and myriads of flies swarmed over everything. Every particle of food had to be kept closely covered until the last moment before you

[1] Some of the boats were towed in by a Government steamer.

popped it into your mouth.

John Scott, as A.G.A., was responsible for law and order in the camp, sat as Police Magistrate, and was Koddu Superintendent; I was Assistant Koddu Superintendent; Stevenson was Superintendent of Police. Stevenson and I shared a bungalow. I was also Additional Police Magistrate, and when I had time helped with the supervision of the camp. The work of the Koddu Superintendents was onerous and exhausting. In theory the fishing ended each day in the early afternoon, the dhows raced back before the wind blowing from the sea, the divers dumped their oysters and the Government had taken its share and the koddu was cleared by the late afternoon. This ideal timetable rarely worked out in practice. For the dhows to get back to the shore from the Banks reasonably early in the afternoon, they required a fairly brisk south-west wind. Very often they got a light or contrary wind or no wind at all, and they had to tack or even row. When this happened, the boats would drop in one by one all night long and even on into the following day.

At one time we were fishing a Bank nearly twenty miles away and the boats, with a favourable wind, took four or five hours to get in, but the wind was consistently unfavourable and day after day they took twelve, twenty-four, or even thirty-six hours to reach the shore. A Koddu Superintendent had to be in the koddu the whole time, keeping order among the hundreds of shouting, gesticulating Arabs in the light of flickering oil lamps and torches and taking over the Government's oysters. In the day one trudged up and down the koddu through the sand under a blazing sky. 'It is like walking about hour after hour', I wrote in a letter, 'in a hell twice as mad as the coaling at Port Said. It is merely coolie work supervising this and the counting and issuing of about one or two million oysters a day, for the Arabs will do anything if you hit them hard enough with a walking stick, an occupation in which I have been engaged for the most part of the last 3 days and nights.' The heat and the flies made everyone feel ill and at the most hectic moment Stevenson went down with malaria and Scott was also ill. I was almost continually in the koddu night and day and, when not there, patrolling the camp or trying police court cases. In a letter to Lytton I wrote: 'The work is consequently going on day and night and I have only been about 3 or 4 hours in bed out of the last 72.'

I think that my recovery from typhoid had given me a new lease of life and, as I often said at the time, a new inside. I know I felt extraordinarily well and completely untirable. But I also experienced in the sands of Marichchukaddi one of those sudden, instantaneous cures which at the moment seem a divine miracle and exhilarate one so that for a time one becomes immune to all the ills of the flesh. When I left Jaffna, I was suffering from an eczema which is very usual in Ceylon. But the heat and continual walking in the sand of the koddu made it infinitely worse and my thighs and scrotum were covered and inflamed with an intolerable rash. The pain and discomfort of walking about for five or six hours on end in the sun in this condition were appalling. I bore it for three or four days and then, after I left the koddu one morning, I went to the Medical Officer and asked him whether he could do anything. He gave me a lotion which I immediately put on. The result was, as I said, literally to me a miracle. When I put the lotion on I was in a raw and bleeding state, and I had to go back to the koddu in the afternoon. By that time, I was more or less comfortable—and I had been in acute discomfort for days—and when I left the koddu about midnight, I was recovered.

There was a great deal to be said against our rule of Ceylon, which, of course, was bleak 'imperialism' or what is now fashionably called colonialism. One of the good things about it, however, was the extraordinary absence of the use of force in everyday life and government. Ceylon in 1906 was the exact opposite of a 'police state'. There were very few police and outside Colombo and Kandy not a single soldier. From the point of view of law and order nothing could have been more dangerously precarious than the Pearl Fishery camp, a temporary town of 30,000 or 40,000 men, many of whom were habitual criminals. As the Fishery went on, the town became fuller and fuller of a highly valuable form of property, pearls. There was one danger which was a perpetual nightmare to us and which I will deal with later, but apart from that we four civil servants never even thought about the possibility of our not being able to maintain law and order. And we were quite right. In the koddu we had an interpreter, some police constables, and a few Tamils whose duty it was to take over the Government's shares of the oysters and see that no one touched them. Otherwise I was single-handed and had to keep order among a thousand or more Arabs pouring into an enclosed space dimly lit, carrying heavy sacks and baskets of oysters, and all desperately anxious to find a good empty compartment and to get out of the koddu as quickly as possible with their share of oysters. At the time it seemed to me quite easy and natural to do this with a loud voice and a walking stick, though I was by nature, as I have already said more than once, a nervous and cowardly person.

The Arabs fascinated me, both in themselves and because of the contrast between them and the Tamils. The Tamil crowd was low in tone, rather timid, depressed and complaining in adversity. The Arab superficially was the exact opposite. At the end of the Fishery I went in a small steamer, packed with about 1,000 Arabs and Tamils, to Paumben in India. The men swarmed everywhere over all the decks and overflowed into the three small cabins and into the box of a saloon. The sea was rough all night and they were seasick most of the time. In a letter to Lytton describing this I contrasted the behaviour of the Semitic with that of the Dravidian, perhaps somewhat unfairly. The Tamils, I wrote, were 'huddling together, squabbling and complaining, but the Arab is superb, he has the grand manner, absolutely saturnine, no fuss or excitement, but one could see when day broke that every Arab had room and to spare to stretch full length in his blanket on the deck.'

The Arabs were not always calm; when they rushed up the beach with their great sacks of oysters, talking at the top of their voices, shouting, laughing, the noise was tremendous, and it was wonderful when above the tumult one heard a voice from the sea crying trailingly and melodiously 'Ab-d-ul-la! Ab-d-ul-la!' The men of each boat always kept closely together, and among the Arabs were a certain number of negroes, said to have been or even to be slaves. Every Arab seemed to have his own copper coffeepot. In one boat there was a gigantic negro—he must have been six foot five inches or six foot six inches—he was wrapped about with several sacks, and, tied together with a rope, dangling and clattering on his back were always 15 or 20 copper coffeepots which he carried for his companions. One of the ways in which the Arab was different from the Tamil was the way in which he treated the white man in authority. The Tamil treated one as someone apart; he would never dream of touching one, for instance. The Arabs, on the other hand, although extremely polite, treated me as a fellow human being. If anything went wrong or there was a dispute which I had to settle, they would surround me and make long eloquent guttural speeches, and often if one of them got excited, he would put his hand on my shoulder to emphasise the torrent of his words. Once towards the end of the

Fishery, when they all knew me well and I had got to know some of them quite well, one of them before he left the koddu rushed up to me, put one hand on my shoulder, made a short speech, and then took off his camelhair head-dress and the noseclip which hung round his neck and gave them to me.

It was this attitude of human equality which accounted for the fact, oddly enough, that I hit them with a walking stick, whereas in the whole of my time in Ceylon I never struck, or would have dared to strike, a Tamil or a Sinhalese. When all the boats were coming in together, the koddu became a struggling mass of packed human beings, Arabs hauling in their sacks of oysters from the beach or carrying them out to sell at the other end. To get through the crowd from compartment to compartment in order to see that the division of the oysters was properly made—as I had to do—I simply had to fight my way through, shouting 'Get out of the way—get out of the way', and the Arabs were vastly amused when I used my walking stick to clear a passage through them.

One scene in the koddu, connected with the Arabs, of a very different kind, tragic and beautiful, I shall never forget. I had been in the koddu all night and the last Arabs and the last oysters were leaving in the early hours of the morning. I was just going to leave myself when an Arab came in from the beach and told me that one of his men had died when diving out on the banks and that the body and the rest of his crew were still on board. As smallpox had broken out in the camp, I kept all the Arabs on board and sent for the Medical Officer. When he came, I went down to the shore with him. Four men waded out to the boat: the corpse was lifted out and placed on their shoulders. Forty years ago, when the scene was still vividly in my memory, I wrote down a description of it, and I think it is better to quote it here verbatim rather than to write it afresh all over again. The four men 'waded back slowly; the feet of the dead man stuck out, toes pointing up, very stark over the shoulders of the men in front. The body was laid on the sand. The bearded face of the dead man looked very calm, very dignified in the faint light.' The doctor made his examination, and when at last he said it was not smallpox, I told the sheik in charge of the boat that he could remove the body. An Arab, the brother of the dead man, was sitting on the sand near his head. 'He covered himself with sackcloth. I heard him weeping. It was very silent, very cold and still on the shore in the early dawn. A tall figure stepped forward, it was the Arab sheik, the leader of the boat. He laid his hand on the head of the weeping man and spoke to him calmly, eloquently, compassionately. I didn't understand Arabic, but I could understand what he was saying. The dead man had lived, had worked, had died. He had died working, without suffering, as men should desire to die. He had left a son behind him. The speech went on calmly, eloquently, I heard continually the word Khallas—all is finished. I watched the figures outlined against the grey sky—the long lean outline of the corpse with the toes sticking up so straight and stark, the crouching huddled figure of the weeping man, and the tall upright sheik standing by his side. They were motionless, sombre, mysterious, part of the grey sea, of the grey sky.

'Suddenly the dawn broke red in the sky. The sheik stopped, motioned silently to the four men. They lifted the dead man on to their shoulders. They moved away down the shore by the side of the sea which began to stir under the cold wind. By their side walked the sheik, his hand laid gently on the brother's arm. I watched them move away, silent, dignified. And over the shoulders of the men I saw the feet of the dead man with the toes sticking up straight and stark.'

There was so much work and so much illness during the two months of the Fishery that we had very little time for social life. It was rare for us all to be free of an evening for dinner and bridge and 'Funiculi, funicula', which was what Mrs Lewis pined for. This was no doubt a pity for we all got on very well together. Scott, the A.G.A., who had been a scholar of King's, I had known for some time and liked. Stevenson was an amusing Irishman and talked incessantly like an Irishman in a novel; he was also extremely able and became Sir Malcolm Stevenson, K.C.M.G., Governor of Cyprus. A curious incident happened to us one night. We had been dining with the G.A. and were walking back to our bungalow. The night was very dark and we had a boy with us lighting our way over the sand with a dim hurricane lamp. Stevenson was discoursing to me and at one point stopped characteristically and faced me so that the fountain of words should be as little impeded as possible. We stood facing each other a few feet apart and, as he talked he slowly twirled round and round, a few inches in front of my nose and of his, a walking stick. Suddenly the stick caught on something on the ground and whizzed it up in the air between us. As it fell back on the ground, Stevenson brought his stick down on it. The boy rushed up with the hurricane lamp and there upon the ground by our feet was a tic polonga, a Russell's viper, one of the deadliest of Ceylon snakes.

I always liked the job of patrolling the camp late at night. One or other of us invariably did this to see that the police were on their beats and awake and that nothing suspicious was going on. The danger which perpetually hung over our heads was that some gang of malefactors would set fire to the camp and then, in the panic which followed, start looting. This had been tried more than once and had in fact a year or two before succeeded. In a fresh wind the wood and cadjan huts went up in flames like tinder and on that occasion nearly the whole camp was destroyed in an hour or two. When one patrolled, however late it was, there were always people walking about or sitting in front of their huts. Very often a pearl dealer or merchant would invite one to sit down with him and have a small cup of Turkish coffee. As the Fishery went on and they got to know me, they would show me some of the pearls they had got from purchased oysters or bought from other people. Once I saw an almost naked coolie walking round the dealers' quarter, clutching something tightly in his hand. I guessed it to be a pearl and asked him to let me see it. He opened his hand for a second, just long enough for me to see one of the largest and most perfect pearls I saw during the Fishery.

The Fishery came to an end early in April and I returned to Jaffna via Colombo. I had been away from it to all intents and purposes for the better part of six months, ever since I was stricken with typhoid, and I found changes in it which changed the rhythm of my life. To start with I lived with the Assistant Conservator of Forests, G. D. Templer, in a largish bungalow down on the shore of the lagoon or sea. It was an official bungalow with the offices of the Forest Department in a building at the back. Templer shared my liking of all kinds of animals and we acquired quite a menagerie, beginning with five dogs and eventually including a leopard, a spotted deer, and a monkey. The deer roamed about the large compound, the monkey when we were not in the bungalow was chained to a pillar of the verandah and usually sat on the roof which the chain was long enough to allow him to reach.

The leopard had been found when a cub in the jungle by a Forest Officer who gave him to Templer. When he was small, the dogs were very fond of him and they used to romp with one another up and down the verandah. He was also great friends with the deer; he used to stalk the deer and suddenly jump on his back with his foreleg over the shoulder in true leopard manner, and the deer would then shake him off and butt him round and round the compound, both of them obviously enjoying the game. The leopard came to a sad end. As he grew up, he failed to realise his own strength. He would playfully bat a dog as he always had done, but he was now so strong that a playful tap sent the unfortunate dog head over heels, and, when he was some way from being full grown, none of the dogs would go near him. Now when he caught one playfully by the ankle or tried to jump on to one's lap, it was rather painful. The clerks in the Forest Office and our boys became frightened of him, and we had to keep him tied up to a coconut tree whenever we were not in the bungalow. He was a very affectionate animal and the only living creature to which he showed any positive dislike was the monkey. One day when Templer and I were out, he broke his rope, climbed on to the roof, and caught the monkey. The Forest head clerk bravely beat him off the monkey with a broom. When we came back, we found the monkey badly torn, but we doctored him and he recovered. A week or so later, when we got up one morning, we found the leopard dead—his rope had got over one of the fronds of the coconut tree and he was hanged. It is just possible that climbing about on the tree, he slipped and hanged himself; but I have little doubt that his death was contrived by the clerks and our servants.

The deer also occasioned a tragedy, which might have been very serious. He was a beautiful and charming beast; he had a passion for cigarettes and tobacco, and whenever we had a meal, he would come up on to the verandah or into the sitting-room and wait patiently by the table until he was given a cigarette. But as he and his horns grew, though he remained very affectionate to me and would let me do anything with him, his temper with other people became uncertain. One afternoon when I returned from the kachcheri I found a small crowd in the compound, a woman and three children weeping and wailing, and the latrine coolie lying on the ground with a nasty wound in his thigh. The deer had attacked him, knocking him down, and gored him. I took him off to the hospital and, though seriously ill for a time he recovered. In the evening reluctantly we shot the deer.

I do not know why I am so fond of animals. They give me the greatest pleasure both emotionally and intellectually. I get deep affection for cats and dogs, and indeed for almost every kind of animal which I have kept. But I also derive very great pleasure from understanding them, *their* emotions and *their* minds. They are, too, as I have said, usually amazingly beautiful. I was always condemned by Lytton on this account for being sentimental and many people, particularly intellectuals, would agree with him. I daresay that to some extent they are right. I daresay that there is sentimentality in my affection for my dog and my cats, for the leopard who hurled himself into my lap, for the marmoset who lived with me for five years. But I think there is also something more to it. If you really understand an animal so that he gets to trust you completely and, within his limits, understands you, there grows up between you affection of a purity and simplicity which seems to me peculiarly satisfactory. There is also a cosmic strangeness about animals which always fascinates me and gives to my affection for them a mysterious depth or background. I do not think that from the human point of view there is any sense in the universe if you face it with the gloves and the tinted spectacles off, but it is obvious that messiahs, prophets, Buddhas, Gods and Sons of Gods, philosophers, by confining their attention to man, have invented the most elaborate cosmological fantasies which have satisfied or deceived millions of people about the meaning of the universe and their own position in it. But the moment you try to fit into these fantasies my cat, my dog, my leopard, my marmoset, with their strange minds, fears, affections—their souls if there is such a thing as a soul—you see that they make nonsense of all philosophies and religions.

Before I leave this subject of animals, which, I know, will irritate many of my readers, I want to describe a curious incident which I saw take place in the bungalow by the sea. I have often heard of people who have a magnetic power over animals, but this is the only time in my life that I have seen an exhibition of it. Templer had a fox terrier bitch which normally was completely good-tempered and obedient. She had a litter of puppies in a basket in the corner of our bathroom and the moment they were born she went madly savage, refusing to allow anyone, including Templer, to come into the room. The moment that Templer tried to go in she flew at him and in the narrow space he found it impossible to get hold of her without being severely bitten. I tried with the same result. Next day an Irrigation Engineer who was in charge of a large irrigation work in the Northern Province looked in on us. He was a big, dark, gentle, shy, silent man called Harward. We told him what was happening in the bathroom and he asked us what we wanted done with the bitch and her puppies. We said we wanted to get her and her basket into another small room so that we could use the bathroom. He said that he thought he could manage that. He opened the door of the bathroom. The bitch immediately sat up in the basket growling; Harward walked straight up to her, patted her on the head and made her lie down, and carried the basket with the whole family quietly in it into the other room.

The bungalow by the sea was in many ways a very pleasant place. It is true that Jaffna is upon the sea, but the sea looks and behaves as if it is a lagoon. This is because the town and peninsula are almost completely shut in on the west by islands. Every now and again I had to sail out to these islands in a Government boat, a kind of dinghy, on Customs duty, and all along the shore of the long island facing Jaffna one could see a long pink line of flamingos wading in the shallow waters. On the sandy shore in front of our bungalow there was practically no rise and fall of tide and rarely a wave. There was always a strong smell of sea and seaweed. Not very far from us at that time lived two young English girls with their widowed mother. They used to take a walk on the beach in the (comparative) cool of the evening, and Templer and I got into the habit of joining them. One of them, Gwen, was pretty, lively, sweet-natured and I became fond of her and she of me. In 1906 it was highly improper in Ceylon that these two young women should wander about on the beach with two young men after dark and I often pondered over why their mother, a most respectable lady, allowed it. After the fierce heat of the day a gentle, languid, and pleasant melancholy would settle over the lagoon and over us as we lay on the seaweedy sand platonically—if that is the right word—in each other's arms. For many years, long after she married and had a family, she used occasionally to write to me, and even up to today whenever I suddenly get the strong smell of seaweed, as in the town of Worthing, I get a vivid vision of Gwen and the sands of Jaffna.

Besides Gwen I have a curious memory of another woman upon those sands. One day I had been away for over twenty-four hours from Jaffna on an enquiry. When I got back in the late afternoon and walked into my room in the bungalow, I was wearing a pair of white flannel trousers. Three minutes later I looked down and saw that the trousers half-way up to the knee had turned black. They were black with fleas and the whole floor of the room was black with thousands of fleas. I dashed into the compound, tore off the trousers and shouted to my boy to bring me a clean pair. Then I wandered out on to the beach and stood there in the depths of gloom, for I did not see how I could possibly get rid of such a plague and swarm. As I stood there, a very old, bent Tamil woman of the fisher caste hobbled by. To my immense surprise she stopped, came up to me, and said: 'Why is your honour so sad?' 'I am sad', I said, 'because I have just come back to my bungalow after being away out there for a day or two, and now I find the floor of my room black with thousands of fleas.' 'If your honour will wait here for a little,' she said, 'I will bring you something which will rid the house of the fleas. There is no need for your honour to be sad. We will get rid of the fleas.' She hobbled away and after five or ten minutes reappeared with a handful of some herb. She told me to take it and make my boy spread it on newspaper on the floor of the bungalow and set fire to the paper and that when the herb burnt all the fleas would leave the house. I thanked her and did what she said. To my great astonishment, the thing worked; the miracle was accomplished; half an hour later there was not a flea in the place.

Although the white population of Jaffna was so small, it contained a high percentage of curious characters. One of the most curious exhibits was Sir William Twynam, K.C.M.G. When I knew him he was seventy-nine years old, living in a house not far from our bungalow on the seashore, a straight-backed, lean, scraggy old man, with a skimpy beard, with that slightly wild, worried look in the eye which you see in many bad-tempered horses. If you had put him into armour with a lance in his hand he would have passed anywhere as Don Quixote, though I think he was the last person to tilt at windmills. He had retired after fifty years in the Ceylon Civil Service, all of it spent in Jaffna, and over forty years as Government Agent, Northern Province. On his retirement he bought a house and continued to live in Jaffna. It was said that he had started life in the Navy and came out to Ceylon as a midshipman on a man-of-war. His boat put into Trincomalee and he was sent ashore with a company of men to buy provisions. They got into a row with some of the inhabitants and the midshipman and his men fought their way through a hostile crowd into a Hindu temple where they were besieged. They were eventually rescued by an armed force under a lieutenant. Twynam was taken to Colombo, court-martialled, and summarily dismissed from his ship and from the Royal Navy. He was stranded in Colombo practically penniless.

At this time the Government Agent at Jaffna was P. A. Dyke, known as the Rajah of the North, for he ruled his province as a paternal despot. It was said that he was over forty years G.A. in Jaffna, so that the Northern Province had only two G.A.'s in eighty years. In forty years he went back on leave to England only once, and the story was that when he got out of the train at Victoria and took a fourwheeler, the cabman was rude to him and he was so infuriated that he immediately returned to Jaffna and never left it again. Dyke, hearing of Twynam's plight and thinking that he had been harshly treated, offered him a place in the Civil Service in the Northern Province. Twynam accepted and spent the remainder of his life in Jaffna.

In my day every new civil servant when he came to Jaffna went and paid his respects to the great man. Whenever I went he was holding a kind of small durbar of chief headmen, for he was still a kind of underground power in the peninsula. He was a formidable old man though quite friendly to me. I never had the courage to ask him whether it was true that he had been dismissed from the Navy. But he did tell me one day that when he first came out he had spent some time in Colombo and had seen strange sights at a military parade on Galle Face. The parade took place at midday in the hottest season of the year and the troops wore thick stocks round their necks and high collars. Dozens of men fainted and were just pulled out of the line and just left on the ground to recover—or not to recover for, according to Twynam, it was quite common for ten or twelve men to die of sunstroke during a parade in Colombo in the 1840s.

A major change for me in Jaffna, when I returned to it from the Pearl Fishery, was that Lewis, the G.A., was transferred to Kandy and the Central Province, and his place was taken by Ferdinando Hamlyn Price. Price, who was fifty-one and had had 25 years in the Civil Service, was a very odd character. He was a Welshman, and looked exactly like the man whom every foreigner regards as the typical Englishman, and indeed there are hundreds of men in the British Isles who at the age of fifty look like F. H. Price—tall, thin, athletic looking, baldish, with a long hatchet-face, an impassive, unflinching, implacable eye, an air of natural unshakable superiority and of good-humoured tolerance of so many obviously inferior (but well-meaning, so far as they go) persons. He was a terrific snob and was—or believed himself to be—a Welsh landowner and gentleman—and he believed that practically no one else in Ceylon was a gentleman. He had three passions: regularity in his everyday life, horses, and golf. He was reputed in the Service to be very slightly mad, and I think that perhaps he was. As a young man he used to race in Colombo, riding his own horses. One day in a race on Galle Face the girth of his saddle broke and he was flung off on to his head. It is true that he had a bad scar and dent in his forehead and it was said that after the accident he became slightly mad.

The above description would on the face of it make Price out to have been an unpleasant man. But in fact he wasn't, for in human beings the character is rarely all black or all white. Price was absurd and, when he was nasty, he could be very very nasty. But he had some very good points and in the end I came to like him and he liked me. In the business of life, using the word business in a strict sense, I owe a great deal to him, for he taught me very valuable lessons and methods in administration, lessons and methods which are applicable to all *business*. He was congenitally and incorrigibly lazy, and, as soon as he found that I was extremely competent and the opposite to him so far as laziness was concerned, he made me do all my work and nearly all of his. His day and mine were regulated by a rigid iron routine. He did not come to the kachcheri, but did his work—such as it was—in his house. All the Government business and papers and persons had to come through me and practically the only person whom he would ever actually see was myself. If anyone came for an interview, they had to see me and, if they wanted to go beyond me to him, they had to put what they wanted to say in writing. This applied even to Government servants. He would never see the head clerk or the kachcheri Mudlayar, who was a kind of A.D.C. to the G.A. and head of all the headmen—even these officers if they wanted to say anything to him had to put it in writing.

Price was not one of those people who lay down general principles for life, business or anything else, but I learnt from him two golden rules which ever since I have found applicable in many departments of life. The first is never to use two words where you can express your meaning clearly in one. Price himself seemed to me to write on the principle that he could express his meaning in one word where anyone else would require a minimum of ten. The second rule is that, both in business and in private life, 99 out of every 100 letters received by you, which require an answer, should be answered on the day on which you receive them. This is, I believe, one of the foundations of office efficiency and one of the great discoveries for saving one time and worry. Ever since the year 1906 I have practised it in my private life and have insisted upon it in every government office or business for which I have been responsible. Whenever I came new into an office in Ceylon, I would find 10, 20 or 30 great files waiting on my table to be dealt with and only 5 to 10 per cent of the ordinary routine letters would be answered on the day they were received. The average time for a person to get a reply to a letter of his from a Government office would probably be a week to ten days. On my second day in the office I always sent for the head clerk and said to him: 'Every letter received in this kachcheri after this week must be answered on the day of its receipt unless it is waiting for an order from me or from the G.A.' The answer of the head clerk was always that in this office the number of letters received daily is so large that it would be totally impossible to answer them in the same day. And the answer to that was: 'You are receiving in this office 500 letters a day, or 13,000 a month. Nine out of ten of the letters which you answer today were received in the office five or six days ago. But the number of unanswered letters at the beginning of the month is on the average the same as the number of unanswered letters at the end of the month. So you are in fact answering about 500 letters every day, for otherwise the number of unanswered letters would continually increase and eventually you would be answering letters today which you received months and years ago. Therefore if you once catch up—as I insist upon your doing—you will find that you save yourself and everyone else an immense amount of time and worry.' I then took the head clerk with me and visited every room in the kachcheri examining the table of every clerk to see exactly what he was doing, what letters he had on his table unanswered and on what date they were received. This was a formidable undertaking, particularly in a kachcheri like Kandy where there must have been over 100 clerks, and I went down into the very bowels of the earth, into that bottomless pit (in those days) of official darkness and despair, the Record Department, the registration and filing department. I do not believe that any civil servant had ever before really inspected the filing departments of the three kachcheris in which I served. They were all monuments of official incompetence, bottlenecks of delay—in the Kandy Kachcheri there were mountains of unregistered and unfiled letters and minutes.

I told the head clerk that he should let everyone know that I proposed to inspect the whole kachcheri and every clerk's desk in the same way monthly until I found that the Record Department was up to date and every letter was being as a general rule answered on the day of its receipt. All this made me extremely unpopular and I got the reputation among the Tamils, and later among the Sinhalese, of being a strict and ruthless civil servant. But in every place I insisted upon and succeeded in making a domestic revolution, and even in Kandy, at the end of my time there, letters were being answered on the day of their receipt. I don't think I was ever popular with my office staff; they thought me too severe and too opinionated. But as time went by they completely changed their view of my methods of business organisation, and nearly all of them agreed that my revolution had not only enormously increased efficiency but made their own work easier. This is not wishful thinking and complacency, for I have two pieces of evidence. When I left Jaffna for Kandy in 1907, one of the leading lawyers, a respectable and respected man in Jaffna, V. Casippillai, who had nothing to gain by flattering me, wrote to me:

Jaffna
23rd August, 1907

Dear Sir,

I very much regret that I was not able to have seen and bid you goodbye ere your departure from Jaffna, as I was laid up with a sharp attack of bronkitis (sic) from which I have not quite recovered yet. Very few here worked as hard as you have done or earned a reputation for more conscientious discharge of duties and I can bear testimony to the fact that very many of your subordinates who had evinced much displeasure at your relations with them at the outset had to confess that they had never had a superior who exacted so much work and at the same time treated them so kindly, holding the balance between all parties—justice being your motto.

Wishing you a long and prosperous career
I remain
Yours truly
V Casippillai

The second piece of evidence came from Kandy. The amount of Government work in Kandy was very heavy all through the kachcheri and I had a severe struggle against the head clerk and others before I was able to put through my revolution. But once the revolution was made and delays got rid of in the office, the more the work the more effective is efficiency. One day after I had been transferred from Kandy to Hambantota, I had to go up country on official business. In the late afternoon I got into the train at Colombo for Kandy and, seeing the head clerk of the Kandy kachcheri on the platform, I asked him to come in my carriage and have a chat. We talked about old times and then suddenly he said to me that when I first came to the kachcheri and said that everything must be brought up to date and that practically all letters must be answered at once, there had very nearly been an open revolt against me. Nobody in the office, including himself, had believed the thing in the least degree possible. But everyone, including himself, agreed that, once the change had been made, the thing had proved to be feasible and everyone's work became easier. Five minutes after this, to me, eminently satisfactory testimonial, I literally saved the head clerk's life. Half-way to Kandy the train was drawing into a station, I suppose it was Ambepussa, and before it had stopped he impetuously opened the carriage door in order to get out and buy himself an orange or plantain. His foot slipped and he fell between the train and the platform, or would have done if I had not caught him round the waist and held him up until the train stopped.

My unpopularity in Jaffna was not undeserved. I meant well by the people of Jaffna, but, even when my meaning was well, and also right—not always the case or the same thing, my methods were too ruthless, too much the 'strong man'. The difficulties and the friction made me for the first time dimly perceive the problems of the imperialist. It is curious, looking back, to see how long it took me to become fully conscious of my position as a ruler of subject peoples. But I remember the moment when for the first time I became fully aware of it and the awareness brought my first doubts whether I wanted to rule other people, to be an imperialist and proconsul. The Jaffna Tamil Association twice reported me to the Governor and asked for my dismissal—an unusual distinction for a civil servant of only two years' service. In both cases the G.A. was directed to call upon me for an explanation.

The first case arose from an order which I had posted in the verandah of the Kachcheri. The amount of spitting which went on in the verandah was extremely unpleasant. The notice said that spitting on the verandah was forbidden and the peons were ordered to turn out anyone who spat. One day one of my own clerks spat and I told him to clean the spot. 'He refused', I wrote at the time, 'but, when he saw I meant it, he did it. Of course I knew he was of a caste to hate doing it, but he was also a person who wanted a lesson given to him. There are other things like that: I expect a row.' The way I did this was, of course, crudely wrong, but the Governor accepted my explanation and there was no row. But I wrote, also at the time, the following about the complaints of the Tamils: 'They don't like the "strong measures" of Price and myself, and so of course they take the paying line that we are anti-native. In any case they have pitched on things which are of course not anti-native but in the main true.'

In their second complaint the Jaffna Association pitched on something which in fact was not true. They said that one of their most respected members, Mr Harry Sanderasekara, a well-known lawyer, had been deliberately hit in the face by the Office Assistant, Mr Leonard Woolf. Mr Sanderasekara had been driving in his trap down the main street of Jaffna and he met the G.A., Mr Price, and the O.A., Mr Woolf, who were riding up the street in the opposite direction. As they passed one another, Mr Woolf turned his horse and deliberately hit Mr Sanderasekara in the face with his riding whip.

When I first read this document, I was dismayed, because I could not understand how or why such an accusation could have been made against me. I knew and liked Sanderasekara and had had business with him several times in kachcheri and Court on a friendly basis. Then suddenly I remembered vividly an incident which seemed to explain his misunderstanding and accusation. Shortly after Price took over as G.A., he and I were riding up the main street of the town, and, when we got to the top of it where it debouched into the esplanade, I asked him to stop and look back down the street, for, if he did so, he would see clearly how people had encroached upon the old line of the street by building verandahs and stoeps out on to the highway. I remembered the long straight street in the glare and dust, the white houses and verandahs, and women's heads peering through blinds or round doors to see what the white men were stopping for. I remember that my horse had been restless, continually fidgeting and turning round and round as I pointed out with my riding whip to Ferdinando Hamlyn Price the old line of the street. And then I suddenly remembered that at some moment as my horse was dancing about, I had caught a glimpse out of the corner of my eye of a trap with Mr Harry Sanderasekara sitting in it.

I gave my official explanation in writing to His Excellency the

Governor and to the Central Government in Colombo. I said that I had never deliberately hit Mr Sanderasekara or anyone else in Jaffna or anywhere else in the world with a riding whip. But I did remember how restive my horse had been as I pointed down the street with my whip, and I could only assume that, as the horse wheeled round, Mr Sanderasekara was driving past and the whip, without my being aware of it, had passed near his face. The Governor and the Government accepted my explanation, but I doubted—and doubt—whether the Tamil Association and Mr Sanderasekara believed or accepted it. It shocked me that these people should think that, as a white man and a ruler of Ceylon, I should consider the brown man, the Tamil, to be one of 'the lesser breeds' and deliberately hit him in the face with my riding whip to show him that he must behave himself and keep in his place. For that is what all this meant. And perhaps for the first time I felt a twinge of doubt in my imperialist soul, a doubt whether we were not in the wrong, and the Jaffna Tamil Association and Mr Sanderasekara in the right, not right in believing that I would and had hit him in the face, but right in feeling that my sitting on a horse arrogantly in the main street of their town was as good as a slap in the face.

As time went on, I spent more and more of my time with Price and Mrs Price. They made me lunch with them every day when the kachcheri was open. Mrs Price was the exact opposite of Mrs Lewis. She was a real Victorian lady, daughter of the head of the Natural History Museum, far away now in Cromwell Road and Queens Gate and the quiet security of Kensington. I think that the life with Price and Ceylon into which Fate had cruelly pitched her terrified her, but, being a lady, she concealed it, except for the unhappiness terribly stamped upon her face. She was rather silent and extremely nervous. The curious thing about her was her handwriting which was very bold and beautiful, and she always signed her letters as if with conviction and enthusiasm very large:

> Yours very sincerely,
> Geraldine Rose Price.

She was an eminently nice person, and, if one had ever been able to get through the impenetrable reserve, her ladylikeness, her deep distrust of human beings, I am sure that one would have found an exceptionally sweet nature. I came to like her very much, and she liked me and every year after I left Jaffna I was asked by her to come and spend Christmas and the New Year with them. The following letter gives, I think, the flavour of her character:

The Old Park,
Jaffna Kachcheri,
Jaffna.
30th October, 1907.

Dear Mr Woolf,

If you have not made any other plans for Christmas, we wondered whether you would like to come back to Jaffna? If so, we should be so pleased if you will stay with us and hope you will be able to manage to spend both Christmas and the New Year here. We could then have plenty of golf, and perhaps our new greens will be ready that we are beginning to make here.

Jaffna is looking very green now, very different to when we went away. No calamity happened while we were away, and we found all the animals well on our return and we ourselves were much refreshed by the little change. Twilight says that he also hopes you will be able to spend Christmas here.

Yours very sincerely,
Geraldine Rose Price.

P.S. Could you tell me something about Mr Wedderburn? I was wondering whether you would care to bring him with you. Would he do? We have never seen him.

G. R. P.

The more I saw of Price, the more strange I found him. It fascinated me to watch that eye of his which positively glittered and with which he 'fixed' his victim in order that by its help he could 'deal with' people, as he called it. He was one of the few people I have known who had absolutely no heart: his harshness was incredible, as I once wrote to Lytton, and with his astonishing grasp of situations it was only his absolute lack of imagination which made him obviously not a great man. He suffered too from being a kind of aristocrat and a schoolboy who had never grown up into the world of reality and 1906. He had an instinctive grasp of a 'situation' and of the person with whom he was 'dealing'. I got on well with him because I understood him and he knew that I understood him and that it was no good his trying to 'deal with' me for I was impervious to the glittering eye. Also I did an enormous amount of work for him and was as intelligent as he was.

When he found out the kind of person I was, he tried to absorb me into their life, and life for the Prices was a fantastic routine. To some extent he succeeded, though I always obstinately refused to be really absorbed. The routine was as follows, so far as I was concerned. I went to the kachcheri very early, attended to the tappal (the daily mountain of letters), prepared the papers which I considered I should discuss with him and took them over to him in his house. Having settled with him what should be done, I returned to the kachcheri and worked until one o'clock. At one o'clock to the second, I went across to The Old Park and lunched with the Prices. The lunch was practically always the same and we drank Madeira, a wine which Price thought that a gentleman should drink for lunch in whatever climate he might live, a wine which I think is uninteresting and which no one, whether a gentleman or no gentleman—for there was one of each at Price's table—or indeed a lady, should drink in a climate like Jaffna's. At lunch conversation was easy, but fundamentally dull, as indeed nearly all conversation was in Ceylon. All shop was forbidden in the presence of a lady. Price had a passion for betting—he would bet on anything—and I have a milder, not passion, but liking for any kind of gamble. Every day we had a sweepstake on guessing what the rainfall had been in the previous 24 hours. As Office Assistant, I was administrative maid of all works, and among my infinite duties I was responsible for the elementary meteorological records, including the daily rainfall statistics. So every morning, when I went over to lunch, I had in my pocket a paper recording the rainfall during the 24 hours ending at noon on the previous day. Mrs Price had in her possession three pieces of paper on which each of us had at the previous day's lunch written what we thought the rainfall of the previous 24 hours had been; she also held three rupees, for each of us had deposited a stake of one rupee. The one whose guess was nearest to the actual rainfall pocketed the three rupees, and we then proceeded with the same routine all over again. As the rainfall for day after day between the monsoons was always nil, the routine was nearly always crazy.

I should like here to leave Price for a moment at his lunch and say something about rain. We do not know what rain is when we live in a place like England. In a place like Jaffna, and again in Hambantota, where I spent my last three years of Ceylon life, it is strange and entrancing. For weeks and months, between the South-West and North-East Monsoons, there is no rain at all—a clear sky, a burning south-west wind day after day sweeping across the brown parched earth. Then one evening some time in October a cloud appears upon the horizon. It does not reach one and fades away and next day the glaring sky and parching wind is on one again. This goes on for a day or two. And then suddenly the rain comes, and you hear it coming from miles away in the breathless evening, the patter patter patter of the rain on the palms and trees, creeping slowly towards one until suddenly the sun is blotted out and with a rush and a roar of wind it is upon one, a deluge of water from heaven. Every year that this happened, it seemed to me more and more miraculous, for the whole earth changed around one in an hour. I remember one year riding in the morning from my bungalow on the seashore to the kachcheri through a dead brown world. Everything was completely dried up, not a sign or sound of life anywhere, not a drop of water, not a speck of mud in any ditch or pond. While I was working at the kachcheri, the monsoon broke, the heavens opened, and I rode back in drenching rain through a world which had completely changed in an hour. The ditches were rushing rivers; the ponds were full, the earth was already turning green, the swish of the rain upon the trees was terrific, but deafening, drowning all other noises was the ecstatic chorus of millions of frogs from every ditch and pond and field and compound, a wild, mad, maddening, corybantic, croaking and creaking orgasm of sound and of wet, wallowing frogs.

To return to Price, after lunch I returned to the kachcheri. At half-past four or five, I went and had tea with the Prices, and then rode to the esplanade. On the esplanade we had made a primitive and not very interesting golf course. Price and I played golf. Mrs Price sometimes walked with us and sometimes went for a ride with her dog Twilight. I had given Twilight to Mrs Price and they were devotedly inseparable until he was killed and eaten by a leopard in the Mannar jungle before their eyes. He was a white whippet-like dog of dubious parentage on the father's side, his mother belonging to me. He once performed on the Jaffna esplanade a feat which, if I had not seen it, I should not have thought possible. There were usually on the esplanade little companies of five or six crows foraging, and Twilight would rush at them and send them swirling up into the air. One evening as they flew over his head he made one enormous leap into the air and caught a crow by its two feet and pulled it down and killed it.

Golf was to Price what Communion Service and its ritual are, I imagine, to a High Church parson. He was only a very moderately good player and so was I. As I have already said, I like all games and I like to play them seriously if I play them at all. But I would never put golf very high in the hierarchy of good games; it is too slowly long drawn out and therefore the anger against one's opponent, which in tennis and rackets, for instance, merely adds an occasional, momentary spur to one's efforts or exhaustion, in golf is apt to smoulder unpleasantly and sadistically. Price played it without any overt anger, but with cold and implacable seriousness. He induced me to order a set of clubs from Scotland, from the famous player and club maker, Auchterlonie.

In August 1906, the Assistant Government Agent, Mannar, was ill and took a month's leave and I was sent to Mannar to act for him. I was extremely pleased, partly to get away from Jaffna by myself for a month, and partly because it was almost unheard of for anyone with only a year and a half's experience to be appointed A.G.A. I enjoyed that month enormously. The Mannar District was 400 square miles in extent. It consisted almost entirely of uninhabited jungle; the only town was Mannar on the island of Mannar, where was the kachcheri, the Residency, and the Court. The island is really one of the islands which form Adam's Bridge between Celyon and India and is connected with the Ceylon mainland by a causeway.

I was the only white man in the 400 square miles of the District, and here for the first time I learnt the profound happiness of complete solitude. For a month I never spoke to anyone except clerks, headmen, Tamil villagers, and my own Tamil servants. My life and my work were entirely my own responsibility and there was no one whom I could consult about anything connected with either. I think this kind of complete solitude, with the necessity of relying absolutely upon oneself and one's own mind, is, when one is young, extremely good for one. I experienced it again during my three years in the Hambantota District. I acquired a taste for it which I have never lost, not for the permanent solitude of the hermit, or even for long periods of it, but for interludes of complete isolation. Even today, when evening falls and the door is shut in the street or in the village, and all life except my own and my dog's and my cat's is for the moment excluded, and for the moment there is cessation of the incessant fret and interruption of other people and outside existence, I enjoy the wordless and soundless meditation and the savour of one's own unhurried existence, and psychologically I am almost back again in the empty silent Residencies of Mannar and Hambantota or camping in the thick uninhabited jungles.

I learnt a great deal in my month as A.G.A. I spent most of my time riding about the District, exploring the jungles of the mainland and the small island of Mannar itself. The island is 18 miles in length and about two miles across. I had a curious expedition when I had to go and hold a land enquiry about 14 miles from Mannar town and about five miles from the other end of the island. I arranged to sleep in a tiny bungalow on an estate belonging to the Chief Headman, and I rode there in the morning, my luggage and servants and food going on in a bullock cart. There were no proper roads, only sandy tracks. The enquiry ended in the late afternoon and I decided to ride to the northern tip of the island before dark and look across Adam's Bridge. At the tip of the island is Talaimannar and there I came upon an extraordinary spectacle, the graves of Adam and Eve. The graves were two enormous, smooth mounds of sand side by side, each about 30 yards long, five yards in width, and about two or three foot high in the centre. Each of them was completely covered from end to end with a white cotton sheet. They were surrounded by a large enclosure of wooden fences with a gate at one end in charge of three Muhammadans. It was they who told me that these mounds were the graves of Adam and Eve and that they would very much like me to come inside if I would take my shoes off. I tied my horse to the palisade, took off my shoes, and went through the gate. There was very nearly a strange catastrophe. I heard behind me a shout of horror and, turning round, saw my dog trying to follow me into the enclosure. I was just in time to stop him and make him lie down by the horse outside. Thus were the graves of our first parents saved by a hair's breadth from defilement by the dog of an infidel. Everyone was delighted, and in the small crowd, which, as always in Ceylon, had appeared out of nowhere and the wilderness of sand and was now following me, there were smiles and shaking of heads and lifting of hands. It was a red letter day for the 22 inhabitants of Talaimannar as well as for the acting A.G.A.

The acting A.G.A.'s adventures were not over. I stayed talking to the Muhammadans about the graves so long that, when I got on my horse and started to ride back to the place where I was to sleep, I found that I had left it much too late. Darkness began to fall and soon I had completely lost my way. The sandy track in the wilderness of sand was quite invisible and there were no villages and no inhabitants. All I could do was to look at the stars and ride south and trust to luck. My horse then performed one of those curious feats of instinct which always astonish me. He suddenly insisted upon going off at a right angle from the direction in which I was riding him. As I had no idea where I was and he seemed to know where he was, I let him have his head. After a mile or so he brought me straight to my carts and servants and bungalow and dinner. He had never been in that bit of country in his life before and he only stopped for two or three hours in the morning near the bungalow, but on a moonless night, across trackless sand, he had smelt or sensed a mile off his horsekeeper and his food and made off unhesitating, undeviating towards them. The bungalow was little more than a one-roomed hut with a tiled roof and I slept on my camp bed under a mosquito curtain. I always sleep well anywhere, but I was vaguely conscious of half waking up occasionally during the night to hear a strange persistent whirring noise in the room. It was due to hundreds of bats flying backwards and forwards in the small room, and, when I got up in the morning, my watch on a stool by the side of the bed was no longer visible for it was coated over completely with bats' dung, and the floor and top of the mosquito curtain were also black with it.

My month at Mannar went only too quickly and I decided to ride back to Jaffna all the way along the coast to Elephant's Pass, a roadless journey with the sea on one side of one and the jungle on the other. Two or three evenings before starting, I sent for my horsekeeper in order to give him some instructions and the servants said that they could not find him. I had had my suspicions for some time that he was drinking, so I went out to the back to the stables and there I found him dead drunk. I have an intense dislike of drunkenness and almost a physical horror of drunken people, and in engaging servants I always told them that the one thing I would not tolerate was drunkenness and that they must clearly understand that, if they took the job, one condition of it was that if they ever got drunk, no matter where or when it was, I would instantly sack them on the spot. I had little doubt but that my horsekeeper had banked on the fact that there was not another horsekeeper in the whole Mannar District and that I could not carry out my threat. Next morning I sacked him, but found myself in a quandary. There was not a man in Mannar who had ever touched a horse or would have the courage to touch my horse. For a day or more the chief headman vainly tried to find me someone who would do so. But at the last moment a strange wild man of the jungle appeared and said that he would go with me to Jaffna as horsekeeper, though he had never had

13 The author in Jaffna

14 Jaffna Hindu temple

15 Fisherman on Jaffna lagoon

16 Pearl fishery: preparing to dive

17 Pearl fishery: Arab divers with nose clips

18 Pearl fishery: boats arriving from the banks

19 Pearl fishery: carrying the oysters into the koddu

20 The Empress Eugénie

21 The author with the Ratemahatmayas outside the Kandy kachcheri

22 Fetching water from the tank of a village in the jungle

23 The author with Hambantota kachcheri staff, mudaliyars, muhandiram, and Engelbrecht

24 The author with Hambanbota kachcheri staff and Father Cooreman

anything to do with a horse. He belonged to a small, remarkable caste of elephant hunters—the name, I rather think, was in Sinhalese Pannikkiya. They had a method of catching elephants handed down from time immemorial. Two of them went out into the jungle each carrying a strong rope. When they found a suitable elephant, they followed it, if necessary for days or weeks. They had to get it into such a position near a big tree as would enable them to creep up to it, slip a noose of the rope over one of his hind legs and tie the other end to the tree, which had to be strong enough to withstand the fury of the captured elephant. Eventually they had to contrive to get the other leg tied by another rope to another tree and I think they finally tamed him in the usual way by bringing up tame elephants who took him prisoner, as it were, between them. The Pannikkiya, who had spent a fairly long life in this precarious profession, was, I learnt without surprise and with relief, not afraid of my horse. He came with me to Jaffna, a taciturn man and not a very skilful horsekeeper, but a godsend under the circumstances. I had to arrange to return him safely to his jungle.

In Jaffna I acquired another horsekeeper, an admirable silent little man who remained with me until I left Ceylon in 1911. Sometime, I think it must have been in 1909, he came to me one day in Hambantota in a terrible state, saying that his wife was dying and that the Tamil doctors had given her medicine, but it did no good. Would I come and see her and give her English medicine? I went over to the room which they lived in by the stable and took her temperature. It seemed to me that she had a violent attack of malaria and I dosed her with quinine and covered her up with blankets. She recovered and their gratitude was extraordinary. He came to me soon after she had recovered and with great hesitation said that they knew that I was very fond of rice and curry, that the curries which the cooks made for English gentlemen were never really good curries because no men, only women, could make good curries—now he and his wife—for I had saved her life—were willing that she in future would always cook curries for me. She did and they were delicious curries.

When I got back to Jaffna in September, the routine of work and the Prices re-established itself, but my month in Mannar led to an incident which threw a strong light upon the hole in Price's psychology at the spot where, if he had had a heart, you would have found it. Though the whole thing concerned me intimately, completely fascinated, with a grim objectivity I watched him 'dealing with' the situation. I think perhaps that I can best show what happened by quoting the account of it which I wrote to Lytton at the time:

March 24, 1907 Jaffna

I am sick and tired of things and I suppose I'm more than a fool for being so. I can look back and see myself astonished at my present state. You, I believe, when we meet will think of me as you and I used to speak of the vague, battered angels. It is only this that has put me out. By a series of accidents the Assistant Agency at Mannar became vacant. Government wired to the G.A. telling him to send me and actually appointed me to act as Assistant Agent. It was where I acted before for a month, but it is almost certain that this time I should have remained there. There are no white people there and it is nearly all jungle, but I should have liked it above everything. Besides it is practically unheard of for anyone to get a District after only 2¼ years out here. When the wire came, the G.A. was away. I could have gone at once, but knowing that he would not like me to go, I waited for his permission. I have described him to you: he has been very nice to me, but is a master of intrigue and has no heart at all. I foresaw the whole thing, but I seemed to be fascinated by wanting to see how he could contort and manage it. *He* wanted me above all things to stay here, because I do much more work for him than he could get most Office Assistants to do. But of course he could not 'stand in the way of my career'. His line was that I was too young and that I should learn so much more by serving another year as Office Assistant. I was determined—partly because he had really been nice to me, I have almost lived in his house for a year—not to go without his full consent, but of course I checkmated that argument. I put him in such a position that I was practically bound to go or he would have practically to go back on his word. I went to bed on Thursday wondering how he would manage it but certain that he would prevent me going. He took his own way, quite wonderfully, for it showed that he had grasped my position absolutely. It would take too long to explain the minutiae of his method. But the end was that he wired to Government asking to be allowed to send Leak (the man who is theoretically my senior and superior here) instead of me *for the present* as it would be more convenient. What showed me that he had so completely grasped my position was that when he gave me the telegram he said: 'of course if you prefer it I will tear this up now and you can go off tonight.' At any rate the wire went and Leak is to go to Mannar. The position I had forced him into on Thursday was that he was to wire to Government asking to be allowed to send *no one* for a day or two, that he was to write to the Colonial Secretary and to say that if I was to get the place permanently he (Price) would not stand in my way, but if I was only going to act for a little time, he proposed to send Leak. Nothing more has been said of this arrangement. I never mentioned it again and I let him send his telegram because I was fascinated by watching his method. My whole object now is to force him to ask me the reason for my present coldness: but I think he is too wily. But he nearly from over-eagerness to justify himself gave himself away. When the wire of Government came approving his proposal, he asked me (damn him) whether I was pleased; the violence of my 'No, not at all' absolutely threw him out and it was only his wife's coming into the room which saved him and, I suppose, me.

So I suppose I shall have another year in this accursed place.

I did not have another year in the 'accursed place', for five months after I wrote this letter I was moved at a moment's notice to Kandy where Lewis was Government Agent; he had asked for me to be sent there as his Office Assistant. Price and I never mentioned Mannar again. I don't think I bore him ill will, for I had always known what he was like and it had even amused me to see him run so true to form. But I was glad to leave Jaffna and there is nothing more to say about my experience there except one curious incident which happened shortly before I left.

I have twice in my life had someone deliberately attempt to swindle me and both times escaped unswindled by the skin of my teeth. The first time was in the Jaffna kachcheri and I defeated the swindle by a deliberate forgery. One afternoon a Colombo Sinhalese sent his card in and asked me to see him. I cannot now remember what his business was, but it was something to do with the purchase of salt or it may have been land from the Government. I did not know anything about him and I was that afternoon extremely busy, but one was continually engaged in that kind of transaction and I had the clerk in and told him to put the thing through in the usual way. Some weeks later when the papers came up before me, I saw at once that the man in some complicated and ingenious way had tricked me into doing something which I ought not to have done and had thus deliberately swindled the Government. I could have taken a case against him, but it would have meant a long, tedious operation, and I suddenly saw that, with some slight risk, I could defeat him at his own game. It entailed either altering or destroying a document, but I was so infuriated that I did it. I then sent a letter asking the man to come up and see me. When he appeared, I told him that I had discovered his attempt to swindle the Government, but luckily he had forgotten or overlooked the snag (which I had deliberately created). I refused therefore to proceed with the transaction and told him that, if he thought he had a case against us, he must go to the Courts where I should be glad to meet him and reveal his business methods. I have never seen a man more astonished. I heard no more from him.

The other attempted swindle took place in Kandy and, if it had succeeded, it would have been entirely my own fault. I was sitting in the kachcheri late one afternoon holding a most exasperating enquiry—it was, I think connected with a Kandyan divorce case. The Ratemahatmaya, the interpreter, the three parties to the case (the two husbands and wife), several witnesses were in the room in a circle round my table. The enquiry had dragged on all the afternoon, because the witnesses and indeed the principals came from some remote mountain village and were so overawed by the Kandy kachcheri that they became practically speechless and what they had to say had to be dragged out of them by me, the Ratemahatmaya, and the interpreter. As the day went on my room in the Kandy kachcheri always became more and more hectic with an unending stream of people, clerks, peons, and headmen, bringing in documents and letters which required my signature or asking me to settle some difficulty. I was therefore always doing two or three things at the same time, concentrating in the centre of my mind on the main business—in this case the villagers and the enquiry—and attending on the periphery of my mind almost automatically with the routine stuff which the peons and clerks were continually putting on my table.

That afternoon a peon suddenly came into my room accompanying a white man whom I did not know. That immediately annoyed me. The longer I was in Ceylon, the more prejudiced I became against 'white men'. I had given a strict order to all in the kachcheri that, if a European wanted to see me, he was not to be brought into my room until he had sent in his card, explained his business, and I had said that I would see him. I did not mind much if a Sinhalese or Tamil wandered into my room and began pouring out his story—a not infrequent incident—partly because it made it more difficult for peons, clerks, and headmen to establish an effective barrier between the people and the O.A. or A.G.A. and exact exorbitant tips before a request or complaint could reach me. But I was infuriated when I saw a rather unpleasant looking white man introduced into my room by the peon without my permission. I let him stand in front of my table and went on with my enquiry as if he were invisible. Eventually I said to him: 'What do you want?' 'I want to get married', he said, 'the day after tomorrow, and I have come to ask you, Sir, to issue a special licence.' Among my other duties was that of Chief Registrar of the Province and special licences could only be issued from the Kandy kachcheri. I turned angrily upon the peon and said: 'Why the devil do you bring the man here? Take him off to the registrar's room, tell Mr Jayasuria to prepare the documents, and bring them to me for signature.' Quarter of an hour later the man and the peon reappeared and a sheaf of papers was laid on my table. I glanced through them and signed my name in various places and gave them back to the peon without looking at the white man or saying anything to him. They went out, but almost immediately afterwards the peon came back and, putting the papers in front of me and pointing to a place, said: 'Master hasn't signed here.' My enquiry had just reached a catastrophic climax and I was listening intently to the hesitating but crucial evidence in Sinhalese of a villager. I glanced at the paper which the peon had put before me, its image registering only on the periphery of my mind, and automatically signed my name. The peon went out and I returned to the enquiry, but three minutes later the image of the paper which I had signed jumped from the periphery of my mind to its centre and through the Sinhalese words of the witness I suddenly became conscious that, like an imbecile, I had been tricked and had endorsed a cheque. I shouted for the peon and told him to run after the man as fast as he could and bring him and the papers back, if necessary by force. A curious scene then took place. As soon as I looked at the man carefully, I saw that he was one of those louche but plausible international crooks who used to drift like the spores of some contagious disease from one Asiatic city to another. He had been reluctantly hauled back into my room by the peon and under my angry pressure he reluctantly handed back the papers to me. I found as I had suspected, that he had obtained my endorsement to a cheque which would mean almost certainly that he would get his licence for nothing and ten or twenty pounds into the bargain. I tore his cheque up and told him that unless he paid for the licence in cash I would not give it to him. He tried to bluster, but I had him turned out of my room and out of the kachcheri. The clerks told me later that he had returned and paid in cash for the licence. The rest of his story I heard much later. He had somehow or other got himself engaged to the rather plain daughter of a respectable and fairly flourishing business man in Kandy. He bluffed his future father-in-law into providing him with the cash which he had so very nearly extracted from me. I cannot now remember whether he did or did not marry the unfortunate lady. At any rate almost immediately the bottom fell out of both her world and his. He had been swindling people up and down the country with dishonoured cheques, and warrants for his arrest were issued in Kandy, Nuwara Eliya, and Colombo. He bolted and managed to get on to a boat bound for Malaya. But in Malaya he was caught and sent back to Colombo where they tried him on many charges of obtaining money by false pretences and sent him to jail.

3
Kandy

I travelled from Jaffna to Kandy to take up my new appointment on Monday, 19 August 1907. It is a curious fact that I cannot remember anything about leaving Jaffna or arriving in Kandy or the journey, which must have taken a whole day, except two or three hours in the middle of it, and those two or three hours I remember after 53 years as vividly as if they had happened 53 minutes ago. I had to change trains at a station called, I think, Polgahawela and, as I had some time to wait, I went to the Rest House and lay in a long chair on the verandah. It was late evening and I was the only person in the Rest House. I had again on me that delicious feeling of setting out alone on a voyage into the unknown. The feeling was intensified by Polgahawela. What a soft liquid gentle Sinhalese word this—Field of Coconuts—was when one compared it with Tamil places like Kangesanturai and Kodikanam! And the place itself, the air, the trees, the sky itself were as different from those that I had left a few hours ago as the Sinhalese language from the Tamil. I had left behind me the bareness, austerity, burning dryness of the sands of Jaffna and now I was bathed, embraced by the soft, warm, damp, luscious luxuriance of the tropics. Here life was full of trees and changing leaves and, after the parched brown earth of Jaffna, it seemed to be embowered in ferns and flowers. As I lay back in my chair and looked up into the sky through the great trees, I saw through the branches the brilliant glittering stars, and all round the branches and the changing leaves were hundreds of tiny little brilliant glittering stars weaving a continually moving pattern—hundreds of fireflies. My two and a half years in Jaffna, the Prices, Gwen and the seaweedy sands on the shore, my bungalow on the wall of the Fort—all this seemed already to have faded away into a long-forgotten dream.

As soon as I got to Kandy, I found that I had indeed entered into an entirely new world. I am glad that I spent a year of my life at the age of twenty seven in Kandy, for life there was unlike any that I have ever known elsewhere, but I did not like it in the way that I liked Jaffna and Hambantota, and it did a good deal to complete my education as an anti-imperialist. Kandy was to a large extent

Europeanised, it was a town of about 30,000 inhabitants, it was full of white men. There were far more Government servants, of course, than in Jaffna; there was a battalion of a Punjabi regiment with a Major Colquhoun and a subaltern whose name I have forgotten; there was a gunner, a captain, a very nasty man, and an Army Pay officer, a major, one of the great Indian Lawrences, a very nice man; there was a white solicitor, a white manager of the bank, a white superintendent of Bogambra Prison, and white shop assistants. And all round on the hills and mountains right up to Nuwara Eliya were tea estates and white planters who were always in and out of Kandy. In addition—and this to me in many ways was very distasteful—there was always an air about Kandy of European cosmopolitanism and 'society', for it was a beauty spot easily accessible from Colombo and its harbour, and so there was a perpetual stream of travellers, 'passengers' as we always called them, to it, staying for anything from a night to a fortnight in the Queens Hotel down by the Lake.

There was a bungalow for the Office Assistant, a curious building up on a bank behind the great Temple of the Tooth, the Dalada Maligawa. It was a dark house, rather gloomy. For the first three months another civil servant lived with me, the Superintendent of Police, now Sir Francis Graeme Tyrrell. I do not like to share a bungalow or house, for the moment comes quite often when I want to be alone, and one of the unpleasant things about my first three years in Ceylon was that I almost always was living in someone else's bungalow or had someone else to live in mine. But of all the people I lived with out there, Tyrrell was far the best stable companion. He was very reserved, but very good company at the right time, unusually good-looking and with great personal charm. He was four years my senior and is one of the few of my Ceylon contemporaries who is still alive at the age of eighty-four. When he went on leave, my sister Bella came out at the end of 1907 to stay with me. She was with me until I was transferred to Hambantota in August, 1908, and her presence made a great difference to my life in Kandy.

The work in Kandy was, as I have said, very strenuous. I used to get up at about 6.30 in the morning and have my early tea on the verandah. For physical enjoyment there are few things better than the delicious hour and a half after dawn in a semi-tropical place like Kandy. Everything in Kandy sparkles, including the air; it is wonderfully soft and cool before the sun gets up high overhead. About seven a peon brought me four or five boxes containing all the letters. He opened them and I separated them out for the various departments, writing orders on them if necessary. In this way I was able to know exactly what had come into the office every day on the day. It was a pretty long business, but all the letters were over in the kachcheri by the time it opened and I went across to it. It meant that I worked without a break from seven to twelve, when I returned to the bungalow for tiffin. In the afternoon I worked in the office from one to five and often later, and more often than not I had to work on difficult papers after dinner in the bungalow. After the office was the sacrament of tennis. Night after night we all went up to the head of the Lake to the tennis courts, a grander and more social ritual than that of Jaffna with a continual flutter of females including a fluctuating stream of visitors, planters, army officers, and their wives and daughters.

After tennis I usually went down to the Kandy Club. In those days in an Asiatic station where there was 'the Club', it was a symbol and centre of British imperialism although perhaps we might not be fully conscious of it. It had normally a curious air of slight depression, but at the same time exclusiveness, superiority, isolation. Only the 'best people' and of course only white men were members. At the same time there was none of the physical luxuriousness, spaciousness, or at least comfort of a London club; it was, indeed, a poky, gloomy, and even rather sordid building. The habitués were the four or five civil servants, Major Colquhoun, the Gunner Captain, whose name I cannot remember, Lee, the solicitor; every now and then, particularly at week-ends, there would be an invasion of planters. The atmosphere was terribly masculine and public school. Even if we were not all gentlemen, we all had to behave, sober or drunk, as if we were, although when some of us were drunk—and drunkenness was not infrequent—it often seemed to me a very curious form of gentlemanliness. The Club was used for four purposes: to have a drink in, to play bridge, to dine in, to play billiards. As far as I was concerned the purposes, when I went to it, were performed in that order. I went to it after tennis and had a drink and played a rubber or two of bridge. Sometimes I stayed and had dinner there, and, if I had not too much work waiting for me in my bungalow, played billiards or bridge again after dinner.

I can still feel what I felt the first evening that Tyrrell took me down to the Club. I was the new boy again, nervous and uncomfortable. Freud says in one of his books that civilization consists in the renunciation of instinctive desires and that the newcomer to a civilized society, the child born into it—the new boy in fact—has to learn again and for himself the renunciation. I am not naturally what is called a good mixer or a good clubman, and I have always felt acutely that what applies to the newcomer into a civilized society applies to me when I have to plunge into the (to me) icy waters of a circle of four or more strangers gathered intimately together. I have to learn all over again to adjust the mask of my words, the façade of my feelings, to the hail-fellow-well-met or the not-hail-fellow-well-met formula of the school cricket field, dinner in the college hall, or the Kandy Club. I was particularly ill at ease during the first weeks in Kandy. The narrow circle in Jaffna, in which after two and a half years there was nothing new for me to learn about anyone, had made me forget how to accommodate myself to a roomful of strangers. The consequence was that I immediately disgraced myself. It was at bridge, which was absurd, for I was quite a good bridge player, quite up to the standard of the Club. But I was set down to play a rubber with a cantankerous old judge, called Templer, the hard drinking, sardonic Major, and the Chairman of the Ceylon Planters Association, Turner. I was the judge's partner, and I was terribly—and quite unnecessarily—nervous, and that was undoubtedly the explanation of why almost at once, holding quite a good hand which included six diamonds, I did not bid. When the hand had been played, 'I suppose, Woolf,' said the angry judge bitterly, 'in Jaffna you don't bid diamonds unless you have thirteen of them.' Inside I was as angry as the judge both with myself and with him, and I was also miserable. It was a good example of how much deeper pain goes than pleasure, and unkindness than kindness, that I was not in the least consoled when, having played the very next hand extremely well, I was highly praised by Turner and even Colquhoun, and got a grudging acknowledgment from my partner.

In a week or two, of course, I had found my social feet in Kandyan society, bid diamonds when I had six of them, had readjusted my mask, façade, and carapace to my new environment, and so was accepted as a good fellow, a good bridge player, and a fairly good tennis player by most people—and even grudgingly by Judge Templer. Kandy was a terribly social place and after my sister came to stay with me, we were hardly ever alone, for she was an extremely sociable person, the kind of person who under the most unfavourable circumstances can help to 'make the party go'. Living in a kind of hill station, we were invaded socially from so many different sides. Apart from the large permanent circumambient population of planters, there was a continual coming and going of very important officials who, like the greater fleas, always bring in their train a number of less important officials. The Governor himself had a Residence, The King's Pavilion, and Sir Hugh Clifford, who for some time was acting Governor, liked the place so much that he spent a good deal of time there. He was a formidable man, but by a piece of luck I happened to impress him as extremely competent, and this not only had a considerable effect upon my future career in Ceylon, but brought me into direct contact with him and his exalted circle in Kandy far more often than a mere Office Assistant to the Government Agent of the Central Province could have expected.

The most exalted region into which I stepped, partly by an accident, but also partly with Clifford, was that of an Empress, a real historical Empress or ex-Empress. She was the Empress Eugénie of France. She was—strangely, I think—a friend of Sir Thomas Lipton, who made his fortune out of tea, and early in 1908 he lent her his yacht to go round the world in. She arrived in Ceylon in February, and, as she had been born in 1826, she was then over eighty-one years old. One day in March a telegram came from the Colonial Secretary to the G.A. saying that Her Majesty the Empress would arrive the following day in Kandy, that the Governor had lent her the King's Pavilion where she would stay for a week, that she must be met at the railway station on arrival, and that everything should be done to make her visit a success. The G.A. was, as usual, out of Kandy, so I put on my best clothes and went down to the station to meet her. It was an absurd ceremony and it was the only time in my life that I have taken part as a protagonist in that kind of royal reception. I took the stationmaster with me and two or three policemen to see that no one got in the way of our procession down the platform and I had arranged for a carriage to take Her Majesty to King's Pavilion. When the train stopped two ladies-in-waiting and two gentlemen-in-waiting first got out of the carriage. I introduced myself to one of the gentlemen who told me that his name was Count Clary and he introduced me to the other three and to the Empress when she descended from the railway carriage. I told her that I represented the Government Agent and I hoped that she would let me know if there was anything at any time which we could do for her. The Empress seemed to me to be a tiny little bent old woman dressed completely in black with a black straw hat and a heavy black veil. I could not really see her face. The two ladies formed up one on each side of her and she began to walk slowly down the platform, while I, with the two gentlemen on either side of me, followed behind her. We crawled along at a snail's pace, stared at by a small crowd of spectators, and I was immediately given a lesson in the art of royal or diplomatic conversation by Count Clary. For no sooner had we begun to move than he looked up at the sky which was the bright blue, clear, cloudless sky of Kandy, and, in a tone of voice which was obviously calculated to put at his ease even an English official, said 'And do you often have thunderstorms here, Mr Woolf?' By the time we had reached the end of the platform, he was telling me that his grandfather had spoken to a man who had been born in the seventeenth century.

The Empress must have assumed that I was in fact the G.A. and so the equivalent of a Préfet d'un Départment in France, for I received the following letter from Count Clary:

Wednesday, 4th March
King's Pavilion, Kandy.

My dear Mr. Woolf,

Her Majesty, the Empress, wants me to ask you to tea for tomorrow Thursday, at 4.30 p.m. If you have a previous engagement, just let me know, and it won't matter in the least, as Her Majesty would be sorry to disturb you.

Come in ordinary day-clothes.

Yrs very sincerely
Clary

On Thursday in ordinary day-clothes I went up to the Pavilion. The whole business seemed to me absurd, for the ceremonial was exactly what I imagine it would have been if the old lady, Eugénie-Marie de Montijo de Guzman, Comtesse de Téba, had still been the wife of Napoleon III and Impératrice des Français. The fact that she had ceased to be Empress of the French thirty-seven years ago appeared to make no difference to the etiquette of her Court in King's Pavilion, Kandy. It seemed to me not inappropriate that the old lady in her make-believe Court should be, under a misapprehension, entertaining a young very pseudo-Government Agent. I was met by Count Clary with immense politeness and conducted by him into one of the smaller rooms—all rooms in King's Pavilion are very large—where once more I was introduced to the other three members of the retinue. After five minutes' fluent conversation one of the ladies-in-waiting left the room and returned immediately saying that the Empress would receive me. I was then led off by her and Count Clary to the enormous central room. Here a large square had been walled off, as it were, by screens and inside it a kind of throne room arranged with chairs and sofas. At the far end Her Majesty sat as upon a throne in solitary state. I felt vaguely that I ought to bow and kiss her hand, but that was beyond me, and instead we shook hands. A chair was put in front of her and I was invited to sit on it, while Clary and the lady-in-waiting stood on each side of the Empress. After a few minutes she rose and we moved in slow procession into another room where tea and the other gentleman- and lady-in-waiting awaited us.

We all sat round the table and the Empress talked or asked me questions. If you look her up in *Petit Larousse*, that monument of lexicography, all you are told about her is 'Célèbre par sa beauté, elle eut une grande influence sur l'empereur, qu'elle poussa à défendre les intérêts catholiques dans le monde.' Most women who have been so beautiful that their beauty (and often little else) is recorded in dictionaries and encyclopaedias—indeed also women of great beauty who have never been sufficiently famous or infamous to have their names recorded in *Petit Larousse*, when they are old or very old, retain in the shape of face or features or in the expression something from which you can see how beautiful they must have been. This was not true of the Empress Eugénie. In 1908 her face to me seemed positively ugly. Other accounts by people who knew her well do not agree with this; for instance, Ethel Smyth wrote of the Empress in *Impressions that Remained*:

> I remember saying to the Duchesse de Mouchy that it was hard to believe that she could ever have been more beautiful than now, and the reply was: 'I think in some ways she is more beautiful now than when she was young, because years and sorrow have done away with the accidents of beauty—youth itself for instance, and colouring—and revealed the exquisiteness of design.'

Well, there you are—I may have been blind to all this, though I must say that what the Duchesse says about the 'accidents' of beauty seems to me a little suspect—to call youth and colour accidents is to beg nine-tenths of the question.

The Empress was extremely affable, lively, talkative. Like nearly all great or very well-known people whom I have met, she asked innumerable questions and would not stay for an answer. All that I can remember of her conversation is that she made 'curious thin little jokes' (as I wrote to Lytton), all of which I have naturally forgotten, and that she gave a very long, vivacious, but slightly silly, account of how when driving to the Peradeniya Gardens that morning she had seen a dog and a chicken fighting in the middle of the highroad. She was anxious to know whether dogs and chickens habitually fought in Ceylon, but when I said 'No', I do not think she really stayed even for that answer. I was given a very regal, but warm, good-bye, and as I was making my final bow, Count Clary, with some assumed hesitation, said that, as I had been so good as to ask Her Majesty to let me know of anything which I could do for her, there was one thing Her Majesty would very much like to see, if that were in any way possible. Her Majesty had heard that the Buddha's tooth was sometimes shown to people and she had a great desire to see it; was there any possibility of my being able to arrange this? I said that I thought I might be able to arrange this for the afternoon of the day after tomorrow, and would let Count Clary know definitely later.

The facts about Buddha's tooth were strange. In 1908 in the great Dalada Maligawa, which means literally The Palace of the Tooth, but is always translated The Temple of the Tooth, there was housed one of the most sacred Buddhist relics, Budda's Tooth. (The whole Maligawa was originally the King's Palace, the Temple, in Sinhalese vihare, being embedded in it.) In my day the relic was kept in a small locked inner shrine in the centre of the vihare; in the shrine was a table and on the table five bell-shaped caskets, called karanduas, one within the other like Chinese boxes, and under the last and smallest casket lay the tooth. The tooth could never be taken out or shown without the consent of both the Manager or Guardian of the Temple, the Diyawadana Nilame, in 1908 a fine old Kandyan chief and Ratemahatmaya, called Nugawela, and the Government Agent. In fact both the G.A. and the Diwa Nilame, as he was usually called, had a key to the shrine, and without the two being present the door could not be unlocked. In practice I, as O.A., kept the G.A.'s key, and arranged with Nugawela Ratemahatmaya for unlocking the door if and when the Tooth was to be shown.

The relic was shown annually at the great festival or Perahera every August, and otherwise only to very distinguished persons. In my year in Kandy I opened the shrine only three times, once for the Perahera, once at my request for the Empress, and once at the Diwa Nilame's request for Reginald Farrer, the Himalayan botanist, who had become a Buddhist. At the Perahera the Tooth was taken out of the Temple, placed on the back of an elephant and carried round the Temple in a procession before enormous crowds of Sinhalese who flocked into Kandy for the festival. If shown to distinguished persons, the caskets were taken off so that the visitor could see the Tooth, but it was not touched.

The reason for the institution of a joint guardianship of the relic by the Buddhists and the non-Buddhist Government was the disorder and ill-feeling which had arisen in the past and during the course of its unfortunate history. According to tradition, after being kept for 800 years in India, it was brought to Ceylon in the fourth century A.D. About 1,000 years later the Indians of the Malabar coast captured it and took it back to India, but it was recovered and again brought to Ceylon by King Prakrama Bahu III in the fourteenth century. In the next two hundred years the island suffered from the chaos of lawlessness and war, and the Tooth was hidden in various places, including Gampola. There seems to be no doubt whatsoever that in 1560 it was discovered by the Portuguese, taken to Goa by Don Constantine de Braganza, and there publicly burnt by the Archbishop in the presence of the Viceroy of India. However a short time afterwards there were at least two 'authentic' Buddha's Teeth in Ceylon. The present Tooth was established in the Maligawa by the Kandyan King in 1566 and it has remained there ever since. I have seen it, as I said, at close quarters three times and I should say that, whatever else it may be, it has never been a human tooth. If my memory is correct, it is a canine tooth, about three inches long and curved. Sir James Emerson Tennent, in his book *Ceylon* written in 1859, says: 'Its popular acceptance, notwithstanding this anomalous shape, may probably be accounted for by the familiarity of the Kandyans, under their later kings, with the forms of some of the Hindu deities, amongst whom Vishnu and Kali are occasionally depicted with similarly projecting canines.' But I think one can find a likeness to the Tooth nearer home than the Hindu deities; in my recollection its shape closely resembles that of the teeth of the Sinhalese Devils or Yakku who play such an important part in the everyday beliefs of the ordinary Buddhist Sinhalese and are always represented in their sculpture and mural paintings with projecting canine teeth curved upwards.

I got hold of the Diwa Nilame and he agreed to show the Tooth to the Empress, and as Sir Hugh Clifford was in Kandy, I told him about it for he had not seen the relic and I felt sure he would like to be present. He met me outside the Maligawa and we waited in the road for the Empress to arrive. When she came, an absurd procession formed up. Clifford was a very tall man, over six foot high, with a broad strong body and a large head and face. He and the Empress led the procession and they walked so slowly that it was like a slow motion picture, and the Empress in the black clothes, black hat, and black veil of the eternally black French widow was so short and bent that Clifford could hardly get his head down low enough to hear what she said through the thick veil. I followed behind with the ladies- and gentlemen-in-waiting, making the bright diplomatic synthetic conversation which is appropriate when one walks officially in procession behind an Empress of the French and the Colonial Secretary of a British Crown Colony. It all passed off extremely well. Nugawela, the Diwa Nilame, in full Ratemahatmaya costume—you can see exactly what he looked like, for he is sitting third seat from the left in the front row in plate 0—was very dignified and impressive and the Empress was suitably impressed. I earned a good deal of unearned kudos from the Colonial Secretary.

Despite the concentrated intensity and long hours of my work in Kandy I lived a strenuous social life. For an hour and a half every day I took violent exercise either at tennis, squash rackets, or hockey. Rackets I played with the Superintendent of Police, Alexander; he was a fine figure of a man and an Oxford Blue and he was so much better than I was that, although we must have played dozens of games, I beat him only once and that must have been by pure accident. I played hockey with the Punjabi regiment. They were absolutely mad on hockey and the subaltern asked me to come and play in their practice games whenever I liked to do so. It was a rather exacting business; they played like demons and some of them were very good, but they got frantically excited and, when they lost their tempers, dangerous.

There were three battalions in the regiment, one Moslem, one Hindu, and one, I think, mixed. Our men were Hindus and the two other battalions were in Colombo. Once a year they had an inter-battalion hockey tournament and the subaltern took our first team down to Colombo to play in it. The whole regiment was mad with excitement. For some reason the British officers never played in the tournament though subahdars did. Our team got into the final and in the second half they lost their tempers and the two sides went for one another with their hockey sticks. The officers, who were watching the game from the touchline, rushed into the mêlée to part the combatants, but before they could stop the fight two players had been laid out insensible.

I liked the Punjabis, but they could be curiously savage. On Saturdays we sometimes got up two scratch teams to play hockey; some planters, keen on hockey, used to come in to play; about six or seven men from the regiment, the subaltern, myself, and Lee, the solicitor, completed the 22 players. In one of these games I was much interested by what was obviously a 'racial' incident. I was playing back, with a planter playing half-back on my wing in front of me, and he was obviously Eurasion, but not Ceylonese. One of our opponents, the outside-left forward facing us, was one of the best of the regimental players. For some reason, which seemed to me purely 'racial', he took against the planter, and, whenever he got near him, instead of hitting the ball took a full-blooded swipe at the unfortunate planter's shins. I knew the Punjabi quite well and had often played with him, and I tried gently and tactfully to dissuade him from pursuing this vendetta. I was entirely unsuccessful and there followed a very painful scene. The planter, having received a crack on the shin for about the tenth time, lost his head, his nerve, and his temper; bursting into tears and shrieking wildly he went for his small, eel-like, elusive tormenter. We seized the two of them and the Punjabi was sent—smiling—off the field.

In writing an autobiography I find that every now and again I am in considerable doubt whether I ought or not to include some trivial or highly personal incident. Having been for 40 years both an editor who has to publish reviews by other people and a reviewer myself, I am very rarely surprised by what reviewers say. But I was slightly surprised (and much amused) to find that some reviewers of *Sowing*, the first volume of my autobiography, were irritated—almost outraged—by the fact that, though an intelligent man, I wrote quite simply about some incidents and my own reactions to them. For instance, the reviewer in the *Times Literary Supplement* said that he was 'startled' because I remarked that 'I remained a virgin until the age of twenty-five; the manner in which I lost my virginity in Jaffna, the Tamil town in the north of Ceylon, I will relate in a later chapter.' The reviewer goes on to say: 'Surely most people would find it natural to say either more or less about this event', and he complains that 'again and again throughout the book the reader is given like occasions to wonder how such an intelligent man can claim to have such simple reactions.' What amuses me in this is the writer's profound ignorance, not merely of my psychology, but of the way in which the mind and heart of all men, intelligent or unintelligent, work. Of course, many of the reactions of intelligent people are just as ridiculous, silly and simple as those of the most unintelligent; the only difference is that in ordinary life we are clever enough to conceal the fact from the world in general and even from the not quite intelligent enough intellectuals. But if one has the temerity to write an autobiography, then one is under an obligation not to conceal. The only point in an autobiography is to give, as far as one can, in the most simple, clear, and truthful way, a picture, first of one's own personality and of the people whom one has known, and secondly of the society and age in which one lived. To do this entails revealing as simply as possible one's own simplicity, absurdity, trivialities, nastiness. Now it seems to me that almost any incident which has stuck in one's memory for fifty years—such as the hockey match which I have just described and one or two things which I am about to describe—are probably relevant either to the picture of the personality or to the portrait of the age.

The first incident was rather ridiculous. I woke up one morning feeling giddy and sick and, when I got out of bed, the room went round and round me and I had to sit down on the floor and crawl back into bed. I sent for a doctor and he, to my surprise, immediately diagnosed correctly the disease. He said that I had caught a cold in a nerve at the back of my neck and that if I stayed in bed for a day, I should be perfectly all right. For the next 24 hours I stayed in bed, doing my kachcheri work there, and as the giddiness had completely gone off, I got up next day and worked in the kachcheri. In the evening I was due to dine with Mr and Mrs Middleton and their rose-like daughter, Rose. He was a Judge of the Supreme Court and was in Kandy holding the Assizes; he and Mrs Middleton were pleasant people, but almost impossibly respectable. The Judge had rapped me on the knuckles for not having attended his Court officially, as Deputy Fiscal, at the opening of the Assizes. I had therefore to be on my very best behaviour for the evening, which I anticipated as pretty dull, though Rose was admittedly an attraction. They were living in a house on the other side of the Kandy Lake, which was perched perpendicularly above the road and reached from the road by a flight of 25 or 30 stone steps. I went by ricksha and told the ricksha boy to come back for me about ten. The evening was pretty dull and after dinner at about a quarter to ten, as Mrs Middleton was showing me some photographs, I suddenly felt the appalling giddiness come upon me again. Rather foolishly I thought that, if they saw me stagger about, they would think I was drunk. So I said nothing and held on grimly until ten, shook hands and by an act of will and just holding on to chairs and tables got myself fairly steadily out of the house and on to the terrace. There I was faced by the terrifying flight of steps. I managed somwhow to get down upright half-way, but then lost my footing and fell straight on to the ricksha, to the amazement of the boy, who certainly thought I was drunk. I managed to crawl into my own bungalow and bed. Next morning when I woke up I was all right and I have never again had a return of the disease.

The next Kandy incident is one of those curious affairs of the heart which I find always fascinating and almost tragic to observe, as they reveal the unending complications of the human mind and the human heart. I was very friendly with a young man in Kandy, Christopher Smith. He came to me one day and asked me whether I knew the Misses Robinson. I only just knew them. They were the daughters of a planter, and Mrs Robinson had taken a house in Kandy for a month or two and was living in it with her two daughters, Ethel aged 22 and Rachel aged 19. The two girls had a passion for riding and had brought their horses with them. Smith, who was 28, was extremely good-looking, intelligent, charming, but given to fits of moodiness, silence, and indecision. He told me that he was much attracted by Ethel and that almost every evening he rode with the two young ladies round the hills above Kandy. The difficulty for him was that he always had to take Rachel as well as Ethel and he therefore was never able to be alone with Ethel. Would I, like a good fellow, come and ride with them and contrive to be with Rachel so that he might have a duologue with Ethel? I must say that I didn't much fancy the job, but I liked Christopher—whom of course in those days I always called Smith just as he always called me Woolf—very much, and so I weakly agreed.

In 1907 Kandy and its surroundings were enticingly beautiful. It was half-way between the low country and the high mountains and enjoyed the best of every climate and every world. The great lake, which was the centre of the European part of the town, lay in a hollow with the hills gently rising up all round it. These hills had been little built over and they were so covered with sub-tropical trees and flowering trees and flowers that the buildings were hardly visible. In the hills round and about the town a series of Drives and Rides have been constructed and named after the wives of Governors of Ceylon, Lady Horton's Walk, Lady Longden's Drive, and so on. They are extraordinarily romantic, winding in those days through unspoilt Kandyan mountain country with views of the Lake, of lovely Kandyan villages with their terraced paddy fields, of more distant mountain peaks, or the beautiful Dumbara valley.

Every evening for some weeks Smith and I used to ride with the two girls through these exquisite, gentle, flowery, deserted roads. I have said before that I do not know whether Kipling's stories were photographs of Anglo-Indian society and therefore of Ceylon society in 1907 or whether we modelled our lives upon the lives of Mrs Hauksbee, Otis Yeere, and Mrs Mallows. I remember sometimes in those rides with Rachel suddenly waking up, as it were, in the middle of Lady McCarthy's Drive or Lady Horton's Walk from a rather gentle, romantic dream, and asking myself whether I was indeed Office Assistant to the Government Agent, Central Province, who would have to go to the Bogambra Jail before breakfast next morning to see a man hanged, and who was now talking to a planter's daughter merely in order that Christopher Smith might talk to her sister, or whether in fact we were living a story by Kipling Under the Deodars.

I have always been greatly attracted by the undiluted female mind, as well as by the female body. And I mean the adjective 'undiluted', for I am not thinking of the exceptional women with exceptional minds, like Cleopatra or Mrs Carlyle or Jane Austen or Virginia Woolf, I am thinking of the 'ordinary woman', undistinguished, often unintellectual and unintrospective. The minds of most women differ from the minds of most men in a way which I feel very distinctly, but which becomes rather indistinct when I try to describe it. Their minds seem to me to be gentler, more sensitive, more civilized. Even in the many stupid, vain, tiresome women this quality is often preserved below the exasperating surface. But it is not easy to catch it or bring it to the surface. You can only do so by listening to and by being really interested in what they say (and it is extraordinarily difficult ever to be interested in or listen to what anyone else, particularly a woman, says, because one is always more interested in and thinking about what one will say oneself after she has stopped talking).[1] I think I have taught myself gradually to be interested in what women say to me and to listen attentively to what they are saying, for in this way you get every now and again a glimpse or rather a breath of this pure, curiously female quality of mind. It is the result I suppose partly of their upbringing, which is usually so different from that of the male in all classes, and partly of fundamental, organic differences of sex. And that again I suppose is why, as a male, I get a romantic, even perhaps a sentimental, pleasure from feeling the quality.

It is necessary to say all this if I am to make clear to myself and therefore to my readers the nature of the relationship which developed in the long evening rides among the hills of Kandy between myself and Rachel. But first I had better deal with the protagonists, the *causa causans* of our rides, Christopher and Ethel. I became extremely uneasy about the whole business, because, as it seemed to me, Ethel was falling more and more in love with Christopher and he was completely unable to decide either to attach or detach himself. The situation was complicated by the fact that the moment was rapidly approaching when he was going back to England for six months. Nothing that I said could bring him to make a decision and eventually the day came for our last ride. He appeared in my bungalow in the morning and said that he could not face a last ride and that he had therefore sent round a message to say that he could not manage a ride, but would come round to the house in the late afternoon and say goodbye. He was not going to propose, and he besought me to come with him as he could not face a tête-à-tête with Ethel. I went and I do not think I have ever spent a more painful three-quarters of an hour.

As for Rachel, I liked her very much and reached the maximum of

[1] Goethe shows in an amusing passage in *Elective Affinities* (quoted by H. O. Pappe in *John Stuart Mill and the Harriet Taylor Myth*) that he had noted this phenomenon: 'Ottilie followed the conversation attentively though she took no part in it. The next morning Eduard said to Charlotte: "She is a pleasant and interesting girl." "Interesting," Charlotte replied with a smile, "why she never said a word." "Did she not," Eduard rejoined while he seemed to retrace his thoughts, "how very strange!"'

intimacy with her allowed by the extraordinary etiquette and reticencies of the age. It must be remembered that up to the end of our acquaintance she wrote to me as Mr Woolf and I wrote to her as Miss Robinson. I had for her a real affection without ever at all falling in love with her; although she was not in the least intellectual and cared for few of the things for which I cared most, I liked the feel of her mind in the way I have described above, and so said to her what really came into my mind and listened, because I was interested in what she said. In the last letter she ever wrote to me, which was to tell me that she was engaged and would shortly marry, she reminded me—of what I had forgotten—that I had once given her a long dissertation upon matrimony and what her attitude to it should be. When I was transferred from Kandy to Hambantota, I did not see her for nearly two years, but then had a curious meeting with her. I had been told by the Government to go up country and meet the Government Agent of the Province adjoining my District to discuss with him what new regulations we considered necessary for the control of rinderpest which was ravaging my District and his Province. I had a two-day journey by road and train right up into the central mountains in order to meet him, and the place of our meeting was quite close to Rachel's father's tea estate. Mrs Robinson wrote and asked me to spend the two nights I would be up there on the estate. I accepted with alacrity.

I found it extremely pleasant to meet Rachel again and her mother and father were very nice to me. In the early morning before my meeting with the G.A. she lent me a fiery little chestnut horse and we went for a long ride. I had just spent a long time in the most solitary life in the dry heat of the low country and here suddenly I was galloping through the cool sparkling mountain air by the side of a young woman of whom I was fond. I had lived in Hambantota a life of complete chastity except for one curious night in Colombo when I had had to go there for my examination in Sinhalese. In all that time the only white women I ever spoke to were the wives of the irrigation engineers and that casually and rarely. I seemed now to be in a completely different world, the comfortable and comforting femininity of the Robinsons' bungalow—Mr Robinson was an English country gentleman who had reconstructed his English environment on the top of a Ceylon mountain—compared with the austerity of my bungalow in the bare sandy compound down there in Hambantota.

My sister Bella, when she was staying with me in Kandy, had

once gone up and spent a few days with Rachel on this estate[1] and she had written to me that Mr and Mrs Robinson had spoken so warmly of me that she thought they would like me as a son-in-law. They were so nice to me now that I could not help rather uncomfortably remembering this. And before dinner on my last evening Rachel took me for a walk on the estate. We had slipped into a long silence and suddenly the narrow path turned round a great rock and brought us out on to a broad ledge with a sheer drop thousands of feet down to the sea level and the low country, and with a superb, terrific view over the miles and miles of jungle to, in the dim distance, the line of the sea and the coast—and somewhere there Hambantota and my bungalow. A strange, painful feeling came over me. I felt as if somehow I had been taken up into this high mountain and was being shown all the kingdoms of the earth and was being tempted, but the temptation was not the kingdom of the earth below, but in the girl beside me. I may be quite wrong about this, but I felt Rachel herself was waiting and I stood by her in miserable silence until we turned away and walked back silently to the house. In the house Mr and Mrs Robinson were waiting for us and I spent a very uncomfortable evening. I had a long journey before me next day, as I had decided to bicycle straight down the mountain side to my district instead of going half-way round the island through Colombo by train. So I had brought my bicycle with me to the estate and before dawn I got up and was given a cup of tea, and I said goodbye to Rachel. I saw her and her mother and father only once or twice again, though she used occasionally to write to me even after she married. As dawn was breaking, I climbed by a rocky track to the top of the mountain, a coolie carrying my bag and bicycle, and then through the clouds and mist over the top and down on to a road. There I tipped the coolie, tied my bag to my bicycle, and coasted mile after mile down through the deliciously cool fresh mountain country until I reached the plain and jungles of the low country which from the ledge high up on the mountain last night I had looked down upon with Rachel by my side. At midday in the dry burning heat I came to the boundary of my District, and there

[1] In a letter to Bella when she was on the estate I made what I think is rather a good joke. I was keeping for Mrs Lewis, the G.A.'s wife, while she was away from Kandy, her parrot. Unfortunately my cat killed and ate the parrot. I wrote the appalling news to Bella, adding: 'Nothing can be done except to say: Requiescat in Pussy.'

waiting for me by the roadside was my horsekeeper with my horse and my dogs. I got on the horse and rode the weary miles to Wirawila and Tissamaharama in regret for Rachel, dejection, and yet at the same time with a kind of relief.

That, I suppose, was in 1909 or 1910; I must return to Kandy and 1907. There was too much work at Kandy, though I never really mind having too much work. Some of it I liked very much, but a good deal of it was boring or to me uninteresting. One was continually having to deal with the planters and their estates and labour, and there was much business connected with the sale and settlement of Crown Land. All this I found dull and irritating. On the other hand everything to do with the Sinhalese seemed to me enchanting. The Kandyans fifty years ago, both the Ratemahatmayas, the feudal chiefs and headmen, and the villagers were generally, and often also individually, the most charming people I have ever come across. They were typically mountain people, independent, fine mannered, lively, laughing, in their enchanting villages hidden away in the mountains, and isolated, unchanged and unchanging. It was extraordinary to deal with them after the rather dour Tamil of Jaffna living behind his cadjan fence under the remorseless sun in the unending plain. There was so much work in the kachcheri that I very rarely got out of Kandy itself for an enquiry in these remote villages, but the first time I did, I was astonished by my reception. I rode up 24 miles into the hills to a place called Urugala and arrived there after dark in a thunderstorm. Half a mile from the village the headmen and villagers met me in procession and brought me in with tom-toms and dancers. Then I had to stand in the rain for ten minutes while each member of the crowd came and prostrated himself, touching the ground with his forehead.

In a letter to Lytton describing this, I tried to defend the system, arguing that the Europeanising of non-Europeans is a mistake, that it is best for every race to remain 'as it was before Adam' (a curious and somewhat exaggerated idea). The Kandyan, I said, grovels on the ground and touches your boots, but has retained his independence and his manners. This letter reflects my growing awareness of the problem of imperialism and my personal relation to it in the plains of Jaffna, the mountain villages of Kandy, and later the jungles of Hambantota. For a long time I was uneasily ambivalent, exaggerating as in this letter, my imperialist, stern Sahib attitude to compensate for or soothe a kind of social conscience which began to condemn and dislike the whole system. Kandyan society in my day—quite apart from the O.A. to the G.A. Central Province, the G.A., the Governor and Government of Ceylon, and far off in London Edward VII by the Grace of God and the British Raj—quite apart from this extraordinary, hierarchical, and complicated engine of Empire and imperial government, Kandyan society in these villages was purely feudal. The Nugawelas, Rattwattes, and all the other great Kandyan landowning families were feudal chiefs, and the procession, and tom-toms, and prostrations which greeted the O.A. were merely an example of manners ordinarily displayed by the villager to the feudal chief, and now displayed towards the highly sophisticated product of St Paul's School and Trinity College, Cambridge, who, by a cynical joke of history, represented Edward VII by the Grace of God in the village of Urugala on 14 September 1907.

I do not think that anyone who has got close to a feudal society like this one in Urugala and all the other Kandyan villages, who to some extent has lived within it and has observed it passionately, sympathetically, and at the same time critically, can truthfully deny that on the surface it has socially a satisfying depth, harmony, beauty. And it was perhaps not only or entirely on the surface. I cannot believe that I was altogether mistaken and self-deluded when riding, walking, and talking to the smiling men and women in those villages. I felt that there was some depth of happiness rather than pleasure, of satisfaction, which is a good thing and which the western world is losing or has lost. Moreover, I was up above in the feudal hierarchy, one of the super-Chiefs, the Princes, or the Boyars, and, however much one may dislike the fuss and ceremony of social systems—and I do hate them—one cannot be impervious to the flattery of being a top dog liked by the underdogs. I certainly, all through my time in Ceylon, enjoyed my position and the flattery of being the great man and the father of the people. That was why, as time went on, I became more and more ambivalent, politically schizophrenic, an anti-imperialist who enjoyed the fleshpots of imperialism, loved the subject peoples and their way of life, and knew from the inside how evil the system was beneath the surface for ordinary men and women.

Another thing I liked about the Sinhalese was their religion. I am essentially and fundamentally irreligious, as I have explained in *Sowing*, but, if one must have a religion, Buddhism seems to me superior to all other religions. When I got to Kandy, I had already passed my examination in Tamil and I now had to take the Sinhalese examination. There is in the Maligawa a curious octagonal building, called the Oriental Library, because it contains some Pali texts; in my day the librarian was a Buddhist priest called Gunaratana. He became my pundit and taught me Sinhalese. Gradually I got to like him very much; we became friends and I used to go up into the Octagon of an evening when I could find time and sit with him on a kind of verandah overlooking the Lake and talk to him about Buddhism. It has to be admitted that he was the only real Buddhist whom I met in Ceylon, the only one who understood, believed, and practised the 'higher' doctrines of this strange religion. As he explained it to me, it was a philosophy rather than a religion, a metaphysic which has eliminated God and gods, a code of conduct civilised, austere, springing ultimately from a profound pessimism. I could never myself believe in the Buddhism of this priest; it seems to me to be, like all metaphysics, a dream which is after all nothing but a dream. But it is a civilised and a humane dream of considerable beauty and it has eliminated most of the crude anthropomorphic and theological nonsense which encrusts other religions. There is another thing about Buddhism which appeals to me. I like the way in which every now and again a Buddhist will throw up his worldly life and withdraw into a life of solitude and contemplation. I know, of course, that these withdrawals are not unknown in other religions. But the Buddhist does not withdraw in order to do penance for his sins, to mortify or crucify himself or other people in order to obtain redemption, as others do. In the instances which I came across in Ceylon, he felt a sudden urge to leave the weariness, the fever, and the fret of his business and pleasures, his family, friends, and enemies, his loves and hates, and subside into solitude and simplicity. I once in Anuradhapura saw a man sweeping the courtyard round one of the dagobas. He was dressed like a sweeper, but there was something rather strange about him. I got into conversation with him and found that he had been a wealthy business man in Colombo; he was highly educated and spoke perfect English. Suddenly at the age of about fifty he had felt an irresistible desire to throw it all up and to follow the path of the Buddha which led him, not to penance or mortification of fakirs, saniyasis, dervishes, or monks, but to a life of gentle contemplation sweeping the courtyard of a dagoba. It is not a withdrawal and occupation which would ever appeal to me personally, but I respect the man to whom they appealed and the religion which inspired him.

There was much to be said against Buddhism and its priests fifty years ago in Ceylon. There were two establishments, both in Kandy, in which the Ceylon priesthood received its training, Malwatte and Asgiriya. My pundit, when he got to know me, talked frankly about things and he was, as a purist, greatly concerned at the maladministration and the corrupt teaching of Buddhism in the two establishments in those days. He had himself a very poor idea of the ordinary Buddhist priest turned out by them. I often came across priests in the course of my official duties, and I must admit that my experience confirmed what he said. They were often very nice people, but their minds and their everyday life had as little connection with the Buddhism of the Buddha and my pundit as those of the ordinary village Rector in England have to do with the Christianity of Christ. The religion of the man in the street, the villager in the village, also had nothing to do with my pundit's religion, but Buddhism, perhaps wisely, accepts this and recognizes that different people must be given different beliefs, a different Buddhism, according to the stage of spiritual development attained by them. In practice, the result was that the religion of the vast mass of Sinhalese villagers consisted to a considerable extent of superstition and devil worship.

I shall always remember, as typical of this Buddhist flock and their Buddhist shepherd, a saffron-robed priest who came to my tent after I had had dinner one evening when I was on circuit in one of the remotest spots in my District of Hambantota, the roadless country in the foothills of the mountains of Sabaragamuwa. I gave him a chair and we sat together, first in the dusk and then the bright moonlight, outside the tent in a lovely meadow—so rare in that district—looking towards the graceful hills and beyond them the misty mountains. We talked and many villagers came and squatted round us near enough to take a respectful, but often amused, part in the conversation. The tranquillity and loveliness of this summer of the snakeless meadow—though I daresay the meadow swarmed with snakes—but that is what it felt like to me, so that when I looked across the meadow to the hills the tranquility and loveliness brought a few sentimental tears into my eyes. But there was no sentimentality about my Buddhist priest. He was a character, a card, a humorist, a realist. He flung himself about in his chair, cracked his jokes, violently rubbed his face and nose with his hand. He was a priest of a small vihare in the neighbourhood, and all he thought about was its revenue, what he could get out of the land or the Government or anyone or anything on earth. He wanted to get something out of me—what it was I have completely forgotten. He talked and talked, and laughed, and watched me with his cunning beady eyes, and the villagers put in a word now and then, laughed respectfully when we laughed, and looked at one another, I noticed, occasionally out of the corner of their eyes. And I realised with amusement that he was not really a Buddhist priest; he was just like them, a villager, but in a saffron robe.

Yet, when all this has been said, Buddhism, even in its debased or most unsophisticated form, even in the devil-worshipping villager and his villager priest, was in many ways a good religion. The way of life as preached by Gautama Buddha is extraordinarily gentle, unaggressive, humane, far more so, it seems to me, in its verbal presentation and attitude than even that preached in the Sermon on the Mount. I think this gentleness and humanity somehow or other filters down even through the debased Buddhism into the minds and everyday lives of the most ignorant villagers. On poya days, the days of the full moon, I used to like to go and sit in the Maligawa in Kandy and watch the ceremony, the ceremony of a civilised religion. The villagers, whole families, men, women, and children, would flock in with their offerings of flowers. For hours the priest would sit reading from the sacred books, and all round him sat the people in family groups with their little children and babies, occasionally talking or eating, but imbibing unconsciously, it seemed to me, something of this doctrine of quietude and gentleness. It differed entirely from the scenes of worship in Roman Catholic countries, where people still flock into churches and cathedrals, for there was none of that horrible insistence upon sin and crucifixion, and much less tawdry worship of bad statues.

Since in the previous paragraph I have said something about Buddhism and Christianity as they appear to me, I ought to say something about Hinduism and Muhammadanism, both of which I have had to observe to some extent at close quarters. I had a good deal to do with Muhammadans and their religion for some time in Hambantota, as I shall explain later. From a purely practical point of view there is something to be said for this religion, just as there is for Judaism, to which it bears a family likeness. But it is too hard, formal, and hostile to the infidel to have any appeal to me. Hinduism, which was all about me for my two and a half years in Jaffna, is entirely different. In its ordinary, everyday form it repels me—the multiplicity of its florid Gods, their grotesque images, the ugly exuberance of the temples, the horrible juggernaut processions with the terrible retinue of fakirs, saniyasis, and beggars. All this prejudiced me against Hinduism and made me, I think, blind to some of its manifestations during my years in Ceylon. When I visited the island again after fifty years in 1960, on my way to Mannar I met in the Anuradhapura Rest House Sir Kanthiah Vaithianathan. When he heard that I was going on to Mannar, he asked me to come and see him at his house there and also the Hindu Tiruketheesvaram temple which he is restoring at great cost. He explained to me, as we went round, the symbolism behind the images and the ceremonies, and in his very clear and sincere exposition I got for the first time some idea of what 'higher' Hinduism meant to a civilised man like my host. Like the esoteric Buddhism of my friend the priest Gunaratana, this esoteric Hinduism was a metaphysic rather than a religion. Yet it seemed to me inferior to Gunaratana's Buddhism, because it was a tiresome symbolism and therefore had never completely disentangled itself from the crude, uncivilised superstition connected with the Gods and Goddesses and their ceremonies.

To return to the Kandyan Sinhalese and my relations with them, as I have said, I was too much tied to my office in Kandy and only rarely could get away into their villages. But I got to know a good deal about them from enquiries which I had to hold in the kachcheri, and in particular from the strange procedure with regard to Kandyan marriages and divorce. This procedure was characteristic of the inveterate empiricism of British imperialism and British administration in Ceylon. The Kandyans have—or had in 1907—some very curious marriage customs or laws. There were two forms of marriage, *bina* in which the husband lived in his wife's house, and *diga* in which the wife lived in the husband's house. In certain cases polyandry was legal and customary, the woman being married to two brothers; the rights of each husband with regard to sleeping with the wife were strictly defined according to a timetable, for each had so many nights in a month. The British allowed these laws and customs to continue, but for some strange reason their administration was kept entirely in the hands of the Government Agent. That meant that in practice the marriage and divorce, in fact all the matrimonial affairs of these Kandyan villagers, were handed over to me, a young man who had been only two or three years in Ceylon. This fantastic system seemed to work quite well; at any rate the enquiries which I had to conduct in the kachcheri, particularly the divorce cases, fascinated me. From them I learnt a very great deal about the way of life of the villagers and the way their minds worked. Both the woman and the man had a right to a divorce on the ground of adultery, desertion, mutual consent, or inability to live happily together. It was the last ground which produced the most revealing cases, for they meant that one of the parties wanted and the other party did not agree to a divorce. Sometimes half the village might be called as witnesses and all the afternoon my room would be full of villagers. I am afraid that I must often have irritated my staff, headmen and clerks who had to be present, by allowing cases to drag on all the afternoon and witnesses to pour out their interminable stories, for if I encouraged them so that they forgot their fear and shyness in the strange atmosphere of my room, I would often get remarkable glimpses into the minds and domestic lives of people who, though on the surface so remote from myself, were to me fascinating, being often lovely to look at, charming, lively, gay, and sometimes tragic. Also it was extraordinarily interesting that every now and again you learnt in one of these cases what it was so rarely that you heard in Ceylon, the woman's side of the case. Not often, it is true, even in the Kandy kachcheri, but occasionally a woman bringing a case or resisting one would shed her genuine or assumed shyness and suddenly reveal in a torrent of words what her life, what her side of the picture was like up there in the mountains.

The most unpleasant work which I had to do in Kandy—and indeed everywhere in Ceylon—was connected with the prisons. The Government Agent held the office of Fiscal in his Province and the Office Assistant was Deputy Fiscal, and the powers and duties of the Fiscal were, I suppose, roughly those of the Sheriff in England. One of the Fiscal's duties was to be present in a prison when anyone was hanged or flogged and to certify that the sentence had been duly carried. The G.A. or A.G.A. was expected to pay surprise visits occasionally to any prison in his territory and make a thorough inspection of it. No G.A. under whom I served was ever present at a flogging or hanging; he left that job to me. In Jaffna I had to be present when a man was flogged, and in Kandy I had to see six or seven men hanged.

The flogging of a man with a cat-o'-nine-tails is the most disgusting and barbarous thing I have ever seen—it is worse even than a hanging. The man is tied by his arms and legs to an iron triangle which is about six foot high and he is given the lashes by a warder in presence of the Deputy Fiscal, a Medical Officer, and the Superintendent of the Prison. His back is literally flayed by the lashes and every ten lashes he is examined by the Medical Officer who has to stop the flogging if in his opinion the man is not in a condition to stand any more punishment.

In Kandy executions took place in the Bogambra Prison in the early morning before breakfast. To be present at them was a horrifying experience, and the more I had to witness, the more horrible I found them—and I think this was the experience of almost everyone who had to be present. Kandy was, as I have already said more than once, a lovely place and it never looked more lovely than in the early morning when I stood in the Bogambra Prison in front of the gallows and everyone waited for me to give the signal to the executioner for the 'drop' which would hang the man. I stood rather above the gallows, and in front of me in the fresh air and gentle sunshine just after dawn I looked across to the lovely hills surrounding the Lake. The procedure was that I first went to the condemned man's cell, read over to him the warrant of execution, and asked him whether he had anything to say. Some said no; several of them asked that their bodies after execution should be handed to their relatives; once the man said to me: 'I have been guilty of a crime; I am glad to be punished.' I think that all the men I saw hanged were Buddhists and were accompanied to the gallows by a priest. After I read the warrant, the condemned man was led out of the cell, clothed in white, on his head a curious white hat which at the last moment was drawn down to hide his face. In most cases they seemed to be quite unmoved as they walked to the scaffold, but one man was in a state of terror and collapse and had to be almost carried to the gallows by the warders, and all the way he kept repeating some words of a Sinhalese prayer, over and over again, and even as he stood with the rope round his neck waiting for the drop. The man was led up on to the scaffold by the warders, his arms were pinioned, and the hat drawn over his face. I had to stand immediately facing him on a kind of verandah where I could see the actual hanging. On the steps of the gallows the priest stood praying. In two out of the six or seven hangings which I had to certify something went wrong. In one case the man appeared not to die immediately; the body went on twitching violently and the executioner went and pulled on the legs. In the other case four men had to hang one morning and they were hanged two by two. The first two were hanged correctly, but either they gave one of the second two too big a drop or something else went wrong for his head was practically torn from his body and a great jet of blood spurted up three or four feet, covering the gallows and the priest praying on the steps.

I gave these repulsive details because those who support capital punishment in the 20th century pretend that it is a necessary, humane, civilised form of punishment. As a form of punishment, it is disgusting and, as I saw it, disgustingly inefficient. From the point of view of society and criminology, in my opinion, it is completely useless. The men whom I saw executed had all committed unpremeditated crimes of violence, killing from passion, anger, or in a quarrel. Not one of them was deterred from killing by the fact that hundreds of other men in Ceylon had been hanged for precisely similar killings. All the evidence, in all countries and at all times, goes to show that capital punishment is not a deterrent of crime; in fact, by the mystique of horror which it creates it tends to induce pathological or weak-minded people to imitate the crimes for which men have recently been executed. This is particularly true today when uncivilized 'popular' newspapers with gigantic circulations exploit—sensationalise and sentimentalise—the horrors, particularly of sexual murders of children, and a series of similar crimes follows. It is characteristic of these journals and their millionaire proprietors that they are hysterically in favour of retaining capital punishment as a deterrent while, by exploiting and sensationalising rapes, murders, and hangings, they increase the number of murders and murderers (as well as their own incomes).

In Ceylon I saw for several years the working of the criminal law from the inside, in my small way, as administrator, as magistrate and judge, and as a public servant intimately concerned with the police and prisons. I have remarked in a previous chapter that I was never a lenient judge or magistrate. This was because I am convinced that it is absolutely essentially that 'law and order' should be strictly maintained, and that means that everyone knows what the law is and what are the penalties for breaking it. But that in turn means that the judge, whatever his private opinion may be about the goodness or badness of the existing law, must apply it to the man in the dock without fear or favour, impartially, justly, objectively, strictly, even sternly. In fact, I should say that the best chance of getting uncivilised laws abolished or changed is that they should be strictly applied by civilised judges who abhor them. Sitting on the bench or visiting the prisons in Jaffna, Kandy, or Tangalla fifty years ago, I felt again and again that much of our criminal law was both uncivilised and stupidly inefficient as a method of punishing or deterring crime. I am sure that it still is both in Ceylon and in Brtain. In those days the prison system was more barbarous and iniquitous even than the law. The prisoners were confined in cages like those in the lion house in the Regent's Park Zoo, two, three, or even four men sometimes in a cage. The buildings were horrible. The prisoners hammered coconuts into coir or walked round and round the yard holding on to a moving rope which, I imagined, was a modern version of the ancient treadmill. I think the prison system has been considerably improved since those days. When I was in Jaffna in 1960 I met the Superintendent of the Jaffna Prison and he showed me over it. It was extraordinarily interesting to see it again after fifty years. There was no treadmill; the atmosphere of hopeless gloom and sordidness no longer existed; here at any rate was some small progress from barbarity to civilisation.

I was only a year in Kandy in the post of Office Assistant, for having arrived there in August 1907, I left in August 1908, to take up my duties as Assistant Government Agent, Hambantota, in the Southern Province. I had less than four years' service and this was extraordinarily rapid promotion, for I was the youngest A.G.A. and three years younger than the next youngest A.G.A. But it was not, I believe, my achievements in the everyday duties of an O.A. which won me this promotion; it was due to the Colonial Secretary, Sir Hugh Clifford, and I won his good opinion rather fortuitously. I think I first created a favourable impression on him by the way in which I dealt with the Empress Eugénie and Buddha's Tooth. The next episode clinched things. Clifford was a tremendous 'lady's man', and while he was Acting Governor, a glamorous lady, the wife of an officer in the Indian Army, visited Kandy for a few weeks. One evening, riding with Rachel in Lady Horton's Walk, a carriage passed us in which sat Clifford and the lady, and even that brief glimpse showed that the lady had made a conquest of the Acting Governor of Ceylon. Some days later Clifford sent for me and asked me whether I could manage to arrange a first-class show of Kandyan dancing in the grounds of King's Pavilion. He would have a few friends dining with him the following Thursday and he would like after dinner to give them a first-class exhibition of this famous Kandyan dancing. He hoped that, if I could do this, I would come and dine with them and manage the thing afterwards for him, including the payment of the dancers. I said I could do this and I went to my old friend the Diwa Nilame, Nugawela Ratemahatmaya, and asked him to get the very finest show of Kandyan dancing ever seen in the Kandyan district. He really did so and it was superb. He turned out all his retainers and headmen and an enormous company of dancers, tom-tom beaters, and musicians. He had about 100 torch-bearers and the dancing took place on the lawn in the light of the torches. The glamorous lady, for whom all this was done, was properly appreciative, and Clifford was immensely pleased. The only person slightly cynical about it was myself, and perhaps too Nugawela Ratemahatmaya. But I think it convinced Clifford that I was extraordinarily competent, and, when shortly afterwards an A.G.A. had to be appointed to Hambantota, on his own initiative—so he told me years later—he said that the post should be given to me. So on 27 August 1908, I took the train from Kandy to Hambantota, reflecting that the fate, the whole life even, of an insignificant civil servant can be fortuitously determined by Empresses, the Buddha's Tooth, lovely ladies, amorous Governors, a few torches and dancers.

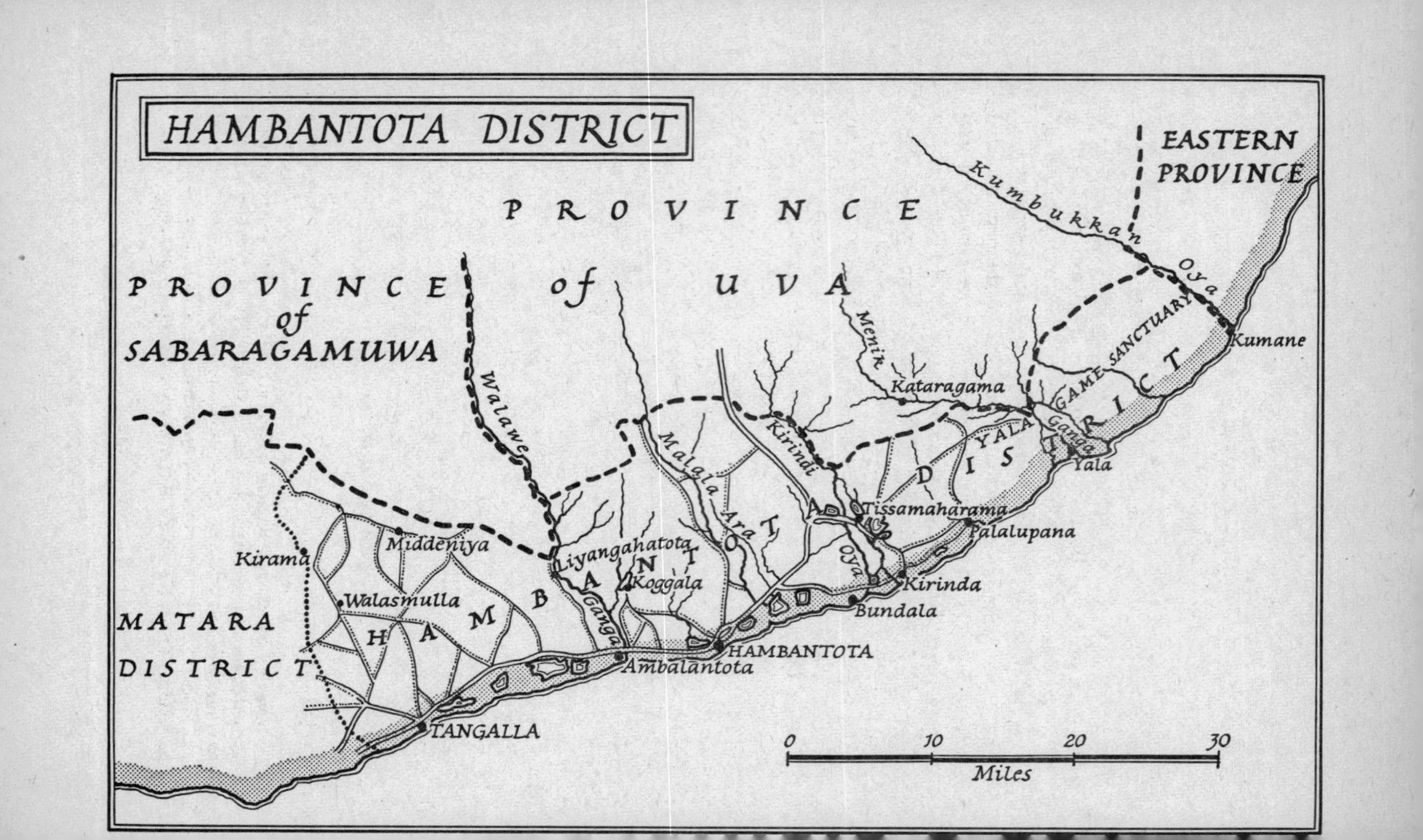
HAMBANTOTA DISTRICT
PROVINCE of UVA
PROVINCE of SABARAGAMUWA
EASTERN PROVINCE
MATARA DISTRICT
HAMBANTOTA DISTRICT
YALA
GAME SANCTUARY
Kumbukkan Oya
Kumane
Menik
Katargama
Kirindi
Walawe
Malala Ara
Ganga
Oya
Yala
Tissamaharama
Palalupana
Kirinda
Bundala
HAMBANTOTA
Ambalantota
Liyangahatota
Koggala
Middeniya
Kirama
Walasmulla
TANGALLA
0
10
20
30
Miles

4
Hambantota

I arrived in Hambantota as Assistant Government Agent and 'took over' from my predecessor on Friday, 28 August 1908; I finally left it on leave for England on Saturday, 20 May 1911. During my first years in Ceylon I had kept in close touch with the England and Cambridge which I had known, for Lytton and I wrote to each other continually. But gradually our letters thinned out and sometimes weeks or months passed without our writing. If two people are separated for years and by thousands of miles, they can write to each other either every week or only at long intervals. After two or three years I ceased to write to Lytton once a week, partly because I buried myself in my work and partly because I buried my past.

When I first came out to Ceylon, I was to some extent embittered and disappointed. My interests were passionately of the mind, though I was never, like Lytton and others of my friends, exclusively intellectual. I suppose that at the back of my mind, and in its depths, I wanted to be a writer. When I got to Ceylon, I found myself back at school. Nobody thought or talked of the things which I was passionately interested in. What I thought and felt about this I had to conceal from everyone in Jaffna and Kandy (except perhaps from Gwen on the seashore and Rachel in the mountains); my letters to Lytton were in part rage and lamentation, and in part a desperate effort to maintain contact. But after a time I seemed to harden my heart against the past and against regret for the past. I became almost fanatically interested in the country and the people and in certain aspects of my work. I think that my state of mind is honestly and accurately described in the following letter which I wrote to Lytton about a month after I arrived in Hambantota:

2nd Oct., 1908

Hambantota
Ceylon

I have often been on the point of writing in the last months and never quite reached it, perhaps because I knew that it would never be the time until you did. Sometimes too I thought of that astonishing letter of Ainsworth, do you remember it? the one I mean which dropped on you after an interval of months dividing it from the deluge of the previous delirium. And then last mail I really thought you had written, a letter in your handwriting with the Okehampton postmark and when I opened it it turned out to be from someone whose whole letter was about hunting on Dartmoor and returning to Ceylon. And by the same post came a postcard with Hunter's Inn on it. God, it seemed all so old. And before I had quite recovered from it, the next day when no mail should have come your letter came.

The scene had changed here too and one changes inside too. After all I am today and to be impinged upon by innumerable todays, the change is inevitable. I have no connection with yesterday: I do not recognize it nor myself of it. I am of and in today moulded and marked by innumerable things which have never touched you and when I come back and find you all the same, someone will say quite truly as Moore once said of Sanger or Crompton or someone who had almost reached the twilight: 'Really they seem to be interested in none of these things.'

And I suppose I am happy too, happier I expect as far as quantity goes than you. I work, God, how I work. I have reduced it to a method and exalted it to a mania. In Kandy I worked about ten hours a day and played tennis tournaments and went to intolerably dull dinners and duller dances and played bridge and drank and became the bosom friend of planters. So as a reward a month ago they sent me here as Assistant Government Agent. A 'reward' because it is what they call 'a charge', I am on my own in my district which is about 1000 sq. miles with 100,000 people in it and I am supposed to be very 'young' to have got it. So I live at the Residency Hambantota. There are no Europeans in Hambantota itself[1] . . . 26 miles away on one side are two Europeans a judge and a Supt. of Police and 20 miles away on the other is another an Irrigation Engineer. There is also another Irrigation Engineer who suffers from chronic indigestion and fever 20 miles away in the jungle I don't quite know where. But the house, really it is worth coming to Ceylon to live in it. It must originally have been built by the Dutch with walls of astonishing thickness and an enormously broad verandah and vast high rooms. It stands on a promontory right away from the town and right over the sea. Day and night you hear the sea thundering away almost at the gates of the compound, which is vast with nothing in it but sand and three stunted trees and is surrounded by a wall which the wind which blows here unceasingly has blown into ruins.

The District of Hambantota which was now committed to my charge lay in the extreme south of Ceylon. Bounded on the south by the sea it was about 100 miles in length; its breadth was never more than 30 and in places was only about 10 miles. Except in the north-west it was entirely flat; it lay in the dry zone, the low country. It had three divisions: Magampattu in the east, East Giruwa Pattu in

[1] This is not quite accurate; there was a Belgian missionary, Father Cooreman, who had a Sinhalese school. He was a very nice man, but I rarely saw him.

the centre, and West Giruwa Pattu in the west. Magampattu was almost entirely covered with jungle. It contained the small town of Hambantota, but otherwise only small scattered and usually poverty stricken villages. Twenty miles east of Hambantota was Tissamaharama with a major irrigation work and a resident white Irrigation Engineer. Here was a great stretch of paddy fields irrigated from the tank and a considerable population of cultivators. Besides producing rice at Tissa, Magampattu also produced salt. All along the coast eastwards from Hambantota were great lagoons or lewayas. In the dry season between the south-west and the north-east monsoons the salt water in these lewayas evaporates and 'natural' salt forms, sometimes over acres of the mud and sand. Salt in my day was a government monopoly, and it was my duty to arrange for the collecting, transport, storing, and selling of the salt—a large-scale complicated industry. Magampattu was also famous for its game and wild animals. In the extreme east there was a Government Game Sanctuary of about 130 square miles in which no shooting was allowed; I had a Game Sanctuary Ranger and some Watchers to look after it. There was a small area to the west of the Sanctuary in which only resident sportsmen might shoot. The issuing of licences to shoot big game—elephant, buffalo, and deer—was in my hands and in the open season sportsmen from all over the world used to come to Hambantota for big game shooting. I got to know a great deal about these sportsmen and the business of big game shooting; the more I learned, the less grew my love and respect for those who shoot and for those who organize the shooting.

West of Magampattu, separated by a fair-sized river, the Walawe Ganga, lies East Giruwa Pattu and then West Giruwa Pattu. Here the scenery changes completely. The jungle disappears; there is more water, more rainfall; it is quite populous with prosperous villages, with rice and dry grain and coconuts. In the north-west corner, where the foothills of the mountains begin, the country is as lovely as anything in the Kandy district. Yet it was Magampattu and the eastern part of the district which really won my heart and which I still see when I hear the word Hambantota; the sea perpetually thundering on the long shore, the enormous empty lagoons, behind the lagoons the enormous stretch of jungle, and behind the jungle far away in the north the long purple line of the great mountains, from which I looked down that evening with Rachel.

One's memory in connection with places is curiously erratic. There are two things about my house in Hambantota which I remember vividly. If you walked towards the sea across the compound, you came out upon a hillock of fine white sand, which was the tip of the promontory. To the right was an absolutely straight stretch of about two miles of the sea shore, dazzling white sand. All the year round day and night, if you looked down that long two-mile line of sea and sand, you would see, unless it was very rough, continually at regular intervals a wave, not very high but unbroken two miles long, lift itself up very slowly, wearily, poise itself for a moment in sudden complete silence, and then fall with a great thud upon the sand. That moment of complete silence followed by the great thud, the thunder of the wave upon the shore, became part of the rhythm of my life. It was the last thing I heard as I fell asleep at night, the first thing I heard when I woke in the morning—the moment of silence, the heavy thud; the moment of silence, the heavy thud—the rhythm of the sea, the rhythm of Hambantota.

The second memory is of sight, not sound. In the early morning when I was having my early tea upon the verandah, regularly every day at exactly the same hour a long line of about 30 or 40 flamingos flew over the sea along the two-mile stretch of coast from west to east. When they came to the headland upon which the Residency stood, they made a right-angle turn to the left and flew inland immediately over my house to the great lagoon which lay to the north of the town. It was a lovely sight and every morning I used to go out into the compound and watch the marvellous manoeuvre. The birds flew in perfect formation single file, and as they flew along over the sea the line was gleaming black and white. Then as each bird in turn wheeled to the left high up in the air above the house, it suddenly changed in the bright sunshine from black and white to a brilliant flash of pink.

During my years in Hambantota I lived a life of intense solitude. It was a social solitude—I had no social life. In the day, of course, except when I was on circuit in the jungles of Magampattu, I was surrounded with people and continually talking to people. But that was my work; the people were Sinhalese talking Sinhalese. They did not come to my house nor did I go to theirs. When I went on circuit to Tangalla, 26 miles to the west, the largest town in my District, I found Southorn, the District Judge, and Hodson, the Superintendent of Police, and we dined together. When I went on circuit 20 miles east to Tissamaharama, I found Wilson, the Irrigation Engineer, and we would dine together. But such meetings were, at the most, once in a month. Occasionally the head of a department or some high official would come to my District on official business and he would stay the night with me. Twice in my three years I had to entertain the Governor on an official visit of some days. During the open shooting season, there was always a trickle of European 'sportsmen' into and out of the District, Princes, Counts, Barons, and less exalted people, soldiers, planters. All of these people I had to deal with in one way or another. Otherwise I never saw a European and I had no social life at all. I worked all day and after dinner I worked or read. I learned in Hambantota to like solitude and I do not think I ever felt what people call loneliness.

In my letter to Lytton I said that I had exalted my work to a mania. This was quite true. After three years in Ceylon I had put out of my mind and out of my life, almost deliberately, everything which until I left England I had considered most important. I immersed myself in, I became obsessed by my work—but only with one side of my work. I disliked the European side of it, the white sahib side of it, the kind of second-rate (as it appeared to me) pomp and circumstance which surrounded one in Kandy and Colombo. I am deep down within myself an extremely ambitious person, desiring success. At the same time I despise success and those who pursue it, even to some extent those who attain it. It is usually much less satisfactory in attainment than in anticipation, while failure is even more bitter when it falls upon one than it was when one feared or foresaw it. I am sure that I wanted to be successful in the Ceylon Civil Service, to be thought well of in the Colombo Secretariat, to win promotion. Yet I do not think that at any time I ever worked with that consciously in my mind. This was partly because after two or three years in the Civil Service subconsciously, at the back of my mind, I knew that it was highly improbable that I would make my permanent career in it. I did not want to be a successful imperialist, to become a Colonial Secretary or a Governor, His Excellency Sir Leonard Woolf, K.C.M.G.

In the main my obsession with work was stimulated by two things, both of which were immensely developed and encouraged as soon as I found myself in charge of the District of Hambantota. I fell in love with the country, the people, and the way of life which were entirely different from everything in London and Cambridge to which I had been born and bred. To understand the people and the way they lived in the villages of West Giruwa Pattu and the jungles of Magampattu became a passion with me. In the 2¾ years in Hambantota, it is almost true to say, I worked all day from the moment I got up in the morning until the moment I went to bed at night, for I rarely thought of anything else except the District and the people, to increase their prosperity, diminish the poverty and disease, start irrigation works, open schools. There was no sentimentality about this; I did not idealise or romanticise the people or the country; I just liked them aesthetically and humanly and socially. But I was ruthless—too ruthless, as I shall show—both to them and to myself.

The second impulse which determined my mania for work was a passion for efficiency. I think I have always had this dangerous passion. If I have to do something, I almost always immediately get a consuming desire to find out 'the best way to do it', the most economical, quickest, most efficient, the most methodical. This desire is theoretically admirable and its results are often admirable; but it is very dangerous for it tends to become a ruthless obsession so that one forgets that efficiency is a means to an end, not an end in itself. My promotion to Assistant Government Agent enormously encouraged this desire for efficiency. Suddenly I found myself on my own, responsible for a vast variety of administrative operations, and my experience had already shown me that administration was almost always and everywhere slow, unintelligent, badly organised. I set out to make the Hambantota District the best administered in the island, and I do not think that I deceive or flatter myself when I say that I succeeded. I will give an example or two which will, I think, prove this and will also show the kind of life which I had to lead and the kind of work that an 'imperialist' administrator performed in a British Crown Colony fifty years ago.

The first example concerned an operation which was not routine or part of the everyday administration. In my last year I had to take a Census of the District. It had to be done through the village headmen and the organization was extremely difficult. Nearly the whole population was illiterate and the enumerators were not much better in many places. For days and days I went round and round the District personally instructing the enumerators, held a 'preliminary' census, and checked every enumerator's schedules filled up at this preliminary census. There was always a good deal of competition among the A.G.A.'s to see who could get his District returns in first.

Mine was a difficult District because in many places there were long distances between the scattered villages and no roads. But the Mudaliyars (Chief Headmen) and their subordinate headmen had learned in the last two years my passion for efficiency and intolerance of inefficiency. The enumerators had been drilled so that they really knew how to fill in the forms. The Census night was 10 March 1911. I organized a system of bicycle relays to get the returns in promptly. It worked so well and the messenger was so eager that he woke me up at 4.30 a.m. to give me the West Giruwa Pattu returns. On March 11th and 12th, the Mudaliyar of Magampattu, the Head Clerk of the kachcheri, and eight other clerks sat with me from 7.30 a.m. to 7 p.m. each day checking returns. On March 13th I wired the figures to the Superintendent of Census in Colombo and he replied that they were the first District returns to be received by him. The final figures, showing an increase during the past decade of only 5,617 or 5·3 per cent, which was less than I had expected, were:

Magampattu	11,799
East Giruwa Pattu	12,948
West Giruwa Pattu	85,740
Total	110,487

As A.G.A. I was responsible, as I have said, for the Government salt industry. As soon as salt formed in a lewaya, I had to arrange, through the Salt Superintendent and the Chief Headmen, for its collection. The collectors had to be recruited from the villages and they often had to come considerable distances. This required careful timing and organization, for unless the salt was promptly collected a shower of rain might destroy it or it might go wrong and turn into epsom salts. After collection I had to arrange for the transport of the salt from the lewaya to the Government salt stores at Hambantota or Kirinda. After tenders had been called for, this was done on contract at so much per ton by contractors in Hambantota who owned, controlled, and hired bullock carts. We sold the salt from the stores either to the Hambantota contractors and carters who transported it in the bullock carts, right up the long straight north road down which I had bicycled from Rachel's tea estate, and sold it up country to traders and planters, or to a large Colombo firm, Delmege Forsyth & Co., for transport by sea to Galle and Colombo.

Some little time after I arrived as A.G.A., when I called for tenders for the removal of salt from the lewayas, it was clear that the contractors were forming a ring with a view to forcing me to pay 20 or 30 cents a ton more than before. I felt that their idea was that here they had a much younger and less experienced A.G.A. to deal with and that I would yield to pressure. For a time I refused to give a contract at all and hired carts direct from the carters. Up to a point this was eminently successful, but it was a slow laborious business and the contractors knew that it could not go on indefinitely. So they tried a new dodge. They offered to remove salt from a distant lewaya at Rs. 1·70 per ton. Then suddenly they all stopped work and left the lewaya and put a pistol at my head saying that they would not remove the salt at less than Rs. 2 per ton. In my official diary I record that

> In the evening I got hold of the previous contractor and I was determined that he should take another contract. Eventually with great difficulty and a certain amount of pressure I induced him to enter into a contract to remove 10,000 cwts. a month until all the salt on this side of the lewaya is removed. As he will probably pay the carters about Rs. 1·50 a ton, I feel that I have scored. He undertakes with me to do it at Rs. 1·80 per ton, which is the old rate.

In the diary I discreetly do not specify how exactly I applied 'a certain amount of pressure'. It was rather unconventional. The Salt Superintendent brought the contractor to me to the kachcheri where I was working late in the afternoon after everyone else had left. I tried unsuccessfully every possible means to induce him to take a contract at Rs. 1·80 per ton; he stood out for Rs. 2. At last I said to him: 'I have been sitting here working since 9 o'clock this morning and I want some exercise and fresh air. I am going for a walk on the Tissamaharama road. There is, of course, no need for you to come, but I shall be very glad if you will, so that we may go on discussing whether you agree to Rs. 1·80.' He was, I think, rather pleased to be asked to go for a walk with the A.G.A. and the Salt Superintendent, and he would be seen by all his friends and enemies walking with us through the town. We discussed the matter as we walked in the usual squirrel cage of fruitless argument. When I got to the first milestone on the Tissa road I stopped and said: 'Now, Abdul Rahman, will you take Rs. 1·80?' and when he shook his head, I said: 'I am going to walk on to Tissa and I should like to go on discussing the matter with you, but don't come, if you don't want to.' He felt, I think, that it would be rather awkward or rude to turn back by himself and so we set out for the second milestone. The Tissa road is very straight and bare through scrub jungle and by the side of the lagoon; it seems to take a long time to walk a mile on it. The evening was warm and fine; the world about us was completely empty except for the darkening sky above our heads and the unending road beneath our feet. Abdul Rahman was not a good walker and the Salt Superintendent, a large Malay, showed signs of wilting. At the second milestone I stopped and said: 'Now, Abdul Rahman, will you take Rs. 1·80?' and when he shook his head, I said: 'I am going to walk on to Tissa which, if we go on at this pace, we shall reach about two in the morning, for we have another 18 miles to go. I am very fond of walking and I think the Salt Superintendent is too. But I don't want you to come on if you would rather not.' Off we set again, but after a bit, Abdul Rahman stopped; he looked at the Salt Superintendent and shook his head; then he turned to me with a smile: 'Well, Your Honour, I'll take the Rs. 1·80.' We walked back, my companions limping slightly, but the best of friends. The tale of Abdul Rahman and his Rs. 1·80 became a legend in the District in various versions, and I never had any more difficulties with the contractors.

In several ways I revolutionized the salt industry in Hambantota. I completely altered the system of paying the collectors so that they were paid on the spot. Hitherto they were given payment vouchers which could only be cashed in the Hambantota kachcheri, a system which led to a regular trade in vouchers by middlemen who bought them at a considerable discount from the collectors. This made it much easier to get labour for the collecting, and it was largely owing to this that the amount of salt collected in 1910 beat all previous records. We collected and stored 224,352 cwt. The largest total collection previously was 189,563 cwt. in 1893.

When collection was going on, I often suddenly got on my horse and rode ten or twenty miles to pay a surprise visit. No one knew when this severe A.G.A. might not appear riding on the horizon and discover someone not doing his work or taking an illicit commission on the sly. One day I became suspicious or received a hint that a certain amount of hanky-panky was going on over the removal of the salt from the lewayas into the Government stores. The salt was bagged and weighed at the lewaya and the weight of salt marked on the outside of each bag just before transportation. They were weighed again on receipt at the store and the weights recorded. Between receipt at the store and sale a certain maximum amount of wastage was allowed; it followed that if the weight of salt in a bag was marked as less than in fact it was and so recorded as received in the store, a pleasant little primrose path was opened for dishonesty. So one afternoon I suddenly appeared in the Hambantota stores when I knew that they were receiving salt from a lewaya. A cart had just arrived and I checked the weight of each of its bags. I found that there was an excess of 36 lb over the weight given at the lewaya. I tried another cart of 18 bags and found an excess of 15 lb. I then found that in practically every case in which I had not been present, the weight of a cartload, according to the checkers at the stores, had been *less* than the weight as given at the lewaya.

It was clear from this that the weighing at the lewaya, for which the head guard was responsible, and the weighing at the store, for which the checkers were responsible, were both inaccurate and in every case the recorded weight was less than the actual weight, the inaccuracy therefore being on the side which would show the least wastage when a store was emptied. By this time the Salt Superintendent had arrived on the scene and I told him that the checkers and the head guard must be suspended for six months from all Government service. The checkers pleaded that it was unfair to rely on figures obtained by checking only two carts. I agreed to go on checking carts, on condition that an additional six months' suspension would be given for every cart which confirmed my deduction. Looking back it seems to me that there were unnecessary severity and relentlessness in this decision. The checkers foolishly agreed and we weighed another cart. The weight recorded on the bags was 51 lb less than the actual weight.

My third example concerns a terrible catastrophe which fell upon my District early in 1909. An outbreak of rinderpest had occurred in the island and there were cases of the disease in the Uva Province which adjoined my District. On 18 February there were three cases of the disease among bulls in Hambantota town. These bulls had been transporting salt in carts to the tea estates in the Uva Province and had become infected there. They had been turned loose with another 250 head of cattle out on the Maha Lewaya adjoining the town. I had the sick bulls isolated and rode down to the lewaya in the evening, had all the cattle there rounded up and counted; I put them in charge of watchers and ordered them to see that none were removed and no other cattle brought to the lewaya.

This began a struggle against catastrophe which lasted for a whole year. I never worked as hard or as despairingly and relentlessly as I did during those twelve months trying to stop the spread of the disease and to save some of the people's cattle. Rinderpest is a terrible disease and to see an outbreak of it in a place like the Hambantota District is horrifying. It is extremely infectious and, if introduced into a herd, practically every animal caught it and the mortality rate was very high. It attacked all cattle including the buffaloes. It is a cruel and disgusting disease; often I have come upon a diseased bull or buffalo wandering about in a field or jungle with half its face eaten away by maggots. The only possible way of stopping or controlling the outbreak was to insist upon (1) the immediate isolation of any infected animal and all contacts, (2) the continual tethering or impounding of uninfected cattle. The difficulty of doing this was tremendous. There were no fences or hedges and all cattle were allowed habitually to wander about everywhere. In open places near towns or villages, like the lewayas, you would always see herds of two or three hundred cattle. In Magampattu one had to think not only of the domestic cattle and buffaloes, but also of the large numbers of wild buffalo which soon became infected and spread the disease to the tame buffaloes.

Cattle and buffalo were the people's most valuable property; the prosperity of the whole district depended upon them. It was almost entirely an agricultural district and rice, the most important crop, was dependent for ploughing and threshing upon cattle and buffaloes. Everywhere the only form of transport was the bullock cart, and in Hambantota town, as I have already said, there were a large number of carters, many of them Muhammadans, who depended for a living upon the transport of salt, and so upon their bulls who pulled the carts. As the disease spread, the Government made regulations that all cattle should be tethered or impounded, and that all infected or stray cattle should be destroyed. For months I spent hours and days trying to control the disease and limit the disaster, riding hundreds of miles in order to try to enforce the regulations and shooting stray cattle and buffaloes on the roads and in villages as a warning. The kind of thing which I did is shown by the following extract from my official diary for 26 June 1909:

I have received several complaints from the G.A. Sabaragamuwa that rinderpest is being spread from East Giruwa Pattu into Sabaragamuwa at Kachchigala. This is a most inaccessible place but as the Mudaliyar of East Giruwa

Pattu who has been removed from service has not been able to effect anything I decided to make a forced march up there. I bicycled early in the morning to Mamadola 14 miles where my pony met me. From there rode to Wetiya on the Liyangahatota road (5 miles). Here were two bulls suffering from rinderpest in a gala. Struck across country to Abesekaragama (3 miles) where 'the Abeskera of Abesekaragama' (an old dismissed Vidana Arachchi of the old type with any amount of influence) met me and showed me all his cattle enclosed in the paddy fields. Then on to Metigatwela wewa (about 3 miles) where I found a very different state of affairs, buffaloes straying about round the tank. I shot two, one of which was diseased, the whole of one eye and part of one side of the face had been eaten away by maggots but the wretched beast was still straying about. I got some rice at Metigatwela and then rode on to Uswewa (2 miles) and Kachchigala (1½ miles). Here I found no stray and no diseased cattle but after enquiry I found that the headmen have undoubtedly been remiss. I am going to punish them and prosecute the chief offender. From Kachchigala there is a path to Kandaketiya (1½ miles) and from there to Talawa (4 miles) which I reached about 7.30 p.m.

Next morning at Talawa a villager told me a curious story about buffaloes. I had several times during the outbreak been told that buffaloes which got the disease would often break out madly and travel long distances to die in the place where they had been born. According to this Talawa villager the disease had been brought to the village in the following way. Four years before a man in Talawa sold a she-buffalo to a man at Alutwewa, a village about 8 miles away. For four years this buffalo never came back to Talawa. But, he said, a week or so ago she got the disease at Alutwewa, broke out of the pattiya 'as if she were mad', and was found the following morning lying dead in the fold at Talawa in which she had been born.

These forced marches in a desperate attempt to save something from the disaster were not only exhausting—for riding and enquiring for 12½ hours with only 'some rice' at Metigatwela under the Hambantota sun is a pretty strenuous day—it was also terribly depressing. I remember one day in particular when in the evening I felt acutely the failure and futility of what I was doing. I had spent the whole day driving and riding round a heavily infected area, destroying animals and warning owners wherever I found stray cattle that I should have to destroy them if I found them straying again. Late in the evening I drove through a small village which I had already visited in the morning. By the side of the road I came on two cows straying, one already showing symptoms of disease. I sent for the owner and he proved to be a man whom I had warned earlier in the day. I felt that I must, as one said, make an example, and I took my rifle from my trap and shot the two animals. It is not a pleasant business to ride and drive through villages and shoot the cattle and buffaloes of the villagers whom one knows and likes.

The whole village seemed to have turned out and the men were standing on the road round the bodies of the animals; there was a hostile murmur from the small crowd. I explained to them that the owner had been warned, that by not impounding his animals he was infecting them and helping to spread the disease to other people's cattle all over the country. As I walked to my trap, they followed me and, as I drove away, I still heard the dull hostile murmur of their voices.

It was the only time in my three years in the Hambantota District, in my seven years in Ceylon, that I heard that note of communal hostility against myself or the Government from villagers (though I did hear it once from a crowd of carters in Hambantota). It is a very disturbing sound. I was profoundly depressed. I knew that the order to impound cattle was practically futile, because it would not be obeyed and could not be enforced. I knew that the villagers did not believe what I said to them; to them I was part of the white man's machine, which they did not understand. I stood to them in the relation of God to his victims: I was issuing from on high orders to to their village which seemed to them arbitrary and resulted in the shooting of their cows. I drove away in dejection, for I have no more desire to be God than one of his victims.

I spent the night in a tent or circuit bungalow—I forget which—not many miles from the village, and I had arranged to meet there the Muhandiram or chief headman of the area to discuss with him these rinderpest difficulties and problems. The Muhandiram was a very intelligent Sinhalese, English educated; he had been sent to Hambantota from another district where he had held a higher post—in fact he had been demoted for some error or offence. I liked him and talked quite freely to him as I would have to a white man. He came to me after I had eaten my dinner and we strolled out to a headland discussing the administrative problem of enforcing the rinderpest regulations. When we came to the end of the headland, we looked eastwards from a low sandy cliff over the sea. It was the days of Halley's comet. The head of the comet was just above the horizon, the tail flamed up the sky until the end of it was almost above our heads. The stars blazed with the brilliance which they have only on a clear, still, black night in the southern hemisphere.

And at our feet the comet and the stars blazed reflected in the smooth, velvety, black sea.

We stood in silence; it was a superb spectacle; as a work of art, magnificent. And I suppose it was what is called awe-inspiring. But there is something about these spectacular displays of nature, about the heavenly bodies and the majestic firmament which, while I admire them as works of art, also irritates me. From my point of view—the human point of view—there is something ridiculous about the universe—these absurd comets racing round the sun and the absurd suns flaming away at impossible speeds through illimitable empty space. Such futility is sinister in its silliness. I turned to the Muhandiram and asked him what he thought about the comet and the planets and the stars. His answer depressed me even more profoundly than the Sinhalese villagers. He believed quite seriously in all the astrological nonsense which the *Daily Express* supplies to its white readers today. Our lives and characters, he said, were determined by the position of the constellations at the moment of our birth. I foolishly tried to convince him of the absurdity of such an idea. I might just as usefully have tried to prove to the President of the Royal Society that the earth is flat and the sun goes round it. He told me that at a female child's birth the horoscope predicted the year, day, and hour at which her menstruation would begin, and it was always accurate. If I would tell him the place and hour of my birth, he would have my horoscope drawn and it would prove to me that my life and character had been determined by the position of the heavenly bodies at the time of my birth.

The incidents of those twenty-four hours in the rinderpest ravaged district of Hambantota were no doubt trivial, but they could be read as a moral tale about imperialism—the absurdity of a people of one civilisation and mode of life trying to impose its rule upon an entirely different civilisation and mode of life. As I stood with the Muhandiram looking at the great comet blazing in the sky and in the sea, I was ruminating on this moral tale and it was the cause of my dejection. For my attitude to the Hambantota villagers was entirely benevolent and altruistic; I was merely trying to save from destruction some of the most valuable of their few possessions. Following me and murmuring as I walked to the trap they had less understanding of my ways, my intentions, my affection for them than the half-bred bitch walking at my heels. They were the nicest of people and I was very fond of them, but they would have thrown stones at me or shot me in the back as I walked to the trap, had they dared. And the Muhandiram, through whom I was attempting to impose our rule upon them, so quick-witted, so intelligent, so anglicised and Europeanised—scratch the surface of his mind and you found that he believed that Halley's comet, the blazing constellations above our heads, the planets in their courses, the spiral nebulae, the infinite galaxies flaming away into space, had been created and kept going through billions of billions of years in order that a grubby little man in the Hambantota bazaar could calculate the exact day and hour at which the Muhandiram's infant daughter would have her first menstrual period.[1]

The destruction and devastation caused by the disease were terrible. Less than a year after the outbreak began I went to the Game Sanctuary and rode through it to see the effect there. The disease had died out among the wild buffaloes, but immense numbers had died. I recorded that 'I have not seen 25 buffaloes, though I went about to look for them, where last year I must have seen two or three hundred.' Among the village cattle, the herds roaming on the lewayas, the cart bulls, the valuable tame buffaloes used in large numbers for agricultural purposes under the great irrigation works, like Tissa, and in rice cultivation under village tanks, the mortality was appalling.

The sights which one saw continually filled one with despair. For instance, I was driving to Tissamaharama from Hambantota one afternoon, during the height of the outbreak, to stay the night there and hold some enquiries, when I was stopped near Wirawila, where the road passes through thick jungle, by a headman, a Vidana Arachchi. I knew him well, a gnarled little man who had some knowledge of the jungle. There was a well-known water hole about 1½ miles through the jungle on the left of the road, and he told me that it was in a terrible state as there were bodies of dead buffaloes in and around it. It was the dry season and there would be no water for miles round except in this water hole. The Arachchi asked me to come and have a look at it. It would be the night of the full moon, so I told him that I would and that I would spend my night at the water hole. I was very fond of sitting up over a water hole in this way and just watching the animals come and drink; I took my rifle and sent

[1] Of course, one must admit that he may be right, and that that is the object of the universe.

my horsekeeper with the trap to Wirawila, telling him to come back and pick me up at six the next morning.

It was a fantastic night. The scene round the hole was indeed terrible: in the water hole itself were the carcasses of four wild buffaloes and a sambhur; round the rock were four dead wild buffaloes and two dead pigs. At first I did not think that I could stand a night there. But I wanted to see whether animals would come to drink and what would happen. Walking round the hole I came upon the body of a wild pig, obviously partly eaten by a leopard. The Arachchi agreed with me that the leopard would probably return to it at dusk and he asked me to shoot it as leopards were causing destruction among the village cattle who had so far escaped the disease. We piled up some branches on the ground about three or four yards from the carcass—the ground was very awkward and that was the best we could do. We lay on the ground behind the branches and I rested my loaded rifle on them. The light began to fade and a mongoose appeared, and disappeared into the belly of the pig. A leopard is the quickest and most silent of all jungle creatures. I was looking the whole time intently at the carcass and then suddenly with no warning, without my seeing a movement of his approach, there was the leopard standing upright a few yards from me, staring straight into my eyes. I looked straight into his eyes, fascinated, so fascinated by his ferocious eyes and his magnificent beauty that I could not shoot, did not think of shooting. The Arachchi made a tiny movement to attract my attention, for he thought I did not see the leopard. At the same moment there was a sudden violent scuttle of the terrified mongoose out of the pig. The next moment there was no leopard there; I did not see a movement of his departure any more than I had seen a movement of his arrival. It was as though some colossal hand had wiped him instantaneously out of the picture or the world. The Arachchi shook his head; he obviously thought I was either cracked or afraid; if I had had time to think, I should certainly have been terrified, but in fact in this instance I had been so entranced by the beauty of the creature that there was no time for fear.

We walked back to the water hole and on the way I saw a most extraordinary sight. It was now bright moonlight and about 100 yards off down an opening in the jungle was a jackal. He was entirely alone, performing what seemed to be an intricate dance. I have twice in my life seen March hares in the Sussex water-meadows performing their extraordinary dances. The jackal seemed to be doing the same thing. Leaping into the air, almost turning somersaults, silently and all by himself, after the mongoose and the leopard's cold eyes staring into mine, he seemed to be part of a completely silent, slightly mad, sinister world.

It was a wonderful place for watching animals come to drink at night. The water hole itself, long and narrow, was in the middle of a great square plateau of solid rock, about 400 to 500 yards each way. It was surrounded on all sides by thick jungle and was raised above the jungle so that the tops of the nearest trees were level with it. On one side of the water hole and about 5 or 6 yards from it rose a great rock or gigantic boulder, 12 or 15 feet high and quite smooth and flat on the top. One could lie on it all night and get a fine view of the water hole and, raised up there, of an immense sea of trees and changing leaves, stretching away below one, beneath the light of the moon, into infinity and eternity.

The wind had dropped; the moon was so bright that I could have read small print in its light. After the ferocious heat of the day the freshness of the midnight air was delicious. Watching at a water hole like this is enthralling. As the night goes on the silence of the jungle grows deeper and deeper, but every now and again it is broken by a soft, sibilant shiver of all the leaves of all the trees for miles round one. This colossal whisper dies away as suddenly as it floats up out of the trees—complete silence to be broken again by strange snufflings and shufflings of some invisible creature nearby, the rattling of a porcupine's quills, the sudden snarl far off of a thwarted leopard, the bell-like call of a deer, or the tortured howling of jackals.

That night for several hours nothing came out on to the rock to drink until, between two and three in the morning, a great crashing and cracking began down there in the jungle and slowly drew nearer and nearer to the rock. Then an immense head appeared out of the trees in the moonlight and an elephant shouldered himself up on to the rocks. He was followed by another and another and another until there were ten elephants lined up along the water hole. The old bull stood at one end of the line and down at the other end were two or three tiny calves standing between their mothers' forefeet. The whole line waited for a few minutes, each beast swaying, fidgeting, lifting up one foot after another in that pattern of eternal restlessness from which no elephant for a single moment seems able to escape.

The whole line swayed and fidgeted and flapped their ears, but the only sound was the slight shuffling of their feet upon the rock. At length, the bull put his trunk towards the water, but he did not drink—it was too foul to drink; he stood still for a moment, flapping his ears, and then, raising his trunk and trumpeting, he turned away from the water hole and lumbered off. Orderly, one after another, keeping the line in single file, the other elephants followed the bull.

After that I fell asleep. I have always found it difficult to keep awake all night at a water hole. Though one is lying or sitting on hard, bare rock, one is overcome with sleep, and, though I have often woken up soaked with dew and stiff in every joint, I have never slept more profoundly or dreamlessly. That night I was terribly hungry because I had intended to dine at Tissamaharama and the only food which I had had since midday was two or three biscuits. But I slept like a log until I was woken up by the sun again on my face. As I walked the 1½ miles through the jungle to the road, two magnificent elephants broke through the trees one on each side of me, making off towards the distant river. They too must have visited the water hole and found the water undrinkable.

It was extremely difficult to get any idea of whether or not the enormous amount which we did for a year or more to combat the disease and save some of their cattle for the cultivators had any effect. What filled me with despair was that as soon as I thought that at last we had got to the end of the outbreak, the disease would start up again in some God-forsaken spot and the horrible business would begin all over again. I thought at the time that we had succeeded to some extent in saving cattle in the populated parts of West Giruwa Pattu. In the jungle-surrounded arable areas of Magampattu, like Tissamaharama, where tame buffaloes were being continually infected by diseased wild buffaloes, I did something by large-scale removal of uninfected buffaloes to remote places where they might escape infection. For instance, I removed 450 buffaloes from Tissa to three different places, and 283 survived the outbreak. If they had remained at Tissa, I do not think that 30 would have survived.

The loss of practically all the cattle under the great Tissa Irrigation Work was a terrible disaster. The people did not plough their paddy fields; the usual method of preparing the fields for sowing was what is called 'mudding', i.e. buffaloes are driven round and round the wet fields until the soil is properly stirred up. By the middle of 1909 there were so few cattle left alive that it became clear that unless something was done, there would be practically no cultivation of rice in the autumn. I got from Colombo some light English and American ploughs and some Agricultural Society instructors to give demonstrations. The struggle against the conservatism of the cultivators was extremely interesting. At first they would not look at the ploughs; 'Hamadoru,' they would say to me, sorrowfully shaking their heads, 'no bull could pull that plough; you would want an elephant!' However we persisted. One of the difficulties was to get bulls and train them; I got the Mudaliyars to obtain some bulls and took them down to the Hambantota lewaya in order to train them and myself to plough. It was literally ploughing the sand, and amused not only me, but the inhabitants of Hambantota town. Then I took the ploughs and bulls to Tissa and gave demonstrations there. Almost at once I got applications for 80 or 90 ploughs, which I immediately ordered from Colombo. In the end 3,140 acres were cultivated, of which 2,420 were ploughed, 570 mudded, and 150 worked with mamoties. The yield of the ploughed fields was considerably higher than the others, but to turn buffaloes into a paddy field and drive them round and round was much less trouble for the cultivator than ploughing with a badly trained bull, and after I left the District I believe that everyone gave up using the English ploughs.

The Hambantota District used to be called a 'sportsman's paradise'. There was a great deal of 'big game' in the jungles of Magampattu: leopard, bear, elephant, buffalo, sambhur deer, spotted deer, and pig. Both in Magampattu and in the two western pattus snipe were plentiful in the wet season, and on the lewayas and irrigation tanks there was good teal shooting. Before I came to the District I had done very little shooting, but I soon began to do quite a lot of it. The food which one got normally in a place like Hambantota was very dreary, particularly the eternal aged stringy curried chicken. Apart from sport, therefore, one shot for the pot: deer, jungle fowl, peafowl, teal, pigeons, snipe, golden plover. I had the extraordinary luck to win in a sweepstake two years running: £17 in the Colombo Turf Club Grand National sweepstake, and then at the end of 1908 on a Rs. 10 ticket £690 in the Calcutta Turf Club Melbourne Cup sweepstake. I spent some of the money in fitting myself out with gun and rifles.

I am a terribly bad shot with a rifle and not a good shot with a gun. But, like almost everyone from the Tolstoys of the world downwards, shooting and hunting at first fascinated me. The excitement is tremendous, whether you are stalking a deer in the jungle, shooting snipe in a paddy field, or waiting in the evening on a tank for the sound of the whistling of the teal as they fly in to roost on the dead trees and give you the chance of a shot at them as they circle high over your head. I always remained a very poor shot, but I got to know the ways of the jungle and of its birds and beasts quite well so that I was a fairly good tracker. But, like many other sportsmen, the more I shot the more I came to dislike the killing. In my last year I spent as much time as I could afford in the jungle, observing the animals and sitting up at night over water holes, but I gave up shooting except for food.

I had under me a Game Sanctuary Ranger and Game Watchers to look after the Game Sanctuary and also generally the shooting and protection of game outside the Sanctuary. The Game Sanctuary Ranger was a strange man. His name was Engelbrecht, a Boer from the Orange Free State. A considerable number of Boers who fought and were captured in the Boer War were sent to Ceylon and were interned in camps up country. Engelbrecht was one of them. When the war was over, the prisoners-of-war were repatriated to South Africa on condition that they took the oath of allegiance to the king and his successors. Engelbrecht was the only one of them who refused to take the oath, on the not illogical ground that he knew who the king was and what he was like, but he knew nothing about his successors. Nothing would move him, for he was, as I found, one of the most obstinate men in the world (and also a very stupid man). So the Government sent him down to Hambantota on a miserable allowance to live in a disused prison, the idea being that he would find life so hard and dreary that he would give in. But the Boers are a stiff-necked race and Engelbrecht was a Boer of the Boers. One of my predecessors who was A.G.A. Hambantota in 1906 reported to the Government that Engelbrecht was living in the greatest poverty and squalor and something ought to be done about him, and he recommended that the Boer should be appointed Game Sanctuary Ranger on a small salary. The Government agreed.

Engelbrecht was a first-class shot, a good tracker and shikari, and he soon learned a great deal about the Ceylon jungle and its ways; he taught me three-quarters of what eventually I learned about shooting and tracking. He was a cold-blooded man, the only man whom I have known who seemed to me to be completely without fear and without nerves—I saw him, as I shall tell, perform in cold blood an act of incredible bravery and foolhardiness. He was tall, straight, and very thin, his hair and beard reddish, his eyes small, very light blue with a glint in them every now and then of icy malignancy. He behaved to the Sinhalese as the Boers behave to the negroes in Africa and, not unnaturally, he was hated in Hambantota. This led to some nasty incidents.

Being Police Magistrate as well as A.G.A. I used to walk over from the kachcheri to the Police Court to try cases in the afternoon when I was in Hambantota town. One afternoon when I got to the Court I found half the male population of the town packed into the Court, on the verandah, and all round the building. There was one woman, a good-looking Sinhalese carrying a baby. There was obviously going to be a *cause célèbre*, and I was rather surprised that neither anyone in the kachcheri nor the Court Interpreter had warned me of it. We began with the usual string of nuisance and similar cases in which the accused always pleaded guilty and was fined a few rupees. Then the woman's case was called and the defendant pushed his way through the crowd of spectators and came and stood below the bench. The defendant was Engelbrecht. It was a paternity case by the woman against him. He denied paternity. There was, however, very good evidence that he had been living with the woman in the old prison, and she unwrapped the naked baby and held it up to show me that it was a white baby. It was extremely interesting to watch the faces of the men packed in and around the Court. There was none of the usual stir and movement, no smiles, lifting of eyebrows, shakings of the head. They stood quite still, expectant, their eyes fixed first on the woman, then on Engelbrecht, then on me. I knew them well enough by now to know exactly what was passing through their heads. 'He is a white man, this swine. The A.G.A. doesn't really know what he's like; he goes out into the jungle and shoots with him. What will the A.G.A. do?' I found for the plaintiff and made a maintenance order. There was no sound from the crowd; their faces remained impassive, rather grim; but there was a distinct drop in tensions, a kind of soundless sigh of relief as they filed out of the Court.

I do not think that Engelbrecht ever mended his ways, and the people revenged themselves upon him twice in a horrible and cruel way. He travelled, of course, always by bullock cart when on circuit in the jungles and Game Sanctuary. He had two magnificent cart bulls—I do not think I have ever seen a finer pair of bulls. One morning he woke up to find the bleeding heads of his two bulls placed one on each side of his doorstep. After enquiry, I had little doubt that the people who had done this were the brothers of the woman who had borne him the child. But the people of Hambantota saw to it that there was no evidence which could possibly have led to a conviction.

The second case was even more unpleasant. One day Engelbrecht shot a she-bear and then found a small bear cub in the grass nearby. He took the cub and reared it. He had a small Sinhalese boy who drove his bullock cart and the bear became passionately devoted to the boy. I have never known a more charming animal than this bear. He was half-grown when I first knew him, and, when I was on circuit in the jungle or Game Sanctuary with Engelbrecht, he would follow us all day like a dog along the tracks, only stopping to dig out an ants' nest if he came upon one. He slept with the boy on a mattress under the cart, and when I was travelling with them, the last thing at night I always went to have a look at the pair fast asleep under the cart with their arms round each other's necks. One day when Engelbrecht was out in the jungle on circuit, the boy got a thorn in his foot which became badly poisoned so that Engelbrecht had to return at once to Hambantota. When he got to his lodging in the prison, he shut the bear in and carried the boy up to the hospital. The bear somehow or other managed to get the door opened and started off snuffing along on the scent of Engelbrecht's boots up the road to the hospital. Everyone in the town knew the bear and knew that it was harmless; but they also knew that it was Engelbrecht's, so some of them beat it to death in the street.

Engelbrecht's act of fearless foolhardiness took place just after dawn one morning in the Magampattu jungle. The Assistant Superintendent of Police at Tangalla was a young civil servant called Hodson. He had never been in the jungle proper and had done no big game shooting. He very much wanted to begin, so when I had to go on a short circuit to the Game Sanctuary, I took him with me. On the way back we camped one night near some great rocks which had caves in them. Just after dawn next morning, we went out with Engelbrecht in order to give Hodson a chance to shoot a deer or possibly a bear or leopard. We were walking slowly in single file, Hodson in front with his rifle, near the rocks when a leopard crossed our path about 25 yards ahead. Hodson fired and hit the beast for we found and followed a trail of blood right up to the rocks and into a cave. The cave had a large entrance about 12 foot long by 20 foot high, but at least half the entrance was blocked by an enormous rock or boulder about 6 foot long and 6 foot high. The rock itself sloped sharply up to the actual lip of the cave so that, as we three stood peering into the darkness, we could rest our elbows and therefore our rifles on the floor of the cave. A wounded leopard is one of the most dangerous of all animals, and to follow him into a dark cave is sheer madness, as Engelbrecht knew even better than I. At first one could see nothing in the cave, but when our eyes grew accustomed to the semi-darkness Engelbrecht and I both saw the tail of the leopard protruding from behind the boulder. I had two rifles, one a Service ·303 which fired smokeless cartridges and which Engelbrecht was carrying and the other, which I was carrying, an old single-barrelled ·450 firing black powder cartridges. Engelbrecht said that if I would stand at the extreme right of the opening, he would fire at the tail which would make the leopard get up and give me the chance of a shot. When he fired, the tail did not move, but another leopard—obviously the wounded animal's mate—lept out of the shadows and disappeared into the back of the cave. (He got out through a hole at the back of the cave.) The wounded leopard was growling so that we knew it was still alive. Engelbrecht then cut down a sapling and said that he would climb on to the boulder and poke the leopard out with the sapling so that I could get a shot at it. I protested that it was madness, but he said that we could not leave it now and I feebly gave way. We had with us three of the game watchers and I remember at this point suddenly catching sight of the three men each perched on the top of a small tree, looking down upon us with horror—and the sight did not reassure me.

Engelbrecht climbed on to the boulder: he was unarmed and he knew that I was about the worst shot with a rifle in the world. But he poked down at the leopard. At first there was only a burst of savage growls, and then suddenly the leopard sprang into view. I could see him quite clearly sitting up, slightly sideways, three or four yards inside the cave. I fired and jumped aside to the left in front of the boulder and Engelbrecht, Hodson, and I cowered down pressed together in the narrow space away from the opening. When I fired the whole cave was filled with smoke and out of the smoke a foot or two from us whizzed the leopard turning head over heels. He fell upon the rocks below, turned another somersault round another boulder, and there again was the end of his tail jutting out beyond the rock. Very very cautiously we crept down with our rifles ready and peered round the rock. He was dead; by a complete fluke, which I don't think I should have succeeded in bringing off once in twenty times, I had shot him through the heart.

I saw some remarkable sights in the Magampattu jungles. The Game Sanctuary itself was a fascinating place. Its western boundary was the Menik Ganga, a biggish river which, however, often had a mere trickle of water in it and only filled when there was heavy rain up country. I used to go and inspect the Game Sanctuary whenever I could spare the time, camping on the west bank of the river. West of the river where shooting was allowed, the game was as shy as everywhere else. As soon as you crossed the river into the Sanctuary, everything changed and you were in the Garden of Eden. Immense herds of deer, buffaloes before the rinderpest, pig, elephants roamed about in the open paying hardly any attention to you. The northern boundary of the Sanctuary was also the northern boundary of my District and the southern boundary of the Province of Uva; the eastern boundary was a river, the Kumbukkan Oya, which was the western boundary of the Eastern Province. The Game Watchers were expected to keep a broad track cleared all along the northern boundary, and on one of my circuits I decided to inspect the whole length of this to see that the work was really done. I camped on the side of the river and set out on foot early in the morning with Engelbrecht, ten Game Watchers, three coolies, and my dog-boy. It was a good two days' walk and we intended to spend the night in a cave. The coolies carried my camp bed and our food. That morning I saw something which I had been told sometimes happens in the jungle, but about which I had always been a little sceptical. We were walking single file along the track when some way ahead on the top of a small tree were eight or nine monkeys, chattering and shrieking, jumping up and down, up and down, their arms raised above their heads as if they were imploring heaven, their eyes fixed upon the ground. We crept slowly up to the tree and when we got quite near it, I heard from behind a big bush just under the tree click, click, click, click; it was a leopard clicking his teeth and when I fired through the bush, I saw him leap into the jungle and disappear. So the story was not a sportsman's yarn. The leopard lies under a tree on which he has seen monkeys and begins to click his teeth together. The monkeys get wildly excited and jump up and down, up and down with their arms above their heads and sooner or later one of them misses his footing, falls to the ground, and is eaten by the leopard.

In the afternoon it began to pour with rain. About six o'clock we got to some big caves and decided to spend the night there. It rained all night and was still raining in the morning. We were in a quandary, for, although when we left our camp the river was almost dry, the rain was so heavy that it would fill rapidly and if we did not hurry back to the camp we might find ourselves cut off from it for two or even three days by the river in flood. We turned back in pitiless rain. 'The rain was wet,' I recorded in my diary, 'but the jungle was far wetter, and I think I was wettest. Most of the jungle was under water. In most places one walked in mud and water above the ankle, in many above the knee. . . . The last three miles was through a lake of mud with some firm patches. A cold bath in this district is often a luxury, but to stay in it for seven hours is excessive. I have never been colder than when we reached the dripping tents at Talgasmankada.' In fact, we only just got back in time, for when we forded the river the water was up to our armpits and the stream running so strong that one kept on one's feet with difficulty.

But we were not by any means out of the wood. It rained heavily all night and in the early morning reached the tents. It was an amazing sight, a terrific flood sweeping down trees, the remains of huts, drowned cattle, buffaloes, deer. The roads were said to be so flooded as to be impassable to our carts so we decided to stay where we were. The river soon flooded the camping ground and we had to move everything into the watchers' huts, already occupied by them and my two ponies. The river continued to rise and flooded the watchers' huts, so that we had to abandon them, cut a path through the jungle, and pitch the tents on some high ground in an opening. Next morning I determined to try to push on at all costs and we started off at 6 a.m. The carts, with the water above the axles, took 6¼ hours to do 2½ miles. We had some food in an open space at 1 and all round us the deer were out in the open as the jungles were flooded. We took the whole afternoon to do another 1½ miles through water two or three feet deep. At Yala the watch station was under water and had been abandoned; the Watchers' families and their cattle were living on rough platforms made of sticks.

I saw two other rare sights in the Magampattu jungle. One day I had been out with one of the Game Watchers and was returning to my camp in the late afternoon. We suddenly came upon two bull elephants fighting. When we first saw them they were standing forehead to forehead pushing violently and playing a sort of ju-jitsu with their trunks, each trying, I think, to get its trunk round the foreleg of the other. After a time they backed slowly away from each other, and when they were separated by about 50 yards, they charged at full speed and met with a violent crash forehead to forehead. Then the pushing began again, followed again by a charge, and this went on for some time. It was a terrifying sight, this silent struggle of the two enormous beasts in a kind of arena of trodden grass, crushed bushes, and broken trees which they had made with their tramplings and chargings. In the jungle the wild elephant was always to me the most alarming of all the animals. Coming upon him suddenly, as I so often did, in thick jungle he seemed to me gigantic towering up above me; there is, too, something primeval and malignant about him, his pachydermatous greyness, his wicked little eye, the menace of his trunk, the slow, relentless, ceaseless fidgeting. Coming face to face with a buffalo, a bear, or a leopard one felt pretty sure of what he would do, and in 999 cases out of a 1,000 one was right; I never felt that I had any idea of what an elephant would do: he might pay no attention to you at all or dash off in a panic into the jungle or come lumbering after you. Though I was terrified by the fighting bulls—and so, I think, was the Watcher—we could not tear ourselves away from the spectacle. We dodged about behind bushes and trees watching sometimes only ten or fifteen yards away from them, and always ready to bolt out of the way when they backed from each other in preparation for the charge. But suddenly one of them must have scented us, for he stopped fighting and turned in our direction. We made off as quickly as we could, and about two or three hundred yards away we came upon a cow elephant feeding peacefully.

I saw the other strange sight one day when I was out with the same Watcher in thick jungle. We heard quite near us the most extraordinary guttural roaring noise. I had never heard it before and I asked the Watcher what it was; he said that he did not know, he too had never heard anything like it. We crept through the jungle towards the sound and came to a small pool with a large dead tree lying across it and on the tree lay an immense crocodile making this strange roaring. The whole thing was disquieting. A large crocodile, covered with slime and weeks, is more sinister and primeval than even the elephant; to see this creature lying flat on the dead tree, with his mouth wide open, and making this terrific choking roaring, was staggering. I shot him, and we then found that there was a large tortoise firmly stuck in his throat. I suppose that he had tried to eat it by breaking its shell and the tortoise slipped into the back of his throat; it was so firmly wedged that he would never have been able to get it out. He would have died a horribly lingering death—the jungle is a terribly cruel place.

It is difficult to know exactly why I found the jungle so fascinating. It is a cruel and a dangerous place, and, being a cowardly person, I was always afraid of it. Yet I could not keep away from it. I used to love going off entirely by myself—without Engelbrecht or the Game Watchers—and wander about ostensibly to shoot something for dinner, but really just to wander. I liked the complete solitude and silence and every now and again the noises which break the jungle's silence and which, as one learns its ways, tells one of the comings and the goings around one. For a few moments one had succeeded in getting oneself out of the world of one's fellow men—which I always do with a sigh of relief—into a world of great beauty, ugliness, and danger. The beauty was extraordinary and you never knew behind what tree or bush or rock you might not suddenly see it. You slink slowly round a rock in thick jungle and there in a small opening are five or six dazzling peacocks. I once climbed up a large rock, about 40 or 50 feet high, in the middle of the jungle, and standing on the top was a superb sambhur deer, his antlers silhouetted against the sky. When he saw me, he went off down the rock at full speed, and, when he was half-way down, he just launched himself out into space, falling with a crash on bushes or small trees, and disappeared into the jungle. It was a magnificent sight, the great deer with his forelegs and hind legs flat out and his antlers flat on his back catapulting himself off the rock into the air. Another time on a game track I turned a corner and there in the fork of a tree twelve foot from the ground hanging over the branch was the body of a full-grown stag, and on the body lay a leopard eating it. We stared at each other for a moment, and then the leopard just poured himself off the tree as if he were made of elastic or even some miraculous fluid, and disappeared into the jungle.

This kind of beauty of wild animals I never get tired of. But the jungle and jungle life are also horribly ugly and cruel. When I left Ceylon, and wrote *The Village in the Jungle*, that was what obsessed my memory and my imagination and is, in a sense, the theme of the book. The more you are in jungle, particularly if you are alone, the more one tends to feel it personified, something or someone hostile, dangerous. One always has to be on one's guard against it or against—one never quite knows what. I twice lost myself in jungle, a terrifying experience, and each time it was due to carelessness, to forgetting for an instant to be on one's guard against the treachery of the jungle. The first time was only for ten minutes or a quarter of an hour, but it gave me a nasty jar. I often had to go from Hambantota town to Tissamaharama to deal with irrigation, cultivation, and judicial work there. My carts went by road, but there was a track through the jungle which one could ride on and cut off about 12 miles of the cart road. I nearly always rode by this track. At one point I used to dismount, tie my pony to a tree, and push my way through 200 or 300 yards of thick jungle north of the track into an enormous open clearing, circular, about half a mile or more in diameter. One used sometimes to see deer, peafowl, or jungle fowl in it and that was why I used to go there. One day I did this and, after roaming about for five or ten minutes, decided to go back to my pony. I had not noticed that the sky was overcast. When I turned to go back, I could not find the place at which I had entered. Normally when the sky was clear all I had to do was to enter the jungle, go due south, and I would soon strike the track on which I had left the pony. Now I was faced with a circle of jungle a mile or more round this open space, and the wall of trees and leaves was exactly the same all round the circle—and I could not tell which was south and which north. I tried again and again to creep and crawl 200–300 yards through the jungle, first in one place and then in another, but I could not strike the path. It is a golden rule in jungle, when you want to find your way back exactly to the place you started from, to break twigs and boughs as you pass, which will guide you back on your return journey. I had carelessly neglected to do this because the distance was so short. But, although the distance was so short, I was hopelessly lost for there was no means of knowing in which direction the track lay. However, after trying again and again, and marking the places where I had already tried, I at last thought I heard my pony some distance off, as I was crawling under the thorn bushes. And so it was.

The other time I lost myself was even more idiotic and unpleasant. When I went to Tissa, I sometimes used to start after I had done a day's work in Hambantota and spend the night at Weligatta circuit bungalow eight miles along the Tissa road in order to get to Tissa as early as possible next morning. My carts and servants went by road and I rode, cutting across country through scrub jungle. One evening, when I was doing this, I arrived at the bungalow before the carts. I tied my pony to a tree and went off into the jungle north of the bungalow. I had often seen peafowl in the neighbourhood and I thought I would try to find the big trees on which they roosted. I moved about rather aimlessly for half an hour and then decided to go back to the bungalow. I knew exactly how the road and the tracks ran and that, if I walked due west, I would come out either dead on the bungalow or a little to the north of it on the Tissa road or a little to the south of it on a path to a village, Bundala. I also knew that I had already crossed and would have to recross a fairly distinct game track running north-south. It was not long to sunset; I was in thick jungle, and I set off towards the light of what I took to be the setting sun.

After slow progress through thick thorn jungle for about a quarter of an hour, I came to the conclusion that something was wrong, because I had not crossed the game track and the jungle was much thicker and thornier than it was in the neighbourhood of Weligatta. I climbed a tree and found that I had made a fool of myself. There had been a heavy rainstorm, and the western sky was still covered with a black cloud, the eastern sky was bright with reflected light from the west. I had been walking due east instead of due west; I was now in dense jungle, with a great deal of impenetrable thorn bush, and I was probably three-quarters of an hour's walk from the bungalow; there was probably another ten minutes of daylight. I made a push for it, but after five minutes it was clear that I had not a chance of getting out before it was dark. The jungle was soaking wet and so was I. I had a copy of the rinderpest regulations in my pocket and a matchbox with a few matches in it. I decided that I would light a fire under a big tree while there was still light and resign myself to a night in the jungle.

It was only with my last match that I got the damp paper and damper wood to start a bonfire. I built up an enormous fire, but it was really an extremely unpleasant night. To keep a fire going for 8 or 9 hours requires an immense amount of wood. I can sleep anywhere and I slept on the ground close to the fire, but every hour I had to wake up and forage about for more wood. It was a wearisome business and there was considerable danger from snakes as one fumbled about in semi-darkness—there was no moon—for wood. I got so sick of it that at three o'clock in the morning, having satisfied myself about the points of the compass from the stars which I could glimpse through the trees, I decided to start back for the bungalow. I built up an immense fire so that I would be able to return to it if I failed to get through. After five minutes I found it impossible in the darkness to get through the dense thorn bushes, but when I tried to find the fire, it was invisible. I had to lie down and sleep where I was. The sun woke me and it took me just under an hour to get out walking due west and coming out of the jungle within two hundred yards of the bungalow. I found my servants and villagers and headmen in a great state over my disappearance. The only effect upon me was a more than usually severe attack of malaria.

The instinct for direction or the 'homing' instinct is very mysterious and variable. I noticed that with the Game Sanctuary watchers it varied enormously. Some of them were not really very good at finding their way instinctively back through the jungle to the last place where we had camped. On the other hand there was one Watcher who, at any moment anywhere, could stop and go straight back to the exact spot he had left five or six hours ago in thick jungle. In Chapter Two I gave an example of the homing instinct of my horse; I had a still more extraordinary display of it with a dog in Hambantota. I bought a bitch, a half-bred hound, from an advertisement which a planter up country had put in the newspaper. When the bitch was delivered to me, she had obviously been very badly treated and was terrified of me and everyone else. After a week she suddenly realised that I was never going to beat her and she attached herself to me as no other dog has ever attached itself to me. She had a puppy whom I called Mermaid. When Mermaid was about three months old, I decided that the time had come when she could come out on circuit with me. Up to that time she had never been more than, say, half a mile from the bungalow, taken along the road for a walk with the other dogs morning and evening by the dog-boy. I had at this time three other dogs besides Mermaid, and one Friday evening I rode out with the four of them across country to meet my carts eight miles away at Weligatta where I proposed to spend Friday and Saturday nights. The first six miles or so was through scrub jungle and then one came out of the jungle on to a great dry lagoon about a mile long. Mermaid followed admirably with her mother and the two other dogs through the jungle. When we got out on to the sand of the lagoon, the pony began to gallop and started off in front of us a great herd of cattle. Before I knew what was happening cattle, dogs, and pony were tearing and thundering across the lagoon in the wildest excitement. We must have gone a quarter of a mile in this mad way when I suddenly remembered Mermaid, pulled up the pony, and was horrified to find that she was not with us. She must have been frightened by the thundering of hoofs on the sand and bolted back into the jungle. I went all round the edge of the jungle searching and calling for her, but she had completely disappeared and when it became dark I had to abandon the search. I gave up all hope of her for, as I said, she had never been more than at most half a mile from my bungalow, the jungle was thick scrub, and she would probably be soon picked up by a leopard. I stayed Saturday at Weligatta and went back late on Saturday afternoon to Hambantota. At nine o'clock in the evening, after dinner, I was sitting reading on the verandah when suddenly out of the darkness there shot a white body and Mermaid hurled herself into my lap. She was dead beat, lame, bleeding from scratches; she had taken over 24 hours to find her way back through a pathless jungle and then—what must have been even more confusing and terrifying for her—the town of Hambantota.

The District, as I have said before, was famous for its big game shooting and in the open season a considerable number of white people, both residents in Ceylon and visitors to the island, came and applied for licences to shoot elephant, buffalo, and deer. As time went on and my experience of the jungle, shooting, and shooters increased, I became more and more prejudiced against my fellow white men. I may have been sometimes over-severe. Engelbrecht reported to me once that two planters, to whom I had issued licences to shoot deer, had shot deer in the river bed which was the boundary of the Game Sanctuary. I issued summonses upon them and had them brought up before me in Hambantota before they could leave the district. After enquiry it was clear that one of them had shot a deer in the bed of the river. I told him what I thought of him as a 'sportsman' and said that, quite apart from that, I considered that the bed of the river was within the Sanctuary and I proposed to prosecute him for shooting within the Sanctuary. I could try him as Police Magistrate, but if he objected to being tried by me, I would get another P.M. appointed to try his case and would let him know the date of the trial. But if he would rather have the case dealt with by me on the spot, I said I would fine him Rs. 50. He was extremely angry, but he eventually paid the fine and departed.

I found the international 'sportsmen' even more uncongenial. Before the Crown Prince of Germany visited Ceylon, the Governor sent his A.D.C. down to Hambantota to discuss with me whether I advised his coming to my District to shoot. I managed to get out of this, but I had some curious experiences with royal and aristocratic sportsmen. Big game shooting was organised in Colombo as big business. The would-be hunter or party went to a Colombo firm which undertook to provide them at Hambantota with bullock carts, trackers, tents, food and to organise the shoot for them. The sportsmen came to me for licences and a strange company they were. One Sunday morning when I was working in my bungalow my boy brought me three cards and said that three gentlemen wanted to see me. A Prince, a Duke, and a Count came into my room: one was a Bourbon, one an Orleans, and one a Napoleon. I issued licences to them. In the afternoon I happened to see the expedition start from the town. There were four bullock carts. The two in front contained an immense number of boxes, tents, and furniture. The third was empty, and walking beside it were the three sportsmen. The fourth contained a bevy of ladies who seemed to me most unsuitable for the jungles of Magampattu; their normal place of domicile was, I guessed, a Colombo brothel.

One day I received from the Government in Colombo a telegram informing me that Baron Blixen, a Danish cousin of Queen Alexandra, was coming to shoot in my District, and I was to help him in every way possible. I found that the Baron was one of a party of Scandinavian aristocrats who were coming to shoot. Two days later the party arrived and their leader Count Frijs called on me, accompanied by his daughter. The Count was a tall, very good-looking Swede; the Countess made my heart, chaste and chastened by two years in Hambantota, turn over in my breast. She was the dream Scandinavian Countess of the glossy woman's magazine and of the unsophisticated (or indeed sophisticated) male heart. About twenty-one years old, she had the yellowest of corn-coloured hair, the bluest of sky-blue eyes, the most delicate, soft, rose-petal pink complexion. And they were charming, with all the charm and perfect manners of the aristocrat who wants to get you to do something for him. What they wanted of me was first to give them licences to kill a large number of wild animals, and secondly to look after Queen Alexandra's cousin when he arrived in Hambantota. For Baron Blixen was not with them; he had become slightly unwell in Colombo and would not be well enough to come to Hambantota for a day or two. The Count, his lovely daughter, and the rest of his party proposed to set off at once to the jungle and begin their shoot; the famous Herr Hagenbeck of Colombo—famous in the world of zoos and circuses—would in a day or two bring the Baron to Hambantota and hand him over to me, and would I have the great goodness to take charge of the Baron and bring him to Count Frijs?

I promised Count Frijs that I would do what he asked of me and they departed for the jungle in a shower of thanks and smiles. I had to go to Tissamaharama to hold an enquiry, and I left directions for Herr Hagenbeck and the Baron to be sent on to me there. They arrived in a motor-car two or three days later. Baron Axel Blixen was a middle-aged man with mutton-chop whiskers, watery eyes, and a distant resemblance to the Prince Consort. He was extremely nervous, and, holding my hand in his two hands, besought me not to leave him alone in the jungle, but take him and hand him over to County Frijs. I reassured him, but, as they had made no arrangements where to meet the rest of the party, I had to send out messengers in various directions to try to find them. Meanwhile Baron Blixen had to spend the night with me in the Tissa Rest House. In the late afternoon I asked him whether he would like to shoot something; we could either go out in the Irrigation Engineer's punt on to the tank just before sunset and shoot teal, or I would take him round the tank and give him a shot at a crocodile. He chose the crocodile. We set off round the tank and after about half a mile I pointed out to him a large crocodile lying by the water's edge about 30 yards from us. The Baron took careful aim and fired, and his bullet hit the ground less than 15 yards from his toes and more than 15 yards from the crocodile's toes. Next day a messenger arrived with a note saying that Count Frijs was at Palatupana, and, having delivered Baron Blixen there, I returned to Hambantota, once more in a shower of smiles and gratitude. Some two or three weeks later the party returned to Hambantota, and the Baron came up to see me. He had had a most successful shoot and he asked me to come and see his trophies. His shooting had improved enormously since the evening at Tissa. I cannot now remember exactly what he showed me, but certainly several deer and I rather think a bear. His terror that I should abandon him in the Ceylon jungles before he found Count Frijs may, of course, have affected his shooting, though I have never seen anyone else, even myself, make quite such a bad shot. I should add that the Baron was an extremely kindly and courteous man. One of my mother's sisters had married a Dane and lived in Copenhagen. When Baron Blixen got back to Denmark with his trophies, he called upon my aunt, told her about his meeting with me, and was enthusiastically grateful for all that I had done for him.

I do not know how the Baron came to shoot so badly at Tissa and so well at Palatupana. But I know that it was a common practice for the tracker supplied by the Colombo organiser of the expedition to stand by the sportsman's side, particularly in the case of a dangerous animal like a bear or buffalo, and shoot at the same moment as the sportsman. A great deal of this big-business organised safari or whatever they called the thing in Colombo was despicable butchery. The most contemptible 'sport' was the shooting of elephants; I used to take every excuse to refuse licences to shoot an elephant, and I unsuccessfully tried to get the Government to make a regulation that the A.G.A. should stop the issue of licences, except in the case of a particular elephant in a particular place which he was satisfied was either a rogue or was habitually causing damage to crops.

As time went on, I became, I think, more and more severe and unrelenting, particularly in relation to my fellow white men, and this sometimes got me into hot water. One incident, in which I still think that right was in the main on my side, had, I heard, a bad effect upon my reputation among some people who never heard my side of the happening. Whenever I was in Hambantota town, I used to bathe in the evening in the bay. There was a very ancient, derelict jetty, the top of which was quite sound and was six or eight feet above the sea. From the end of it, there had once been a flight of steps down to a landing stage, but the wooden steps and platform had long ago disappeared and only an iron skeleton, covered with barnacles, remained. I used to dive from the jetty itself into the sea, but to get out on to the iron skeleton of the landing stage required great care, agility, and experience. The only safe way was to swim quietly up to it and allow a wave to lift you up above it so that, as the wave fell, your two arms were left supporting you on the iron girder and you could then gingerly get your feet upon the girder, avoiding the lacerating barnacles. There was always a fairly heavy swell rolling into the bay. I am not a very good swimmer but continual practice had taught me exactly how to get out of the sea on to the girder. One day a civil servant, whom I will call X, came to Hambantota for a night on some business and stayed with me. He said he would like to bathe in the evening; I explained how I got out of the water, but asked him not to try to do it, unless he was a first-class swimmer, and instead to come back to the shore. When I had got out on to the jetty after our swim, he began to follow me and I implored him not to do so, but to swim straight back to the shore. He would not do so, and being a heavy, fat man, he was soon in difficulties and his legs and arms bleeding from the barnacles. I really thought he was going to drown and went back into the water to help him swim to shore. It was an extremely unpleasant experience, for he was exhausted and we were swept together under the jetty. I only just got him and myself to the shore.

About three months later another civil servant, whom I will call Mr Y, came for a night and stayed with me. We went down to bathe; I told him of my experience with Mr X and said that he must not on any account try to get out of the sea on to the jetty; if he did so and got into difficulties, I should let him drown for I was not going to repeat the very unpleasant experience of rescuing Mr X. Mr Y did exactly what Mr X had done and was soon in great difficulties. I refused to go in to help him, and eventually, having swallowed a great deal of sea-water, exhausted and angry, he struggled ashore. I too was angry, especially when I heard that it was being widely said that I had behaved in a cowardly and ruthless way to Mr Y. Nothing was ever said about Mr X.

I also got into hot water with my superiors, particularly the Government Agent, C. M. Lushington. I thought Lushington to be a rather stupid man and prejudiced against me as being too young for my post and 'jumped up' by Sir Hugh Clifford. Shortly after I was made A.G.A. he recommended the appointment of a headman in my District without consulting me, a very unusual proceeding. I protested to Government, recommended someone else, and won my point. He several times opposed innovations which I introduced or recommended, and here again once or twice I got my way against him. No doubt I was arrogant and offensive, and he had a good deal to complain of against me. At the end of my time in Hambantota, in fact just after I went on leave, I was sent by Lushington a copy of the following letter which he had received—I am sure with great pleasure—from the Colonial Secretary:

19th May, 1911
Colonial Secretary's Office
Colombo.

Sir,

I am directed to request you to inform Mr Woolf that His Excellency the Governor has observed that the tone of his comments in his diary and in endorsement No. 205 of 26th April to the Government Agent, Southern Province, regarding the acquisition of land required for the Public Works Department Store at Tangalla, leaves much to be desired.

2. His Excellency accordingly desires you to instruct him to comment with more restraint and discretion upon the orders of his Superior Officer.

I am, etc.
A. N. Galbraith
for Colonial Secretary.

In my last year at Hambantota, and as the time for my leave came nearer and nearer—I was due for a year's leave at the end of 1910 but, owing to the Government's difficulty in finding a successor, had to wait until 20 May 1911—I became more and more doubtful about my future. What may be called the imperialist side of my profession had become consciously distasteful to me. If I was very successful in my career, as I now was certain I should be, I would be promoted sooner or later to the Central Government and Colombo, and would go on to become a Colonial Secretary and Governor. The prospect filled me with despondency though the temptation of power and position was felt by me. Not for the last time, confronted with a choice of worldly goods or paths, I thought of the French poet:

Si le roi m'avoit donné
Paris sa grand' ville
Et qu'il me fallût quitter
L'amour de ma vie!

Je dirois au roi Henri
Reprenez votre Paris;
J'aime mieux ma mie, o gué,
J'aime mieux ma mie.

And, of course, just as the Paris which the world offers you and tempts you with is not always the same, ranging from perhaps a

Governorship at one moment of your life to an editorship or what is called security at another, so *l'amour de ma vie* and *ma mie* are not always the same. The *ma mie* for which I was prepared to sacrifice Paris was in one case no doubt Virginia, but it has also been occasionally in my life a kind of independence or freedom denied to you in Civil Services and similar occupations which bring you pomp and power.

On the other hand I became completely immersed, not only in my work, but in the life of the people. The more remote that life was from my own, the more absorbed I became in it and the more I enjoyed it. In July 1910, I had to go and superintend the famous Kataragama Pilgrimage. Kataragama was not actually in my District; it was a tiny village in dense jungle in the Uva Province, but it had no roads to it and was so far from any inhabited place in Uva that it was practically inaccessible to the G.A. of that Province. It was about ten miles from Tissamaharama and the A.G.A. Hambantota always had to look after it. It was a very curious experience. The pilgrimage, which took place every three or four years, was famous in Ceylon and all over Southern India. In the old days great numbers of pilgrims used to come from India. They trailed along the south coast of Ceylon through Galle and Matara into the Hambantota district. From Hambantota town to Kataragama there were practically no villages and neither food nor shelter was obtainable. Among pilgrims there are always a large number of sick people who are brought to the temple to be cured by the God. These unfortunate people trailed along the unpopulated Magampattu road and along the jungle track from Tissa to Kataragama, half starved, many of them falling sick and dying on the way. There was something even worse than this: very often they brought with them from India cholera or smallpox, and the pilgrimage more than once was the cause of serious epidemics in Hambantota which spread through the island. Eventually the Government made strict regulations for the pilgrimage. It was allowed only at intervals and no one was allowed to come to it except on a ticket issued by the Ceylon Government. A limited number of tickets were sent to the Government of India to issue to would-be Indian pilgrims and a certain number were reserved for people in Ceylon. I had 75 tickets and 300 applicants.

I rode to Kataragama from Tissa in the early morning of 8 July and I stayed there 14 days, until 22 July when the pilgrimage ended. There were between 3,000 and 4,000 pilgrims. Many of them were town dwellers who had never seen a jungle. They had travelled by sea and train to and through a strange land; men, women, and children had trudged 180–200 miles along the roads and on the jungle track to find themselves dumped for a fortnight with three or four thousand other people in a clearing in dense jungle. For Kataragama in 1910 was little more than a large clearing in the unending jungle. It had two temples, one at one end of what might euphemistically be called the village street—it was only a very broad path between boutiques and sheds—and the other at the other end. The religious set-up of the temples and the pilgrimage was most confusing. The temples were Hindu and the priests were Tamil Hindus; the Managers were Sinhalese Buddhists. Buddhists as well as Hindus came to the pilgrimage, and low caste people, dhobies and pariahs, were allowed into the temple, which would never be allowed in an ordinary Jaffna Hindu temple. Every evening the image of the God was carried in procession to the other temple—a kind of juggernaut procession with the pilgrims following or rolling over and over in the dust before the God's car. In the other temple was the God's wife or concubine and after visiting her he returned to his own temple. On the last day of the festival the priest and all the pilgrims went to the river with the image of the God, and there, standing in the middle of the river, the priest 'cut the waters' with a knife—and the festival was over.

One day during the festival I climbed the Kataragama hill, a pretty high rugged hill some distance through the jungle from the temples. It took me four hours' strenuous walking and climbing, but I got a fine view from the top of the miles and miles of jungle stretching to the Uva and Batticaloa hills and mountains. A Sinhalese villager came with me to show me the way and we got talking about the God and the temples. According to this Sinhalese the Kataragama Deviyo (God) was Kandeswami and originally had his temple on the top of the Kataragama hill. One day he thought he would like to cross the river and live in Kataragama. He asked some Tamils who were passing to carry him across. They said that they were on the way to Palatupana to collect salt and could not do so, but they would carry him across on their way back. A little while afterwards there came by some Sinhalese and the God asked them to carry him across the river into Kataragama. They did so at once. The God at that time was a Tamil, but he married into a Sinhalese family in Kataragama and became a Sinhalese God, and that is why now the temple kapuralas are Sinhalese. This was the story of a Buddhist Sinhalese villager. When I told his story to my servant, a Hindu Jaffna Tamil, he said that that was 'all tales': the God is Kandeswami and no one else. But he could not explain how the dhobies and pariah are allowed into the temple if it is really a Hindu Kandeswami Koyil.

The only really bad sleepless night I can remember to have had in my life was in the village of Kataragama. The pilgrimage is a kind of Ceylon Lourdes, and hundreds of sick people dragged themselves or were dragged through the jungle to be cured by the Kataragama Deviyo. My bungalow—the only one in the village—was just above the temple. The pilgrims used to spend the night round the temple and one night when I went to bed, a child was screaming and crying in a terrible way in the courtyard of the temple just below my room. After a bit, I could not stand it, called my boy, and told him to go down into the temple and ask the parents either to do something to pacify the child or remove it from immediately under my window. My boy returned, but the child went on crying and it cried all night, 'in the night, with no language but a cry', a terrible, unending, tortured cry. I felt in my bones that it was no good doing anything more; my boy would have had the thing stopped if he could; there was something behind it which I would learn in the morning. So I lay awake hour after hour tortured by the tortured howling of the child. In the morning I asked my boy what it all meant. He was very sorry, he said; the people, a mother and father, had come from India with the child. The child was blind, and they had come to Kataragama to ask the God to give him sight. The God had not heard their prayers and they thought that perhaps if they made the child cry long and loud enough, the God would hear him. They had therefore pinched the child and had even pricked him with pins to make him cry. I went down to the temple and found the parents. They were South Indian villagers, unhappy, tired, bewildered; the child was blind. I asked them whether they would come with me and let the District Medical Officer, a Sinhalese, look at the child's eyes. They agreed, for they were resigned to agree to anything. According to the D.M.O., there was nothing that he could do. The child was blind and neither Kandeswami nor science could give him sight.

It was these kind of strange, alien psychological encounters which fascinated me—the mixture of pathos and absurdity, of love and cruelty, in such horrible and grotesque incidents. I ought to have hated my 14 days supervising the pilgrimage. The heat during the day makes life intolerable; I wrote at the time, 'one cannot exist in the bungalow after 10 a.m. without wearing a hat of some sort while the glare is enough to warrant smoked spectacles. In this condition one sits in a perpetual sandstorm waiting for the sun to go down and for the mosquitoes to come out and take the place of the eyeflies. I hope that the Kataragama God sees to it that the supervisor of the pilgrims acquires some little merit from this pilgrimage.' Yes, despite the physical miseries and the complete isolation, I enjoyed my fortnight and left Kataragama with slight regret. The complete self-confidence of the British imperialist in 1910 was really rather strange. Here was I, an Englishman aged 29, who had collected in the middle of the Ceylon jungle nearly 4,000 men, women, and children, gathered together from all over Ceylon and Southern India. I was responsible administratively for everything connected with the well-being of these people and for the maintenance of law and order. If anything had gone wrong during the pilgrimage I should have been blamed. But we were so firmly convinced that, if one white civil servant was there, nothing could possibly go wrong, that I had no staff and no police. I had the District Medical Officer to look after the health of 4,000 people and the village headman to maintain order among them. Our self-confidence was fully justified. I had little or nothing to do except to answer questions, listen to complaints, keep an eye on what was going on, particularly during the processions. In the early morning or late afternoon I used to take my gun and wander off alone into the jungle and down to the river, and I was able to find out a good deal about the illicit shooting of deer and a kind of large-scale traffic in dried meat which, I had long known, went on all along the northern boundary of my District. I enjoyed the meditative isolation of my pilgrimage to the Kataragama Deviyo.

Sometimes the good that men do is not interred with their bones, it lives after them to be turned into evil. When the pilgrimage was over I wrote to the Government Agent and recommended that the Government should make the Kataragama temple authorities provide accommodation for the pilgrims. I pointed out that the authorities got between three and four thousand pilgrims to come to Kataragama and the revenue which they obtained from offerings must have been pretty considerable. There was not cover enough in the village to shelter 1,000 people; there had been heavy rain during the pilgrimage and the result was much malaria and pneumonia. The authorities, I said, should at least provide temporary cadjan buildings and cut drains round them.

I left Kataragama on 23 July 1910. I saw it again on my visit to Ceylon on 16 February 1960. The jungle track from Tissa had been converted into a good road over which I was comfortably driven in a car. My recommendation had certainly been carried out, but the Kataragama that I knew had disappeared. There was now a large car park by the side of the river and a bridge over the river; there was now shelter for the pilgrims. There were many things connected with the Kataragama of 1910 which were evil and which to me were repellent. I dislike superstition wherever I find it, whether among primitive and simple people or sophisticated ninnies. But at least there was something fundamentally genuine, primitively real there in the jungle. The people believed what they believed simply and purely. The beliefs were deplorable, no doubt, but the purity, simplicity, and their motives for taking the terrible journey to the temple I respected. Even the temple authorities, though they were, like most Church authorities, greedy and disingenuous, seemed to have some faint belief in what they preached or professed. The pilgrimage was an authentic, spontaneous explosion of the hopes and aspirations of ordinary men and women who lived hard and bewildered lives. The Kataragama of 1960 is the exact opposite. Like Lisieux and other famous European places of Christian pilgrimage its whole atmosphere is that of the commercialised exploitation of credulity. Walking up what was before the village street, you passed boutique after boutique, selling flowers and fruit, to be offered in the temple and *mutatis mutandis* you might have been passing the shops in Lisieux or even in London's Victoria Street, selling their candles and images of the Blessed Virgin. I went into the temple, where in 1910 I had often gone to talk about arrangements for the procession with the priest, in order to see what things were like in 1960. I took the usual offering of fruit and flowers, but was advised that the offering would not be received by the God unless a rupee, as a minimum, was included. When I saw the priest—I have seen his spit and image in many cathedrals, churches, and temples—I had no doubt that he was the God's financial adviser. The only thing which he was interested in was my rupee which he abstracted at once. What surprised and saddened me was to find that even educated Sinhalese would drive all the way from

Colombo to Kataragama to worship in this temple, despite or because of its commercialised religion.

In the last half of my time in Hambantota I had, I think, an extraordinary wide and intense knowledge of the country and the people. If a man came into the kachcheri or the Court, more often than not I could tell from his looks which village he came from. The knowledge was indeed reciprocal; if the A.G.A. knew the people, the people got to know the A.G.A. Many of them did not like his severity. I always encouraged the headmen and villagers to talk quite freely to me. One day, camping in a village in West Giruwa Pattu, I had a crowd of petitioners who kept me at work until the evening. When the enquiries were over, I stayed talking to them for a bit. Halley's comet was blazing in the sky. The villagers informed me that they did not like the comet and that it was an evil age for the people. The village headman then gave me the following list of evils which had come upon them:

1. the road tax,
2. the V.C. tax,
3. the irrigation rate,
4. the taxes on carts and guns,
5. the restriction of chenas,
6. a strict Assistant Government Agent.

He invited me to take as my model a previous Assistant Government Agent who had allowed chenas freely and, when he left the District, wept among weeping headmen.

When I visited Ceylon again after 50 years I had a curious instance of the long memory of grievance and of my severity. Hardly any of the headmen or government officers who had worked under me were alive. But on my last day in Colombo, a man who had been chief headman of one of the pattus when I was A.G.A. came to pay his respects to me at the Galle Face Hotel. After desultory conversation, he suddenly said to me: 'Do you remember, Sir, when you made me shoot the buffalo?' I said no, I did not remember it. 'You heard', he said, 'that there were stray buffaloes, affected with rinderpest, in the village of Liyangahatota, and you sent a message to me to meet you in the village with the village headman. We found the buffaloes in a large stretch of paddy field, and saw that one of them was badly diseased. When we tried to get near them, they ran off. Then you told the Arachchi to go and drive the sick buffalo down the field to you so that you could destroy it. The Arachchi said it had gone savage and would attack him. You insisted, but when he got near the animal, he became afraid and ran away. Then you gave me your gun; you were riding a horse and you said that you would go and drive the buffalo down to me and that I was to shoot it. This we did. Then you asked who owned these buffaloes and why had they been allowed to stray? It turned out that it was the Arachchi himself who owned the buffaloes. You fined the Arachchi 10 rupees for not carrying out his duties as headman and not seeing that the buffaloes were impounded. Then, as Police Magistrate, you tried him as owner of the buffaloes for allowing a diseased animal to stray and you fined him 25 rupees. Ten days later the man came to me with 20 rupees to pay his fine, but he could not pay the other 15 rupees and I had to pay it for him. It was too severe, Sir—was it fair, Sir, was it fair?' After 50 years I felt I could not be quite certain of the answer. *Was* it fair?

For some time in 1910 I was bombarded with anonymous and pseudonymous letters, all in the same handwriting, abusing me and threatening me. They were the result of two incidents. Information about what was happening or going to happen in the District used to reach me from many different sources, often unsolicited. I was told—very confidentially—that in a latrine that I was having built in the town the work was being done in a most dishonest way with the connivance of the Government officer responsible. What should have been solid cement according to the estimate was rubble with a very thin coating of cement. When it was reported that the building was completed and certified by him as properly built according to specification, I told him to meet me at the place with a pickaxe. He fell on the floor in a faint. When I examined the building it proved to be a complete swindle and the Government officer was dismissed. I had a suspicion that the anonymous letters came from his father.

The other incident in which the same family was involved was more interesting. Gambling was illegal in Ceylon, partly because it often led to violent crime and disorder. One day I came back from circuit to Hambantota town a day earlier than expected and I was told by someone that about 100 strangers had come to the town from all along the south coast, even from Galle and Matara, far outside my District, for organised gambling, and that my Police Sergeant was conniving. I made arrangements with someone other than my informant to let me know at once if gambling began again.

Two nights later after midnight a message came to say that the gambling was going on. The following entry in my diary describes what happened:

I sent word to Mr Doole, Mudaliyar of East Giruwa Pattu, whom I had instructed to remain in Hambantota for the purpose, to keep watch and inform me of a favourable opportunity as watchers were said to be 'keeping cave'. At 1.30 a.m. Mr Doole came to my bungalow and told me that gambling was going on in two houses. At 2 a.m. we got to the first and after sending men round to the back door I went on to the verandah. Eight persons were gambling and one was lying asleep on a couch. Among them were the Police Sergeant himself, the Vidane Arachchi of Tissa, and the Mudaliyar's clerk. It was an extremely diverting sight to see their faces when I put my head in at the door. I prosecuted them all except the Sergeant in the Gansabhawa this morning and they were fined. I am dealing with the Sergeant departmentally.

It was, of course, depressing to find that one's severity was much resented and anyone who tries to insist that a large number of persons, particularly government servants, shall work hard and efficiently, is bound to be unpopular. On the other hand, my vanity was flattered because it seemed to me that, as time went on, in many ways the people seemed to trust me more and came to me to settle their disputes and solve their difficulties. It was in this kind of work that I became most deeply absorbed. There was, for instance, a large village in the extreme west of the District in which a tremendous dispute over the ownership of land had been going on for a long time and had caused an immense amount of litigation and even some crimes of violence. The whole thing was characteristic of village life in Ceylon 50 years ago. The kernel of the trouble was 48 acres of land, the ownership of which was in dispute between the villagers on one side and the Court interpreter of Tangalla on the other. When I went to the village, both sides agreed to submit the matter to me for arbitration. I held the enquiry in the village, sitting from 8 in the morning to 4 in the afternoon in the middle of a crowd of about 250 excited partisans. I decided that 18 acres belonged to the interpreter and 30 acres to the villagers. But I had become convinced that as long as the interpreter owned any land in the village, there would be trouble, and I induced him to agree to sell and then to buy the 18 acres. It then became necessary to assess the price to be paid. After five and a half hours of strenuous negotiation I got the villagers to agree to pay Rs 5,000 in two annual instalments. But if I thought that that settled the dispute, I was very much mistaken. First of all the whole thing broke down because the villagers began to quarrel among themselves as to how the land was to be distributed among them. I refused to accept defeat and went down again and again to the village, enquiring minutely into the claims to ownership. It took me six months to get 44 people to agree to my decision as to who should be the owner of 44 lots and to my assessment of what each should pay to the interpreter for his lot. They then actually, to my astonished relief, deposited Rs 5,051 to be drawn by the interpreter when the deeds were executed. Then other difficulties arose involving more enquiries and negotiations, and it was another six months before all the parties met in my presence and the deeds were signed and the money paid over.

Another big dispute which I settled interested me greatly. There was in Hambantota town a mosque and quite a large number of Moslems, chiefly Malays. I knew that a great deal of ill-feeling had arisen among them, when the Hakim died, over the selection of a successor. Some of them wanted Mr Doole, a chief headman, to be appointed, others wanted a Mr Bahar who was the Government Salt Superintendent. I was rather concerned by the growing ill-feeling, but it was very difficult for me to interfere. Then one day a card was brought in to me and I was told that a gentleman wished to see me. The gentleman proved to be a rather melancholy, but tough-looking Englishman. He said that his name was Hadji Salam Robertson; he had been an officer in the Leicestershire Regiment, but just after getting his company he was converted to Muhammadanism, had resigned, and had made the pilgrimage to Mecca. He was travelling through the East and went from place to place lecturing on the Moslem religion, the lore and law of which he had studied deeply. He was going to give a lecture in Hambantota and he and the local Muhammadans wanted me to take the chair. I agreed to do this provided that the local Muhammadans confirmed the invitation. I told him about the Hakim dispute and asked him to try to get the rival factions to agree over an appointment. He said that he would do so, but that if they could not agree, the right procedure was for them to remit the dispute to Constantinople for settlement.

The lecture took place; it was interesting and nearly all the Moors and Malays attended, but I noted at the time that I rather doubted whether they understood much of it. But, to my surprise, shortly after it the leaders of the two factions came to me and asked me to try to settle the dispute. I found it to be a curious and rather dangerous situation. There were two mosques in the town, one old, and one new. A section of the Muhammadans whom they called Karawas or Fishers had been excommunicated from the old mosque and they had built a new mosque of their own. Mr Doole was the leader of the old mosque party and Mr Bahar of the Fishers. I arranged for the rival leaders and the trustees of the two mosques to come to my house. It was clear from the discussion that the ordinary people were quite ready for a settlement and would choose a Hakim acceptable to both parties—it was the leaders who would not agree. I could not induce them to accept a compromise but I made it clear to them that I would not allow the formation in Hambantota of two dangerous factions headed by two of the chief Muhammadan Government officers. They went away and two rival Hakims were elected, which was quite irregular. Some time later I received a letter from Mr Doole saying that there would be a serious disturbance at the mosque at next Friday prayers. Mr Bahar and the Fishers had announced their intention of praying at the old mosque and Mr Doole and his party were going to resist them: every man had been told to come 'taking one sandal in the hand'. Two hundred and fifty men were assembled on one side and 150 on the other. Everything seemed to be prepared for very serious trouble. I sent for the leaders, talked frankly to them, explaining to them exactly who would be held responsible if there were a disturbance. I told the Government officers concerned that, as they had roused up the people, I should hold them personally responsible to calm them down. I noted in my diary that 'the warning was sufficient and it was not necessary to fall back upon the police force of Hambantota which consists of one sergeant.' In fact a few days later the leaders again asked to see me. We had a meeting and after prolonged discussion a settlement was proposed to which they said all would agree. Three days later it was announced that the Hakim dispute was ended.

These were sophisticated disputes among sophisticated people, and they were dangerous because they might easily have led to large-scale violence. What fascinated me more were the queer problems and disputes which quite often the unsophisticated villagers put before me. For instance, one day noticing a man who looked rather ill, I asked him what was the matter with him. He said he was suffering from 'yak leda', which means devil sickness. How, I asked him, did he catch devil sickness. Well, he said, one night he went to look at the wells, which he was in charge of, and in the dark he ran against what he thought was a devil. It turned out to be an old woman, but he had been ill with devil sickness ever since.

In a remote village on the coast a curious female trade existed. The village women used to swim out 300 yards from the shore, dive down, and fish up big coral stones. They swam back with the stones and stacked them in heaps called fathoms, 6 foot by 6 foot by 6 foot. The stones were sold for building purposes at Rs 4 to Rs 6 per fathom. The output was about 300 fathoms a year and I was told that as many as 2,400 women work off and on—a number which seemed to me quite incredible. When I went to see the diving, the women told me that they never got malaria. One day when I was passing near the village, a large deputation of the women stopped and asked me to help them. The stones which they had fished up had been seized by the Forest Department on the ground that they were 'forest produce'. I wrote to the Assistant Conservator of Forests that I did not think that even the law, which everyone knew was an ass, could include the sea in the legal definition of a forest. The Assistant Conservator of Forests released the stones from seizure.

It was very rare for village women to put their problems before one. I had in fact, I think, only one other case. One day on circuit in a rather remote part of the District I was riding along a path when I was stopped by a number of women belonging to the Berawaya or tom-tom beater caste with a strange request. By immemorial custom they were not allowed to wear jackets; the most that they were allowed for covering of their breasts was a narrow strip of cloth which they wound over their breasts and under their armpits. They asked my permission to wear jackets, giving as their reason that they could not pound rice decently owing to this strip of cloth. I told the petitioners that it was not for me to tell the Sinhalese women what clothes they could or could not wear, but that I would have a talk with the village headman. I knew the Vidana Arachchi to be a crusted conservative, and I had small hope of his agreeing to any change. At first he said that the tom-tom beating caste had never been allowed to wear jackets, but, after some discussion and cogitation, he said that if the women did not put their arms into the sleeves, they might be allowed to wear jackets just hanging round their necks. I told the women that they had better do this and they were quite satisfied; I felt sure, that after another 50 years, the Berawaya women's arms would be in the sleeves. But one had to be careful about caste customs and demands to change them. I once had to help the police quell a serious riot in Jaffna which arose in the following way. When a high caste man died, his corpse was carried out of his compound to cremation or burial not through the gate, but part of the cadjan fence was torn down and the corpse was carried out through the hole. Suddenly one of the lower castes announced that they would follow the same practice and the higher caste objected. When a man of the lower caste died and the corpse was about to be carried out, a large crowd of the higher caste gathered outside the house and when the dead man's relations began making a hole in the fence a fight began. There were soon a hundred or more men fighting savagely on the road and in the compound. Before we got to the scene and stopped the fighting, a dozen men had been seriously injured.

The nicest case which I was ever asked to settle was in a large village of West Giruwa Pattu called Walasmulla. I was holding enquiries and also conducting a sale of Crown land situated in a neighbouring village. I was surrounded by a large crowd of villagers. Suddenly in the middle of the proceedings the crowd parted and an old man with one side of his face shaved and the other unshaven rushed into the ring and fell at my feet. He complained that the barber in the bazaar (and he was apparently the only barber in Walasmulla), after shaving one side of his face, had refused to shave the other unless paid 50 cents. The correct price of a shave in Walasmulla was 5 cents. I sent for the barber and he appeared accompanied by some hundreds of spectators. After enquiry, I told the barber that he must complete the shave and he would be paid nothing, but if he cut the old man, he would have to pay him 50 cents. The old man was in deadly earnest, but the barber, who had the face of a rogue and a humorist, appeared to be greatly amused. We adjourned to a coconut tree in the compound of the Rest House and there the operation of shaving the old man was completed before me and an enormous crowd of spectators. The spectators were obviously delighted and amused and this revealed a characteristic of the Sinhalese which always endeared them to me. The relations between Europeans and some Asiatic peoples are made difficult because the Asiatic does not seem to share the European's sense of humour. This is not the case with the Sinhalese. They are a humorous people and they have the same kind of sense of humour as the European. Even in a remote village I felt that I could make a joke which would be appreciated.

Just before I left Hambantota an incident occurred which

proved—what I knew only too well—that one never knew what might not happen and that, even in the quietest place, peace was precarious. There was very little crime in Hambantota town and the police force consisted, as I have said, of one Police Sergeant. During my three years there the various races and religions had lived amicably side by side. But a night or two before I left, when I was taking my dogs for a stroll near my house, a man came running towards me shouting: 'Come, Sir, quick—they are killing one another in the town. Come, Sir, quick.' We ran as hard as we could to the town and on the way he told me that the Buddhists and Moslems, armed with sticks and stones and with the posts which they pulled out of the fences, were fighting one another in front of the mosque. When I got to the spot, I found a large crowd of angry people, but the fighting was practically over. A number of Sinhalese Buddhists were being besieged in a house by angry Moslems. There were six or seven Moslems wounded and covered with blood and one Sinhalese, a Government servant, who lived near the mosque, had tried to stop the row when it began, and had been hit by a stone in his face. I was immediately surrounded by a crowd of people telling me different stories. I noticed three or four people who, I was sure, were not residents of the town and would therefore be more or less unbiased. So I got hold of them and took them straight away, accompanied by most of the combatants, to the Police Court. I had the Court opened and by the light of lamps began at once to record evidence.

It was soon quite clear what had happened. There had been a Buddhist procession through the town. Because they might easily result in religious disturbances, religious processions with tom-toms were not allowed except on licence. The licence prescribed through what streets the procession might go and always contained a clause forbidding the beating of tom-toms while the procession was passing a place of worship belonging to a different religious community. In this case the row had begun when the Buddhist procession, contrary to the terms of the licence, beat their tom-toms while passing the mosque. Some Moslems tried to stop this and the Buddhists fell upon them and severely handled them. The Moslems in the bazaar, hearing what was happening at the mosque, rushed to the spot in large numbers, tearing up the fences as they came in order to provide themselves with weapons. The Buddhists, seeing that they would be overwhelmed, sought sanctuary in the house where I had found them being besieged.

This, of course, was not quite the story told to me in the witness-box by the strangers, who were themselves Buddhists and Sinhalese. But as they had no time to get together with their co-religionists and prepare their evidence—which was my object in starting proceedings at once—they very clearly gave it all away. After recording sufficient evidence to show beyond doubt what had happened, I adjourned and went to bed. Next morning the leading Moslems and Buddhists came to see me, and the following entry in my official diary shows what happened:

The leaders on both sides wished to settle the matter of yesterday amicably. No one had been seriously hurt. There has also never been any religious feeling in the town and there is no doubt that, if cases with proctors on each side had been engaged on, such feeling would be engendered. I therefore said that if the persons responsible on each side would plead guilty to charges which I would frame against them I would allow the cases of hurt &c. to be withdrawn. This was done and I fined one side for disturbing a religious procession and the other for tom-toming without licence, the Muhammadans Rs 35 and the Buddhists Rs 60. The penalties were, of course, light, but as a matter of expediency much will have been gained by allowing the religious ill-feeling to die out at once.

My last day in Hambantota, I spent visiting the schools. I had built and opened a Government Tamil school in the town and had made primary education compulsory. Father Cooreman, a Belgian Roman Catholic missionary, had a Sinhalese school in the town. I visited these two schools and the last entry in my diary records that 'the numbers have gone up very well since we began to enforce attendance and there are signs of some knowledge being driven into the heads of the youth of Hambantota.'

Next day I departed for Colombo, and from Colombo, with my sister Bella, now married to the Assistant Director of the Peradeniya Gardens, I sailed for England.

5
Epilogue

Our boat left Colombo on 24 May 1911, and arrived at Marseilles on 10 June. We took the train across France and next day, Sunday 11 June, got back to London. I went and stayed with my family at Putney, for my mother and brother and sisters were still living in the house to which we had migrated from Kensington nearly 20 years before. What I found in England and my life in London after June 1911, belongs to the third volume of my autobiography, if I ever write it. Here I am merely concerned with the ending of my life in Ceylon.

When I got to London, I was still in doubt about my future which I have referred to in the last chapter. But I had a year's leave before me and I decided to dismiss the whole matter from my mind for at least six months and enjoy myself. I did enjoy myself. I found my Cambridge friends living in or about Bloomsbury: Lytton Strachey, Saxon Sydney-Turner, Virginia and Adrian Stephen, Vanessa and Clive Bell, Duncan Grant, Maynard Keynes. After Jaffna, Kandy, and Hambantota, the Prices and Lewises, Gwen and Rachel it was a plunge—a slightly icy plunge—into an entirely different world, almost a different universe. But I was received by them all as one of themselves and slipped without much difficulty into the kind of place which I had occupied in 1904 when I sailed for Ceylon. And yet perhaps not entirely the same, for I think the seven years in Ceylon left a mark upon my mind and even character which has proved indelible, a kind of reserve or withdrawal into myself which makes me inclined always to stand just a little to one side of my environment. But for a time I did dismiss Ceylon from my mind. I saw a great deal of them all and went to the Russian Ballet and the *Ring* with them, and dined with Vanessa and Clive and with Virginia and Adrian, and stayed with Virginia in a house which she rented in Firle near Lewes. And I went up to Cambridge, and stayed with Moore and Lytton on Dartmoor.

In the autumn Virginia and Adrian took a large house in Brunswick Square. They let the ground floor to Maynard Keynes and they offered to let the top floor to me. I agreed and in December went into residence there. I had been feeling for some little time that I must make a decision about Ceylon. In October I began writing *The Village in the Jungle* and I realised that I was falling in love with Virginia. By the end of 1911 I had come to the following conclusions: (1) If Virginia would marry me, I would resign from Ceylon and try to earn my living by writing; (2) If Virginia would not marry me, I did not want to return to Ceylon and become a successful civil servant in Colombo and end eventually with a governorship and K.C.M.G. But if I could go back and immerse myself in a District like Hambantota for the remainder of my life, as Dyke and old Sir William Twynam had immersed themselves in Jaffna, I might welcome it as a final withdrawal, a final solitude, in which, married to a Sinhalese, I would make my District or Province the most efficient, the most prosperous place in Asia. At the back of my mind I think I knew that this last solution was fantasy. The days of paternalism under a Dyke or Twynam were over; I had been born in an age of imperialism and I disapproved of imperialism and felt sure that its days were already numbered.

In May my leave would be up. So in February, being still in doubt about the future, I decided to try to get my leave extended. On 14 February 1912, I asked the Secretary of State for the Colonies to extend my leave for four months. I received from him the following letter:

Downing Street,
16 February, 1912

Sir,

I am directed by Mr. Secretary Harcourt to acknowledge the receipt of your letter of the 14th February applying for an extension of your leave of absence from Ceylon; and to request that you will be so good as to state the nature of the private affairs to which you refer.

I am, Sir, your obedient servant
H. J. Read
for the Under Secretary of State

I replied that I could not state the nature of my private affairs, and the following correspondence then continued to its destined end:

Downing Street
29 February, 1912

Sir,

I am directed by Mr. Secretary Harcourt to acknowledge the receipt of your letter of the 20th February with regard to your application for an extension of your leave of absence.

2. Mr. Harcourt regrets that he is unable to grant you an extension without a more explicit statement of the nature of the private affairs to which you refer than is contained in your letter under acknowledgment. This explanation may, if you wish, be given in a confidential letter which will not be communicated to the Government of Ceylon, except in so far as you may agree to its being communicated to the Governor confidentially.

3. If, however, you would prefer not to state the exact nature of the private affairs, Mr Harcourt will ask the Governor whether an extension can be granted to you on the ground of service, without making any reference to the reasons for which you desire it.

I am &c.
H. J. Read
for the Under Secretary of State

To the Under Secretary of State

1 March, 1912

Sir,

I have the honour to acknowledge receipt of your letter of 29 February.

2. I should prefer that the course proposed in paragraph 3 of your letter under reply should be followed, i.e. that the exact nature of the private affairs be not stated and His Excellency the Governor be asked whether an extension can be granted to me on the ground of service.

3. I have the honour to submit that unless my private affairs absolutely necessitate it, I do not desire to prolong my leave and that if circumstances subsequently permitted of my leaving England before the expiration of the four months extension now applied for, I would immediately report the fact to you so that, if desired, I might then resume my duties.

I am &c.
Leonard Woolf

From the Under Secretary of State

Downing Street
23 April 1912

Sir,

I am directed by Mr. Secretary Harcourt to inform you that the Governor of Ceylon has now reported that the extension of absence for which you applied cannot be granted.

2. Mr. Harcourt, therefore, regrets that he must call upon you to resume your duties at the end of the leave already granted to you, which expires on the 20th May.

I am &c.
G. V. Fiddes

To the Under Secretary of State

Sir,

With reference to your letter of 23rd April I have the honour to report that as I am unable to assume duties on May 20th I regret that I must resign my post under the Ceylon Government from that date.

I am &c.

Leonard Woolf

From the Colonial Office (in handwriting)

29 April, 1912

Dear Sir,

I am desired to write to you with regard to your letter of the 25th and to say that, before accepting your resignation, Mr. Harcourt would like to give you an opportunity of reconsidering the question.

In accordance with your wish, the Governor of Ceylon was only asked whether you could be given an extension of leave 'on the ground of service.' He has replied that this cannot be done and it is of course impossible for Mr. Harcourt to overrule him. The grant of leave on the ground of urgent private affairs is, however, another matter and is one for the decision of the Secretary of State.

If, as would appear from your letters, your private affairs make it impossible for you to return to Ceylon at present, Mr. Harcourt, on being satisfied as to their urgency and importance, would probably be prepared to grant you an extension. If, however, you are still unwilling to state the exact nature of these affairs, Mr. Harcourt will have no alternative but to accept your resignation.

It is for you to decide whether you will now state their nature. If you do so by letter, the matter will be absolutely confidential and, if an extension is granted, the Governor will only be told that the leave is granted on the ground of private affairs, the nature of which has been explained to the satisfaction of the Secretary of State. Or if you are unwilling to state them in writing, do you care to come and tell me about the matter in person? Anything you tell me will go no further. It will only be necessary for me to report that I am satisfied that there is proper ground for granting an extension.

Yours faithfully,

R. E. Stubbs.

I did not feel that I could explain to Mr Harcourt or Mr Stubbs that I had come to dislike imperialism, that I did not want to become a Governor, that I wanted to marry Virginia Stephen, and that, if I didn't marry her, I would like to continue to be a Ceylon Civil Servant provided that they would appoint me permanently Assistant Government Agent Hambantota. I merely thanked him for his letter and said that my resignation must stand, murmuring to myself as I signed the letter:

> Mr Secretary Harcourt,
> Reprenez votre Paris;
> J'aime mieux ma mie, o gué,
> J'aime mieux ma mie.

To which Mr Secretary Harcourt replied:

Downing Street,
7 May, 1912

Sir,

I am directed by Mr. Secretary Harcourt to acknowledge the receipt of your letter of the 25th April, in which you tender your resignation of your appointment in the public service of Ceylon.

2. Mr. Harcourt understands that you are not prepared to accept the suggestion which has been made to you privately that you should state confidentially the nature of the urgent private affairs on account of which you desire an extension of your leave of absence, in order that the question of granting you an extension might be considered. He regrets, therefore, that he has no alternative but to accept your resignation which will take effect from the 20th May.

I am &c.
H. J. Read
for the Under Secretary of State

INDEX

Compiled by Patricia Utechin

INDEX